Case Studies in Courageous Organizational Communication

This book is part of the Peter Lang Media and Communication list.
Every volume is peer reviewed and meets
the highest quality standards for content and production.

PETER LANG
New York • Bern • Frankfurt • Berlin
Brussels • Vienna • Oxford • Warsaw

Alexander Lyon

Case Studies in Courageous Organizational Communication

Research and Practice for Effective Workplaces

PETER LANG
New York • Bern • Frankfurt • Berlin
Brussels • Vienna • Oxford • Warsaw

Library of Congress Cataloging-in-Publication Data

Names: Lyon, Alexander, author.
Title: Case studies in courageous organizational communication:
research and practice for effective workplaces / Alexander Lyon.
Description: New York: Peter Lang, 2016.
Includes bibliographical references and index.
Identifiers: LCCN 2016032916 | ISBN 978-1-4331-3124-0 (hardcover: alk. paper)
ISBN 978-1-4331-3123-3 (paperback: alk. paper) | ISBN 978-1-4539-1875-3 (ebook pdf)
ISBN 978-1-4331-3593-4 (epub) | ISBN 978-1-4331-3594-1 (mobi)
Subjects: LCSH: Communication in organizations.
Classification: LCC HD30.3 .L96 2016 | DDC 658.4/5--dc23
DOI: 10.3726/978-1-4539-1875-3
LC record available at https://lccn.loc.gov/2016032916

Bibliographic information published by **Die Deutsche Nationalbibliothek**.
Die Deutsche Nationalbibliothek lists this publication in the "Deutsche Nationalbibliografie"; detailed bibliographic data are available on the Internet at http://dnb.d-nb.de/.

The paper in this book meets the guidelines for permanence and durability of the Committee on Production Guidelines for Book Longevity of the Council of Library Resources.

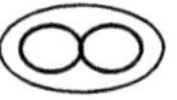

29 Broadway, 18th floor, New York, NY 10006
www.peterlang.com

Printed in the United States of America

Contents

Acknowledgments

This book was only possible because of a long list of people for whom I thank God. My good friend Julien Mirivel helped me identify the focus of the book early in the process. He was an instrumental sounding board and source of encouragement. Joe Chesebro challenged me to "just make an outline," which I did. I would like to thank Mary Savigar and the team at Peter Lang who believed in the project and were excited to publish it. I'm also blessed to have supportive parents, Ken and Alicia Lyon. My mother, with a PhD in English, was particularly helpful in the writing process throughout this long adventure. My wife, Erin, provided numerous rounds of feedback at various stages of the book's development. My son, Soren, was very patient with me as I typed away but equally relieved when the book was done. Students in my advanced undergraduate and graduate organizational communication courses at The College at Brockport, State University of New York inspired many of the case studies in this book. Numerous cases—such as Foxconn (Jennifer Zhang), Miami Dolphins (Nick Wockasen), Nalgene (Julie Goonan), Boy Scouts (Mark Shipley), Domino's (Kelsey Hartigan), JetBlue (Andrea Sillick), and Abercrombie & Fitch (Tia Kennedy)—came to my attention through in-class projects, discussions, and during back-and-forth exchanges between teacher and student that I can only describe as ideal. I would also like to thank the anonymous reviewers at each stage who pushed my thinking forward. Lastly, I would like to acknowledge the long-time guidance and inspiration of two mentors, Stan Deetz and Robert R. Ulmer.

Introduction to Courageous Communication in Organizations

When I was visiting a friend's house, his young son, Michael, was hitting a rotten stump with a hammer. My friend bought the hammer at a yard sale as a special gift to signal a new level of responsibility for his 6-year-old son. The hammer instantly became Michael's favorite item in the world. At first, Michael was handling his grown-up tool well, but he quickly grew bored of pummeling the poor old stump. As several other children played in the yard around him, Michael looked for new objects to hammer—some dirt, the driveway, and then the tire of his father's new Jeep. His father called out a few times, "Please don't hammer that!" "Be careful, Michael!" Michael's choices went downhill quickly. We soon spotted him on the swing set, twirling his hammer above his head like Thor as other children played just inches away. Michael's father had seen enough and said, "That's not what hammers are for. Give me that!" The experiment was over. Michael surrendered the tool.

This book juxtaposes 31 real-world case studies that show both problematic and productive communication approaches. The cases feature some of the most well-known companies in the world such as Google, GlaxoSmithKline, Nestlé Purina, the Miami Dolphins, General Motors, JetBlue, Taco Bell, Massachusetts General

Hospital, Merck, Zappos, Comcast, the Boy Scouts, and many others. Some of these organizations are not so different from Michael. They gravitated toward a few key "tools," systems, and philosophies and often overused them. As employees, we may do the same. We develop shorthand ways of interacting with others and pull out default solutions when problems emerge. These ways of responding become metaphorical tools we use almost automatically to handle everyday situations. Organizations develop strongly preferred ways of seeing and doing things to reduce the ambiguity of life and move the ball forward (Weick, 1979, 2000). Unfortunately, like Michael, they sometimes use tools for the wrong purposes that do more harm than good. Deetz, Tracy, and Simpson (2000) put it this way:

> Old habits and automatic responses are hard to recognize and change. … As with riding a bicycle, one's early learnings never quite go away. Most people carry about thousands of social recipes for handling routine life events. They have used these over and over again for most of their lives. And most have worked reasonably well or they would have gone away some time ago. When ways of responding become entrenched, even repeated failure rarely leads to change. Many people assume if they just do what they usually do only with more strength and tenacity they will succeed. Only focused attention can make these automatic response patterns visible, let alone provide a motivation for change. (p. 40)

This book is fundamentally about examining four common ways of viewing and practicing communication in organizational settings and suggests an alterative. Specifically, many organizations view and practice communication as a tool for ***control***, as flowing ***top-down***, as ***secretive***, and as ***impersonal***. I agree that communication like this still has a viable place, but I suggest that these four approaches have been overplayed to the point of hurting many organizations' effectiveness. As the quote from Deetz et al. suggests, these approaches may have been useful at a certain time and place, but a continued emphasis on them in today's environment will not take organizations to the next level. This book makes these four common approaches more visible and suggests alternative ways of viewing and practicing communication in organizations that is more courageous. This chapter defines communication from various perspectives, describes a model of courageous communication, and outlines the rest of the book.

Models of Communication

Three models of communication have relevance here. The first two are necessary steps to understand the third. The classic model of communication is often referred to as the ***information transfer model***. Sometimes called the *transmission* model, it is the first one taught to most college freshmen. In it, a speaker or *sender encodes* a *message* and sends it through a *channel* to a *receiver* or listener who *decodes* the message (Shannon & Weaver, 1948). The model presents a one-way, linear conceptualization of communication and has been critiqued as a narrow view of a rather complex process (Craig, 1999). It sees communication as mainly the process of transmitting information or data from one point to another. The message flows through the metaphorical pipeline to its destination. It has been called a "container" model because the meaning of a message is contained in the words. This objective, fixed model was developed and articulated by Claude Shannon and Warren Weaver in late 1940s when people were still making sense of the telephone and related technologies. A sign of the times, this theory explains the way a telephone or radio works quite well but misses many important aspects of face-to-face communication.

In the 1960s, Paul Watzlawick built on the work of Gregory Bateson to develop the ***transactional model of communication*** (Watzlawick, Bavelas, & Jackson, 1967). It compensated for some of the limitations and frustrations with the first model. From this new view, communication was a two-way process, a transaction or exchange between communicators. This model allowed for important aspects of face-to-face communication like the *context*, *nonverbal cues*, and *feedback*. When considering nonverbal communication, for example, both individuals in a conversation were always sending a message of some kind whether they spoke or not. Even listening silently or perhaps not listening well sends the other person a message. For this reason, the oddly worded statement, *you cannot not communicate* is associated with this model. In other words, we are always communicating. From this model's view, meaning is not fixed or contained in words. Rather, it is established in the minds of the communicators as they interact back and forth and is socially determined. In this book, I refer to the concepts in both models because they often provide the most useful labels to explain an issue.

However, the third and most salient model for this book, the ***constitutive model of communication***, was articulated best by Robert Craig (1999). He explained what the previous models missed. Communication is constitutive. It does not merely transmit information that already exists. Communication creates and establishes our lives and relationships. In a similar fashion, Karl Weick wrote how "organization" was far too fixed a term to represent the way various workplaces functioned. Instead, he (1979) preferred to discuss the constantly active processes of "organizing" that establish our workplaces. In other words, the process of organizing comes first and builds what we look at and describe in more concrete terms over time (e.g., the building, the brand, etc.). In the same way, communication is the main generative process that creates our relationships, organizations, and society. Craig (1999) explained it this way:

> Communication, from a communicational perspective, is not a secondary phenomenon that can be explained by antecedent psychological, sociological, cultural, or economic factors; rather, communication itself is the primary, constitutive social process that explains all these other factors. (p. 126)

Said more simply by Manning (2014), "Communication is not a mere tool for expressing social reality but is also a means of creating it" (p. 433). This is the view I take in this book. Communication is not a secondary activity that serves more important functions (e.g., finance, accounting, IT, etc.). It is the central generative activity in organizational life. Improving communication is not so much about expressing ourselves more clearly. It is about transforming our organizations through different communication practices (Deetz, 1995). For better or worse, our daily communication practices create our organizational realities. For this reason the model of courageous communication below holds up an ideal to which organizations can strive.

Courageous Communication

As we look at the landscape of corporate scandals since 2000, clearly courage in organizational settings is in short supply. Therefore, case studies and research on courage are sorely needed. Jablin (2006), who noted this gap, stated that courage is obviously more complex than "doing the right thing" or "following your convictions" (p. 100). These notions appeal to a higher sense of duty, moral obligation, and a firmness of mind that all resonate, but courage is clearly more layered. As Jablin (2006) explained, the word is often tossed around in conversations about professional life but is seldom developed as a specific set of concepts, ideals, and practices. In professional settings, courage has clear communicative features. In a foundational text titled *Managerial Courage*, Hornstein (1986) described what many of the case studies in my text show. Organizations put forth constant energy to maintain the status quo and the way things have always been done:

> Organizations always harbor powerful forces which discourage employees from questioning the value of established practices. By carefully dispensing perks and promotions, and by using a host of other organizational blackjacks, these forces easily find persuasive means of communicating that individual self-interest is better served by silently assenting to what is than by openly speaking out on behalf of what might be. (p. 2)

Hornstein described the "menacing protection" by organizations to reinforce traditional practices even when continuing to do so can cause the organization "illness and even death" (p. 2). He explained that, at its root, courage often means expressing ideas that run contrary to the group's current consensus or at other times, perhaps, resisting the temptation to jump on the latest fad or bandwagon. Hornstein's text has clear communication implications throughout.

Jablin (2006) elaborates on Hornstein and his own perspective on courage as a fertile but still seldom explored area of organizational communication. He stated that the most obvious cases of courageous communication in organizational settings involved both internal and external whistleblowing, various aspects of the leader-follower relationship such as upward communication or dissent, what is not talked about, openness, and organizational socialization and assimilation processes. This list is not comprehensive but offers a starting point for reflecting on courageous communication activities in organizational settings. Jablin also suggested that courage can be (a) offensive, "as the courage of the charge, the attack" or to take action to change a situation for the better, or (b) defensive, "standing one's ground under the face of attack" (p. 106). Similarly, May (2012) stated,

> Ethical organizations have employees who have the courage to identify, assess, and resolve ethical dilemmas that may negatively affect the organization or its stakeholders. Courageous organizations have the courage to admit mistakes, reject conformity, respond to injustice, and defy standard industry practices or laws that may be unethical. In addition, courageous organizations seek not only to respond to ethical challenges but also to anticipate them; they exhibit the positive courage to be ethical. (p. 11)

At its center, thus, courage involves taking risks often by doing what is unpopular by ethical, organizational, or industry standards. Inspired, in part, by the work of Hornstein, Jablin, and May this book offers an expanded model of courageous communication.

Courageous communication goes against the consensus, the way organizations commonly handle issues and moves toward something better. For the purposes of this book, I define courageous organizational communication as follows: *Communication is courageous when it a) stands against common but minimally effective and even harmful practices and b) pursues more effective and sustainable strategies, even if doing so is unpopular in a given context.* As such, I present four dominant communication tensions that most organizational members have experienced at one time or another. As implied by the earlier descriptions of courage and shown in the rest of this book, many organizations have traditionally favored *controlling*, *downward*, *secretive*, and *impersonal* communication. These four approaches represent the status quo and default communication "best practices." I suggest four alternatives of the courageous communication model:

- Courageous communication moves from controlling to ***collaborative***
- Courageous communication moves from top-down to ***upward***
- Courageous communication moves from secretive to ***transparent***
- Courageous communication moves from impersonal to ***engaging***

Each of these four components is defined and spelled out in detail in the text's four sections.

Clearly, some level of controlling, top-down, secretive, and impersonal communication will always exist in organizational life as a matter of necessity. To use Hornstein's phrase, they are "established practice[s]" for a reason. The research and case studies in this book show, however, too many organizations overemphasize these traditional approaches to communication in ways that have done more harm than good. I offer the four elements of courageous communication not as replacements for but alternatives to these traditional approaches. Further, like any concept, other ways of articulating courageous communication certainly exist and should by all means continue. As noted, the term "courage" is not easily defined. The four central components or themes here advance a particular view of courageous communication that gathers the types of practices many readers will admire under one conceptual roof.

This model has both practical and ethical justifications. From a practical standpoint, the case studies show the untapped advantages of collaborative, upward, transparent, and engaging communication. Despite the benefits, these practices often involve going against the grain. The players in the cases who followed these courageous practices did so for the good of the company, often in the face of resistance within the organization or in contrast to broader industry "common sense" or accepted "best practices." In addition to practical advantages, another key element of courage is that it calls us to a higher standard that goes beyond self-interest. Thus, each of the four research themes of the book corresponds to four ethical standards to ground this view of courageous communication in a clear moral foundation. First, the practice of collaboration is informed by a *dialogic* ethic in contrast to more linear or monologic approaches to communication. Second, the call for more upward communication is grounded in the *utilitarian* standard of *promoting the greatest good for the greatest number of people*. Third, the need for transparent communication is supported by the ethical standard of *significant choice*. Fourth, engaging communication is drawn from the *I-Thou* ethical perspective on communicating with others. Taken separately, each of these four research themes and ethical standards can stand on their own. Taken together, the case studies show courage as their common characteristic.

The Format of This Book

Within these four themes, the 31 case studies here span a wide range of industries and issues: airline, pharmaceuticals, Internet and telecommunication, manufacturing, food service, healthcare, and many others. The cases also touch on a wide variety of issues from food safety, college sports, frivolous lawsuits, product design, defective products, customer backlash, employee treatment, mismanagement, and others. In about half the case studies, organizations made decisions and took actions that made a situation worse. These aligned closely with the traditional default communication practices that many organizations use: controlling, top-down, secretive, and impersonal. In the other half of the case studies, the organizations made decisions and took actions that the book positions as courageous. These organizations' actions aligned closely with collaborative, upward, transparent, and engaging communication, even though they experienced some degree of organizational or industry pressure to do otherwise.

It would be tempting to see these counter-point themes as sorted into "bad" and "good." The spirit of this book, for example, is not to say that control is bad and collaboration is good. More accurately, the book looks at what can happen when practices like control, top-down communication, etc. are emphasized too much. Of course, in some cases it is difficult to see any good or to empathize deeply with those who made mistakes. When a space shuttle disintegrates on reentry or a company goes bankrupt, something went very wrong indeed that deserves attention. As such, this book does not take a "right vs. right" approach common in some useful case study books (e.g., May, 2012), but in the majority of cases, plenty of room for disagreement and diverse opinions exist. Even cases that look unambiguous on the surface provide space for different opinions and a variety of entry points for robust discussions. Further, the case studies generally focus on a particular issue that cannot possibly capture all of the nuances people experience at work over the long run. But they do allow us to look at a snapshot of a particular time and place. Sometimes the snapshot shows an organization at a good moment and sometimes at a moment they wish wasn't caught on camera. All of these moments are instructive and serve as a catalyst for further discussion. They offer an opportunity to draw out lessons and consider the nature of courageous communication in organizational settings. Many of the organizations featured are familiar and have existed for decades, but some are newer. With some exceptions, I chose 2000 and forward in terms of when the central activities featured in the case took place. My goal was to select not only cases from the last few years but also to provide enough variety of issues and industries to show relevant practices discussed across time and contexts.

The reader may also notice a strong theme of leadership. This is intentional because people clearly influence organizations. Since I assume a constitutive view of communication, leaders come into focus because they shape their contexts profoundly. Those who hold official positions have a special responsibility to make decisions on behalf of those that follow them. This book, however, is meant for employees and leaders at every level. Thus, terms like "leader," "manager," "supervisor," "follower," "employee," and "member" include the full range of scenarios. Even a new hire and front-line employee can lead by example at any given moment. Sometimes the use of these terms grows out of specific research discussed in a given segment. In other instances, I use these terms interchangeably to include the widest variety of contributors to organizational life.

The book's four parts discuss collaborative, upward, transparent, and engaging communication. Each section features a theme in the model of courageous communication: (a) The beginning of each case-study chapter provides a brief overview of the issues to provide a conceptual vocabulary and research context for the cases that follow. (b) The central feature in each part is a collection of seven to eight mid-length case studies. Both the number and average length of the cases provide the reader multiple industries, issues, and angles. (c) Each part of the book then concludes with a tips, tools, and resources chapter that draws from the case studies and existing literature to ground the advice. It is important to note that the order of the book's major sections is not particularly important. I chose to begin with control because it emerged as a recurring and perhaps root element supporting top-down, secretive, and impersonal communication to various degrees. Like Michael who wanted to use his beloved hammer in some not-always-helpful ways, organizations must look for better communication tools to create long-term success. My goal, thus, is to equip readers with a conceptual vocabulary, a robust set of case studies, and some practical skills to apply to the workplace.

References

Craig, R. (1999). Communication theory as a field. *Communication Theory, 9*, 119–161.

Deetz, S. A. (1995). *Transforming communication transforming business.* Cresskill, NJ: Hampton Press.

Deetz, S. A., Tracy, S. J., & Simpson, J. L. (2000). *Leading organizations through transition: Communication and cultural change*. Thousand Oaks, CA: Sage.

Hornstein, H. A. (1986). *Managerial courage: Revitalizing your company without sacrificing your job*. New York, NY: John Wiley.

Jablin, F. M. (2006). Courage and courageous communication among leaders and followers in groups, organizations, and communities. *Management Communication Quarterly, 20*, 94–110.

Manning, J. (2014). A constitutive approach to interpersonal communication studies. *Communication Studies, 65*, 432–440.

May, S. (2012). *Case studies in organizational communication: Ethical perspectives and practices*. Thousand Oaks, CA: Sage.

Shannon, C., & Weaver, W. (1948). *The mathematical theory of communication*. Urbana, IL: University of Illinois Press.

Watzlawick, P., Bavelas, J. B., & Jackson, D. D. (1967). *Pragmatics of human communication: A study of interactional patterns, pathologies, and paradoxes*. New York, NY: Norton.

Weick, K. (1979). *The social psychology of organizing* (2nd ed.). Reading, MA: Addison-Wesley.

Weick, K. (2000). *Making sense of the organization*. Malden, MA: Wiley-Blackwell.

Part I

Moving from Control to Collaboration

1

Controlling Communication and Case Studies

Most conversations are simply monologues delivered in the presence of a witness.

—*Margaret Miller*

Years ago, I worked briefly for a very controlling supervisor who had a raw style of interacting. Several times a day, she reminded everybody about important procedures and pointed out almost every mistake we made. She was clearly the most experienced person in our department and had excellent technical skills. Still, her clipped, corrective communication short-circuited what might have otherwise been pleasant or even inspiring conversations. Instead, she micro-managed everybody to the point of frustration, did little to help the organization achieve its goals, and hurt her own credibility. Strictly speaking, control is not "wrong," is clearly one component of a manager's responsibility, and has a place. However, she mistakenly overused it as a stock response. This chapter looks at the various ways people use control counterproductively. The first part introduces the conceptual landscape of control, and the second presents four case studies where control played a damaging role: Enron, Foxconn, Jim Beam, and the Miami Dolphins.

Controlling Communication

At its core, controlling communication flows in a linear, one-way direction. People with this approach spend their time steering conversations, telling others what to do, and imposing their ideas into others' heads. This ***monologic form of communication*** involves "some form of control, utilization, domination, or manipulation" (Yoshikawa, 1977, p. 103). You may have experienced, for instance, leaders with an ***autocratic style***, which aligns closely with notions of control. As Cherry (2014) writes, "Autocratic leadership involves absolute, authoritarian control over a group" (para. 1). These leaders limit others' participation in decision making, seek little input, and communicate through directives (Eagly & Johannesen-Schmidt, 2001). While autocratic leaders can be effective in certain situations, conversations with them are usually about deadlines, priorities, and other task-related activities and emphasize their power distance over followers. Perhaps for these reasons, even if people anticipate a favorable outcome when working under autocratic leaders, they are more likely to exit a group compared to those working with democratic leaders (Van Vugt, Jepson, Hart, & De Cremer, 2004). The way a leader relates to others, thus, often matters more to people than the outcome of the work.

Research has long recognized that some level of authority and control is an expected part of leaders' job descriptions. As Richmond, Davis, Saylor, and McCroskey (1984) explain, most researchers who have studied power and control conclude that leaders are, in part, "responsible for directing, coordinating, and guiding subordinates' activity so that organizational objectives may be reached" (p. 86). Most leaders' years of experience qualify them to help employees learn new skills or guide them. However, even early research on an autocratic approach frames this style in an unflattering light that may resonate with readers' experiences. For example, Rosenfeld and Plax's (1975) foundational study contrasting autocratic and democratic styles showed that individuals with the former also typically lacked insight about themselves, manipulated others for their own benefit, did not consider others' feelings, and did not make "any show of treating [others] as people" (p. 208). A controlling approach is not limited to leaders. Employees at all levels may respond this way if positioned to do so.

An often unspoken belief is that a controlling approach is the best way to get things done. Most of us know people we would characterize as micro-managers or even bona fide "control freaks" who manage others' tasks and insist that things be done their way. This mindset has led to unfortunate expressions like "managers think, employees do," "do as you're told," or "good employees [like children] are seen and not heard" that distance employees from a sense of agency and initiative. Controlling individuals may check in on others' tasks on a daily basis and readily point out perceived mistakes before duties are even completed. These conversations do not normally involve a two-way, back-and-forth exchange of ideas or provide the opportunity for others to voice their opinions. Even though frequently discussed in a negative light, control is sometimes necessary, at least in low doses. When less restrained, however, a control-oriented person can frustrate others' drive. More recent research has gone beyond the simple autocratic-democratic continuum and delves deeper into the various ways controlling communication emerges in the workplace.

Types of Control

Organizations today employ a variety of strategies in addition to "bossy" or overly directive individuals. Our daily work experience is often layered with intersecting systems that act as obstacles and feel like stifling restrictions. ***Simple control***, the most basic and common form, consists of an authority figure telling a subordinate what to do. As Bullis and Tompkins (1989) explain, this type "involves simple overt direction and supervision. Straightforward commands are issued. Compliance with commands is monitored and contributors are corrected as needed" (p. 288). Depending upon its intensity, simple control most closely resembles the autocratic style mentioned earlier and is sometimes overused as a primary strategy for interacting with others. Organizations also establish ***bureaucratic control*** through the numerous steps, rules, and procedures employees must follow to accomplish work (Tompkins & Cheney, 1985). Workers at all levels sometimes complain about "bureaucracy" or "red tape" that encourages *in*-the-box thinking. The sometimes-hundreds of rules employees must follow make innovation difficult. ***Technical control*** (Bullis & Tompkins, 1989) has many developing forms. Essentially, it integrates simple or bureaucratic control into technology. The assembly line is a typical example, but cell phones, computers, and countless other technologies control our tasks and even tie us to work after hours. Video surveillance, swipe cards, and other monitoring technologies keep track of keyboard strokes, email content, phone calls, and visited websites. Simple, bureaucratic, and technical controls share the same goal: compliance of individuals to organizations' rules, policies, and procedures.

Groups, teams, and social relationships also exert control. Several overlapping terms capture these inherently communicative dynamics. For instance, we experience ***cultural control*** when the norms, rituals, and values of an organization guide our behavior (Deal & Kennedy, 1982). Strong cultures guide actions in organizationally prescribed directions. New members often learn the ropes by following or violating expectations they did not know existed. While many expectations remain unspoken, they shape activities nonetheless. We experience a general sense of ***social control*** (e.g., Mumby, 1993) in our groups and interpersonal relationships. Our ties and connections in a network bind us to others in a web that shapes and reinforces attitudes and values (Yang & Kim, 2013). Group members maintain their influence and social currency in the group, in part, by conforming to the group's norms, expectations, and mutual interests. At a more intense level, we police ourselves and fellow co-workers to ensure that everybody conforms to sometimes unreasonable expectations. Tompkins and Cheney (1985) call this ***concertive control*** because the group acts "in concert" to control themselves and each other. As Papa, Auwal, and Singhal (1997) describe, "the locus of control shifts significantly from management to workers who collaborate to create rules and norms that govern their behavior" (p. 221). Some research (e.g., Barker & Cheney 1994) shows that concertive control can be even more powerful than traditional top-down supervisory control because everybody in the group enforces expectations rather than a single supervisor. No clean lines separate the daily reality that these three terms describe. Cultural, social, and concertive forms blur together, and all emphasize the relative intensity of cohesiveness, pressure, and conformity. Social cohesion has its benefits including increased coordination, teamwork, and collective well being (Putnam, 2000). However, an overemphasis on cohesiveness and harmony in groups has been a long-acknowledged potential contributor to bad decisions (e.g., Janis, 1982). While these types may have their place, employees today frequently experience numerous forms simultaneously, which undermine the sense of purpose, initiative, and creative problem solving that keeps organizations effective.

The aim of argument, or of discussion, should not be victory, but progress. (Joseph Joubert)

Unintended Consequences of Control

A controlling approach is not always a bad idea. Organizational crises (e.g., Ulmer, Sellnow, & Seeger, 2013), for example, occur when response time is short, the organization is under potential threat, and leaders *must* take decisive and often controlling action. By definition, however, crises are not everyday occurrences. In most situations, organizations need just enough control to coordinate activities and keep people safe. When employees notice control or see it as excessive, this approach has unintended consequences.

Two common responses to heavy-handed control are resistance and imitation. Neither response helps organizations succeed. ***Resistance*** occurs when employees feel dominated, the organization has encroached too far into their territory, their dignity and worth as a person has been challenged, and their freedom and choices have been too limited. In response, they resist the organization's control by creating space and distancing themselves from the organization's power

(Mumby, 1997). When leaders emphasize control too intensely, it engages some employees' fight-or-flight response to reclaim the threatened territory. Some, for example, resist by doing the bare minimum while others may actively confront or openly question and critique a managerial policy. Some resistance like telling unflattering jokes about managers or privately complaining is relatively harmless. Other employees engage in more harmful activities like stealing, breaking or sabotaging company property, or calling in or quitting without notice. Some who are burned out or frustrated by the organization's power moves even lash out at unsuspecting co-workers or customers. Resistance like this has a negative impact on the organization. When employees are focused on resisting, little work gets done.

Another common response to control is imitation. Studies show that a variety of behaviors and attitudes, even harmful ones, are ***contagious***. For instance, Sy, Côté, and Saavedra (2005) showed that group leaders' moods shaped the group's mood and attitude noticeably. People in supervisory roles have a disproportionate influence over a group in that followers are likely to take on the behaviors, attitudes, and tone of leaders (Zenger & Folkman, 2013). Porath and Pearson (2013), for instance, showed that managers' incivility was often a direct consequence of their own supervisor's incivility. This is not surprising given the normative and constitutive influence of communication (Craig, 1999). Our communication practices shape our organizations. Those who lead set a powerful example. Controlling people, thus, can create cultures where other employees then see directive, one-way communication as proper interaction with everybody. Control, thus, has unintended "blowback" that we must consider. Thankfully, the reverse is also true. Positive features of leadership are even more contagious than negative features (e.g., Cherulnik, Donley, Wiewel, Tay & Miller, 2001; Zenger & Folkman, 2013).

> *O, it is excellent to have a giant's strength, but it is tyrannous to use it like a giant. (William Shakespeare)*

Dysfunctional Levels of Control

As the case studies later in this chapter show, some leaders and organizational cultures have what I characterize as dysfunctional levels of control driven by a personal reason rather than by what is best for the whole organization. For some people, control can become a self-justifying preoccupation, a distraction from the organization's actual purpose of serving the public in a valuable way. When this happens, we see additional attempts at control beyond those mentioned earlier.

It becomes an adversarial, fearful, and habitual process in the form of turf wars, bullying, and systematically distorted communication.

Turf wars. Many subgroups in organizations develop an *us-versus-them* mentality. Departments, teams, and various peer groups who should be working cooperatively nurture intense rivalries. This happens when resources become scarce, "healthy competition" becomes too intense, and leaders unwisely pit their followers against each other. Internal ***turf wars*** can become so familiar that our efforts to dominate another group seems normal, desirable, and justified. As shown in two related articles on the same organization (e.g., Lyon, 2005; Lyon & Chesebro, 2010), some departments became virtually obsessed with discrediting others. These groups spent hours each day creating disparaging nicknames and labels for each other, spreading rumors, gossiping, manipulating, and refusing to work with their perceived opponents. These activities were counterproductive and expensive placeholders that prevented the organization from investing its time, effort, and attention to the common goal of helping clients. The organization received increasingly poor customer feedback and ultimately went out of business.

Workplace bullying. In the past decade, researchers have begun to study workplace bullying in earnest. Similar to schoolyard bullying, it involves "persistent, verbal, and nonverbal aggression at work that include personal attacks, social ostracism, and a multitude of other painful messages and hostile interactions" (Lutgen-Sandvik, 2006, p. 406). The statistics should concern us. Approximately 30% of workers in the U.S. report being bullied at some point in their careers, up to 25% of organizations report bullying, and 80% of workers have witnessed bullying (Lutgen-Sandvik, 2006; Lutgen-Sandvik, Tracy, & Alberts, 2007). Bullies exist at all levels including leaders, co-workers, and even subordinates who "bully up." In most cases, however, supervisors and managers are the culprits (Lutgen-Sandvik et al., 2007). At its core, this negative tactic dominates the target emotionally and even physically. In these contexts, people may mistake this behavior as the best way to get results. In contrast, research above shows that bullying hurts the organization by lowering productivity, retention, and employee satisfaction and by increasing confrontation and retaliation. Neither the bullies nor their targets do anything that resembles working.

Systematically distorted communication. In contrast to a back-and-forth conversational pattern, some communication feels monolithic. When only one voice dominates interactions, the perspective a listener gains likely represents a narrow agenda. As Deetz (1990) explains, these conversations usually involve at least one person who seeks to "divert, distort, or block the open development of understanding. When discussion is thwarted, a particular view of reality is maintained at the expense of equally plausible ones usually to someone's advantage" (p. 235). Perhaps you've experienced the frustration of not being allowed a voice in decisions that directly impact your work. For a variety of reasons, however, some people in organizations do not believe or simply forget that others have valuable insights to offer. Thus, ***systematically distorted communication*** (Deetz, 1992) occurs when conversational lopsidedness gets built into the norms, expectations, and structure of the organization and become "routine, patterned, and reproduced" (Lyon, 2007, p. 379).

Deetz (1990, 1992) provided a comprehensive list of the ways people shut down others' voices in interpersonal and organizational settings. For instance, some will only invite individuals with the "right" expertise, qualifications, credentials, or connections to key discussions. Those with credentials that are not positioned as good enough experience a ***disqualification*** from the discussion. Another approach to closing off communication is ***objectification*** when the dominant view is positioned as the objective truth while alternative views are treated as meager, subjective, and rooted in personal opinion. Perhaps the most common way to tilt conversations is simply to avoid undesirable topics altogether or ***topical avoidance***. Touchy topics (e.g., moral failings, illegal activities, inappropriate conduct, etc.) are simply not broached and considered taboo. Various systematically distorted communication practices can accumulate to repressive levels and are limited by individuals who determine what gets said and what does not.

Turf wars, workplace bullying, and systematically distorted communication are examples of a controlling approach gone too far. Too, many acceptable types like simple control, bureaucratic control, technical control, cultural control, and so on may stifle an organization's chances at effectiveness and long-term success if they become intense. The following four cases demonstrate what can happen when organizations overemphasize control.

Case Studies on Controlling Communication

Enron's Controlling Culture Covered Leaders' Tracks

In the late 1990s, Enron Corp. was known as one of the largest and most successful companies in the US. Just a few years later, however, the mere mention of the name "Enron" was used to symbolize all that can go wrong in corporate America. The company was the center of the first and largest corporate scandal of the 21st century. For years, Enron existed as just another traditional gas and oil company in the 1980s' sluggish energy market. As the federal government deregulated the energy industry, Enron's founding President and CEO, Ken Lay, looked for new ways to make money. To do so, he hired a soon-to-be controversial figure, Jeff Skilling, who quickly became Lay's key confidant and right-hand man. Together, they fought to shed Enron's old image and business model as a traditional energy company and transform the company into an energy trader or clearinghouse. From their view, Enron no longer needed to own actual hard assets such as gas, oil, pipelines, refineries, etc. Instead, as Lay and Skilling envisioned it, Enron's expertise and big ideas would transform Enron into a "new economy" company that was able to make money every time smaller energy suppliers and large customers bought and sold virtually any type of energy.

These leaders envisioned Enron as a new stock market of sorts for energy as the company simultaneously fought to dominate the energy marketplace. The company's future was no longer bound by its direct ownership of hard assets. As Enron's president, Skilling wrote the following in Enron's (1999) annual report to stockholders:

> Enron is moving so fast that sometimes others have trouble defining us. But we know who we are. We are clearly a knowledge-based company. … We are participants in the New Economy, and the rules have changed dramatically. … The fluidity of knowledge and skills throughout Enron increasingly enables us to capture value in the New Economy. (p. 2)

Enron's bold but ambiguous vision for the future seemed to work, as least at first. In the end, much of Enron's growth and apparent success was the result of a combination of illegal accounting practices, the deception of stock analysts, and essentially stealing money by exploiting confusing rules in the newly deregulated California energy market. When the truth came out, Enron went bust in 2001. Leaders ran the company into the ground and declared bankruptcy shortly before their fraud was exposed in 2002. The meteoric rise and catastrophic failure of Enron marked a turning point in corporate America. This case examines how company leaders' management style allowed them to keep their wrongdoing hidden for so long.

Aggressive Communication and Leadership Approach

Hindsight allows outsiders to see what many Enron insiders knew all along. Enron's leaders' apparent success continued because of two main ingredients: (a) The sheer cleverness of their illegal activities and (b) the high level of control over Enron's culture that kept those illegal practices hidden. While Ken Lay had a reputation for being folksy and diplomatic, Jeff Skilling used aggressiveness and a combative style to get what he wanted. Some employees called Skilling "Darth Vader," a nickname Skilling was reportedly proud of (Schwartz, 2002). Skilling was a self-admitted control freak (Schwartz, 2002), though he prefers the phrase "'controls' freak,'" referring to the strict control systems and processes he put in place at Enron ("Skilling Claims," 2002, para. 3). He earned at least part of this reputation through his combative communication style. Enron vice president Sherron Watkins, explained that Skilling made sustained direct eye contact, "spoke in clipped, flat, supremely confident tones" and often used foul language to intimidate others (Swartz & Watkins, 2003, p. 12). According to Watkins, Skilling took the approach, "I'm right—you know I'm right—so why argue?" (p. 43). Skilling preferred to hire people like himself that he called "guys with spikes. He liked [individuals] with something extreme about them" (Gibney, 2005). For example, Andy Fastow, who eventually became the chief financial officer (CFO) at Enron, was the first person Skilling hired in 1990. Fastow regularly and publicly yelled, threatened, and cursed to get things done. Another high-level executive and close ally of Skilling, Cliff Baxter, was "blunt, blustery, and bombastic … [had] a towering ego and a volatile personality" (McLean & Elkind, 2003, p. 65). Lou Pai, a top executive, was described as "Enron's fiercest corporate warlord" (McLean & Elkind, 2003, p. 58). A fellow executive who worked with Pai described him this way, "you don't mess with Lou. … If you got in the way of Lou's agenda, he'd get rid of you" (McLean & Elkind, 2003, p. 58). Skilling and other top executives actively encouraged this aggressive approach. They labeled those with more measured styles "losers" who didn't "get it" (see McLean & Elkind, 2003, pp. 325–326; Swartz & Watkins, 2003, p. 2). Many people at Enron tolerated this aggressive approach, in part, because Enron appeared to be a great success story on paper. Enron's stock was higher than ever. Numerous magazines plastered the executives' faces on the cover. At its peak, Enron was the seventh largest company in the US. In this context, it would have been easy to conclude mistakenly that this level of success perhaps required their muscular, cutthroat managerial style.

Not surprisingly, this approach spread throughout the organization as the primary way to get things done. A junior attorney from Enron's legal department, for instance, believed that Andy Fastow (CFO) had a legal and financial conflict of interest in the company. Rather than hearing the attorney's explanation, Fastow attempted to fire him when he showed Fastow was operating in a way that was bad for Enron. Fastow left the employee a hostile voicemail that was laced with expletives as a warning to never cross him again and called for the junior attorney's resignation. The junior attorney's supervisor stepped in. He told other high-level executives that he planned to go to Jeff Skilling with his concerns about Fastow's handling of the attorney as well as the legal and financial conflicts of interest that could hurt Enron. Other executives told the supervisor, "I wouldn't stick my neck out. … Don't go there" ("House Energy," 2002, para. 193–202). Though it was not known until years later, the silenced attorney was correct. Fastow's activities at the time were ultimately sabotaging Enron's financial future.

Top executives often used this combative style when other people questioned Enron's ever-rising stock price, a rise that defied traditional principles of stock evaluation. In one instance, Skilling publicly called a fund manager an "asshole" during a conference call when he asked Skilling to provide simple financial statements to support Skilling's yet unverified claims about how much money Enron actually brought in and the appropriateness of Enron's high stock value. Rather than apologizing for the outburst, Skilling took pride in his brash approach. In fact, the most combative executives were routinely promoted. Many rose to the top of Enron's ranks. The most noticeably absent figure in this group of combative executives was founding CEO, Ken Lay. By this point in Enron's story, Lay had taken on a political role for Enron. He regularly mingled with the country's president, vice president, and influential lawmakers in Washington, DC. He grew out of touch as he moved away from the day-to-day operations at Enron. He nevertheless endorsed Skilling's style and soon promoted Skilling to CEO. Lay remained the company's president.

Emerging Concerns

People outside of this circle of high-level executives became increasingly concerned about Enron's future. Outsiders and lower-level insiders alike began to ask openly, was this how a company should be led? A former executive emailed Ken Lay to voice his frustration with Skilling's approach.

> I just read an interesting article … [that] focused on how to recognize CEOs and CEO candidates who were not up to the requirements of their job and used Jeff Skilling as an example. I have agreed with views of this journalist for some time, especially since Jeff called a fund manager an "asshole." Publicly calling someone [that] is simply not something any CEO should do and you and Enron's board should have done something about Jeff then. (Shaw, 2001, September 24, para. 2)

As CEO, Skilling had opportunities to address the growing discontent at Enron. Many people were tired of working in such a hostile environment. Further, lots of top executives disagreed with the direction that Skilling was taking the company. By moving almost entirely away from a traditional gas-and-pipeline business model, Skilling and Lay put the company at great risk. Further, Skilling struggled to get some of his famously "big ideas" off the ground, ideas that were supposed to ensure Enron's future.

Instead of adjusting to growing concern at Enron, Skilling fired executives who did not see things his way. He hired an outside consulting firm to interview Enron managers and to determine who agreed and disagreed with his way of doing things (Swartz & Watkins, 2003, p. 113). With this information, Skilling then systematically fired people who disagreed. In one year, Skilling filled 11 of 26 high-level positions with "Skillingites" or executives who were loyal to him alone (McLean & Elkind, 2003, p. 105). Many executives learned about the illegal practices Enron was engaging in over time. Sherron Watkins, a vice president testified before Congress that while she knew of potentially illegal accounting practices, she was not comfortable approaching either Skilling or Fastow about her concerns, "To do so, I believed, would have been a job-terminating move" ("Senate Commerce," 2002, February 26, para. 82). Skilling, Fastow, Baxter, Pai and other top executives, used this intimidating and combative approach, in part, to make sure Enron's ill financial health was not exposed to scrutiny either within the organization or to outsiders.

Skilling's Resignation and Enron's Collapse

On August 14th of 2001, Jeff Skilling abruptly resigned as Enron's CEO. Neither at the time nor since has Skilling ever admitted that he resigned because he believed the company was in trouble. Instead, he cited unspecified personal reasons upon which he would not elaborate. Enron employees' and investors' concerns about the hasty nature of Skilling's resignation were compounded by the growing realization that something deeper was amiss at Enron. The day Skilling resigned, for example, Enron's stock price had already lost over 50% of its value compared to just one year earlier. Shortly after Skilling resigned, Sherron Watkins delivered a letter to Ken Lay explaining her concerns about Andy Fastow's accounting irregularities. When Fastow heard about the letter to Lay, he screamed "at a very high decibel" at a fellow executive, accusing him of ghostwriting the memo ("House Energy," 2002, para. 736). Her letter, however, was far too late to save Enron. By November 2001, just three months after Skilling resigned, Enron's stock was worthless. The company closed its doors in December 2001. Over 20,000 employees lost their jobs along with billions of dollars in retirement funds tied up in Enron stock. Legal investigations began before the company even went out of business.

Throughout the investigation, congressional testimony, and court trials, both Ken Lay and Jeff Skilling maintained their innocence. Both claimed that other executives at Enron, like Andy Fastow, were responsible for the wrongdoing and deliberately hid those actions from them. As Skilling (Beltran, 2002) claimed in testimony to congress, "When I left on Aug. 14, I thought the financial reports accurately represented the financial [state] of the company … Enron was an enormous corporation … Could I have known everything going on in the company?" (para. 3, 5). He told the *New York Times* when he resigned, "I had no idea the company was in anything but excellent shape" (Schwartz, 2002, para. 3). Similarly, Ken Lay told his side of the story. He claimed that he had no knowledge of any wrongdoing and never did anything illegal himself. He simply hired the best people he could, trusted them, and gave the executives "room to run" (Mayberry, 2006, para. 3). In the end, Enron's success was a complete illusion.

Aftermath

By every measure, executives had "cooked the books." The company used manipulative accounting practices to make the company appear financially successful on paper. Enron executives dishonestly "talked up" the stock price and financial health of the company publicly but privately sold off hundreds of millions of dollars worth of their own stock at a fervent pace. This practice is known as insider trading. Investigations ("Enron Execs," 2002) show that Ken Lay profited over $119 million during his last three years at Enron by selling company stock at dramatically overpriced values. Jeff Skilling pocketed $112 million. Andy Fastow made $18.5 million. Lou Pai, "Enron's fiercest corporate warlord," pocketed an astounding $271 million. In total, the top executives made $1.3 billion. For most of them, however, this victory was short-lived. In January 2002, Cliff Baxter, a close friend of Skilling and executive at Enron, committed suicide as the investigation of Enron gained momentum. In 2004, Andy Fastow pleaded guilty to fraud and agreed to cooperate with investigators. He served six years of a ten-year jail sentence before he was released. In 2006, Ken Lay was convicted of conspiracy and fraud ("Enron Trial," 2006). He died of a heart attack after he was convicted but before

Questions:

- How would you describe Enron executives' communication approach? How did it shape Enron's culture?
- To what extent do you think executives' controlling tendencies contributed to Enron's downfall?

being sentenced. Jeff Skilling was convicted of fraud, conspiracy, and insider trading and was sentenced to 24 years in jail, a sentence that was later reduced to 14 years. In most cases, executives were forced to surrender their temporary fortunes as part of their sentencing.

Life Inside Foxconn's Electronics Factory: The Complex Relationship between Employees, Foxconn, and Apple

> *You go in this place and it's a factory but, my gosh, they've got restaurants and movie theatres and hospitals and swimming pools. For a factory, it's pretty nice.*
>
> —*Steve Jobs, CEO for Apple ("For a Factory," 2010, para. 7)*

When the iPhone first came out in 2007, customers lined up for hours outside of a store in New Jersey long before it opened. When the doors finally opened that morning, customers in the line that wrapped around the sidewalk clapped and cheered fervently. One by one, customers exited the store smiling broadly with excited eyes as they pumped their still-boxed iPhone in the air. One satisfied customer dressed in an iPhone costume exited the store to more cheers. Reactions like this remain common today for the release of new Apple devices. Over the years, customers in the US have shared a similar affection and pay top dollar for electronics products like Playstation, Wii, Kindle, and X-Box. Most people, however, do not realize the growing controversy around the way these products are made. All are made by overseas technology manufacturing giant, Foxconn Technology Group (Foxconn). Though its factories are located in China, the company partners with numerous brand-name companies in the US such as Microsoft, Amazon, Samsung, Hewlett Packard, Nokia, Dell, IBM, Sony, and, most notably, Apple.

Foxconn is led by an outspoken and controversial CEO, Terry Gou. The company employs over 178,000 workers at its three large manufacturing facilities located in China. The average employee is 23 years old. Most of the approximately 65% male and 35% female employees work various assembly lines making consumer electronics products. Foxconn recruits young Chinese job seekers with slick marketing. As a former employee explained, the company tells potential applicants, "Hurry toward your finest dreams, pursue a magnificent life. At Foxconn, you can expand your knowledge and accumulate experience. Your dreams extend from here until tomorrow" (Heffernan, 2013, para. 3). They promise the employees onsite apartments close to the factory, swimming pools, movie theaters, and recreational activities. By far, Foxconn's highest profile partner is Apple. While Apple's leaders pride themselves on the company's employee-friendly corporate and socially responsible practices, Foxconn developed a troubling reputation for an extremely controlling culture that mistreats workers on several fronts. In response, a wave of suicides swept through the factory. This case looks at how Foxconn's controlling approach causes its employees undue stress and exhaustion and does little to help the company's profits.

Life and Death at Foxconn

Foxconn exercises various types of control over employees' work lives. For example, Foxconn forces employees to work well beyond China's legal limit. The country limits regular full-time work to 40 hours per week plus no more than 36 hours per month in overtime. However, an onsite investigation by Fair Labor Association ("Fair Labor," 2012) showed that between Foxconn's three factories, 70–80% of employees exceeded China's legal limit of overtime hours. The Fair Labor Associations investigation used 17 investigators and conducted over 1,000 interviews with employees and managers. The investigation found that during the busiest times of year, approximately half of employees worked overtime 11 or more days straight. Marathon shifts are not uncommon. At least one employee died of exhaustion after completing a 34-hour shift (Brownlee, 2010). Incidents like these put pressure on Foxconn leaders to change their policies. Company leaders routinely promise to reduce employees' mandatory overtime requirements. A 2012 investigation of Foxconn, however, shows after more than two years following the employees' death-from-exhaustion, all three factories still regularly exceed legal overtime limits, often making employees work 60 hours or more per week (O'Toole, 2013). An employee interviewed at Foxconn said, "During my first day of work, an older worker said to me, 'why did you come to Foxconn? Don't ever think about it again and leave right now' … Foxconn employees have a saying, 'they use women as men and men as machines'" (Zhang, 2012, para. 10). An Apple spokesperson characterized these practices as "excessive overtime" (O'Toole, 2013, para. 14) and vowed to work with Foxconn to improve employees' situation.

On paper, Foxconn pays their employees in compliance with Chinese legal requirements. Similar to the minimum wage laws in the US and many factories across the globe, this level of pay is often not enough to pay for employees' basic living expenses. However, Foxconn leaders cut corners that reduce employees' pay in ways that do not pay workers for certain types of work the company requires of them. For example, Foxconn's overtime system measures time in large 30-minute units. Employees who work 58 or 59 minutes of an hour (based on when they began, ended, took breaks, etc.) are only paid for one 30-minute unit. Similarly, employees are required to attend meetings before and/or after work in addition to training that takes place outside of employees' scheduled work hours. Foxconn does not pay employees for this time because "management [did] not see these as work and accordingly did not pay for them" (Protecting, 2012, p. 9). Clearly, the company requires employees to attend theses meetings and requires them to stay on the assembly line beyond their scheduled shifts. Employees deserve to be compensated fairly for this time.

In addition to long hours and lean pay, Foxconn is a difficult place to work. In contrast to the slick recruiting messages, the company sends a different message once the employees begin work. CEO Guo's sayings are posted on the walls to remind employees about life at Foxconn. One states, "Growth, thy name is suffering," and another states, "Achieve goals or the sun will no longer shine" (Heffernan, 2013, para. 7). Management also treats employees in demeaning ways to emphasize the power the company has over them. One exhausted worker lied down on the floor for a moment during an extremely long shift. When a supervisor saw him, he made the employee "stand at one corner for 10 minutes like the old school days" (Wrenn, 2012, para. 37). The supervisory style is militant and they forbid employee conversations while working. Managers yell, insult, and belittle as common practice. A report from a workers' rights group in Hong Kong, Students and Scholars Against Corporate Misbehavior (SACOM), stated that "workers have been told to clean toilets, sweep lawns and write confession letters, which are then pinned up on noticeboards or read out to colleagues" (Foxconn, 2012, para. 4). A journalist called for the company to treat its employees humanely, "Foxconn, please don't treat your workers like dogs" (Chang, 2010, para. 13). Foxconn CEO responded to criticisms about working conditions by stating uncaringly, "People are calling us sweatshops. What's wrong with sweatshops?" (Fiegerman, 2012, para. 3). The factories are also dangerous. In a survey of workers, over 43% said they either witnessed or personally experienced some type of work-related accident (Pepitone, 2012). In 2011, for instance, explosions occurred in two different Foxconn plants (Brownlee, 2011). China Labor Watch, a non-profit organization that partners with unions in China for safe working conditions, explained that the blasts were a "result of aluminum dust in the workshop where iPad cases are polished" (Brownlee, 2011, para. 3). In total, three employees died and over 60 were injured in the blasts.

In contrast to Steve Job's "pretty nice" description of Foxconn, employees live "on campus" in company "dormitories." The terms used by the company resemble the way many readers may picture life at college or in a Silicon Valley Fortune 500 company. Employees' lives in these large apartment buildings, however, do not match our common understanding of these words. At times, 20–30 employees share a three-bedroom apartment with up to eight people per bedroom stacked in bunks. Since employees work various shifts around the clock, it is common to live with roommates for months without ever speaking face to face or even learning each other's names. The *Shanghai Evening Post,* a Chinese news agency, sent an undercover reporter to work at Foxconn. His notes describe his experiences:

> The first night sleeping at Foxconn dormitory is a nightmare. The whole dormitory smells like garbage when I walked in. It's a mixed of overnight garbage smell plus dirty sweat and foam smell. Outside every room was fully piled up with uncleared trash. When I opened my wardrobe, lots of cockroaches crawl out from inside and the bed sheets that are being distributed to every new workers are full of dirts and ashes. (sic) (Wrenn, 2012, para. 9–13)

Employees in the apartments are "forbidden from using power-hungry electrical items such as [cooking] kettles or laptops" (Foxconn, 2012, para. 6). If they do, the company confiscates these personal items. The windows in these apartments are covered with prison-like bars.

Employees' Resistance

For some employees, life at Foxconn was simply too difficult to bear. In 2010, 14 employees committed suicide at Foxconn and three more attempted suicide ("Foxconn Worker," 2010). In most cases, employees jump off of the roof of a Foxconn building to their death. Twenty more employees were stopped by other members at Foxconn before they could jump. Further, not all jumpers die. Tian Yu is one of the employees who survived her suicide attempt. She was a 17-year-old girl at the time and attempted suicide after working at Foxconn for a month. In the fall, she "suffered multiple spinal and hip fractures and was left paralyzed from the waist down" (Heffernan, 2013, para. 2). Chinese sociologists described the wave of suicides at Foxconn as a loud cry for help. After this wave of suicides, Foxconn employees twisted the Chinese pronunciation of the company's name to sound like "run to your death" (Moore, 2010, para. 6). When news broke about Foxconn's growing suicide problem in the US, reporters started asking then CEO Steve Jobs about the issue who then put pressure on Foxconn leaders to improve the company's working conditions. Unfortunately, in response, Foxconn did little to improve employees' lives. Instead, leaders took three main actions. First, they installed suicide nets that circled each building. The purpose of the nets was to catch jumpers and prevent their deaths. The nets also served as a deterrent for would-be jumpers because they decreased the likelihood that death would result from a suicide attempt. Second, the company hired counselors to be available to despondent employees. Third, the company forced each employee to sign an anti-suicide pledge in which the employee agreed not to commit suicide and also absolved Foxconn of any legal blame if they did so. This legal document was meant to prevent the company from being sued by families if their sons or daughters committed suicide.

Sometimes, employees resist by fighting back collectively against harsh treatment. In 2012, 150 employees went to the roof in protest and threatened mass suicide if their leaders did not improve their working conditions. They held out on the roof for two days until they were eventually convinced to come down when Foxconn leaders agreed to discuss their working conditions. One of the employees on the roof explained why they took such drastic measures, "The assembly line ran very fast and after just one morning we all had blisters and the skin on our hand was black. The factory was also really choked with dust and no one could bear it" (Moore, 2012, para. 6). Around the same time, a riot involving over 2,000 employees broke out at one of Foxconn's three major factories (Roberts, 2012). The riot was sparked by harsh treatment of employees by Foxconn's security guards, who employees describe as gangsters. Well before the riot, videos taken by fellow employees were broadcast by Chinese TV news sources showing guards beating employees. In a reaction to the riot, Geoffrey Crothall from Hong Kong's China Labor Bulletin, an organization that defends the rights of Chinese workers, stated that Foxconn security guards "have a longstanding reputation of being heavy-handed and harsh with workers" (Dexter, 2012, para. 4). Crothall continued, "[employees] have a greater sense of self-worth. They believe that they should be treated with dignity and self-respect" (para. 11). Rather than with respect, Foxconn's CEO sees employees quite differently. He once stated he "has a workforce of over one million worldwide and as human beings are also animals, to manage one million animals gives me a headache" (Blodget, 2012, para. 2). In many instances, employees simply quit, choosing unemployment over the depressing and suicide-inducing atmosphere of the company. Others feel forced to stay, often because their families are counting on their income.

Apple's Response

Conditions at Foxconn have been a constant embarrassment for Apple's leaders (Adams, 2012) and customers' consciences. Foxconn leaders have repeatedly promised to improve the conditions, pay, and treatment of their employees. All reports, however, show the opposite. Thus, how can a company as successful as Apple do business with leaders like those at Foxconn? The answer is more complicated than we likely prefer. Based only on public statements, Apple certainly appears to care about Foxconn employees. Apple's current CEO, Tim Cook, personally visited Foxconn's facilities in 2012 and released photos of his visit (Elmer-DeWitt, 2012). Deceased CEO Steve Jobs, however, never visited the factories. His statement about Foxconn's pool and restaurants were not based on first-hand knowledge. Further, when asked directly, an Apple spokeswoman would not comment in detail and referred to an earlier statement: "We care about every worker in our worldwide supply chain. We insist that our suppliers provide safe working conditions, treat workers with dignity and respect, and use environmentally responsible manufacturing processes wherever Apple products are made" (Foxconn, 2012, para. 18). Beyond these symbolic gestures, however, Apple's leadership has taken little action as it has in other similar cases. In the past, for instance, Apple cut ties to two other overseas manufacturing plants classified as "repeat offenders" for poor working conditions (Pepitone, 2012, para. 15). It has not done the same for Foxconn.

In addition to reputational problems, Foxconn's heavy-handed approach is ultimately hurting the company's profitability. Over a six-year period, Foxconn's profit margin shrunk, "from 3.7 percent in the first quarter of 2007 to a mere 1.5 percent in the third quarter of 2012" (Heffernan, 2013, para. 16). Not surprisingly, a key reason for decreasing profits is high employee turnover. The Fair Labor Association's investigation ("Fair Labor," 2012) noted that "high labor turnover … undermine[d] efficiency, and [caused] gaps in production and capacity planning" (p. 2) over the period covered by its research. To complicate matters further, some critics claim Apple is pushing Foxconn to meet aggressive deadlines to keep its string of new products flowing into stores. While Foxconn's profits have decreased, Apple's soared over the same period, peaking "at 39.3 percent in early 2012 from initial levels of 18.7 percent in 2007" (Heffernan, 2013, para. 16). Apple has an economic incentive to keep the pressure on Foxconn. Chan continued, "The problem here is not shortage of funds. Apple is the second-most profitable company in the Global Fortune 500" (Heffernan, 2013, para. 16). In other words, Apple can afford to ease its pressure on Foxconn and thereby reduce the need for overtime hours and an unrelenting pace.

Questions:

- What types of control (e.g., simple, bureaucratic, technical, etc.) were most common at Foxconn?
- What changes could Foxconn make to help the company reduce employee turnover?

A former Foxconn manager until 2013 stated, "Apple never cared about anything other than increasing product quality and decreasing production cost ... Workers' welfare has nothing to do with their interests" (Heffernan, 2013, para. 16). While Foxconn has made gradual changes to its policies amid the public outcry, it is difficult to undo a history of harsh and controlling culture overnight. It may be that its worst chapter is behind it but its employees still struggle. Over half of Foxconn employees still exceed the legal limit of overtime (Dugigg & Barboza, 2012).

Jim Beam's Sour Bathroom Break Policy

The Jim Beam company, that makes the best selling bourbon whiskey, was officially founded in 1933 after the end of prohibition in the USA. The Beam family bourbon business, however, goes back over 200 years, spans seven generations, and had several incarnations in that time (www.jimbeam.com). In 2008, the Beverage Tasting Institute of Chicago awarded Jim Beam's "Black Bourbon" the highest rating among the most well known brands of North American whiskey above other famous brands such as Jack Daniels. Despite its outward success, the company is not without its internal controversies. In October 2001, its distillery and bottling plant in Clermont, Kentucky, introduced a strict bathroom break policy for frontline employees. Employees working on the production line were only allowed to take one bathroom break before lunch, one after lunch, and one other unscheduled break per day. The leaders allowed exceptions for employees with medical conditions and a doctor's note. Company leaders put the new policy in place after they concluded that employees were abusing the comparatively more liberal bathroom policy that had been in place for years. This case looks at the way the factory managers approached the issue and how employees were treated as a result.

Employees Push Back

The plant managers' decision to limit bathroom breaks contributed to an adversarial relationship with those employees directly affected. The United Food and Commercial Workers union representing the approximately 100 employees affected at the plant helped employees fight the policy. Through the union, employees claimed that the new policy was both demeaning and unnecessary. In response, Jim Beam defended its new policy explaining that managers "'observed, documented and analyzed break habits of the employees' and consulted with a urologist to make sure that the new policy would be 'reasonable'"

(Schreiner, 2002a, para. 6). Employees who violated the guidelines would be disciplined in writing for taking more than the three breaks permitted and would be fired after six instances of unapproved trips to the bathroom. The state of Kentucky also weighed in on the dispute. The Kentucky Labor Cabinet issued a non-monetary citation to Jim Beam stating that the company's punitive bathroom break policy was illegal. The policy violated a 1998 federal OSHA policy that expects employers to allows "timely access" to bathrooms and not prevent employees from taking these breaks (Tejada, 2002). Jim Beam's policy allows a bathroom break around every two hours and "never more than three [hours]" (Schreiner, 2002a, para. 7). Despite the federal law, company managers believed their policy complied with the law, vowed to fight the citation, and continued the policy.

Employees felt the effects of the new policy right away. For many, these long stretches of time can be too much. During the time the policy was in place, plant managers disciplined 45 of the 100 employees, and some were in danger of losing their jobs. Krystal Ditto, an employee stated, "It's embarrassing to be a 36-year-old woman and have to justify your need to go to the bathroom" (Schreiner, 2002b, para. 9). At the time of her statement, the single mother of two was just one unscheduled break away from being fired. She continued, "Once you get the feeling you have to go, you sit there looking at the clock and see you have an hour to go, and it intensifies. I'm not going to sit there and be miserable" (para. 10). A union representative said that some employees "had urinated on themselves because they were afraid of breaking the policy, and some had started wearing protective undergarments [or adult diapers]" (Schreiner, 2002b, para. 3). Angie Mattingly, a 25-year-old employee, secured a doctor's note for an overactive bladder but also said, "Mother Nature isn't a medical problem" (Tejada, 2002, para. 1). The decision, of course, came directly from the plant managers and did not solicit input from employees who were expected to obey or be fired.

The reach of the policy went beyond the walls of the bottling plant. Jo Anne Kelley, the union local's president, said the policy degraded employees and that company executives told some workers to "practice" going to the bathroom every two hours on the weekends "to put themselves on a schedule" (Schreiner, 2002b, para. 13). Kelly continued, "Basically, we're being asked to train our bladders and other organs to meet their needs, not ours," Kelley said. "Your bodily functions don't have a time clock" (Schreiner, 2002b, para. 14). Within several months of the policy, 29 employees obtained medical waivers and were therefore exempt from the policy. One who obtained a waiver explained, "I've held it and it's miserable. … You can only concentrate on looking at the clock and wondering when break time is going to be" (Schreiner, 2002b, para. 11). Some employees resorted to wearing adult diapers to keep their jobs. Employees' statements are not mere complaints. In fact, the Bladder and Bowel Foundation reports that while urinating six to seven times each 24-hour day is average, some people go as few as four and some as many as ten times per day ("Frequency," n.d.). Ironically, the union representing the employees claimed that the urologist hired by Jim Beam determined the excessive bathroom breaks that concerned company leaders were not motivated "by [employees'] need" to go to the bathroom but more likely by particular employees' "smoking habits" (Schreiner, 2002b, para. 7). Instead of addressing the individuals who took extra smoking breaks directly, the plant managers created a policy that grouped non-smokers and smokers alike.

Ineffective Policies

Three points about Jim Beam's bathroom policy signal the type of relationship managers had established with their employees. First, managers wrote the policy even though they knew that it likely violated federal laws. They imposed the bathroom break policy on top of an already rigid bottling assembly line work process. Second, managers made no claims that the plant's productivity was suffering from too many bathroom breaks from the start. Alternatively, managers could very well have been prompted by a managerial philosophy rather than an actual business need to reduce bathroom breaks. In fact, the policy had a negative effect on the company because it demoralized employees who felt "stripped of their dignity" (Schreiner, 2002c, para. 8) and were preoccupied with fighting back. Third, Jim Beam's policy was applied to employees only. Managers did not limit their own bathroom use. Employees who weren't able to wait would lose their jobs, urinate in their pants, wear diapers, or claim to have a medical condition. Managers did not hold themselves to the same standard. The break policy, thus, added fuel to the fire of a conflict-ridden relationship between managers and employees and piled more rules to an already-restrictive set of workplace policies.

Over time, Jim Beam felt increased pressure from the Kentucky Labor Cabinet's citation and hearing, the public outcry against the company, and employees' collective resistance. The outside entities agreed that it was Jim Beam's managers, not its employees, who were in the wrong. On Friday September 6, 2001, Jim Beam's CEO, Rich Reese, announced that the company would return to its former open-ended bathroom break policy almost a year after the rule went in place: "Our former policy was intended only to manage excessive breaks, and we believe it provided appropriate flexibility. … However, we've listened to the concerns of our employees and have changed our policy" (Schreiner, 2002c, para. 4). Reese also stated that Jim Beam would work with the employees' union leaders toward a "mutually acceptable solution for managing breaks" (Schreiner, 2002c, para. 6). Jo Anne Kelley, union president, stated about the policy change, "I am really glad to hear that they've come to their senses … [and] I look forward to sitting down with them and trying to work in a reasonable and adult manner to reach a solution" (para. 9). She continued, "If we have won, it is a victory for working people all over the country. … If we had lost this battle, it would have been a domino effect. It would have gone all over the country" (Schreiner, 2002c, para. 12). Krystal Ditto, the single mother of two, was relieved when she heard the news: "Nobody should have to go to work with that kind of fear" (Schreiner, 2002c, para. 20).

Jim Beam Employees Are Not Alone

Jim Beam employees are not alone. OSHA cites 30 to 40 employers each year for similar bathroom break policies (Tejada, 2002). These remain a controversial issue in many settings. WaterSaver Faucet Co. in Chicago, for example, recently implemented a bathroom break policy that allowed employees just two bathroom breaks a day (Williams, 2014). Employees must swipe in and swipe out with their ID cards for each trip. If they spend more than six minutes in the bathroom per day, they are punished. The company literally tracks every second of their bathroom breaks and takes workers off the clock while they go. The CEO of WaterSaver admits he has "no hard evidence" (Williams, 2014, p. 4) that employees are doing anything other than going to the bathroom, though he suspects they are avoiding work. Nevertheless, about one-third of employees have been punished for going too often. An employee union representative explained employees' humiliation about the policy: "[managers had] meetings with workers and human resources where the workers had to explain what they were doing in the bathroom" (Williams, 2014, para. 4). In fact, the company keeps a detailed spreadsheet that shows how long each employee's trips to the bathroom take. Employees have picketed the policy without success. As was the case at Jim Beam, managers did not say if they would be applying the same break policy to themselves, though it is unlikely based upon past practices. At WaterSaver, employees are going through their union to get relief from this policy.

However, not all employees respond as calmly as those from Jim Beam and WaterSaver. Consider, for example, the decisive backlash that leaders at China's Shanghai Shinmei Electric Company faced ("Chinese Workers," 2013). In January 2013, it enforced a new policy that limited the company's 1,000 employees' bathroom breaks to just two minutes or they would face fines and termination. In response, employees held 18 managers hostage inside the factory for 36 hours in protest. Employees released the managers only after over 300 police arrived at the company, and managers agreed to reconsider the bathroom break rule. In the US, physical resistance like this is not likely. Still, the ambiguity of OSHA's "timely access" rule will allow this struggle to continue in companies across the country.

Questions:

- If "no hard evidence" existed that employees abused bathroom breaks, why do you believe managers insisted on tightening existing policies even more?
- How might these companies approach the issue of bathroom breaks in a more reasonable way that maintains cooperative relationships with employees?

Workplace Bullying at the Miami Dolphins

The National Football League (NFL) consists of 32 teams. In the past several years, numerous off-field incidents have tarnished the league's reputation. Players from various teams have been accused of domestic violence, illegal drug use, sexual assault, dog fighting, and even murder. Of course, the vast majority of players are not involved in illegal activity. Further, it is easy to blame the NFL's macho culture for attracting players with aggressive, dominating personalities who sometimes live recklessly. The issue, however, is not solely about these players' personal lives. Their choices influence teams on the field and shape the league in profound ways. The Miami Dolphins' workplace bullying incident provides an inside look at how some players' hard-hitting dispositions sometimes damage their organization's culture and perceived legitimacy. The two key players involved were Richie Incognito and Jonathan Martin. This case looks at how these players and team leaders handled the bullying issue.

Miami's Offensive Linemen

Richie Incognito played at the University of Nebraska on the offensive line. He was a talented player but was suspended from the team more than once for breaking team rules, fighting at parties, and even fighting his own teammates in the locker room (Pennington, 2013). His coach required him to attend anger management classes. In 2005, Incognito entered the NFL draft. He is 6′3″, weighs over 300 lbs, and is white. He was arguably the most talented offensive guard available in the 2005 draft. Despite his size, strength, and talent, he slipped into the third round of the draft in part because of his known anger issues ("Richie Incognito," n.d.). While he played for the St. Louis Rams from 2005 until 2009, Incognito quickly solidified his reputation for playing dirty football. He insulted referees during the game, had frequent unnecessary-roughness penalties, and was occasionally flagged for head-butting players. He had the most personal fouls in the league during that time period and in 2009 was voted the dirtiest player in the league (Pennington, 2013). Over the years, NFL coaches benched him repeatedly because he could not control his anger. After numerous unheeded warnings from his coaches and fines from the NFL, the Rams released him. In 2010, Incognito signed with the Miami Dolphins. He quickly asserted himself as the offensive line's unofficial leader on and off the field.

When Jonathan Martin came to the Miami Dolphins in 2012, two years after Incognito, they became teammates on the offensive line. The Miami Dolphins picked Martin high in the second round of the draft. He is 6′5″, weighs over 300 lbs, and is African-American. Together, Martin and Incognito played, trained, were coached, and socialized off the field along with other offensive linemen. Unlike the attention-grabbing Incognito, Martin had a quiet disposition. He was raised in an upper-middleclass home. His father is a college professor and his mother is a lawyer (Hyde, 2012). His mellow demeanor became obvious to observers. For instance, in 2013 mid-season, coaches switched Martin to another offensive position, a move that can often unsettle players. Martin's response sounded mature. He told a *Miami Herald* reporter, "You can approach this two different ways. … You can go in the tank and be one of those guys who bitches and moans and is a cancer in the locker room, or you can be a guy who goes out there and can be a professional and plays as hard as I can" (Salguero, 2013, para. 15). However, on October 28, 2013, Martin's demeanor changed. Early reports indicated that he abruptly left the Miami Dolphins training facility after being mistreated by Richie Incognito and some other players during a meal. Within a few months, the full details of Incognito's relationship with and treatment of Martin were released to the NFL, Miami Dolphins, and public.

A Pattern of Bullying

Shortly after allegations that Martin was mistreated, the NFL hired a law firm to investigate the incident. The firm produced the conclusive, "Wells Report" (Wells, Karp, Birenboim, & Brown, 2014). After a complete investigation, "three starters on the Dolphins offensive line, Richie Incognito, John Jerry and Mike Pouncey, engaged in a pattern of harassment" (Wells et al., 2014, p. 1). The report named Incognito as the leader of the three bullies. The primary targets of the harassment were Martin, two other unnamed teammates, and an assistant trainer. The players at the center of the controversy were Incognito and Martin.

Incognito's bullying was evident in some of the 1,300 text messages exchanged between Incognito and Martin as well as voicemails. The majority of these were mundane and demonstrated that the two worked and socialized together. Some messages, however, demonstrated clear instances of vulgarity and cruelty aimed at Martin. While discussing a lineman trip to Las Vegas organized by Incognito, a flurry of successive texts to Martin suddenly turned cruel. (*Note:* These messages are edited here for the sake of propriety.)

> Incognito: U f****** mulatto liberal b****
> Incognito: I'm going to s*** in ur eye
> Incognito: Goodnight slut
> Incognito: Tell ur ***** sister I said hi
> Martin: Ah yes I missed being demeaned by you boys lol ... Can't wait for this weekend.
> (Wells et al., 2014, p. 96)

Despite Martin's stated intentions to go to Las Vegas, he did not show up with the rest of his teammates and claimed he would be late. When Incognito heard this, he texted the following: "Shut the f*** up weirdo. I'm going to beat ur a** and s*** in ur mouth u f****** f*****" (p. 97). Martin's return text read: "Sounds like my kind of vacation – getting my a** beat & s*** on by a bipolar psychopath" (p. 97). Instead of showing up late, Martin did not show up at all in Las Vegas. In addition to avoidance, these texts show that Martin responded with sarcasm instead of stating his distaste for and anxiety about Incongito's behavior. Martin hoped the taunting would subside once he entered his second year on the team and that he could just ride out the verbal abusive storm until then (Wells et al., 2014). These texts confirm that the messages did not stop. Even off-season, Incognito found ways to attack Martin and assert his dominance. For instance, one day after Martin had posted a comment on social media, Incognito left the following voicemail for Martin:

> Hey, wassup, you half-n***** piece of s***. I saw you on Twitter, you been training 10 weeks. I'll s*** in your f*******' mouth. I'm gonna slap your f******' mouth, I'm gonna slap your real mother across the face [laughter]. F*** you, you're still a rookie. I'll kill you. (p. 99)

The aggressive messages were not limited to Martin. To another player, Incognito discussed his plan to buy a rifle that was "perfect for shooting black people" (p. 103).

In both texts and daily interactions, Incognito made racially charged comments, frequently used "the N word," made continuous homophobic insults, and repeatedly told Martin about the various and detailed, forcible sexual acts he planned to perform on Martin's sister, which are all documented in his text messages.

Martin Response and Departure

Martin never confronted or responded directly or in the moment to Incognito. Instead, he was passive or sarcastic in return. Though Martin often tried to avoid Incognito, it was not entirely possible. Further, Martin described Incognito as "bi-polar." One moment he acted supportive and compassionate toward Martin, and the next moment, he turned abusive (Wells et al., 2014). This confused Martin, who desired to be accepted and respected by more veteran players. In a text message to his mother six months before Martin left the team, he wrote the following:

> I figured out a major source of my anxiety. I'm a pushover, a people pleaser. I avoid confrontation whenever I can. I always want everyone to like me. I let people talk about me, say anything to my face, and I just take it, laugh it off, even when I know they are intentionally trying to disrespect me. (p. 102)

In another message to her, he clearly blames himself for the harsh treatment, "Everywhere I go, I get punked. I have a disagreeable personality, people are always annoyed by me. And I don't know how to stop it. I don't" (p. 104). Similarly, Martin sent the following message to his father:

> I wish I had your toughness dad … People call me a N***** to my face. Happened 2 days ago. And I laughed it off. Because I am too nice of a person. They say terrible things about my sister. I don't do anything. I suppose it's [my] white private school conditioning, turning the other cheek. (p. 107)

For years, Martin had privately suffered from anxiety and depression. During his time at the Miami Dolphins, his condition became much more acute. On October 28, 2013, he simply could not take it anymore. After some typical insults by Incognito at the Miami Dolphins cafeteria, Martin sat down to eat dinner with the other offensive lineman. When he did, Incognito and the other lineman all stood up and walked away to signal that Martin was not welcome at the table, a common hazing move. With that, Martin slammed down his tray of food and left the facility for good. He reached his breaking point and checked himself into a mental health facility.

The Miami Dolphins' Initial Response

The days immediately following Martin's striking departure were filled with speculation. The media quickly took Martin's side and began criticizing Incognito's behavior. Other teammates reached out to Martin to express their support for him and disapproval of Incognito. Not all members of the Miami Dolphins supported Martin, however. Offensive line coach Jim Turner blamed Martin and stood up for Incognito. Coach Turner sent the following texts to pressure Martin in the several days after Martin left the team's facility:

- Richie Incognito is getting hammered on national TV. This is not right. You could put an end to all the rumors with a simple statement. DO THE RIGHT THING. NOW.
- … [Incognito] has been beat up for four days. Put an end to this. You are a grown man. Do the right thing.
- John I want the best for you and your health but make a statement and take the heat off Richie and the locker room. This isn't right.
- I know you are a man of character. Where is it? (pp. 134–135)

Eventually, Coach Turner backed off. Several days after Martin's departure, the Miami Dolphins' leadership released the following press statement ("Miami Dolphins," 2013):

> The Miami Dolphins, including Coach Joe Philbin and Jonathan's teammates, have been in communication with Jonathan and his family since his departure from the club and continue to be in contact. Our primary concern for Jonathan is his overall health and well-being. As an organization, we take any accusations of player misconduct seriously. The notion of bullying is based on speculation and has not been presented to us as a concern from Jonathan or anyone else internally. … We will continue to make Jonathan's health and well-being a focus as we do with all of our players.

When the team's leadership issued this statement, they were not aware of the various voicemails and texts that Incognito sent to Martin. As such, the statement clearly labels "mental health" as the issue for Martin but downplays the possibility that his departure was caused by bullying, a claim the media was already making.

Incognito's View

In the weeks following Martin's departure, Incognito responded in two opposing ways. On the one hand, he texted Martin frequently to offer his support. For example, he wrote, "It's unbelievable all the attention this is getting. All that's important is that you feel better and know we miss u dude" (p. 131). Similarly, Incognito claimed publicly and repeatedly that he and Martin were close friends. He cited the 1,300 exchanged text messages as proof that the two shared a bond. Incognito claimed that if Martin was offended or hurt by his actions, Martin never told him. After all, Incognito pointed out, the two frequently spent one-on-one time together and with the other lineman at restaurants and bars. Incognito claimed (Wells et al., 2014) that if Martin had simply told him to stop, he would have. Incognito interpreted Martin use of coarse language in their exchanges as implied approval of his own. In an *NFL Sunday* interview (Glazer, 2013) on the *Fox* network, Incognito stated the following:

> If I would have known that this was hurting John, we've spent plenty of time one-on-one outside of football, if John would have came to me once or if other teammates would have come to me once and said "Listen, lay off John, he's had enough of it, it's been too much," I would have been the first person not just to change myself but to change people around me.

The interviewer asked Incognito about the potential perceptions of a white man calling an African American "the N word." Incognito agreed that it was not appropriate. His public position on the bullying accusations can be summed up as follows: *I was just joking around and it looks worse than it was. If it bothered Martin, he never let on.*

On the other hand, while claiming innocence for himself and compassion for Martin, Incognito simultaneously sent text messages to teammates that systematically disparaged Martin. He wrote several messages to Mike Pouncey, a fellow lineman who was also implicated, "F*** Jmart [Johnathan Martin] That f***** is never [allowed] back," "F*** that guy if Ur not with [u]s Ur against us," "Snitches get stitches Blood in blood out F****** guy" (p. 133). Pouncey agreed and responded, "He's dead to me" (p. 133). Further, at the same time he was expressing support to Martin privately via texts and denying any wrongdoing publicly, Incognito was attempting to get rid of evidence that showed his abuse. For example, he tried to get rid of a notebook called the "fine book" in which he recorded monetary fines he imposed on the players and himself as well as bonuses the players were awarded for various behaviors. In one fine-book entry, Incognito fined Martin an incredible $10,000 for not showing up to the trip to Las Vegas and badgered him constantly to pay up. Even more incredibly, Martin paid the fine, perhaps to calm Incognito down. In another, he recorded a fine against himself for $200 for "breaking Jmart" (Wells et al., 2014, p. 3). About one week after Martin left the team, Incognito texted two fellow lineman: "They're going to suspend me. Please destroy the fine book first thing in the morning" (pp. 3–4). The attempted destruction of the fine book indicated that Incognito knew he acted inappropriately toward Martin or at least that his actions would look inappropriate to outsiders.

Aftermath: The Evidence Adds Up

The Miami Dolphins suspended Incognito indefinitely after hearing various voicemails and texts about a week after Martin left the team. Team leaders were particularly concerned with the voicemail in which Incognito calls Martin "half-n***** piece of s***" (Wells et al., 2014, p. 99) as well as other racially explicit text messages. After hearing and seeing messages like these, an unnamed source from the team told a *Miami Herald* reporter, "He's done. … He'll never play another game here."

> **Questions:**
>
> - To what extent did Incognito's behavior help or hurt his team's performance and reputation?
> - To what extent do you believe the Miami Dolphin's and NFL's culture made Incognito's behavior seem normal?

The bullying, Martin's public departure, and the media attention that followed hurt the team on and off the field. That season, the Miami Dolphins' offensive line allowed the most sacks in the team's history. The offensive line went further downhill after Martin's departure and Incognito's suspension. In their December 22nd game against the Buffalo Bills, for instance, the offensive line allowed the quarterback to be sacked seven times, a season high. The team scored zero points in the game ("Bills Hurt," 2013). In their final game of the season, Miami scored only seven points against the New York Jets. After the Wells report was released by the NFL in February 2014, Incognito defended himself publicly with vigor. He did not, however, play football for Miami or any other team the next season. In 2015, the Buffalo Bills signed him. Martin played for the San Francisco 49ers in 2014 and retired after playing for the Carolina Panthers in 2015. Subsequently, he has remained relatively quiet about his time with the Miami Dolphins.

Chapter Discussion Questions

- To what extent do you think the organizations in this chapter took control too far? How did employees resist this control?
- What level of control would have helped these organizations become more effective?

- We see in these cases that communication did far more than merely transmit information from senders to receivers. In what ways did communication from the leaders and employees create and shape the organizations' reality?

Key Terms

- Monologic Communication
- Autocratic Leadership Style
- Simple Control
- Bureaucratic Control
- Technical Control
- Cultural Control
- Social Control
- Concertive Control
- Resistance
- Contagious Control
- Workplace Bullying
- Turf Wars
- Systematically Distorted Communication
- Objectification
- Disqualification
- Topical Avoidance

References

Barker, J. R., & Cheney, G. (1994). The concept and the practices of discipline in contemporary organizational life. *Communication Monographs, 61*, 19–43.

Bullis, C. A., & Tompkins, P. K. (1989). The forest ranger revisited: A study of control practices and identification. *Communication Monographs, 56*, 287–306.

Cherry, K. (2014). What is autocratic leadership? *About Health.* Retrieved from http://psychology.about.com/od/leadership/f/autocratic-leadership.htm

Cherulnik, P. D., Donley, K. A., Wiewel, T. S. R., & Miller, S. R. (2001). Charisma is contagious: The effect of leaders' charisma on observers' affect. *Journal of Applied Social Psychology, 31*, 2149–2159.

Craig, R. (1999). Communication theory as a field. *Communication Theory, 9*, 119–161.

Deal, T. E., & Kennedy, A. A. (1982). *Corporate cultures: The rites and rituals of corporate life.* Reading, MA: Addison-Wesley.

Deetz, S. A. (1990). Reclaiming the subject matter as a guide to mutual understanding: Effectiveness and ethics in interpersonal interaction. *Communication Quarterly, 38*, 226–243.

Deetz, S. A. (1992). *Democracy in an age of corporate colonization: Developments in communication and the politics of everyday life*. Albany, NY: State University of New York Press.

Eagly, A. H., & Johannesen-Schmidt, M. C. (2001). The leadership styles of women and men. *Journal of Social Issues, 57*, 781–797.

Janis, I. L. (1982). *Groupthink: Psychological studies of policy decisions and fiascoes*. Boston, MA: Houghton Mifflin.

Lutgen-Sandvik, P. (2006). Take this job and …: Quitting and other forms of resistance to workplace bullying. *Communication Monographs, 73*, 406–433.

Lutgen-Sandvik, P., Tracy, S. J., & Alberts, J. K. (2007). Burned by bullying in the workplace: Prevalence, perception, degree, and impact. *Journal of Management Studies, 44*, 837–862.

Lyon, A., (2005). "Intellectual capital" and struggles over the perceived value of members' expert knowledge in a knowledge-intensive organization. *Western Journal of Communication, 69*, 251–271.

Lyon, A. (2007). "Putting Patients First": Systematically distorted communication and Merck's marketing of Vioxx. *Journal of Applied Communication Research, 35*, 376–398.

Lyon, A., & Chesebro, J. (2010). The politics of knowledge: A critical perspective on organizational knowledge. In H. Canary & R. McPhee (Eds.), *Communication and organizational knowledge: Contemporary issues for theory and practice* (pp. 69–86). New York, NY: Routledge.

Mumby, D. K. (1993). Introduction: Narrative and social control. In D. K. Mumby (Ed.), *Narrative and social control: Critical perspectives* (pp. 1–14). Newbury Park, CA: Sage.

Mumby, D. K. (1997). The problem of hegemony: Rereading Gramsci for organizational communication studies. *Western Journal of Communication, 61*, 343–375.

Porath, C., & Pearson, C. (2013). The price of incivility. *Harvard Business Review, January-February*. Retrieved from https://hbr.org/2013/01/the-price-of-incivility

Putnam, R. (2000). *Bowling alone: The collapse and revival of American community*. New York, NY: Touchstone.

Richmond, V. P., Davis, L. M., Saylor, K., & McCroskey, J. C. (1984). Power strategies in organizations: Communication techniques and messages. *Human Communication Research, 11*, 85–108.

Rosenfeld, L. B., & Plax, T. G. (1975). Personality determinants of autocratic and democratic leadership. *Speech Monographs, 42*, 203–208.

Sy, T., Côté, S., & Saavedra, R. (2005). The contagious leader: Impact of the leader's mood on the mood of group members, group affective tone, and group processes. *Journal of Applied Psychology, 90*, 295–305.

Tompkins, P. K., & Cheney, G. E. (1985). Communication and unobtrusive control. In R. McPhee & P. Tompkins (Eds.), *Organizational communication: Traditional themes and new directions* (pp. 179–210). Beverly Hills, CA: Sage.

Ulmer, R. R., Sellnow, T., & Seeger, M. (2013). *Effective crisis communication: Moving from crisis to opportunity* (3rd ed.). Thousand Oaks, CA: Sage.

Van Vugt, M., Jepson, S. F., Hart, C. M., & De Cremer, D. (2004). Autocratic leadership in social dilemmas: A threat to group stability. *Journal of Experimental Social Psychology, 40*, 1–13.

Yoshikawa, M. (1977). Implications of Martin Buber's philosophy of dialogue in Japanese and American intercultural communication. *Communication, 6*, 103–124.

Zenger, J., & Folkman, J. (2013, November 27). Will your bad boss make you a bad boss too? *Harvard Business Review*. Retrieved from https://hbr.org/2013/11/will-your-bad-boss-make-you-a-bad-boss-too/

Enron References

Beltran, L. (2002, February 7). Skilling: It wasn't me. *CNN*. Retrieved from http://money.cnn.com/2002/02/07/news/enron_skilling/

Enron (1999). Annual report. Retrieved from http://www.enron.com/corp/investors/annuals/annual99/letter.html

Enron execs sold $1.3B in stock (2002, January 22). *CNN*. Retrieved from http://money.cnn.com/2002/01/22/companies/enron_stocks/

The Enron trial: The grilling of Skilling (2006, April 20). *The Economist*. Retrieved from http://www.economist.com/node/6838617

Gibney, A. (Producer), & Gibney, A. (Director). (2005). *Enron: The smartest guys in the room* [DVD]. United States: Mangolia Pictures.

House Energy and Commerce Committee. (2002, February 7). U.S. House Representative James Greenwood (R-PA) holds oversight and investigation subcommittee, Panel IV. *Federal News Service*.

Mayberry, E. (2006, April 25). Enron trial: Ken Lay denies breaking law. *Houston Public Media*. Retrieved from http://www.houstonpublicmedia.org/news/16188

McLean, B. & Elkind, P. (2003). *The smartest guys in the room: The amazing rise and scandalous fall of Enron*. London: Portfolio.

Schwartz, J. (2002, February 7). Enron's many strands: The former C.E.O. *New York Times*. Retrieved from http://www.nytimes.com/2002/02/07/business/enron-s-many-strands-former-ceo-darth-vader-machiavelli-skilling-set-intense.html?pagewanted=all

Senate Commerce, Science and Transportation Committee. (2002, February). U.S. Senator Byron Dorgan (D-ND) holds hearing on financial collapse of Enron. *Federal News Service*.

Shaw, N. (2001, September 24). Email. Retrieved January 27, 2006 from http://sonic.ncsa.uiuc.edu/enron

Skilling claims he knew nothing. (2002, February 7). *CNN*. Retrieved from http://money.cnn.com/2002/02/07/news/enron_roundup

Swartz, M., & Watkins, S. (2003). *Power failure: The inside story of the collapse of Enron*. New York, NY: Doubleday.

Foxconn References

Adams, S. (2012, September 12). Apple's new Foxconn embarrassment. *Forbes*. Retrieved from http://www.forbes.com/sites/susanadams/2012/09/12/apples-new-foxconn-embarrassment

Blodget, H. (2012, January 19). CEO of Apple partner Foxconn: "Managing one million animals gives me a headache." *Business Insider*. Retrieved from http://www.businessinsider.com/foxconn-animals-2012-1

Brownlee, J. (2010, June 4). Advocacy group: Foxconn employee died of exhaustion after 34-hour shift. *Cult of Mac*. Retrieved from http://www.cultofmac.com/45716/advocacy-group-foxconn-employee-died-of-exhaustion-after-34-hour-shift/

Brownlee, J. (2011, December 20). Both Foxconn iPad 2 factories exploded for the same reason. *Cult of Mac*. Retrieved from http://www.cultofmac.com/136398/both-foxconn-ipad-2-factories-exploded-for-the-same-reason/

Chang, C. (2010, May 19). The shocking conditions inside China's brutal Foxconn factor. *Business Insider*. Retrieved from http://www.businessinsider.com/the-shocking-conditions-inside-chinas-brutal-foxconn-factory-2010-5#ixzz2nfF8czgW

Dugigg, C., & Barboza, D. (2012). In China, human costs are built into an iPad. *New York Times*. Retrieved from http://www.nytimes.com/2012/01/26/business/ieconomy-apples-ipad-and-the-human-costs-for-workers-in-china.html?_r=0

Elmer-DeWitt, P. (2012, March 29). Tim Cook's China photo album. *CNN*. Retrieved from http://tech.fortune.cnn.com/2012/03/29/tim-cooks-china-photo-album/?iid=EL

Fair Labor Association (2012, March). *Independent Investigation of Apple Supplier*. Foxconn. Retrieved from http://www.fairlabor.org/sites/default/files/documents/reports/foxconn_investigation_report.pdf

Fiegerman, S. (2012, March 3). Foxconn's CEO is in trouble again, this time for saying, "What's wrong with sweatshops?" *Business Insider*. Retrieved from http://www.businessinsider.com/foxconn-ceo-talks-about-sweatshops-2012-5#ixzz2nfCMlPqM

"For a factory, it's pretty nice": Apple boss Steve Jobs defends conditions at Chinese factory where 10 workers have jumped to their deaths. (2010, June 2). *Daily Mail*. Retrieved from http://www.dailymail.co.uk/sciencetech/article-1283389/Apple-boss-Steve-Jobs-defends-China-Foxconn-factory-conditions-10-suicides.html

Foxconn worker plunges to death at China plant: Report (2010, November 5). *Reuters*. Retrieved from http://www.reuters.com/article/2010/11/05/us-china-foxconn-death-idUSTRE6A41M920101105

Heffernan, M. (2013, August 7). What happened after the Foxconn suicides. *CBS News*. Retrieved from http://www.cbsnews.com/news/what-happened-after-the-foxconn-suicides

Moore, M. (2010, May 27). Inside Foxconn's suicide factory. *The Telegraph*. Retrieved from http://www.telegraph.co.uk/finance/china-business/7773011/A-look-inside-the-Foxconn-suicide-factory.html

Moore, M. (2012, January 11). "Mass suicide" protest at Apple manufacturer Foxconn factory. *The Telegraph*. Retrieved from http://www.telegraph.co.uk/news/worldnews/asia/china/9006988/Mass-suicide-protest-at-Apple-manufacturer-Foxconn-factory.html

O'Toole, J. (2013, December 12). Foxconn's worker hours still excessive. *CNN*. Retrieved from http://money.cnn.com/2013/12/12/technology/foxconn-labor/

Pepitone, J. (2012, March 29). Apple supplier audit finds major wage and overtime violations. *CNN*. Retrieved from http://money.cnn.com/2012/03/29/technology/apple-foxconn-report/?iid=EL

Roberts, D. (2012, September 27). What's behind the Foxconn worker riots? *Business Week*. Retrieved from http://www.businessweek.com/articles/2012-09-27/whats-behind-the-foxconn-worker-riots

Jim Beam References

Chinese workers hold managers hostage after toilet break changes. (2013, January 22). *The Guardian.* Retrieved from http://www.theguardian.com/world/2013/jan/22/chinese-managers-hostage-toilet-breaks

Frequency. (n.d.). Bladder and Bowel Foundation. Retrieved from https://www.bladderandbowelfoundation.org/bladder/bladder-conditions-and-symptoms/frequency

Schreiner, B. (2002a, August 27). Jim Beam fighting citation for bathroom-break policy. *Associated Press Online.* Retrieved from http://www.tuscaloosanews.com/article/20020828/NEWS/208280346

Schreiner, B. (2002b, August 21). Jim Beam fighting citation for bathroom-break policy. *Associated Press Online.* Retrieved from http://www.bigbigforums.com/off-topic-chat/217680-jim-beam-fighting-citation-bathroom-break-policy.html

Schreiner, B. (2002c, September 7). Bathroom policy down the drain [online version]. *Cincinnati Gannett.* Retrieved from http://enquirer.com/editions/2002/09/07/fin_bathroom_policy_down.html

Tejada, C. (2002, August 28). New Labor Battleground: The Employee Bathroom. *Wall Street Journal.* Retrieved from http://www.wsj.com/articles/SB1030483251804972515

Williams, M. E. (2014). Can your employer punish you for bathroom breaks? *Salon.* Retrieved from http://www.salon.com/2014/07/18/can_your_job_punish_you_for_bathroom_breaks/

Miami Dolphins References

Bills hurt Dolphins' playoff hopes with shutout. (2013, December 22). *Associated Press.* Retrieved from http://www.nfl.com/gamecenter/2013122200/2013/REG16/dolphins@bills#menu=gameinfo|contentId%3A0ap2000000302330&tab=recap

Glazer, J. (2013, November 10). Richie Incognito sits down with Jay Glazer [video]. *Fox Sports.* Retrieved from https://www.youtube.com/watch?v=lTqT9wHAq3s.

Hyde, D. (2012, September 29). The education of Jonathan Martin on course. *Sun Sentinel.* Retrieved from http://articles.sun-sentinel.com/2012-09-29/sports/fl-hyde-miami-dolphins-0930-20120929_1_jonathan-martin-harvard-football-coach-harvard-grads.

Miami Dolphins statement on Jonathan Martin [Press release]. (2013, November 3). Retrieved from http://www.miamidolphins.com/news/press-releases/article-1/Miami-Dolphins-Statement-On-Jonathan-Martin/4d417b72-ad82-4ec9-8ce2-1ce6d2a560b2

Pennington, B. (2013, November 8). Prized for his aggression, Incognito struggled to stay in bounds. *New York Times.* Retrieved from http://www.nytimes.com/2013/11/09/sports/football/prized-for-his-aggression-richie-incognito-struggled-to-stay-in-bounds.html?_r=0

Richie Incognito [biography]. (n.d.). Draft Tracker. *ESPN.com.* Retrieved from http://proxy.espn.go.com/nfldraft/wireless/html/player?id=9109

Salguero, A. (2013a, December 23). Dolphins "concerned" about moving Martin. *Miami Herald.* Retrieved from http://miamiherald.typepad.com/dolphins_in_depth/2013/10/dolphins-concerned-about-moving-martin-.html

Wells, T. V., Karp, B. S., Birenboim, B., & Brown, D. W. (2014, February 14). *Report to the National Football League concerning issues of workplace conduct at the Miami Dolphins.* Retrieved from http://63bba9dfdf9675bf3f10-68be460ce43dd2a60dd64ca5eca4ae1d.r37.cf1.rackcdn.com/PaulWeissReport.pdf

2

Collaborative Communication and Case Studies

How effective would our workplaces be if we all knew how to collaborate? How efficient might we become as businesses if we were able to tap into the hidden productivity of the workforce?
—*Marshall, (1995, p. v)*

As organizations grow, they too often add a variety of tighter control systems discussed in Chapter 1. Nowadays, a tight control model is ill suited to contemporary, knowledge- and relationship-driven work in the new economy and information age, which relies increasingly on expertise and specialized skills. Newer, cutting-edge organizations thrive, in part, because of their collaboration, innovation, and creativity. This chapter moves the conversation from control to collaboration by first overviewing collaborative principles, barriers, and benefits and then presenting three case studies that illustrate how different organizations approach collaboration: Virtual-Learn, Bigger Pockets, and IDEO.

The Nature of Collaboration

At its core, the term "collaboration" describes the act of working jointly with others, particularly on intellectual or creative projects. Schwarz (2006) defines this word as meaning "a mutually beneficial relationship between two or more individuals, groups, or organizations who jointly design ways to work together to meet their related interests and who learn with and from each other, sharing responsibility, authority, and accountability for achieving results" (p. 282). Collaboration necessarily means letting go of an individualistic and potentially controlling disposition to make way for sharing work. John Harris is founder and CEO of California Defects Monitoring Program, the world's largest research organization focused entirely on finding the causes of birth defects. In a discussion about collaboration, he emphasized a group approach: "There has to be a shared belief among all of us that the team works better than the individual" (Schwarz, 2006, p. 6). Similarly, Kriss Deilglmeier, the executive director of Stanford University Graduate School for Business Center for Social Innovation, crystallized the collaborative mindset perhaps most concisely: "No one is as smart as everyone" (Schwarz, 2006, p. 6). Thus, working together achieves big goals.

When we collaborate, we view fellow workers as genuine partners who share common goals. Heath and Sias (1999) describe this as a ***collaborative spirit*** or "general intent or principles" that guide participants to share the same "goals, values and behavior" to work in an alliance (p. 358). Heath and Sias list numerous characteristics that grow from collaboration such as trust, integrity, true consensus, shared power, ownership, and alignment in all aspects of the organization. These same authors found that in many cases a lack of adequate back-and-forth communication inhibited true collaboration. In contrast, collaboration was made possible when the *content* of the communication was sufficient (e.g., to maintain a shared mission) and the communication fostered positive *relationships* (e.g., mutual supportiveness, reaffirmation of the collective enthusiasm).

Collaborative communication involves at least a two-way or transactional process and is not simply a linear matter of expressing ourselves so listeners can accurately receive our message. The goal is to use our interactions as co-creative exchanges where ideas are shared back and forth, meanings are collectively generated, and problems and solutions are constructed extemporaneously as the conversation unfolds. You may have had an informal conversation over coffee, for example, when ideas flowed freely. This conversation likely involved joking, "riffing" on each other's ideas, and even temporary misunderstandings that led the conversation in an unexpected but fruitful direction. The collaboration process generates transformed ideas with which neither person entered the conversation.

This approach depends upon genuine dialogue rather than tactical conversations. Martin Buber (1947, 1970) wrote about dialogic communication from a philosophical, ethical, and moral standpoint. To him, human beings are special. They deserve to be heard, understood, and their life experiences respected. As Arnett (2015) explained it, "Dialogue is defined by 'meeting,' not imposing information upon another" (p. 3). Dialogue also goes beyond merely taking turns or sharing data in an orderly fashion. Buber's ***dialogue*** signifies a deeper and more meaningful process of connection. As Yoshikawa (1977) explained, "It is only through the dynamic activity of coming together [through communication], without loss of individual identity that both can experience meaningful reciprocation and growth" (p. 106). Dialogue as honest, authentic communication between equally valuable individuals takes courage because it involves a genuine meeting between individuals where both parties share unique perspectives and appreciate the other. This ethic favors communication with a collaborative spirit.

Collaboration and the Stakeholder Model

The aim of the ***stakeholder model of communication*** is to make decisions and solve problems together. Straus (2002) sums up the two-fold benefits of this process:

> The power of collaboration comes from inclusion, not exclusion. … When the full range of differing interests and points of view is involved … [1] the solution is likely to be much more comprehensive and creative than if a small group of like-minded individuals acted on its own. [2] The inclusion of all stakeholders also naturally creates a broader base of support for the solution and increases the likelihood that it will actually be implemented. (Straus, 2002, p. 39)

A stakeholder decision-making group can make more creative decisions and is likely to gain the full support of all involved. A group of stakeholders is much more than a committee, department, or even a team because of the wide range of people involved and its collaborative spirit.

The term "stakeholder" was coined to contrast many corporations' historic focus on just one group—the owners of the company—and, by extension, the top executives who make decisions on their behalf. However, a ***stakeholder*** is any individual or group that has a stake in, or will be influenced by, an important decision. When working together, stakeholders have "the chance to contribute and collectively shape and implement solutions that represent much more than the sum of their individual ideas" (Sioukas & Sweet, 2006, p. 435). Ulmer (2001) explained, "[I]f organizations are going to be successful, they need to look beyond just their stockholders and expand their view of critical relationships" (p. 593). Stakeholder groups, he suggests, have the capacity positively or negatively to impact the organization.

The actual stakeholders for any given project may vary significantly. The scope, length, and impact of a project will shape who should be at the table. Existing research (e.g., Deetz, 1995; Sioukas & Sweet, 2006; Straus, 2002) suggests several overarching categories to consider when pulling a collaborative group together.

1. ***Those with the formal power to make decisions.*** In most cases, the official leaders of any group or organization are fairly clear. If the "boss" isn't on board in the early stages of a project, the entire effort may be a waste of time.
2. ***Those with the power to block decisions.*** Projects can get held up by any number of groups or individuals. Can somebody in the organization delay or simply ignore a group's effort or request? He or she has a stake in the decision.
3. ***Those affected by a decision.*** This is usually the most diverse category, and investors, suppliers, employees, supervisors, managers, customers, and even host community members of the organization may all have a stake in a group's decision because of the direct impact on their work and lives.
4. ***Those with relevant information or expertise.*** At times, only outside experts can answer certain questions. They are not necessarily primary decision makers because the group's decision may not affect them, but they do protect groups from blind spots.

Individuals and groups who need to be included in a project from start to finish and will be influenced the most are ***primary stakeholders***. Those who play more supporting roles are ***secondary stakeholders***. The broadest range should be included early in a decision-making process. The power of strong stakeholder relationships goes beyond high-quality decisions alone. Strong collaborative relationships can often translate into tangible action. Ulmer (2001), for example, shows how CEO Aaron Feuerstein of Malden Mills, a textile factory, leaned heavily on his long-established stakeholder relationships to rebuild his company after a devastating fire destroyed most of the factory. For years before the fire, Feuerstein proactively developed positive working relationships with primary stakeholders such as employees, the union, suppliers, and vendors, as well as secondary stakeholders such as the local media, other area organizations, the Chamber of Commerce, and the factory's host community in Massachusetts. Ulmer found that stakeholders overwhelmingly describe Feuerstein as acting with "the values of trust, reciprocity, and loyalty" as well as "providing open, candid, and accessible information to these stakeholders when needed" (p. 206) to establish and maintain these relationships. When the fire burned the factory to the ground, Feuerstein stood on camera in front of the still-smoldering building and asked a collection of willing stakeholders to help him rebuild the company. They believed him and worked tirelessly to support his vision to rebuild. Remarkably, with some salvaged equipment and a temporary building, Malden Mills began shipping new products in about a month. By two months after the fire, 70% of employees were back to work, and almost all workers were back on the job within several months as the factory was rebuilt and near full capacity. Feuerstein would not likely have accomplished this had he not built collaborative relationships with stakeholders over the long run.

Collaborative stakeholder relationships are much more than playing "good politics." They represent a shift in thinking about how decisions get made and problems get solved. As Deetz (1995) explained, "Many of the groups that are seen [historically] as external to the conceptual corporation now have to be considered as internal to its system. The corporation is seen as being accountable to many 'investors'" (p. 48). Some readers may be challenged by such committed conceptualizations of collaboration and prefer more traditional ways to solve problems. Indeed, a leader's role shifts from "shot caller" to coordinator. Deetz continued by stating, "The payoff from a more collaborative approach is not only in better corporate goal accomplishment, including economic goals. Learning to participate in collaborative decision making is also a value in itself" (Deetz, 1995, p. 49). To collaborate at the highest levels, we must rethink what "good communication" looks like.

Common Barriers to Collaboration

In addition to a control-mindset, three common barriers hinder our efforts to collaborate effectively. First, rigid structures, hierarchies, or chains-of-command make it difficult to mingle in the "white space" of our organizational charts and outside the official reporting channels. In many ways, a clear structure makes good sense. Like the traditional bureaucratic structures advocated by Max Weber (1947), a highly organized arrangement can create a shorthand way to divide the labor, manage ambiguity, and designate responsibilities. The trouble begins when the structure restrains rather than supports the organization's potential. The challenge is to move away from what Weick (1976, 1979) calls a ***tightly coupled*** arrangement, a structure where the various parts and departments are highly dependent upon each other. The parts of an assembly line, for example, are tightly connected and allow little room for creativity. When organizations are highly structured, workers stay in their prescribed boxes. In contrast, collaboration involves pulling people from various departments across functional areas of the workplace. For instance, Weick suggests that many organizations might be better served by a ***loosely coupled*** structure whereby the parts of an organization have flexible ties that allow people to work freely while still maintaining meaningful connections. Cross-functional teams, multiple stakeholder groups, and lattice structures, for instance, are all loosely coupled, decentralized ways to organize. Loose coupling, thus, still provides clarity organizations need to keep their projects coordinated but allows a space for collaboration, innovation, and creativity. A rigid structure can be a barrier to these outcomes.

Second, when we join organizations, we enter fairly ***politicized contexts***. Each organization accumulates a collective history of battles and choices (Deetz, 1992). Employees and leaders of the past put these long-standing structures in place. Over time, we may forget that these personal views, professional interests, and ideologies became embedded in a culture and codified into official policy, rules, and structures. Changes to those norms expose and threaten that system of beliefs and their identities. Dana Carvey's awkward character, Garth, in the film *Wayne's World* once said, "We fear change." Many people feel uncomfortable when new arrangements displace how we see ourselves, our sense of purpose, and our preferred understanding of work. This is why many leaders genuinely desire a more collaborative process but may be hesitant to embrace wholesale structural changes. The history of office politics, even in the most positive sense, can function as a barrier to collaboration.

Third, most large organizations today employ a high percentage of specialists. Expertise is essential but can also be an intellectual barrier to collaboration for a variety of reasons. The most obvious is that each field of knowledge (e.g., accounting, law, software development, engineering, etc.) has its unique technical vocabulary that takes months to learn and years to master. You may have had the conversational experience, for instance, where two educated professionals had difficulty understanding what the other person does for a living. We spend so much time speaking with individuals within our intellectual subculture that we may get frustrated by others' inability to follow our meaning. These moments help us recognize that our in-group has developed a depth of knowledge but does not necessarily understand other areas of expertise very well. As Lazega (1992) explains, we construct our knowledge in ***epistemic communities*** that, in part, reinforce our preferred interpretations about our expertise.

Specialists, thus, develop group sensibilities about the typical problems they expect to face and the stock solutions they most readily use. This is one reason some groups see their own expertise as very important and other areas of knowledge as only somewhat important. As Peter Drucker, a founder of organizational studies, stated, when left in isolation, specialists can become "intellectually arrogant and unproductive" (Drucker, 1993, p. 271). In his best selling book, *Post-Capitalist Society* (1993), Drucker underscores the simultaneous importance and difficulties expertise poses. He suggests the biggest daily challenge knowledge workers will face in the future is two-fold: (a) workers must understand the basic assumptions, theories, and aims of various knowledge areas, and (b) "take responsibility for making themselves and their specialty understood" (p. 217). Organizations can soften the influence of insular communities by encouraging collaboration outside of the usual subcultures of expertise.

The fourth barrier to collaboration involves the tendency toward ***individualism*** rather than collectivism in Western society. Many people believe, for instance, that the best way to succeed and thrive is to work alone. As Bennis and Beiderman (1997) state, "The myth of the triumphant individual is deeply ingrained in the American psyche" (p. 1). From the founding fathers' emphasis on individual rights, to president Herbert Hoover's notion of rugged individualism, to Frederick Douglass' concept of the self-made man, the narrative of individual success runs deep in our cultural vision of the American Dream. The problem with these individual success stories is that they are frequently more myth than fact. When we look around, we notice that few people actually become successful without the backing of at least an unofficial group of team members and allies. Buying into the philosophy of individual achievement too much creates a barrier between potential partners and ourselves. A healthy dose of ***collectivism***, the belief that gives priority to and puts faith in the group over the individual, is a prerequisite to good collaboration.

The best way to get a good idea is to get lots of ideas. (Linus Pauling, scientist and author)

Benefits of Collaboration

Collaborative communication has many benefits for both individuals and their organizations:

- ***Passion.*** Researchers have known for some time that leaders who use a more democratic style are often more likely to have satisfied employees, especially when the work involves moderate to high levels of complexity (e.g., Gastil, 1994). Collaborative communication by its nature embodies democratic ideals. Employees enjoy having a voice in and, thus, more direct influence over their own work. Further, in contrast to a one-way model of communication, a two-way collaborative process is a natural motivator for employees. Kelley and Littman (2001) describe the motivating "ripple effect" of brainstorming sessions that give people that "fantastic feeling of possibility" (p. 62). Cooke (1989), for instance, showed that higher productivity and greater quality improvements resulted from joint collaborative activities. As Bennis and Beiderman (1997) argue, "The payoff [for collaborative groups] is not money, or even glory. … The reward is the creative process itself" (p. 215). Collaboration cultivates employees' natural drive and initiative.

- ***More ideas.*** The most obvious benefit of collaboration is new ideas that individual contributors would not have thought of on their own. As Gray (1989) explains, collaboration is "a process through which parties who see different aspects of a problem can constructively explore their differences and search for solutions that go beyond their own limited vision of what is possible" (p. 5). Structures and control systems that separate us also rob organizations of the best that employees have to offer.
- ***Increased coordination.*** An active program of collaboration builds a strong organizational culture, which, in turn, fosters more collaboration. As Deetz, Tracy, and Simpson (2000) explain, "Important coordination and control can be achieved without direct supervisory intervention" (p. x). Deetz et al. show how employees generally favor the coordinating forces of a strong culture than the top-down alternative. Organizations that know the value of collaboration give their people "what they need and free them from the rest … [and] aren't places where memos are the primary form of communication. They aren't places where anything is filed in triplicate" (Bennis & Beiderman, 1997, p. 211). In most cases, a strong collaborative culture provides all the coordination organizations need.
- ***Social capital.*** Collaboration also builds the organization's social capital, a term that describes the value found in relational connections (Lyon, 2008). Any time we interact supportively with others, we make it much easier to access the organization's collective expertise and other resources to accomplish our work. Collaboration is one of the main ways employees build trust (Abrams, Cross, Lesser, & Levin, 2003), strong social ties, and mutual obligation toward each other. Many organizations seek to improve working relationships because they know this strengthens processes.

The following cases studies look at the mindset and practice of collaborative communication as opposed to the controlling variety. Each of these organizations pursues a collaborative spirit and innovative communication in its own unique way.

Case Studies on Collaborative Communication

Virtual-Learn: Growth and a Struggle Between "Silos" and Collaborative Efforts at an Upstart*

* *Several years ago, I conducted a field study at a knowledge-driven company that I refer to here a "Virtual-Learn" (a pseudonym). This case is based on longer accounts of this field research (e.g., Lyon, 2005; Lyon & Chesebro, 2010).*

Virtual-Learn was based in a mid-sized city in western US. During the company's first year, it employed approximately 12 to 20 employees and managers. The company's goal was clear: to design online courses for nurses and other medical professionals. At the time, the market for online education was growing rapidly, and great excitement filled the air at Virtual-Learn. The company's online course delivery involved more steps than live classroom teaching. It combined the elements of raw course content (e.g., medical information, healthcare policy, etc.), the online presentation of ideas (e.g., the readable texts, activities, graphics, etc.), and the technological delivery of the course (e.g., web programming, the application that allows students to navigate the course, etc.). Several diverse groups of employees worked together to develop the courses. This case looks at how Virtual-Learn struggled to maintain a collaborative dynamic as the company grew.

Struggling to Maintain a Team Atmosphere

Virtual-Learn developed fairly technical courses that were self-paced. Unlike many online college courses, Virtual-Learn's were entirely automated, and, once posted online, did not require ongoing attention from teachers on the other end. As such, the company employed a variety of experts to design and offer top-to-bottom course curriculums. In the beginning, the 12 to 20 employees all shared a common office space the way most new businesses do. They kept physical barriers to a minimum to allow close interaction among employees. Not surprisingly, the organization quickly developed a team-based approach. While the company did have an official "org chart," it existed on paper only since some departments employed only a single employee. As such, interactions flowed without walls or bureaucratic barriers. If one employee had a question, he or she just leaned over and asked the person seated nearby. Employees handled issues with courses in real time. Each person offered feedback on an on-going basis.

Employees' intellectual, creative, and collaborative work impressed clients quickly. The company secured a few small clients right away. Before long, executives made a deal with a very large client, a chain of hospitals that employed thousands of would-be students. To meet the growing demand, Virtual-Learn expanded and hired rapidly. Within just two to three years of its inception, it peaked at 120 employees. To cope with the growth, the company did what many organizations do, but these decisions ultimately contributed to some undesirable and unintended outcomes.

Several small changes drastically influenced employees' ability to collaborate freely. First, the organization's hierarchy lengthened. Managers and executives moved into private offices and met mostly with each other. As the company grew, the organization added more executive-level members, in part, because the leaders assumed the company's growth would continue. Some of the original executives, in fact, admitted that the company's pyramid had "become too top-heavy" with more executives and managers. Decisions had to be run all the way "up the flagpole" and back down before employees could take any meaningful actions. Under the new structure, only the direct supervisors interacted regularly with front-line employees, which is uncommon for a company of 120 members. Standardized rules, policies, and expectations replaced the cultural norms that developed in the early months of the company.

Second, the company became more divided across departments. In contrast to the original shared space, the organization moved to a larger, segmented office space split over two floors of the building. Visiting other departments often required an elevator. The layout of the top floor included small offices that fit one to three employees. At first, the sometimes-spoken statement, "I have my own office," appealed to some members who enjoyed the privacy and status. These spaces housed instructional designers, editors, nurses, application developers, human resources, and executives. The lower floor offered comparatively more open space or "bullpen" with two main areas that clustered about a dozen employees each. It had some smaller, segmented managerial offices lining the windows and primarily accommodated web programmers, digital illustrators, their supervisors and mid-level managers.

With Walls Came Barriers

Unfortunately, the departmentalized and segmented workspace functioned as natural barriers to working with employees outside of a prescribed area. In addition, the divided physical space coincided with greater division of labor for the company's tasks. Before long, the company was structured into what members called several "silos," one silo or department under each executive with little communication between and among these work areas. As each department grew, employees' work roles narrowed for the sake of efficiency. For example, one editor was particularly good at catching mistakes and consistency issues in the online courses while another excelled at revising a wordy course to enhance clarity. Over time, as the company increased its workload, employees complained that the organization had become "just like an assembly line." Further, the absence of shared space decreased casual and spontaneous interactions with employees from other work areas.

The work process posted along the wall of the halls also showed the strains of growth. These maps showed hundreds of miniscule steps involved in bringing a course from start to finish, steps that the original team did more intuitively while working in a shared space sitting side by side. One instructional designer summed up the increasingly frustrating work experience as "throwing the folder [or course] over the wall" to the next department once he completed his single step, "never to see it again." A researcher at the company explained it in similar terms: "The problem I see happening is that work is too departmentalized right now. Where all the skills are, 'Oh, it's a writing issue, send it to the instructional design department or to edit.' So, what we end up doing is trying to put all the separate pieces together as opposed to developing it all as more of an organic or holistic effort." Technically, nothing about Virtual-Learn's growth, bureaucracy, and office layout forbid the collaboration and teamwork employees desired. Nevertheless, cross-departmental projects almost completely ceased. The original team who formed the company simply did not have enough momentum to continue the cross-functional teamwork once employees and executives were separated by walls, departmental structures, and a growing list of protocols. Further, most new employees had never experienced the organization's earliest and most collaborative months. They were hired into layers of bureaucracy, divided labor, and a protracted chain of command. These new norms overwhelmed the original atmosphere that helped the company grow and so rapidly and attract clients in the first place. This was an outcome of growth and consequences that leaders never anticipated. Even worse, the company's largest client complained about a decrease in quality of the courses the company was producing.

Experiments with Collaboration

Dissatisfaction with the organization's restrictive arrangement led some employees to initiate an experiment with a team approach. With permission from executives, a supervisor pulled employees from each department to make online courses collaboratively to mimic the original process. Instructional designers worked alongside editors, digital illustrators sat side by side with nurses, and software application developers shared computer screens with web programmers. One of the team's goals was to upend the way the rest of the organization was currently structured. Over the next several weeks, the results of this collaboration delighted the team members and their supervisor. The team produced some of the highest quality courses the company had ever made. Hal, a team member, reflected on the experience and looked forward to the way the team approach was "going to help with innovation as far as coming up with new activities for the courses … If people are collaborating in the beginning, then these ideas are coming out right before the course is even really written." His co-worker, Tim, agreed: "Yeah, and in that type of collaboration, new ideas come up that never would." Melissa, an editor, was also energized by the process and explained the benefits of the teamwork:

> This time [with the team approach] I got to see everybody working on the art. I got to see the ugly little tagged up page turn into this cool thing where you push a button and this liver splits up into two pieces and goes to two patients. It was so cool I could have sat there all day pushing the button and watching the liver split, which I didn't *(laughing)*. So, I loved that. I loved the collaboration. I felt like having a—I had a blast with Sally, partly because Sally is a blast—but having a less linear or less compartmentalized relationship—editor-instructional designer relationship—was great because we were in and out of each other's offices throughout the whole thing. She would try something and I was her second pair of eyes.

Melissa highlights several aspects of the teamwork that differ from the "linear" and "compartmentalized" approach the company had grown into. Melissa, Hall, Tim, and other collaborators instantly understood how the team process differed from the more traditional one that most of the company has accepted as a necessary step following growth.

Around the same time, the web programming manager, Dave, took a collaborative approach with his employees. He was one of the few managers who worked alongside his department in the lower-level's shared space. Dave emphasized coaching and mentoring much more than managers on the segmented top floor. His main goal was to get those he supervised "trained up" as soon as possible:

> If everybody knew what I know all of a sudden, it makes my job easier. If I show people how to do something in HTML, or whatever, then they know it. That means they can do it over and over again, and they can teach other people how to do it, and that's easier for me. Because if people know how to do their job at my level – or whatever level, as long as they're getting to a higher level – that means it's going to be easier for me because

> they know what they're doing. It's going to be easier for them because they know what they're doing, and they can do things faster. … you want everybody to move forward and sometimes people pass you. I've seen Jess learn ASP right before my eyes, and he started learning it after me and he knows way more than me. I guarantee it.

In the midst of growing hierarchical and departmental constraints, managers like Dave found opportunities to keep the superior-subordinate relationship open. His "bullpen" space no doubt made it easier for his employees to reach out to him and each other rather than sending emails or scheduling formal meetings.

In another instance, Dave's department hatched an idea to get the entire group more training. Like many organizations, Virtual-Learn had a specified budget for training workshops and professional development so employees could hone their skills. At a certain point in the year, however, that training budget had been exhausted. Undaunted, the department looked for another way to fund the workshop. The group discussed the idea of pooling an existing continuing education tuition reimbursement benefit the company allotted to each employee. Individually, the benefit was relatively modest but large when combined. Dave made a special request to executives to tap each departmental employee's funds to contract an expensive two-day workshop at Virtual-Learn. Since the entire department agreed, the executives approved the plan. A few weeks later, an in-depth training session took their programing and development skills to the next level. Some departments on the upper and more segmented floor attempted to do something similar. However, the managers and supervisors could not agree on a training focus in large part because their jobs had become more specialized, and their work had drifted further away from each other's areas of specialty.

Executives Made the Final Call

Following these various efforts at returning to a more collective, team approach to projects and training, some supervisors asked the executives about the possibility of moving toward a team-based organization. After all, they argued, the team made higher-quality courses, and the company's largest client was primarily concerned with the quality of the courses and not the sheer volume of courses the company delivered. Further, the departments who worked more like teams in the "bullpen" had strong relationships and high

Questions:

- What features of Virtual-Learn's increased structure do you believe made collaboration more difficult?
- Why do you think a team-based approach to course development and training efforts worked so well?

levels of productivity. Despite a strong case for teams, the executives decided against moving back to this approach. They anticipated securing more large clients in the ensuing months and believed the more traditional structure would position them to grow more rapidly. However, the opposite occurred. The company continued to hire more executives and employees but opened a second location that was out of state. The executives believed that an office closer to its largest client would strengthen the relationship and lead to more clients. Unfortunately, the quality of the company's courses continued to deteriorate and Virtual-Learn went out of business about 18 months after some employees and supervisors attempted to move to a collaborative, team-based structure. The company had many issues beyond course quality, especially conflicts among its executives. Whether a team-based structure would have saved the organization is unclear. However, the organization's segmented, traditional hierarchy and departmental structure did little to address the company's issues and hindered collaboration and innovation.

Two-Way Communication at an Online Real Estate Educational Organization: Bigger Pockets

From 2007 to 2012, the housing market in the US crashed (Shiller, 2015). Families who purchased single-family homes for the first time were hit particularly hard by the quickly falling prices. In the early 2000s up to 2007, banks gave out loans in excess of what many first-time homebuyers could practically afford. In the short-run, these subprime loans boosted the percentage of families owning homes from 64% to 69% and looked like a victory for politicians, banks, and society in general (Matthews, 2014). Because home prices seemed like they would keep going up, many families purchased homes and planned to sell them just a year or two later to make a profit. Further, speculation from new and veteran investors was running wild. The increased demand for homes pushed prices up even further. Unfortunately, when the housing prices suddenly fell amid the banking crisis, many new homeowners were stuck with homes they could not afford that were worth less than the amount they owed banks. Sadly, a wave of foreclosures swept across the country and many families declaring bankruptcy. Many investors or house "flippers" were also stuck with unoccupied homes that were no longer worth what they paid.

This resulted in many "accidental landlords" who needed to keep and rent out houses they could not sell without a massive financial loss (Schultz, 2009).

Within this complicated financial mess, two needs emerged simultaneously: (a) many families needed to rent rather than buy single-family homes because of their bad credit, and (b) current and would-be property investors needed to learn how not to lose money in the future. If new property investors wanted to actually make a profit off the houses they were stuck with, they clearly needed a much better education in property management. During the build up and crash, numerous individuals and organizations started to fill this educational gap, especially online. Each company had its own approach to communication. This case study looks at one such online organization called Bigger Pockets. This organization demonstrates refreshing two-way collaborative communication practices with its online community members in contrast to many other real-estate organizations.

The Rental Property Profession

The business of investing in and managing rental properties can be controversial. The business has a questionable reputation at best. Few people, for instance, have entirely positive associations with words like "landlord" and "real estate investor." Nevertheless, the practice of renting homes has been around throughout history. An article in *Forbes* (Landes, 2012), a reputable financial magazine, describes being a landlord as "a viable vocation" that plays an important role in society. Virtually all people at one point in their life will rent a room, apartment, or house. To manage properties well, one must use a specialized knowledge set. The *Forbes* writer stated, "making a living [property investor and manager] isn't always as easy as others would lead you to believe. If you want to earn a living, for example the equivalent of a $50,000 salary, you'll need to profit more than $4,000 per month. That's a lot of pressure" (Landes, 2012, para. 3). The profession requires excellent money management skills. For instance, after all expenses, including a mortgage payment, property taxes, insurance, and maintenance, one property may make an optimistic monthly profit totaling $400 (i.e., "cash flow"). The job often involves taking personal responsibility for maintenance and repairs to reduce expenses, at least for the "easy" repairs, such as dripping faucets, light electrical work, and painting. Property owners who do not do this work themselves hire others to do so and coordinate with a variety of plumbers, painters, and handymen. It is a complicated job that may involve middle-of-the-night calls and great potential financial losses. Owning and managing even one property, such as a single family home, takes the knowhow and commitment of running a small business.

Bigger Pockets' Dialogic Business Model

In 2004 amid the real estate boom and pending crash, Josh Dorkin founded Bigger Pockets (BP) to help people learn about the business of real estate in a down-to-earth way. He built the company in grassroots fashion with a deliberate two-way model of communication. Dorkin, CEO, started his company while still teaching high school and gradually created the original BP website on the side. He wanted to learn more about investing but was frustrated with the manipulative approach most of the real estate educational companies took toward people who wanted to learn. He decided instead to start with a social networking approach and a simple discussion forum where people could chat about real estate investing in peer-to-peer fashion with no charge. He continued to add pages and resources over the years, BP caught on, and it grew into a full-time business. The small company now boasts a staff, over 30 paid contributors, and over 100 other contributors who write articles, contribute to podcasts, and provide other educational materials. The company has built a positive reputation in the industry and has been covered in *Forbes* magazine (Berger, 2015), *New York Times* (Schultz, 2009), *US News and World Report* (Quinn, 2015), and many other reputable news outlets. The BP website boasts over 435,000 regular visitors and the organization's YouTube channel has over 30,000 subscribers and 1.6 million views. While considered modest by some online standards, the level of visitor participation and the sharp educational focus of BP subscribers make the company somewhat unique.

The primary reason for BP's success is how it communicates differently with regular visitors, or "community members," compared to other real estate companies like it. When Dorkin first entered the industry, he was turned off by the high-pressure and hype that plagues the real estate industry. He stated the following:

> [I] very quickly learned that the basics [of real estate are] … pretty simple, but there's a lot of complexity involved in the industry. The books that you can get at the library or the bookstore … don't really dig into all of those details. I found myself looking for a place to get those answers and I went online. Online, I found lots of 'Get rich quick!' and 'You're going to make $1 million next week!' and all of that crap. As a New Yorker, my BS-ometer is finely tuned. So, I wasn't into it. I realized that there wasn't really a good place to go. There were a couple of sites that existed but it seemed like they were in bed with the 'gurus' and while I think some of those guys have good information I don't love the constant upselling, I don't love the fact that somebody needs to spend $50,000 before they can get anything and so I thought 'What can I do here? Let me build my own website. (Tardy, 2014, para. 10)

In addition to providing high-quality information for free, BP posts articles about how to avoid falling prey to the "real estate guru trap" and protecting yourself from predatory "get rich quick" sales people and unrealistic promises. With these goals in mind, Dorkin created a place online for people to share real estate ideas and strategies, get a free education, and build real relationships with other new and experienced investors.

BP is essentially home to what some people call an online "community." Dorkin explained the benefits of his conversation-based community model for education as a counterpoint to the guru or expert model:

> I'm not the guy who's going to go up on TV and hawk some kind of, you know, "I'm the genius real estate guru man!" That's not me. Bigger Pockets was created as kind of a counter to that. It was created to establish a place where the community can be that expert, as opposed to one individual, because I don't care how expert you are, if I take 1000, 5000, 100,000 people and put their brains together, they're going to crush you. That's what we've got and that's what's happening. (Trady, 2014, para. 11)

In contrast to many real estate organizations online, BP does not believe in pressuring people or pretending to have esoteric knowledge. The YouTube channel's self description explains that it is a place where people can come to "Learn the 'secrets' (there are no secrets!) of successful real estate investing" ("Description," 2007, para. 1). In an industry with a questionable reputation, Dorkin's open approach stands out.

What BP Community Members Say

New and established investors instantly notice that interactions on BP are unique in the marketplace. Many credit Dorkin and other BP employees for the help they get. Lisa, an investor with four single-family homes for rent, wrote in the comments section of an interview with Dorkin, "I've used it for the last 5 years because it's the most honest, not trying to sell me everything, type site out there! And, there are many experienced investors that offer to help out" (Tardy, 2014, para. 1). A new investor from Idaho wrote how BP prepared him for his very first rental property purchase, "After 8 or so months of learning and listening to almost every episode of the bigger pockets podcast, I finally pulled the trigger on my first deal!!!" (Kroepfl, 2016, para. 1). Another BP member, Phillip, stated, "The amount of information that is shared freely is amazing. Browse the forums and you will get a better real estate education than most books on the subject" (Tardy, 2014, para. 5). Still another person, Steph, posted this, "I have been a member of

BP for years. I've learned so much from the forums alone. My new addition is the Thursday podcast episodes. I've listened to all of them so far & have received lots of great tips. Keep up the great work, Josh" (Tardy, 2014, para. 7).

Other investors point out the cooperation and sharing they experience from fellow community members. Stone, an investor from Ohio commented, "I constantly run into things for the first time, so I post questions here and get great answers/opinions. It's also great when I can answer a question for someone else. We help each other."* Another member, Troy, commented on the networking he's done through BP, "I met my business partners on here [and] I've met people I share resources with (contractors, properties, banks, etc.)."* Mike, an investor from Illinois, said the following:

> [T]he real value in that is that [the people I have met through BP] are now sharing ideas, strategies, issues, and even though they were newer investors, I've gotten a ton of great stuff from them. … I'm sharing with them and they're sharing with me.*

Dev, an experienced investor from Texas, offered his point of view, "I've spent hundreds of hours over the past 2 years in here helping people, most of whom will never pay me a dime … This is *really* about 'community.'"* For new and experienced investors alike, Dorkin and the BP staff have established a refreshing place to learn about real estate. Many of the relationships that start online extend into face-to-face relationships and even business partnerships. Community members can connect via a zip code search, meet for coffee, and continue to build the relationship. BP stands in stark contrast to less reputable online organizations, in large part, because it insists upon a dialogic and collaborative approach that forms the foundation of its community.

BP's Rules of Communication Engagement

BP's communication approach takes constant work and supervision. Dorkin explained his deliberate philosophy about cultivating collaborative community this way.

> I knew that if I stuck it out, we were going to continue to grow if we stuck to our standard of quality, not selling out, just trying to create this pure, cool place where people can get together and help one another. (Tardy, 2014, para. 45)

Dorkin and BP's other leaders have had to manage this dynamic carefully. BP, for instance, has strict rules about not allowing members to constantly pitch their own "deals" in the forums. If they allowed new community members to do so, it would undermine what BP has built. Dorkins explained: "[Some] people won't like me because we'll throw them out of the community because they come on and all they want to do is spam, spam, spam, pitch, pitch, pitch" (Tardy, 2014, para. 48). BP does allow community members to discuss the services they offer to fellow community members over time but has strict rules for how to do so to preserve the peer-to-peer, no-pressure, no-hype dynamic in the community. For instance, when sending a private message through the BP site to another community member, users must read several statements and agree to BP's terms. One statement reads, "The PM system is to be used for building relationships, never solicitation. As you deepen your relationships with your colleagues, deal making is fine but we are extremely sensitive to spam and if you get reported by users for spam, you can lose your privileges permanently." Maintaining the purity of the BP site is one of Dorkins' biggest challenges. He stated,

> No matter how much [effort] … how many tools you use to kind of stop bad people from joining, they're still going to join and they're going to post crap. And, if you let that stuff stay there, it becomes an instant turnoff to anybody that's looking at your community. ("How Did Joshua Dorkin," 2015, para. 28)

While BP staffers monitor the site daily, most community members also do so in their own way. Most members simply ignore posts from individuals who have a not-so-hidden agenda to make money off fellow BP's members or post links to their own businesses aimed at taking people off BP's site.

Further, part of building an active online community required Dorkin to respond to and have discussions with thousands of people who ask questions and comment. When Dorkin first started, it was all his responsibility, was incredibly time consuming, but was ultimately worth it. He stated, "you have to seed the community and if you don't do it, there's no energy, there's no life. I spent the vast majority of the first few years on the forums all the time. That's a lot of work" (Tardy, 204, para. 52). Corresponding with the CEO of any organization is not common online but it was an important step to jumpstart the community. While Dorkin still contributes to these discussions and answers questions regularly, the overwhelming majority of information shared in the forums these days is user generated. The community now has its own momentum. Thousands of new conversations start each day on a full range of topics for investors at all experience levels.

Dorkin has also had to fight off the temptation to quickly cash in on the vast community he has built. He explained the constant pressure he gets to run his business differently:

> I have hired consultants and I have talked to a lot of people who are very smart who have said "Josh, close it down. You're out of your mind having this open community that's free. The information is free, people would pay like crazy." And I agree. They would, they absolutely would [pay], but they would because we built the community to size. I think starting a community from scratch and saying "You've got to pay to access this," I don't love that idea and, for me, the whole thing with Bigger Pockets is that I said very early on that the information in this community is going to be free, period. If I don't live by that, if I don't stand by that, I feel like I'd be selling myself out. (Tardy, 2014, para. 56)

Instead, Dorkin and scores of contributors provide free high-quality information and structured online courses. The business model thrives because BP's open two-way communication philosophy is very clear. Community members, paid contributors, and Dorkin himself come to BP to learn from each other and help each other meet their own professional goals.

When Josh Dorkin decided to leave his high school teaching job and do BP full-time, he knew the company had to be self-sustaining and profitable. While his business model looks different than most, BP is not simply providing a public service. It functions as a for-profit corporation. Most of what BP does, however, does not make money directly. In addition to the active discussion forums, for example, all of the information offered through BP is free and includes resources like newsletters, articles, videos, podcasts, webinars, and many e-books. Creating and giving away free information is the foundation of BP's two-way communication business model. Community members come to BP for resources, information, and support but it also allows them to share and teach what they already know. They ask questions in the forums that BP employees and fellow community members answer. Discussions are lively, and, in some ways, not unlike those that take place on other vibrant social networking sites. Unlike Facebook, Google+ and others, however, BP's discussions primarily involve peer-to-peer conversations that get fairly technical. These discussions cover topics like the ins and outs of bank loans, how to stop foreclosures, do-it-yourself tips, real estate law, and many others. People post questions and often receive answers in mere minutes. These two-way conversations form the foundation of the BP community. Instead of manipulating, persuading, or selling to community members, BP makes money from advertising and professional level membership fees for experienced investors. These memberships start at just $5 per month and provide access to analytical software and other valuable services. BP is one of numerous other online educational entrepreneurial efforts made possible in the past decade as technologies like social media, webinars, e-books, podcasts, and YouTube have matured from interesting technologies to practical channels to reach an otherwise dispersed community.

Some of these businesses continue to ascribe to the "guru" business model where knowledge flows in one-way fashion at a considerable financial expense. Those like BP, however, seek to build a community in comparatively dialogic fashion.

* *Author's Note:* To prepare this case study, I became a member of the BP online community. I posted three original questions over a 2-month period to gain personal experience in the community forums. I also watched numerous YouTube video podcasts, registered for a webinar, and read numerous blog posts. The last question I posted in a forum was "How has Bigger Pockets helped you personally?" Some of the responses are posted above as indicated. Perhaps not surprisingly, the CEO, Josh Dorkin, responded to my question and we began an email discussion about his company. In short, even my peripheral experience as a newcomer mirrored the positive ones reported by long-standing community members.

Questions:

- Why do you think BP employees have to invest so much time monitoring BP to make sure new community members do not "spam, spam, spam, pitch, pitch, pitch"?
- What do you believe are the key communication differences between the "guru" model and BP's dialogic approach?

IDEO: Collaboration at the World's Most Influential Product Design Firm

IDEO is a global product design firm based in Palo Alto, California. Dave Kelley, an engineer by training, founded the company in the late 1970s. In 1991, it merged with three other firms to become one of the nation's largest. While most consumers have never heard of IDEO, they have very likely used one or more of the thousands of products the firm has designed over the decades. The company has designed a wide variety of products such as the earliest computer mouse, medical equipment, sun glasses, countless toys, and even the mechanical whale for the 1993 movie Free Willy. It has helped design products for clients such as Microsoft, Apple, Proctor & Gamble, Ford, PepsiCo, and many others. Dave Kelley explained, "We're not actually experts at any given [product] area. We're experts on the process of how you design stuff. So, we don't care if you give us a toothbrush, a toothpaste tube, a tractor, a space shuttle, a chair. It's all the same to us. We want to figure out how to innovate by using our process and applying it" (Smith, 1999). In a survey ("15 Top MBA," 2013), Master's of Business Administration (MBA) students from 135 different graduate programs ranked IDEO as one of the top 15 most attractive organizations out of over 14,000. When asked why, MBA students explained that the company was known for an organizational "culture that fosters creativity and collaboration" ("15 Top MBA," 2013, para. 1). One writer put it bluntly, IDEO "is the standard by which all other design firms are measured" (Tischler, 2008, para. 1). This case examines the company's unique process of collaboration. At IDEO, collaboration is the process that fuels the innovation.

Shopping Cart Challenge: The Boss Is Not Always Right

Since IDEO mostly works with other corporate clients, few consumers have heard of it. In 1999, however, the company first captured the national spotlight. The show *Nightline* (Smith, 1999) challenged the company to redesign the common shopping cart, a traditional design that has barely changed in decades. The segment marked a tipping point for IDEO. *Nightline* documented the weeklong challenge as a way to profile the company's collaborative culture and innovative process. Would it succeed in its shopping cart redesign with the cameras rolling? Would IDEO turn out to be just an ordinary company with a good publicist? It was immediately clear in the program that IDEO resists many of the conventional expectations in corporate America, starting with traditional notions of authority. Kelley explained, "In a very innovative culture, a kind of hierarchy of here's the boss, and the next person down, and the next person down" is not going to work. He elaborated, "Is the boss always going to have the best ideas? Not likely." Instead, Kelley said, "status is who comes up with the best idea. It's not who's the oldest, who's been with the company the longest, not who has the biggest title." At IDEO, Kelley explained, developing innovative ideas frequently means openly disagreeing with the people in charge: "You have to hire people who don't listen to you. I don't think corporate America is ready to hear that quite yet." To ensure diverse perspectives, the company employs botanists, physicians, psychologists, engineers, linguists, anthropologists, and even opera singers who all work side-by-side on the same team. The variety of backgrounds and divergent areas of expertise ensure that ideas do not come from a narrow point of view.

Kelley's unconventional approach is reflected in the autonomy employees enjoy when creating their own workspace. Each "office" is customized within an open floor plan that maximizes comfort, creativity, and interaction with co-workers. Many workers' hang their bicycles from the ceiling above their workspace. In contrast to many organizations, employees do not ask permission from their boss about these choices. Kelley explained how this came about:

> The first guy who hung a bike up didn't come and ask me or ask some facilities person if it was okay. He tried it and waited to see if anybody complained. If nobody complained, then another guy hung a bike up. Pretty soon everybody's got their bike up and nobody's complained. It's that whole thing of trying and asking for forgiveness instead of asking for permission. It's the way people come up with new ideas.

To increase collaboration, teams use open and playful spaces that resemble large garages or small warehouses filled with mobile furniture, whiteboards, and even toys. Playfulness, according to Kelley, improves the work processes: "Being playful is a huge part of being innovative. If you go into a culture and there are a bunch of stiffs walking around, I can guarantee you they are not going to invent anything."

This culture helped IDEO's employees collaborate and innovate rapidly on their shopping cart project. The processes they used appeared chaotic on the surface, but followed some important prescribed steps. The first step defined what the real shopping cart issues were rather than simply designing a new cart based upon personal preferences. To do this, the shopping cart team split up and almost immediately left the office to do autonomous research. Kelley explained the advantage of getting out: "The trick is to find these real experts so you can learn much more quickly than the normal way and trying to learn about it yourself." This method of collecting qualitative information is not new and is taught in many graduate programs. Kelley explained. "What you're seeing here is like the social scientists, the anthropologists that study tribes. What is it that they [shoppers] do that we can we learn from that will help us build a better cart?" Kelley's desire to send employees out contrasts with typical corporate expectations. "One of the things you see is that [most] bosses measure who the good people are by who they see at their desks," Kelley explained. "That couldn't be further from the truth." In contrast, "The people who are really getting the information are out [there] talking to the [people who repair shopping carts] of the world and going to meet other experts. It's much more useful than sitting at your desk." The team members returned to IDEO to share what they had learned with each other.

Once the team was confident in its grasp on the existing issues with shopping carts, the group began looking for possible innovations by brainstorming. These sessions that can last for hours. Their goal is to generate as many potential ideas as possible, regardless of the ideas' reasonableness. Kelley explained the need for crazy ideas, "You have to have some wild ideas. Then, you build on those … If everybody only came up with sane, appropriate things, you'd never have any points to take off to build a really innovative idea." While the ideas were wild, the discussion followed some guiding rules that kept the conversation productive. The team discussed them and posted the rules on the walls.

- One conversation at a time
- Stay focused on topic
- Encourage wild ideas
- Defer judgment
- Build on the ideas of others

Over time, IDEO's team leaders have found that deferring judgment while brainstorming is very challenging. The leader rings a bell strapped to his wrist, for instance, to gently remind people not to criticize ideas while brainstorming. The team leader said to the group, "If anybody starts to nail an idea, they get the bell." When brainstorming was complete, the team selected the best solutions.

The team then narrowed down the hundreds of ideas taped to the wall by, voting on them with Post-It notes. This voting once again displayed IDEO's collaborative culture and process. When asked why the bosses don't simply pick the best ideas, the team leader replied, "Because I'm going to be wrong. It's the team that's really able to judge what the best idea is." He continued to recite one of IDEO's guiding philosophies, "Enlightened trial and error succeeds over the planning of lone genius." Once the team selected the best ideas, they built hasty prototypes to make further improvements. The team agreed on the details, made all of the necessary decisions, and built the final product. They unveiled it the next morning to *Nightline's* crew. The design was truly innovative. The team completely removed the permanent basket from the shopping cart and replaced it with removable, handheld, stackable baskets. They expanded the small children's seating area and improved its safety. They also placed numerous hooks to hang conveniently the plastic shopping bags. In addition to impressing customers and employees at a local store, the improvements were so good that the shopping cart won a design award at a subsequent competition. Dave Kelley was not surprised by the team's success. He's seen it hundreds of times. He explained the long-term goal of IDEO's collaborative process, "It's one thing to do a [new] product once in a while but if you can build a culture and a processes where you routinely come up with great ideas, that's what companies really want." It's not often that a major network puts a company's culture under the microscope to put it to the test. In 1999, the public had simply not seen a workplace like this before. The TV special propelled IDEO into the public eye to instant living-legend status and job applications flooded the company. Much of what happened until 1999 was merely a preamble to what IDEO would accomplish in the 2000s and onward, primarily through spreading their creative and collaborative methods.

Innovation and Letting Go of Control

IDEO's success is due in large part to Dave Kelley's reliable processes of collaboration and innovation. He and his brother Tom Kelley, who also helps lead IDEO, have each written books (Kelley & Kelley, 2013; Kelley & Littman, 2001), given many interviews on innovation, collaboration, and creativity, and even gave a popular *TED* talk (Kelley, 2012) entitled "How to build your creative confidence." It's a creative process they call "design thinking." In a *60 Minutes* interview, Kelley explained that the two main elements to design thinking are "[1] having a diverse group of people and [2] having them be good at building on each other's ideas" (Davis, 2013). One of the main obstacles for this type of collaboration is that participants cannot let go of control. Kelley stated, "When you abandon the status quo and work collaboratively, you sacrifice control over your product, your team, and your business. But the creative gains can more than compensate" (Kelley & Kelley, 2012, para. 19). Kelley emphasized the benefits of this approach, "The big thing about 'design thinking' is … you get to a place that you just can't get to in one [individual's] mind." In addition to letting go of control, another issue is that many people fear that they are simply not creative enough to participate effectively in a collaborative process. Kelley explained in his *TED* talk to a large audience:

> When we have a workshop or have clients in to work with us side by side, we eventually get to the part of the process that is fuzzy or unconventional. Eventually these big time executives whip out their Blackberries, say they have to make really important phone calls, and they head for the exits. They're so uncomfortable. When we track them down they say, "I'm just not the creative type." We know that's not true. If they stick with the process, they end up doing amazing things. (Kelley, 2012)

Indeed, IDEO has become successful primarily by going against conventional wisdom. The company started in a small office in Palo Alto California and has now grown to employ over 500 employees at offices in New York, Chicago, Boston, London, Mumbai and other major cities across the globe.

Continued Influence of IDEO's Approach

The shopping cart project was just one of the thousands of products IDEO has redesigned, and clearly not the most significant or exciting. The project did, however, highlight a refreshing corporate culture that continues to thrive and influence all of its client organizations in positive ways. Kelley has since stepped down as CEO but has stayed on at the company as a managing director. The company continues to work on product design but has expanded its services to help other types of clients. For example, it has worked with the Center for Disease Control to address childhood obesity, helped Acumen develop a business model for providing clean water in developing countries, supported the Red Cross's efforts to boost blood donations, and consulted with HBO to predict how its audience would view content five years in the future (Tischler, 2008). Current CEO, Tim Brown, explains some newer directions for IDEO, "we're working in social domains such as wellness, sustainability, and design for markets where people live on less than a dollar a day. This creates opportunities to make a significant impact on people's lives" (Tischler, 2008, para. 2).

Kelley and IDEO's influence extends far beyond the individual products and projects the company develops. An article originally published by *Business Week* featured Dave Kelley and IDEO and stated, "IDEO's impact on the corporate world is far greater than the sum of its sales" ("Power of Design," 2004, para. 5). *Fast Company* consistently ranks IDEO as one of the nation's most innovative companies and is often mentioned alongside organizations such as Apple, Google, and Facebook (Lee, 2010; Tischler, 2008). IDEO is teaching the corporate and non-profit world a new way to achieve excellence through a process that looks very different from most workplaces. Even though the company has been around for decades, "the IDEO way" still sets the standard toward which new companies strive. One writer described "the IDEO way" like this: "the design firm's disciplined yet wild-and-woolly five-step process that emphasizes empathy with the consumer, anything-is-possible brainstorming, visualizing solutions by creating actual prototypes, using technology to find creative solutions, and doing it all with incredible speed" ("Power of Design," 2004, para. 14). These five steps each involve numerous collaborative and creative methods that IDEO applies with much greater fluency than most companies. In these later years of his career, Kelley has dedicated himself to influencing industry through the classroom. Kelley created Stanford University's wildly popular "d.school," a graduate-level program that teaches many of his company's philosophies and methods to Silicon Valley's best and brightest leaders of tomorrow.

Questions:

- How do IDEO's leaders set the tone for its collaborative atmosphere?
- What about IDEO's approach requires employees and leaders to be courageous? What are the risks of this full commitment to collaboration?

Chapter Discussion Questions

- What commonalities do you see in these three cases regarding how each organization approaches communication? To what extent do they use a dialogic approach?
- Why does each collaborative approach in these case studies require a degree of courage for employees and leaders?
- How do the specific communication practices used in these cases studies shape the broader culture of these organizations?

Key Terms

- Collaboration
- Collaborative Spirit
- Dialogue
- Stakeholder model of communication
- Stakeholder
- Primary stakeholder
- Secondary stakeholder
- Tight coupling
- Loose coupling
- Politicized contexts
- Epistemic communities
- Individualism
- Collectivism
- Social capital

References

Abrams, L. C., Cross, R., Lesser, E., & Levin, D. Z. (2003). Nurturing interpersonal trust in knowledge-sharing networks. *Academy of Management Executive, 17*, 64–77.

Arnett, R. (2015). The dialogic necessity: Acknowledging and engaging monologue. *Ohio Communication Journal, 53*, 1–10.

Bennis, W., & Beiderman, P. W. (1997). *Organizing genius: The secrets of creative collaboration*. Reading, MA: Addison-Wesley.

Buber, M. (1947). *Between man and man*. (R. G. Smith, Trans.). London: Routledge & Kegan Paul.

Buber, M. (1970). *I and Thou*. New York, NY: Charles Scribner's Sons.

Cooke, W. N. (1989). Improving productivity and quality through collaboration. *Industrial Relations, 28*, 299–319.

Deetz, S. A. (1992). *Democracy in an age of corporate colonization: Developments in communication and the politics of everyday life.* Albany, NY: State University of New York Press.

Deetz, S. A. (1995). *Transforming communication, transforming business: Building responsive and responsible workplaces.* Cresskill, NJ: Hampton Press.

Deetz, S. A., Tracy, S. J., & Simpson, J. L. (2000). *Leading organizations through transition: Communication and cultural change.* Thousand Oaks, CA: Sage.

Drucker, P. F. (1993). *Post-capitalist society.* New York, NY: Harper Business.

Gastil, J. (1994). A meta-analytic review of the productivity and satisfaction of democratic and autocratic leadership. *Small Group Research, 25,* 384–410.

Gray, B. (1989). *Collaborating: Finding common ground for multiparty problems.* San Francisco, CA: Jossey-Bass.

Heath, G. R., & Sias, M. P. (1999). Communicating spirit in a collaborative alliance. *Journal of Applied Communication Research, 27,* 356–376.

Kelley, T., & Littman, J. (2001). *Art of innovation.* New York, NY: Doubleday.

Lazega, E. (1992). *Micropolitics of knowledge: Communication and indirect control in work groups.* New York. NY: Aldine de Gruyter.

Lyon, A. (2008). The mis/recognition of Enron executives' competence as cultural and social capital. *Communication Studies, 59,* 371–387.

Marshall, E. M. (1995). *Transforming the way we work: The power of the collaborative workplace.* New York, NY: American Management Association.

Schwarz, S. (2006). *Creating a culture of collaboration: The international association of facilitators handbook.* San Francisco, CA: Jossey-Bass.

Sioukas, T., & Sweet, M. (2006). Involving multiple stakeholders in large-scale collaborative projects. In: S. Schuman (Ed.), *Creating a culture of collaboration* (pp. 435–448). San Francisco, CA: Jossey-Bass.

Straus, D. (2002). *How to make collaboration work: Powerful ways to build consensus, solve problems, and make decisions.* Williston, VT: Berrett-Koehler Publishers

Ulmer, R. R. (2001). Effective crisis management through established stakeholder relationships: Malden mills as a case study. *Management Communication Quarterly, 14,* 590–615.

Weber, M. (1947). *The theory of social and economic organizations* (A. M. Henderson & T. Parsons, Trans.). New York, NY: Oxford University Press.

Weick, K. (1976). Educational organizations as loosely coupled systems. *Administrative Science Quarterly, 21,* 1–19.

Weick, K. (1979). *The social psychology of organizing* (2nd ed.). Reading, MA: Addison-Wesley.

Yoshikawa, M. (1977). Implications of Martin Buber's philosophy of dialogue in Japanese and American intercultural communication. *Communication, 6,* 103–124.

Virtual-Learn References

Lyon, A., (2005). "Intellectual capital" and struggles over the perceived value of members' expert knowledge in a knowledge-intensive organization. *Western Journal of Communication, 69,* 251–271.

Lyon, A., & Chesebro, J. (2010). The politics of knowledge: A critical perspective on organizational knowledge. In H. Canary & R. McPhee (Eds.), *Communication and organizational knowledge: Contemporary issues for theory and practice* (pp. 69–86). New York, NY: Routledge.

Bigger Pockets References

Berger, R. (2015, September, 5). Investing podcasts you should download today. *Forbes*. Retrieved from http://www.forbes.com/sites/robertberger/2015/09/05/7-investing-podcasts-you-should-download-today/#2715e4857a0b2a484a2135da

Description (2007, March 14). *Bigger Pockets* [YouTube channel]. Retrieved from https://www.youtube.com/user/BiggerPockets/about

Kroepfl, J. (2016, January 19). The journey has begun. *Bigger Pockets*. Retrieved from https://www.biggerpockets.com/forums/223/topics/268052-the-journey-has-begun----closed-on-1st-property

How did Joshua Dorkin create the most popular real estate podcast on iTunes? (2015, June 1). *Mixergy*. Retrieved from http://mixergy.com/interviews/joshua-dorkin-bigger-pockets/

Landes, L. (2012, August 6). Earning a living with rental properties: Should you be a landlord? *Forbes*. Retrieved from http://www.forbes.com/sites/moneybuilder/2012/08/06/earning-a-living-with-rental-properties-should-you-be-a-landlord/#2715e4857a0b3565cfaf5694

Lyon, A. (2016, January 21). How has Bigger Pockets helped you? *Bigger Pockets*. Retrieved from https://www.biggerpockets.com/forums/223/topics/268637-how-has-bigger-pockets-helped-you-personally?page=1#p1753830

Matthews, C. (2014, July 18). Why the housing recovery is over, in four charts. *Fortune*. Retrieved from http://fortune.com/2014/07/18/housing-recovery-us/

Quinn, M. (2015, March 13). The top 15 personal finance podcasts to follow. *US News and World Report*. Retrieved from http://money.usnews.com/money/blogs/my-money/2015/03/13/the-top-15-personal-finance-podcasts-to-follow

Schultz, J. S. (2009, December 24). Resources for accidental landlords. *New York Times* [blog]. Retrieved from http://bucks.blogs.nytimes.com/2009/12/24/resources-for-accidental-landlords/

Shiller, R. J. (2015, July 24). The housing market still isn't rational. *New York Times*. Retrieved from http://www.nytimes.com/2015/07/26/upshot/the-housing-market-still-isnt-rational.html?_r=0

Tardy, J. (2014). Slow and steady to an amazing online business with Joshua Dorkin. *Eventual Millionaire* [blog]. Retrieved from http://eventualmillionaire.com/joshua-dorkin/#sthash.mwKWH3Bu.dpuf

IDEO References

15 top MBA employers. (2013). *CNN*. Retrieved from http://money.cnn.com/news/economy/mba100/2013/snapshots/13.html

Davis, K. (2013). Design thinking. *CBS, 60 Minutes*. Retrieved from https://www.youtube.com/watch?v=GYkb6vfKMI4

Kelley, D. (2012). How to build your creative confidence [video presentation]. *TED*. Retrieved from http://www.ted.com/talks/david_kelley_how_to_build_your_creative_confidence.html

Kelley, T., & Kelley, D. (2013). *Creative confidence: Unleashing the creative potential within us all.* New York, NY: Crown.

Kelley, T., & Kelley, D. (2012, December). Reclaim your creative confidence. *Harvard Business Review.* Retrieved from https://hbr.org/2012/12/reclaim-your-creative-confidence

Kelley, T., & Littman, J. (2001). *The art of innovation: Lessons in creativity from IDEO, America's leading design firm*. New York, NY: Crown.

Lee, A. (2010). Most innovative companies: Design. *Fast Company*. Retrieved from http://www.fastcompany.com/1547606/most-innovative-companies-design

The power of design. (2004, May 16). *Bloomberg*. Retrieved from http://www.bloomberg.com/bw/stories/2004-05-16/the-power-of-design.

Smith, J. (July 13, 1999). The deep dive [DVD]. ABC's *Nightline.*

Tischler, L. (2008). Most innovative companies. *Fast Company*. Retrieved from http://www.fastcompany.com/713911/fast-50-2008-ideo

3 Tips, Tools, and Resources to Move from Control to Collaboration

Consider this chapter's practical tips, tools, and resources as first steps for collaborative communication. Some are inspired by the case studies and others are drawn from existing research.

Mindset Minute: Do You Believe in the Myth of the Lone Genius?

Chapter 1 mentions that the American focus on individual achievement can be a barrier for collaborative efforts. The same could be said for our views about the creative process. Many people believe they are better off breaking fresh ground on their own. Tom Kelley (Kelley & Littman, 2001), an author and executive at IDEO, describes this belief:

> The myth that creativity flourishes primarily in solitude is an established one. We've all read over and over again how novelists and screenwriters writing in the seclusion of remote cottages or bungalows churn out best-selling novels and blockbusters. But is that the only way to foster innovation? And is it a viable model for business? (p. 87)

In contrast, Kelley shows how Ron Bass (i.e., "Bass & Co.") uses a dynamic, interactive team of six writers and researchers regularly to make commercially successful and critically acclaimed films such as *Rain Man*, *My Best Friend's Wedding*, and *Snow Falling on Cedars*. Creative collaboration and even creative friction can bring projects to new levels. Consider that John Lennon had Paul McCartney, Paul Simon had Art Garfunkel, and even the "Lone" Ranger had Tonto.

Most successes are the result of team efforts when we scratch below the surface of the story. Thomas Edison's improvement of the light bulb was built on other inventors' ideas. Further, he employed dozens of "muckers" or employees who experimented tirelessly to find a long-lasting filament to make the light bulb a commercially viable product. The focus on his individual success camouflages the fact that even one of the best and brightest that ever lived needed (a) to build on others' ideas and (b) had a massive team around him. Companies like IDEO and Bigger Pockets show us the need to let go of this mythical Lone Ranger approach and embrace collaboration. Have you bought into the myth that most creative work is done alone? How might that be restraining collaboration around you? *See Boxes 3.1 and 3.2 for clues about controlling and collaborative mindsets.*

Box 3.1. Control-Mindset Cues.

When somebody says …	What's going on in their heads is …
It's really important to do this correctly.	Do it my way.
I just want to be clear about the expectations.	Conform. It's not negotiable.
I've indicated the mistakes. Please fix them.	Do it like I would do it.
I don't like to repeat myself.	Do it my way or else …
I don't want to micro-manage you but …	I'm going to micro-manage you.

Facilitative Leadership for Stakeholder Interactions

Leaders set the communicative tone in organizations. Agile ones break out of the stereotypical "managerial" persona and bounce effectively between guide and facilitator as needed. For instance, discussion leaders must have their eye on the overall project and act as a *guide* to move forward when the group gets stuck. A guide can help ensure that a group of stakeholders uses meeting time well, moves on to other important agenda items, and meets deadlines. A good *facilitator* also handles overly talkative members diplomatically and draws out less involved members with skill. I recently observed a manager in a major organization, for instance, who spent at least 80% of his time facilitating the team's discussion and only 20% of his time guiding the group with simple prompts to move forward when needed. He nudged them on with simple statements like, "Let's spend five more minutes discussing both sides of this and then make a decision." He rarely promoted his own point of view and only did so toward the end of the discussion if nobody else voiced an important perspective. His team members all contributed with energy, excitement, and initiative largely because of his leadership.

From my observations in professional settings, most leaders believe they are much better facilitators than they are and reverse the percentages of the effective manager described above. They "guide" or tell the group what to do about 80% of the time and only facilitate 20% of the time. Straus (2002) paints a hypothetical scenario about a manager/facilitator, who will look familiar to many readers:

> Bob thought he could build consensus collaboratively by getting all of the key stakeholders in a room together and persuading them to support his ideas. He quickly learned that consensus building doesn't work that way. It's not possible to simply throw people in a room and assume consensus will emerge if you just push hard enough. And proposing a solution at the outset of a collaborative process, as Bob did, typically only divides a group and heightens the conflict. (p. 58)

"Guide" is in quotations because many managers really attempt to steer the group in a predetermined direction, as Straus' quote explains. To encourage more collaboration, leaders should push less and facilitate more. When they restrain themselves from intervening too much, group members will answer the call, and their natural collaborative energy and motivation will far outweigh any induced motivation the leader tries to instill in them.

Collaborative and facilitative leaders are not passive, weak, or unwilling to make decisions. They do not act as if they are not responsible for taking action. Also, they do not believe they must consult with everybody about even minor issues. As Straus (2002) explained, "a facilitative leader has the unusual positional power to act unilaterally, but chooses instead to work with others when appropriate to find win-win solutions to important issues" (Straus, 2002, p. 146). A collaborative and facilitative leader knows exactly how, when, and why to take individual action but also knows the power of the team will be more effective in many cases.

Playing Facilitative and Collaborative Roles

Each member of a group influences the discussion in a variety of ways. Benne and Sheats' classic (1948) work describes the *task*, *social*, and *individual* roles group members play and still has relevance (e.g., Hackman & Johnson, 2013; Hirokawa, 1980). Readers can refer to the roles below as a behavioral inventory to gauge and develop their range of skills, break out of a role rut, and avoid playing less productive parts.

Task Roles

- **Initiator:** Proposes ideas or different ways to approach a group problem or goal. Initiates group discussions and moves into new areas of exploration: "Let's approach this from another angle. How about we …"
- **Information or Opinion Seeker:** Asks for the evaluation of information and opinions of others. Seeks expert information or facts relevant to the problem: "I was curious to hear what people think about …"
- **Information or Opinion Giver:** Provides and evaluates information or opinions in the group: "Here's my viewpoint on that …"
- **Elaborator:** Takes ideas, facts, or opinions introduced by others and builds on them by providing background, examples, or potential next steps: "I'd like to jump off of what Kyle said and add that …"
- **Coordinator:** Shows the relationships between and among ideas. May pull together a few different ideas and make them cohesive: "I think we may be saying the same thing just in a different way because …"
- **Orienter:** Summarizes and clarifies what the group has discussed and accomplished and helps get the group back on track: "It sounds like so far we've agreed on the budget limitations and length of the project. Let's figure out where we stand on personnel."
- **Evaluator**: Evaluates or critiques rationality or practicality of ideas based upon an ideal standard: "If our goal is *x*, then we need some logical steps to move that forward."
- **Energizer:** Stimulates and excites the group to move forward and achieve its goals successfully: "This project is really going to help our company get noticed in a big way."
- **Procedural Technician:** Helps the group by taking care of logistics like scheduling where meetings will take place and arranging for needed supplies.
- **Recorder:** Takes notes or meeting minutes.

Social or Group Maintenance Roles

- **Encourager:** Affirms and supports fellow group members' efforts with a warm and a positive attitude: "That's a really good point, Mark."

- **Harmonizer:** Bridges differences between individuals, reduces tension through humor, mediates conflicts, and helps build a sense of belonging: "Let's keep some perspective here. We're all on the same team, and we all want the same thing."
- **Compromiser:** Willing to adjust his or her position and meet others half way to ensure progress: "I'd be willing to accept that. Does that sound like a fair tradeoff?"
- **Gatekeeper:** Regulates the flow of communication to make sure all group members have a chance to get involved. May limit time and topic to make sure individuals do not dominate the conversation: "Okay, we've heard the case in favor of adjusting the schedule from a few of you. Let's go around the group and hear from some of the others. Ricky, what's your view?"
- **Commentator/Standard Setter:** Expresses group values and standards as a way to evaluate the group process. Gives feedback about how he or she sees the group functioning: "Like we always say, let's focus on solving the problem, not criticizing each other's ideas."
- **Follower**: Mainly listens to other group members and accepts what others say and decide but does not directly contribute to the decision.

Interestingly, Hirokawa (1980) found that both effective and ineffective groups display these behaviors at various times. Thus, just playing different roles is good practice but will not automatically ensure effective group work or leadership. The difference, he found, was that groups who make effective decisions tend to make more procedurally relevant statements. In other words, effective groups invest extra time and effort to make sure all members have a shared understanding of the steps they will use to move forward in the discussion. Hirokawa (1980, p. 321) shows the following excerpt from a group discussion to illustrate.

Member A:	Well folks, what should we do?
Member C:	Um, why don't we, you know, just go around and …
Member B:	I think we should first decide on a set of criteria for deciding what things to take and what things to leave behind.
Member C:	Yeah. That's a good idea. I mean, we shouldn't just toss out suggestions.
Member A:	Yeah. Let's do it.

Notice now group Member B stops to clarify how the group discussion should move forward: "We should first decide on a set of criteria." Small conversational moments like this play a crucial facilitative job that moves groups forward. A talkative group is not necessarily an effective group. Invest a few extra moments

Box 3.2. Collaborative Mindset Cues.

When somebody says …	**What's going on in their heads is …**
We're all in this together.	I see us as a team.
Two heads are better than one.	Your ideas are just as valuable as mine.
Let's brainstorm some ideas.	Let's play with ideas and not critique yet.
Touch base with some stakeholders on this.	This plan needs input from more players.
We should collaborate on that.	I respect what you can bring to this project.

clarifying the procedural steps or structure the group will follow to hear participants' ideas, make decisions, and solve problems. As such, the list of task-and-relationship roles can be used as (a) a suggested way to contribute individually to meetings, and more importantly, (b) as a set of tools to facilitate meetings more effectively. In contrast to task- and-relationship roles, *individual roles* can distract and hinder discussions. The meaning of roles like aggressor, blocker, recognition-seeker, dominator, etc., are fairly clear and may remind readers of a controlling approach. In general, individuals take the attention off of the group effort and use the collective time to act in their own self-interests when they enact these behaviors. What roles do you normally play in meetings? What roles could you begin to practice to become more facilitative and collaborative? What roles should you try to phase out? If you hear people regularly use collaborative language, this is a good indicator that they are truly open to working cooperatively.

Let Go of Fixed Positions and Focus on Deeper Interests

Collaborative interactions work best when all parties are in touch with their deeper motivations and interests rather than fixed, predetermined outcomes they must secure. The classic, best-selling negotiation book *Getting to Yes* (Fisher, Ury, & Patton, 1991) discusses the difficulties of negotiating with articulated positions at the outset. An employee who states that he or she wants "Four weeks of vacation per year rather than two" has just stated a position. His or her boss is likely to respond with a positional statement as well such as, "Our policy is just two weeks vacation. We can't afford to pay for four weeks. We'd go broke." In a straightforward adversarial bargaining scenario, the employee and boss might settle on three weeks of vacation, a solution that neither is thrilled about. Instead, Fisher and Ury suggest each party invest the time necessary to figure out his or her interests or what he or she truly "needs, desires, concerns, and fears" (p. 40) that may hide beneath the positions he or she states.

Managers and employees historically wrestle over vacation time. The employee who wants four weeks, for example, should look deeper into his or her interests and may discover that what he or she really wants is simply more time with family and travel to recharge, not necessarily paid time off. Similarly, the manager may know the organization can allow employees more time off and still thrive; it just can't afford more *paid* vacation time. If each stakeholder is able to (a) articulate his or her deeper interests rather than a fixed position and (b) help each other fulfill those interests in a non-adversarial, collaborative fashion, then solutions they develop may pleasantly surprise everybody. In fact, even though many employees and managers still wrestle over this historic tension today, some organizations are now satisfying both parties' underlying interests through unlimited but unpaid vacation time (Kwoh, 2012). The solution works out for everybody involved. Employees love the flexibility of the policy, and employers say that it reduces turnover, prevents burnout, and helps keep employees creative (Kwoh, 2012). Rather than abusing the policy, virtually all employees are trustworthy, thoughtful, and considerate about coordinating vacations so the organization's productivity remains high. It is essentially a "low cost way to win [employees'] loyalty" (Kwoh, 2012, para. 5). Our openness about deeper interests rather than fixed positions allows space for more creative, collaborative solutions.

Collaborative Problem-Solving Steps

> *The less you strive to control ideas and insist on credit for those that are yours, the more good ideas you are likely to have—and see implemented.*
>
> —*Kelley & Littman, (2001, p. 86)*

Group problem solving and brainstorming are two methods often discussed in tandem as ways to reach creative solutions. In the field of communication, Hirokawa published numerous studies (1988, 1990; Hirokawa & Poole, 1996) demonstrating the effectiveness of groups' ability to create high-quality solutions when they followed articulated problem-solving steps diligently. Further, Osborn (1953) developed what we currently call brainstorming and its many varieties (e.g., silent brainstorming, nominal group technique, etc.) to reach creative breakthroughs that individual people could not make as readily. While these approaches are well known across various fields, few organizations take advantage of them as consistently as IDEO shown in the previous chapter.

Identify and Analyze the Problem

- *Identify the problem*: The goal of this step is leave it with a crystal clear picture of the problem the group is trying to solve.
- *Analyze the problem*: Look at the problem from multiple angles.
- *Articulate criteria for an ideal solution*: How will the group know they have a good solution? The group should specify the criteria an ideal solution should have.

Generate Possible Solutions

- *Brainstorming*: At its most basic level, brainstorming is simply a discussion that emphasizes spontaneity and generates possible solutions from everybody in the group. The most difficult aspect is not judging ideas until the session is over. The following tips will help a group perform effectively:
    - Choose an environment conducive to creativity
    - Set aside a predetermined amount of time
    - Set a goal for the number of ideas
    - Keep it playful
    - Resist the urge to shoot down ideas

Note: The social intensity of a good brainstorming session is much easier for naturally extroverted people. Introverts may require several minutes to warm up and contribute to the discussion with ease. To jumpstart the discussion, you may ask each group member to arrive with a short list of ideas. With these notes in front of them, it will be much easier to enter a fast-paced discussion.

Evaluate and Select Solutions

- *Consensus*: Ideally, everybody supports a direction and agrees on the best solution as long as the consensus is genuine and not assumed.
- *Vote*: When a group can't reach a unanimous decision, voting may be an option, although it can sometimes upset people who prefer another course of action.
- *Rating and Ranking*: If a group is faced with several viable alternatives, group members can individually rate their preferences (e.g., 1 through 5),

and those ratings can be added up to form a collective ranking of solutions and an agreement on the overall best solution.

Test Solutions

- *Prototyping*: One way to test a solution is to "build" a mock up or quick-and-dirty, low-budget version of the intended idea. These versions can help a group catch and address issues early before making a larger investment.
- *Pilot testing*: When possible, test a solution on a small scale to see how well it works.

Implement Solutions

- Put the refined solution into practice.
- Gather feedback as the solution gets implemented to determine if further adjustments would improve it.

These steps are well known but not often followed closely in organizations. Groups and teams may give up too easily or experience a lackluster brainstorming session that discourages future attempts, a norm that IDEO leaders warn against. Because the brainstorming "killers" listed below can drastically reduce the chances of experiencing an effective problem-solving session and sour an organization's attitude toward group problem solving, they should be avoided:

Six Ways to Kill a "Brainstormer" (see Kelley & Littman, 2001, pp. 65–66)

1. ***The boss gets to speak first.*** When the boss speaks first, it sets the agenda too much and automatically narrows the focus. Team members may then simply anticipate and provide what they think the boss wants to hear.
2. ***Everybody gets a turn.*** Turn-taking may seem polite but there's no quicker way to drain the energy out of a room than by having each person around the table share his or her idea in stepwise fashion. Brainstorming should sound more like cooking popcorn than a ticking clock.
3. ***Experts only please.*** The "right" degrees are not important when brainstorming. A good idea can come from anyone. It's important not to be the

expert "snob." Instead, bring in people with real experience and creative tendencies.

4. ***Do it off-site.*** Creative collaboration should happen in your regular work-space. Kelley states, "Remember, you want the buzz of creativity to blow through your offices as regularly as a breeze at the beach."
5. ***No silly stuff.*** Have fun while brainstorming. Silly ideas remind everybody that this isn't like regular work.
6. ***Write everything down.*** You should not approach your brainstorming notes the same way you might if you were taking notes for a final exam. Notes should include sketches, doodles, and ideas but not so much detail that it looks like testable material.

Spatial Arrangement and an Us-Against-Them Mentality

Lastly, many organizations nurture conflict without realizing it, especially the way they use space in meetings. As Glaser (2005) explained, an "'us against them' dynamic is typical in many workplace and customer service interactions" and organizations "must find a way to bring an end to the fight-or-flight behaviors that promote adversarialism" (Glaser, 2005, p. 32). A shared or common space like those at IDEO and parts of Virtual-Learn can break down physical barriers and facilitate cooperation. Glaser (2005, pp. 33–34) suggests that seating arrangements in meetings can either emphasize or ease a competitive atmosphere. When the various parties are seated directly across from each other, the face-off position establishes distinct territories for participants who may otherwise want to work together more easily. Similarly, when a leader is clearly separated from the rest of the group, he or she is nonverbally distinguishing himself or herself from others. Instead, some leaders prefer to alternate seating in ways that blend the various subgroups together. A leader can mix up the seating by providing name tents, pre-arranging the meeting room, or simply asking people to mix up the seating on their own. Thus, readers may want to consider decisions about special arrangements that increase the likelihood of the other collaborative practices mentioned here.

In closing, the information in this chapter represents a first step toward collaborative communication. The tips and tools provide a way to put this method into practice right away. Consult the reference list below for in-depth treatment of collaborative strategies. In particular, the text *Creating a culture of collaboration: the International Association of Facilitators handbook* (Schwarz, 2006) is a robust resource for exploring collaboration to its fullest. Further, Kelley and Kelley's (2013) second book helps individuals build their skills when they do not feel as creative as others. Meanwhile, consider taking the self-evaluation assessment tool below, "Are you a 'control freak?'" for a lighthearted look at your current mindset about controlling communication.

Are you a "Control Freak?"

Want to know if you're a "control freak?" The following lighthearted self-evaluation tool was adapted from Dr. Shelley Prevost's (2012) *Inc.* magazine article "8 signs you're a control freak." Remember, it is not a scientific instrument.

Key:

YES! = That's me! This describes me well.
Yes = I am like this more often than not.
yes = I suppose I am a little bit like this but not all the time.
no = I'm not really like this from what I can tell.
No = This does not describe me.
NO! = Never. I'm the exact opposite.

Instructions: Circle the answer that reflects your honest evaluation.

1. You believe that if someone would change one or two things about their work themselves, you'd be happier. So you try to "help them" change their behavior by pointing it out more than once.

   YES! *Yes* *yes* *no* *No* *NO!*

2. You micromanage others to make them fit your very specific expectations. You like things to be perfect and think other people should want things to be perfect too.

   YES! *Yes* *yes* *no* *No* *NO!*

3. You judge others' behavior as right or wrong and withhold attention until they meet your expectations. Sitting in silent judgment is a good form of control.

   YES! *Yes* *yes* *no* *No* *NO!*

4. You offer "constructive criticism" as an indirect attempt to advance your own agenda.

   YES! *Yes* *yes* *no* *No* *NO!*

5. You change how you act or what you say you believe so someone will accept you. Instead of being yourself, you attempt to draw others in by managing their impression of you.

   YES! *Yes* *yes* *no* *No* *NO!*

6. You present worst-case scenarios as a way to influence someone away from certain behaviors and toward others.

   YES! *Yes* *yes* *no* *No* *NO!*

7. You have a hard time with ambiguity and not knowing something.

   YES! *Yes* *yes* *no* *No* *NO!*

8. You intervene on behalf of people you align yourself with by trying to explain or dismiss their behaviors to others.

   YES! *Yes* *yes* *no* *No* *NO!*

Score:

Number of YES!	________	Number of NO!	________
Number of Yes	________	Number of No	________
Number of yes	________	Number of no	________
	+		+
Total Yes answers	________	***Total No answers***	________

Evaluation:

6–8 total yes answers = You're a control freak and you probably already know it.

3–5 total yes answers = You show clear signs of being a control freak but you restrain yourself in some areas

1–2 total yes answers = You show some controlling tendencies but it's unlikely anybody thinks of you as a control freak at this point.

References

Benne, K. D., & Sheats, P. (1948). Functional roles of group members. *Journal of Social Issues, 4,* 41–49.

Fisher, R., Ury, W., & Patton, B. (1991). *Getting to yes: Negotiating agreement without giving in* (2nd ed.). New York, NY: Penguin.

Glaser, J. (2005). *Leading through collaboration: Guiding groups to productive solutions.* Thousand Oaks, CA: Corwin.

Hackman, M. Z., & Johnson, C. E. (2013). *Leadership: A communication perspective* (6th ed.). Long Grove, IL: Waveland.

Hirokawa, R. Y. (1980). A comparative analysis of communication patterns within effective and ineffective decision-making groups. *Communication Monographs, 47,* 312–322.

Hirokawa, R. (1988). Understanding the sources of faulty group decision making: A lesson from the Challenger disaster. *Small Group Research, 19,* 411–433.

Hirokawa, R. (1990). The role of communication in group decision-making efficacy: A task-contingency perspective. *Small Group Research, 21,* 190–204.

Hirokawa, R., & Poole, M. S. (1996). *Communication and group decision making* (2nd ed.). Thousand Oaks, CA: Sage.

Kelley, T., & Littman, J. (2001). *The art of innovation.* New York: Doubleday.

Kelley, T., & Kelly, D. (2013). *Creative confidence: Unleashing the creative potential with us all.* New York, NY: Crown.

Kwoh, L. (2012, October 26). Go ahead and take off, for as long as you like. *Wall Street Journal.* Retrieved from http://www.wsj.com/articles/SB10000872396390443686004577637730320709396

Osborn, A. (1953). *Applied imagination: Principles and procedures of creative problem solving.* New York, NY: Charles Scribner's Sons.

Prevost, S. (2012). *8 signs you're a control freak. Inc.* Retrieved from http://www.inc.com/shelley-prevost/8-signs-youre-a-control-freak.html

Schwarz, S. (2006). *Creating a culture of collaboration: The International Association of Facilitators handbook.* San Francisco, CA: Jossey-Bass.

Straus, D. (2002). *How to make collaboration work.* San Francisco, CA: Brett-Koehler Publishers.

Part II

Moving from Top-Down to Upward Communication

4

Top-Down Communication and Case Studies

Years ago, I sat in on an exit interview. The lead interviewer asked, "What do you think is already working well at this organization?" and made careful notes about the organization's strengths. Finally, he asked the magic question, "What are some things we could do to make it better here?" The exiting member offered several thoughtful suggestions that very likely would have improved our organization. As she did, the lead interviewer stopped taking notes and listened with a stone-faced expression. In awkward fashion, he then explained in defensive tones point-by-point problems with each of the exiting member's ideas.

Unfortunately, the dynamic in this conversation is too common. This meeting was meant to collect upward feedback, but the conversation flipped back into a ***top-down communication*** pattern. Most organizational members notice fairly early that communication typically flows down the ***organizational hierarchy***. The president or CEO along with the other top executives pass their messages down through the various director- and managerial-level ranks, who continue to pass the messages down through department or shift supervisors, who make sure that employee-level members finally get the message. Nothing is wrong with downward communication. In fact, organizational members at all levels need to know what leaders think, including the goals, priorities, and vision for the organization. However, when organizations overemphasize top-down communication, they inadvertently overwhelm the supply of needed upward communication. The first part of this chapter looks at the way top-down communication functions including common obstacles to effective bottom-up communication. The second discusses four organizations that overemphasized top-down messages: NASA, Netflix, Tropicana, and Merck.

Top-Down Communication Design

Hierarchies are designed to ensure communication flows from the top to bottom. Simply put, traditional organizations use a ***chain-of-command*** structure to push messages down to each subsequent level. Research shows that most managers view good communication as messages that transfer from managers to subordinates, (e.g., Tourish & Pinnington, 2002; Tourish & Robson, 2003), but not the other way around. Consider the variety and volume of ***downward messages*** that bombard us daily. We receive memos, announcements, reminder emails, and mass voicemails. We sit in meetings where the leaders speak most of the time. We go through mandatory training sessions that often do not relate to our positions. We read through binders of material to stay current with organizational policies or industry protocol. Many publicly traded companies post the daily stock price in the elevator or near bathrooms. When I visited an organization, I noticed a newsletter posted above each urinal and on the door of each stall. Its name was "The Toilet Paper" with the tagline, "Keeping you in the know while you go!" No end exists to the amount of downward communication we receive.

Leaders of organizations may also feel stuck in an ill-fitted pyramid-like structure. They, too, get flooded with constant downward communication and have trouble getting important information to those above them. Embedded in the traditional hierarchy are some unspoken assumptions that do not sound particularly impressive when we describe them aloud (e.g., "managers think, employees do"). These unspoken beliefs are at least partially influenced by where the chain-of-command structure originates. It was, essentially, borrowed from the military, the most enduring structure whereby leaders must organize large groups of people. The strong military influence is built into the structure and evidenced in our language. The CEO is the Chief Executive Officer, the COO is the Chief Operations Officer, and so on. Have you ever noticed how members at various levels in organizations dress differently to indicate their "rank"? Organizations use words like territory, targets, triggers, offense, defense, campaign, and battle to normalize top-down communication practices (Lyon & Mirivel, 2011). Not surprisingly, most front-line or employee-level troops are expected to follow marching orders. We all enter organizational hierarchies from the lower levels and with the top-down momentum of this history. Even managers, thus, struggle like Sisyphus to push needed input up to top decision makers in a system that was designed to flow downhill.

Clearly, organizations need consistent downward communication to function effectively, but it is only half of a typically unbalanced equation. Research shows that many organizations need upward communication but do not often handle it effectively. The absence of reliable and systematic feedback can slow organizations' ability to learn and adapt to emerging issues (Bisel, Messersmith, & Kelley, 2012). Employees' input plays a key role in helping organizations function effectively (Detert & Burris, 2007; Gao, Janssen, & Shi, 2011). Kassing (2002) explained that bottom-up communication plays an "important monitoring force within organizations in that dissent can signal organizational problems such as employee dissatisfaction or organizational decline" (p. 198). Unfortunately, employees often pay a price for sharing information that could help their organizations and learn to keep quiet.

Obstacles to Upward Communication

Upward communication does not happen routinely within a traditional chain-of-command structure. Not only are hierarchies designed in top-down fashion, but numerous cultural and psychological aspects make high-quality feedback unlikely. As such, organizations should not put the primary responsibility for upward communication on lower-level employees.

Silence, fear, and distortions. Despite traditional pyramid structures, some lower-level employees will attempt to pass information upward. Some managers hear lots of complaints. However, research shows that managers do not necessarily hear about the critical issues. Detert and Edmondson (2011), for example, found that would-be speakers did not want to offer upward feedback because they believed their supervisors would "be personally identified with, or … feel ownership of, the aspect of the organization in question" (p. 467). Detert and Edmondson (2011) found that subordinates are even less likely to speak up during group meetings to avoid potentially embarrassing the boss. Further, Bisel, Messersmith, and Kelley (2012), argue that the hierarchical structure and the work-for-pay economic arrangement create a ***psychological contract*** between supervisors and subordinates. Supervisors expect to issue orders, and employees expect this too. This unspoken psychological contract reinforces the communicative structure displayed in a hierarchy's design.

Employees also do not share ideas because of outright fear. As Kassing (2002) explained, "From the perspective of employees, expressing upward dissent is a risky proposition" (Kassing, 2002, p. 198). Employees don't want their bosses to "shoot the messenger." Milliken, Morrison, and Hewlin's (2003) research found top fears and beliefs that prevent employees from offering upward feedback (see p. 1462):

1. Fear of being viewed or labeled negatively (e.g., trouble maker)
2. Fear of damaging their relationship with the supervisor
3. Feelings of futility that their feedback will not make a difference
4. Fear of retaliation or punishment
5. Concern about the negative impact on others

Employees may withhold their opinions for years even when they see simple improvements, but their fears are not unfounded. Burris' (2012) research showed that employees who express disagreement were rated as lower performers, less loyal, and more threatening than employees who communicated more agreeable messages. Burris (2012) explains that those who offered upward feedback were rated lower "despite the fact that [they] had information that could objectively increase the decision quality of the group to which they belonged" (Burris, 2012, p. 868). Realities like lower ratings add to employees' reluctance to share important feedback. For these reasons, organizations cannot simply expect employees will pass needed information upward on their own. Consequently, the lack of feedback is an ongoing problem for many organizations (Milliken, Morrison, & Hewlin, 2003).

Ineffective channels and response. In addition to employees' fears, another major obstacle is the lack of dedicated channels and leadership training for handling upward communication. While some modern organizations have adapted their structures to aid employees' participation, many have not (Kassing & Avtgis, 1999). Most current methods resemble the open-door policy or suggestion-box-type solutions that do not typically work (See Chapter 5). In general, many organizations do not provide adequate channels. This can make existing problems much worse, as Kassing and Avtgis (1999) explained:

> ***Latent dissent*** occurs when employees desire to voice their opinions but lack sufficient avenues to effectively express themselves. Consequently, they become frustrated and resort to expressing their contradictory opinions and disagreements aggressively to ineffectual audiences across organizations or in concert with other frustrated employees. (p. 103)

Instead of expressing potentially helpful messages upward to supervisors, employees complain to each other and shake their heads about their out-of-touch leaders. While some employees will still work hard regardless of their feelings, many will not.

Those who do communicate upward, however, follow predictable and unfortunate patterns. In most cases, subordinates "screen, modify, or withhold [negative] upward communications" (Athanassiades, 1973, p. 222). This causes an ***upward***

distortion where employees withhold negative messages and instead communicate favorable ones, especially those that show the employee in a positive light. Not surprisingly, when employees aspire to move up in the organizational hierarchy, they are more likely to distort information in their favor. If they routinely emphasize the good news and leave out the bad, leaders receive an inaccurate picture of organizational reality. Without consistent effort to the contrary, leaders routinely receive bad "intel" or none at all. Upward distortions are one of the main causes for the perception that leaders are out of touch. Consider further the multiplying effect that the hierarchy has on messages at they get edited on each rung up the ladder (see Chart 4.1).

Chart 4.1. The Life Cycle of an Upward Message.

Start at the bottom. Track the message from bottom to top as it flows from the employee up the chain-of-command to the CEO.

CEO's Interpretation:	My idea for a new computer system was a success. It is reducing errors and saving money.
Vice President's Message:	We predict the new computer system will reduce errors and thereby boost efficiency.
Director's Message:	Employees are getting better with the new computers and we predict the new system will reduce errors
Manager's Message:	Employees are taking the time to get comfortable with the new computers and the supervisor thinks mistakes will go down in the long run.
Front-line Supervisor's message:	Employees are having trouble getting used to the new computers. They are claiming there are more mistakes but I'm optimistic they'll get better.
Employee's Message:	The new computer system was a terrible idea. It's slowing production and causing more errors than ever.

Note: Notice how even tiny adjustments at each level distort the intel leaders receive.

This chart assumes that employees and managers intend no ill will and are only slightly altering their message. But Krone (1992) showed that some employees actively deceive their supervisors in an attempt to influence them by concealing their strategy for influencing the supervisor (e.g., discrediting a third party) and/or concealing their desired outcome (e.g., to secure a promotion for themselves). Deliberate changes distort communication even more.

In sum, although organizations need top-down communication, it is often overemphasized at the expense of the upward variety. The case studies below demonstrate how organizations can get carried away with pushing messages down the chain of command while disregarding or squelching information that could have otherwise helped avoid major problems and even disasters.

Case Studies of Top Down Communication

NASA Squelched Safety Warnings from Its Own Experts

The moon landing in 1969 was a turning point in human history. The crew marked the occasion in a fitting fashion. Just before he was scheduled to descend the ladder and take its first steps on the surface, Buzz Aldrin read a passage from the Bible and took communion. He stated, "We wanted to express our feeling that what man was doing in this mission transcended electronics and computers and rockets" (2014, Hafiz, para. 3). At the apex of the mission as Neil Armstrong reached the bottom rung on the ladder, he famously stated, "One small step for a man, one giant leap for mankind." In doing so, Armstrong was claiming a victory not only for NASA and the US but for all humankind. The 1960s and 1970s were the agency's golden era, marked by a steep learning curve, professionalism, and a concern for safety that mimicked military discipline. In the early 1980s with the moon in NASA's rearview mirror, the agency started the Space Shuttle program. In contrast to its moon-landing era of discipline, NASA's culture changed with a growing list of preventable safety incidents marked by the Space Shuttle Challenger explosion in 1986 and the Space Shuttle Columbia explosion in 2003. In each incident, the entire crew was lost. This case explores the specific instances in which NASA ignored forceful safety warnings from its own experts in the hours before each shuttle disaster. This two-part case shows that these tragedies were as much about communication failures and emerging complacency at NASA as they were about technology failures.

Part 1: Problems with the Challenger Shuttle's O-Rings

By the mid-1980s, NASA had launched over two-dozen shuttles into orbit. The Space Shuttle Challenger was the agency's first scheduled launch of the year in January 1986. The mission piqued the public's interest because the crew included an ordinary person on its crew for the first time, a school teacher, Christa McAuliff from New Hampshire. Many school children watched the launch on live TV at school assemblies (Wright, Kunkel, Marites, & Huston, 1989). Unfortunately, to the horror of everyone watching, the shuttle exploded just over a minute after liftoff. In the months following the disaster, NASA investigated the cause of the explosion. A rubber seal or "O-ring," a critical component of the right booster rocket, cracked and caused a hot gas leak that ignited the rocket's hydrogen fuel. This cascaded into a catastrophic explosion of the rockets and shuttle (United States & Godwin, 2003). NASA managers in charge of recommending launch/no-launch decisions ignored heated warnings the night before the launch that the O-rings could fail.

As early as six months before the launch, the engineers from Morton-Thiokol (Thiokol), an outside engineering firm for NASA who worked directly with the O-rings, warned supervisors about problems with the rubber seals. The problem was two-fold. The rocket joints the O-rings were meant to seal moved during launch and put greater-than-expected stress on O-rings. Also, the rubber seals performed poorly at lower temperatures. As a result, engineers noticed that the O-rings retrieved from previous missions' booster rockets had a tendency to erode and wear out a concerning amount. The engineers, however, could not get anybody higher up at Thiokol or in NASA's chain of command to listen. In October 1985, Bob Ebeling from Thiokol wrote a frustrated email entitled "Help!" to warn his supervisors and anybody else who might listen about the seriousness of the issue: "We didn't think we were getting anyone's attention and we thought by using the subject 'Help!' would get them … to read at least the first sentence of the memo" (Bergin, 2007, para. 5). The "pressure to launch," however, was a difficult issue. NASA had 15 scheduled launches in 1986, an increase from nine the year before. The pressure to maintain this pace became more important than growing safety concerns. John Young, the chief of the astronaut office during this period, acknowledged the "urgency to proceed with every launch" was caused in part by the tight launch schedule (Boffey, 1986, para. 28). Managers at Thiokol and NASA also ignored these warnings because, despite some erosion and cracking, the O-rings had performed successfully on all 24 proceeding launches. With each successful launch, the attitude became, "[We] got away with it the last time" (Boffey, 1986, para. 12). NASA lowered its standards with each launch, and the shuttle program continued down the road of "perpetual movement heading for trouble" (Boffey, 1986, para. 12).

The evening before the scheduled launch in January, engineers from Thiokol mounted their most robust arguments against a launch because of the forecasted weather. The O-rings had only been tested in conditions as low as 40°F. The predicted temperature the next morning was just 18°F. Bob Ebeling, the engineer who wrote the "Help!" email explained, "We discussed what might happen below our 40°F qualification temperature and practically to a man we decided it would be catastrophic" (Bergin, 2007, para. 14). The engineers and managers from Thiokol made a call to NASA and recommended that the agency delay the launch until the temperature went up later in the day. Jud Lovingood, NASA's senior manager, told the Morton-Thiokol engineers, "They couldn't make that recommendation. They had to give us a temperature that we could launch with" (Bergin, 2007, para. 16). NASA gave Morton-Thiokol just two hours, until 9pm that evening, to prepare a formal presentation to NASA via teleconference to justify a no-launch recommendation. Ebeling recalled, "The entire Thiokol group recommended no launch" (Bergin, 2007, para. 21). The firm recommended not to launch the shuttle until the temperature reached 53°F and showed data about the retrieved O-rings from past missions as evidence for their recommendation. Instead of taking the engineers' recommendation, NASA managers picked apart Thiokol's presentation. NASA's Jud Lovingood stated, "I thought it was a very poor briefing" (Bergin, 2007, para. 22). Roger Boisjoly, an engineer from Thiokol reflected, "We're always probed on rationale, but that night I was hammered (by NASA engineers) way more than I had experienced as an engineer in the aerospace industry" (Bergin, 2007, para. 24). Boisjoly summed up the unexpected tone of the meeting:

> This was a meeting where the determination [from NASA] was to launch, and it was up to us to prove beyond a shadow of a doubt that it was not safe to do so. This is in total reverse to what the position usually is in a preflight conversation or a flight readiness review. It is usually exactly opposite that. ("Rogers Commission Report," 1986, para. 138)

At one point, a NASA manager asked, "My God, Thiokol, when do you want me to launch, next April?" (Berkes, 2012, para. 13). NASA was unwilling to accept a no-launch recommendation.

At this impasse, both sides paused the teleconference and got off the phone at 10:30 p.m. to speak among themselves. At NASA, Lovingood explained to his colleagues that they would have to accept Thiokol's recommendation if the firm would not change its mind. On the other end at Morton-Thiokol's office, the engineers felt that they had little choice but to change their recommendation from no-launch to launch to satisfy their biggest client, NASA. Boisjoly recalled the following turning point in the conversation at Thiokol:

> But surely the photographs I had showed that the more black that you see between the seals, the lower the temperature, the closer you are to a disaster. I was told I was literally

> screaming at the [Morton-Thiokol senior] managers to look at the photos, but they wouldn't look at them. (Bergin, 2007, para. 29)

Instead, the general manager of Thiokol asked the three senior managers at the firm to reconsider their no-launch recommendation by stating, "take off your engineering hat and put on your management hat" (Bergin, 2007, para. 31). Boisjoly said, "there was never one positive, pro-launch statement ever made by anybody" ("Rogers Commission Report," 1986, para. 101). Despite the lack of support from the engineers, all three senior managers at Morton-Thiokol changed their recommendation to NASA to "launch." Boisjoly added, "it was clearly a management decision from that point" ("Rogers Commission Report," 1986, para. 134). When they resumed the teleconference at 11 p.m., NASA managers did not ask why the firm had changed its recommendation and simply asked the firm to put it in writing and fax it to NASA. When Thiokol's Bog Ebeling returned home visibly shaken after the meeting, his wife asked him what was wrong. He replied in frustration, "Oh nothing honey, it was a great day, we just had a meeting to go launch tomorrow and kill the astronauts, but outside of that it was a great day" (Bergin, 2007, para. 35). At NASA, Lovingood's team downplayed the intensity of the previous night's teleconference to the team's supervisor. The team relayed that Thiokol's engineers had some initial concerns about weather below 53°F but said the meeting "had been concluded agreeably, that there was no problem" ("Rogers Commission Report," 1986, para. 265). Arnold Aldrich, the head of the entire shuttle program, was not informed by anybody at NASA about the weaknesses of the rubber seals in the months prior to this launch and was not informed about Morton-Thiokol's heated warnings the night before. The next morning, the shuttle launched and exploded 73 seconds after takeoff, killing all seven of its crew.

Part 2: Holes in the Leading Edge of Columbia's Wing

In 2003, another shuttle catastrophe occurred. During launch of the Space Shuttle Columbia, a piece of insulating foam separated from the large orange central fuel tank the shuttle rides into orbit. The nose of the shuttle is temporarily attached to the fuel tank by a bipod. The foam detached where the base of the bipod's left leg connects to the fuel tank. When it came loose, the foam struck the heat-resistant tiles that formed the front edge or "leading edge" of the shuttle's left wing at a speed of 545 mph. The impact punctured the tiles. When the shuttle concluded its mission in space over two weeks later, the craft reentered the atmosphere to return to Earth. Upon reentry, the damaged tiles did not hold up. The almost 3,000°F heat caused by reentry quickly burned through the damaged tiles and destroyed the left wing. The shuttle tumbled and was torn apart. The shuttle's disintegration was visible from California to Texas as it streaked across the morning sky at 17,000 mph. In many ways, the events leading up to the Columbia explosion echo the Challenger disaster.

Similar to the Challenger disaster, clear warnings about Columbia's safety surfaced in advance. Some people at NASA raised numerous red flags that managers ignored with increased frequency. Don Nelson, for example, worked at NASA for 36 years. During this time, he was on the initial design team for the shuttle and participated in every shuttle upgrade (Beaumont, 2003). A middle-ranking engineer, he made numerous attempts in his last few years at the agency to refocus leaders' attention on safety. He stated, "what happened is that very slowly over the years NASA's culture of safety became eroded" (Beaumont, 2003, para. 7). He warned NASA's new administrators, but they refused to listen. Instead, Nelson reported, "I received two reprimands for not going through the proper channels, which discouraged other people from coming forward with their concerns" (para. 9). He even wrote a data-filled letter in 2002 to the President of the United States to share these concerns. He listed numerous instances of cracked fuel lines, 3,500 faulty wiring issues, computer failures, hydrogen leaks, and contaminated engine parts. Both NASA and the White House brushed aside insiders' concerns like Nelson's.

In addition, the tendency for foam separation was a known and serious concern, at least at first. From the early 1980s, NASA collected data on foam loss. The heat tiles were not designed to withstand impacts from debris and were damaged frequently by the foam. According to the investigation (United States & Godwin, 2003) of the Columbia disaster, "Foam loss has occurred on more than 80 percent" (p. 53) of shuttle missions, and almost always caused some level of damage. Seven of these events happened at the base of the left bipod leg. Five of these seven occurred on Columbia flights, a disproportionate number. Instead of looking into this pattern of incidents with the Columbia shuttle, perhaps caused by one of its unique design features compared to the other shuttles, NASA "failed to adequately perform trend analysis on foam losses" (p. 131). Without this long-term analysis, NASA was not able to make an informed decision about the true risks of continuing to fly. Unfortunately, while the number of foam strikes increased, NASA leaders admitted, they had no "comprehensive inspection plan to determine the structural integrity of" the tiles (United States & Godwin, 2003, p. 54). Additionally, while the tiles were not designed to withstand the impact from strikes, NASA knew from its experiments that the tiles on the leading edge of the wing "could survive re-entry with a quarter-inch diameter hole" or smaller (United States & Godwin, 2003, p. 56). This area is smaller than previously confirmed damage to less vulnerable tiles on the underbelly of the shuttle. The data alone should have led to aggressive steps toward ensuring the integrity of the heat tiles.

NASA did not put its information on the foam and tiles to good use. Instead of growing more concerned about damage the loose foam caused and lack of a plan for fixing the problem, "managers increasingly regarded the foam shedding as inevitable, and … unlikely to jeopardize safety" (United States & Godwin, 2003, p. 122). Despite this belief, in October 2002, during the mission just before Columbia's, a large chunk of foam detached from another shuttle's fuel tank from the same spot and the "damage it caused" to a booster rocket was "significant" (p. 125). Instead of taking preventative steps on future missions, NASA manipulated the numbers to minimize the perceived risks (United States & Godwin, 2003). It downgraded the perceived risk further when The Flight Readiness Review following the October 2002 mission concluded foam loss, particularly from the base of the bipod, should be labeled as an "accepted risk" and "not safety-of-flight" issue (p. 126). Columbia's post-accident investigation (United States & Godwin, 2003) posed the issue, "It would seem that the longer the Shuttle Program allowed debris to continue striking the [shuttles], the more opportunity existed to detect the serious threat it posed" (p. 121). Instead, as the number of foam strikes went up, NASA made the unsupportable claim that foam shed was less likely in the future. The investigation (United States & Godwin, 2003) described this approach as "gambling" (p. 139). As such, NASA took no steps to improve the quality, strength, or application of the insulating foam.

Post-strike response and decision-making. By January 2003, NASA officials had essentially made their minds up that loose foam had little safety significance. When Columbia launched on January 16, the foam detached and struck the shuttle's wing 82 seconds after take off. NASA employees noticed the foam strike after reviewing high-resolution video of the launch, a normal procedure. The team responsible for evaluating issues like loose foam strikes raised concerns about the loose foam happening on two launches in a row. The group, however, did not believe this posed any danger to the current shuttle mission even though the video and photos taken from the shuttle did not provide a clear view of the damaged area. An early email from a manager in the group downplayed the potential risk. He wrote even before the team met, "Basically the [tile surface] is extremely resilient to impact type damage" (United States & Godwin, 2003, p. 141). In an early meeting about it, a manager of the group wrote in the log, "there was no rush on this issue" (p. 142). Other official notes from these meetings stated, "it shouldn't be a problem" (p. 142). These early opinions were made with no data and framed the issue as a low priority. Despite being given the weekend off, engineers who worked for the team ran computer simulations about the debris strike through a program called "Crater." Their simulations "predicted damage deeper than the actual tile thickness" (p. 145). This result should have signaled trouble. Instead, the engineers discounted the Crater results because, in their view, the program was inadequate, and they believed the tiles were tougher than the results showed.

Early internal communication from NASA also shows that managers felt they could do little during Columbia's mission even if damage had occurred. In a transcript from a meeting six days after launch, an engineer states, "I don't think there is much we can do so it's not really a factor during the flight because there is not much we can do about it" (p. 147). The team involved was more concerned about how the foam strike on Columbia might delay NASA's next launch and realized that the rationale for the next launch was "lousy," which was *foam strikes hadn't caused "safety-of-flight" issues in the past* (United States & Godwin, 2003, p. 148). Nevertheless, they hoped this explanation would be good enough to get a green light for future launches. Initially, the team made several requests for additional photographs and video to be taken of the potentially damaged area, even requesting help from the Air Force at one point. These requests for imagery were ignored or quickly withdrawn because of their expense. According to meeting notes, additional imagery "was no longer being pursued since even if we saw something, we couldn't do anything about it" (United States & Godwin, 2003, p. 154). Even though everybody involved knew of the likely area the foam would hit on the wing and understood the data about the potentially deadly result from its Crater simulations, the decision-makers were not willing to pursue the problem. In the end, the managers' team meeting notes concluded that the potential damage was not an issue for Columbia: "no safety of flight, no issue for this mission, nothing that we're going to do different" (p. 161).

While the team continued to downplay the need for more imagery and potential damage, others had concerns. The press began asking questions about potential trouble on the mission. Some engineer-level employees also wanted to approach the problem more aggressively, particularly by getting more information additional imagery might provide. For example, engineer Rodney Rocha did not send a draft email in which he wrote that it was a "wrong (and bordering on irresponsible) answer … [to] not to request additional imaging help" (p. 157). He only shared a printed version of the message with a colleague because he did not "want to jump the chain of command" (United States & Godwin, 2003,

p. 157). Further, other engineers elsewhere at NASA had concerns a debris strike might cause mission-threatening problems. Because they also lacked data, their concerns were based upon the speculation that a foam strike could disable the tires on the landing gear and result in a dangerous "belly landing." Among themselves, the engineers suggested a possible crash landing in the water without the landing gear and even ran simulations but did not communicate these concerns to NASA managers. Communication between engineers and managers was a problem. Managers did not enlist engineers' help or share data, and engineers were not comfortable expressing their views to managers.

Numerous managers reiterated the claim, "there's nothing we can do." Despite this repeated statement following the foam strike on the mission before Columbia's, NASA had developed two options for handling mission-threatening damage to the tiles (see United States & Godwin, 2003, pp. 173–174). The first plan was to accelerate the preparation and launch of the next shuttle, Atlantis, to rendezvous with Columbia and take the crew back to Earth on Atlantis. Doing so, however, would require a decision by at least the sixth day of Columbia's mission to ensure enough water, food, and oxygen. The Crater computer analysis "predicted damage deeper than the actual tile thickness" on Day 4 of the mission. This data would have allowed enough time to make the decision to rescue the crew with Atlantis. The second involved Columbia's crew repairing the damaged tiles while in orbit. This would result in a temporary rather than complete fix, involve multiple spacewalks, and rely on the less-than-ideal materials and tools available on the shuttle. Part of this option involved dumping any extra cargo into space to reduce the weight of the shuttle and changing the angle or "profile" of the shuttle's re-entry. A changed profile would reduce the buildup of heat on the damaged tile surfaces. Clearly, none of these options offered any guarantees. At the same time, the NASA team responsible for weighing these options never informed the crew that there might be a problem and never told them to take a look at the potentially damaged area. When NASA instructed the shuttle crew on the 17th day of its mission to come home as scheduled, the agency and crew "treated the re-entry like any other" (United States & Godwin, 2003, p. 38). NASA did not even change Columbia's re-entry profile to reduce heat on damaged tile area. Sadly, 14 minutes after re-entering Earth's atmosphere, all seven of Columbia's crew were dead. The shuttle's debris field covered a 2,000 square foot area of eastern Texas. Wayne Hale, the Ascent Flight Director for Columbia's last mission, wrote about the explosion in his personal blog on the tenth anniversary of the mission (Hale, 2013). He repeated a statement he had made in a NASA meeting after the disaster: "We are never ever going to say that there is nothing we can do" (para. 8).

Common Conclusions

The Challenger and Columbia disasters have common features. Budget pressures continually put NASA in a position where leaders, managers, and engineers felt like they had to cut corners. By the time Columbia launched, NASA had lost 40% of its inflation-adjusted budget since the push to reach the moon. This resulted in a steady decrease of technical employees at the agency. The leadership in both instances was also under increased scheduling pressure. As the 2003 investigation put it, "No one at NASA wants to be the one to stand up and say, 'We can't make that date'" (United States & Godwin, 2003, p. 138). At the time of the Columbia explosion, NASA's future was in serious question. The investigation reports, "The Space Station Program and NASA were on probation, and had to prove they could meet schedules and budgets" (United States & Godwin, 2003, p. 131). Perhaps, in part because of budgetary and scheduling pressures, NASA also relaxed its attitude toward safety issues. The Columbia investigation concluded the following: "By the eve of the Columbia accident, [NASA] practices that were in effect at the time of the Challenger accident—such as inadequate concern over deviations from expected performance, a silent safety program, and schedule pressure—had returned" (United States & Godwin, 2003, p. 101). In both cases, engineers had difficulty getting managers to listen or were unwilling to approach them, and managers consistently downplayed risks when safety issues surfaced. Neither the Challenger nor Columbia crews were warned about the potential dangers. In both cases, NASA took no actions that may have increased the likelihood of survival. The shuttle program was cancelled permanently in 2011, but NASA is planning to send astronauts to Mars in the future.

Questions:

- Why did communication flow so easily down the chain of command at NASA but not up?
- What would you change at NASA to make sure top decision-makers receive the information they need to make the best possible decisions?

Netflix "Slid into Arrogance" and Lost 800,000 Customers

Throughout the 1980s and 1990s, most people rented movies from a brick-and-mortar video store in their local town. In 1999, however, Marc Randolf and Reed Hastings started a subscription-based service called Netflix that meant customers didn't have to go out to shop. Customers selected from a vast catalog of movies through the company's website and Netflix mailed the DVDs directly to customers' homes. After viewing, customers could conveniently send the DVDs back to Netflix in prepaid envelopes rather than driving to a store to return a DVD. Customers paid a flat monthly rate and watched and returned as many or as few movies as they wanted to. Since customers paid via subscription and not per movie, the company did not have due dates or late fees like its main competitor, Blockbuster. Further, without the constraint of shelf space, Netflix's massive catalogue of over 100,000 titles allowed customers to see many "small" films they could not see otherwise. Netflix solved the three major inconveniences customers faced: selection, drive time, and late fees. Netflix's success among other factors led Blockbuster to file for bankruptcy in 2010. By this time, Netflix was expanding its online streaming offerings of films and other programming. Blockbuster's bankruptcy and the growth of online streaming both positioned Netflix as the sole dominant player in the market. This case examines a decision that temporarily set Netflix back and shows the dangers of ignoring warning signs in the marketplace.

CEO's Decision to Split Services

In September 2011, Netflix entered a brief but controversial episode. Reed Hastings, the company's CEO, raised the price a whopping 60 percent. Customers fumed over the increase. Hastings apologized for the price increase on the company's blog ("Explanation and Some Reflection," 2011) and explained another related change. The company would be splitting the DVD-by-mail service and the online movie streaming service. He stated the following:

> I messed up. I owe everyone an explanation. It is clear from the feedback over the past two months that many members felt we lacked respect and humility in the way we announced the separation of DVD and streaming, and the price changes. That was certainly not our intent, and I offer my sincere apology. (para. 1–2)

Splitting services was an even more significant change than the price increase. He explained the change as follows:

> It's hard for me to write this after over 10 years of mailing DVDs with pride, but we think it is necessary and best: In a few weeks, we will rename our DVD by mail service to "Qwikster." We chose the name Qwikster because it refers to quick delivery. We will keep the name "Netflix" for streaming. Qwikster will be the same website and DVD service that everyone is used to. It is just a new name, and DVD members will go to qwikster.com to access their DVD queues and choose movies. (para. 10–12)

Hastings explained that as time went on, the online streaming business was developing very differently than the traditional DVD mail business. Both had "very different cost structures, different benefits that need to be marketed differently, and we need to let each grow and operate independently" ("Explanation and Some Reflection," 2011, para. 10). At the beginning of his message, Hastings emphasized, "I slid into arrogance from [Netflix's] past success" (para. 5) regarding his lack of communication, in particularly, about the previous increase in prices. Netflix posted a video explanation to coincide with the blog announcement in which he further explained the reasons for splitting the companies and services entirely. As details came out, it became clear that customers who wanted both services would have to pay for both services separately, use two different websites with unique logins, and pay two separate bills. While the change may have made sense from Hasting's business standpoint, the change would be a major hassle for existing customers. In the following weeks, Hastings gave numerous interviews to essentially apologize for not preparing customers for these changes earlier and reassure them that the split was a good idea.

Public Backlash

Customers' backlash was immediate. Within 24 hours, Netflix's blog was flooded with over 15,000 comments from customers, mostly negative (Lang, 2011). The previous price change was annoying but tolerable. Splitting services completely created clear inconveniences for customers. Some commenters did not restrain their feelings as shown here (para. 5–6):

- "Fire the manager who came up with both the name Quickster [SIC] change and division of services. I'll probably have to drop one or both."
- "Thanks for the explanation and apology. That helps, but your arrogance is still so thick it's palpable. The 'I'm sorry if you were offended' is no apology at all. It just makes things worse."
- "I just got your email, and, as a long-time customer, quite frankly found it to be offensive. And perhaps a devastating mis-calculation for your business. Your best customers are those like myself that use the DVD and the streaming services. But those are the very customers that you are alienating."

Hastings and company spokespeople insisted that splitting the companies would ultimately benefit customers. Once separated, they explained, each business could focus on its core competencies and innovate. Hastings believed that the DVD mail service had peaked and the online streaming business was just beginning. Nevertheless, most business analysts also saw the move to split the company as a poor decision. Michael Pachter, an analyst at the financial services and investment firm Wedbush Securities, stated, “It’s the dumbest thing I’ve ever seen. They went from being about the smartest company to the dumbest in about three months. They had a flawless service that was widely admired and they’re throwing a wrench in it” (Lang, 2011, para. 16–17). Customers expressed their opinion with more than just words. Within three weeks, over 800,000 customers cancelled their subscriptions (Wingfield & Stelter, 2011). Further, investor sentiment turned against the company. Netflix stock price fell from $295 per share in July 2011 to $63 per share by November 2011 and remained low until it began to recover steadily in early 2013. Some stockholders felt the company was so mismanaged that they filed a lawsuit against the company’s top executives (Stempel, 2013).

Hastings’s Apology and Reversal

Ultimately, just three weeks after the initial announcement, Netflix reversed its decision to split the services but would maintain the price increase. The bad publicity and loss of customers was clearly hurting the company in numerous ways. Hastings (“DVDs Will Be Staying,” 2011) explained the decision on the company’s blog:

> It is clear that for many of our members two websites would make things more difficult, so we are going to keep Netflix as one place to go for streaming and DVDs. This means no change: one website, one account, one password … in other words, no Qwikster. (“DVDs Will Be Staying,” 2011, para. 1–2)

For some customers, the damage was already done and they did not re-subscribe. Over the next few months, other customers reconsidered and some gradually re-subscribed to Netflix by the year’s end. Netflix’s stock price saw a modest increase after this reversal announcement but remained low for months. In a follow up statement, Hastings explained his desire to keep Netflix ahead of the industry curve: “there is a difference between moving quickly—which Netflix has done very well for years—and moving too fast, which is what we did in this case” (Stelter, 2011, para. 15). Hastings’ explanations, however, reveal his thoughts about the industry’s future but also his lack of insight into his current customers’ interests.

Did Anybody Ask Anybody?

In the weeks following the reversal announcement Hastings continued to give interviews and do public relations damage control. Reporters asked more probing questions about Netflix's baffling decision-making process for such a poorly received change. A major theme in these interviews was that Hastings had no idea how Netflix customers' would react to these changes. Before the change, Netflix leaders either didn't ask or didn't care. In one interview, Hastings was asked if the company used focus groups to listen to customers' thoughts about the changes. He replied, "Our focus-group work concentrated on trying to understand consumers' perspectives on names other than Netflix" (Goldman, 2011, para. 4). To clarify, Netflix asked focus groups about their opinion on the name Qwikster, and presumably other potential names, to describe the DVD-by-mail service. Another reporter asked Hastings a similar question. The reporter summarized Hastings' response: "he was not sure whether the plan to split the company had been presented to customer focus groups … he assumed it had been … [but] did not recall what those focus groups had said" (Wingfield & Stelter, 2011, para. 11). After numerous interviews and statements from spokespersons, it was clear that Netflix had not gathered any meaningful data from customers about how they would feel about splitting the services.

Following these interviews, Hastings developed the reputation for not understanding customers. At least one customer who was also a good friend of Hastings, for instance, provided his unedited thoughts to the CEO before the change. He explained his conversation to *New York Times* reporters (Wingfield & Stelter, 2011) who retold the story as follows:

> Reed Hastings was soaking in a hot tub with a friend last month when he shared a secret: his company, Netflix, was about to announce a plan to divide its movie rental service into two—one offering streaming movies over the Internet, the other offering old-fashioned DVDs in the mail. "That is awful," the friend, who was also a Netflix subscriber, told him under a starry sky in the Bay Area, according to Mr. Hastings. [His friend said,] "I don't want to deal with two accounts." Mr. Hastings ignored the warning, believing that chief executives should generally discount what their friends say. (para. 1–2)

Naturally, CEOs cannot make important decisions about their company based upon one friend's or one customer's opinion. Neither, however, should we expect companies to read customers' minds in the midst of industry pressures, competition, and organizational deadlines.

The same skills that make organizations and leaders effective on one level (e.g., vision, strategy, decisiveness, etc.) may not necessarily help them understand customers. Gina Keating, a reporter and author of the book *Netflixed* researched the company for two years and interviewed Hastings numerous times. When discussing her research at Netflix, she concluded,

> Many people told me that Reed [Hastings] just doesn't have that human, they called it an emotional IQ, [Hastings' is] zero. … He just doesn't have any kind of empathy toward people in terms of consumers. I think with a lot of great CEOs, there's a little bit of a blind spot there. (Sandoval, 2012, para. 7)

Keating's point has important implications. Netflix should not simply assume they understand or know better than customers. As mentioned earlier, Hastings describes his handling of the price increases alone as resulting from his slide "into arrogance" and implied, at least in customers' eyes, that he perhaps lacked respect and humility in that incident. From customers' standpoint, it was ironic that Hastings acknowledged his arrogance and out-of-touch price increase in the very same message he announced an even more drastic complete split in services.

Bouncing Back

Netflix steadily recovered in the long run. The company had added several million subscribers as of 18 months after the Qwikster announcement and the company is now bigger than ever. The company's stock has continued to climb and was back near historic highs two years after the incident. The lawsuit by investors against Netflix leadership was dismissed about two years after the initial split announcement. The company now remains the dominant player in the movie rental and streaming industry and has restored investors' and customers' trust. It is unlikely the company will make sweeping changes in the future without first gathering and sifting through feedback very carefully.

Questions:

- Why do you believe Netflix did not ask customers or employees for their opinions about potential changes?
- How could Netflix have balanced their top-down communication with more upward feedback to the company's advantage?

Customers Not Juiced about Tropicana's New Logo

Most people have enjoyed a glass of Tropicana orange juice at some point in their lives. Tropicana was founded in the late 1940s in Florida and grew into a breakfast favorite in the US over the next several decades. In the 1980s, the company developed the logo used for many years: a straw speared into a large, bright, delicious-looking orange. In the 1990s, the company expanded sales into Europe, Latin America, and Asia. In 1998, PepsiCo purchased Tropicana. The arrangement was a natural fit for the two beverage giants; Tropicana is arguably the most recognizable orange juice brand in existence, and PepsiCo knows how to market and distribute beverages worldwide. The company has experienced consistent success over the years and occupies impressive portions of most juice aisles at grocery stores. In January 2009, however, it became the center of a surprising controversy. When Tropicana changed its logo, customers and critics alike expressed strong negative opinions about the product's new look. After public outcry and decreased sales, the company re-established the old logo, an uncommon move in corporate America. This case looks at the process by which the new logo was created and the way customers resisted the change.

The Arnell Group and the New Logo

In mid-2008, PepsiCo hired an outside firm, The Arnell Group (Arnell), to help redesign the logos of the various companies it owned, including Gatorade, Mountain Dew, Pepsi, and Tropicana (McCracken, 2009). Arnell is known for its innovation and specialized in branding and marketing campaigns for many well-known companies. Peter Arnell, the firm's founder and public face, has developed and overseen successful marketing campaigns for Samsung, DKNY, Reebok, Bank of America, and many other high-profile companies ("Company Overview," n.d.). According to a former partner at Arnell who now runs a rival branding firm, "Peter is an artist—he's a genius" (Lyons, 2009, para. 3). In many cases, his work generated great interest from customers. For instance, his memorable Superbowl ad in 2003 has been mentioned as one of the best of all time ("Obnoxious Boston Fan," 2014). The humorous Reebok spot featured a fictional football player, "Terry Tate," who unexpectedly tackled various office workers and screamed in their faces to increase their productivity. When Tropicana hired Arnell for its logo redesign, rebranding, and marketing campaign, they clearly selected one of the best in the business. Tropicana's festive and multi-colored logo had many advantages over competitors' logos. It relied on a strong illustrative image rather than just the name of the product and as such was instantly recognizable when customers scanned grocery coolers. Arnell's design went in a different direction that used a mostly white-and-orange color scheme. Its sleek logo was a simple glass of orange juice, and the largest font on the carton read, "100% orange." In contrast, the word "Tropicana" was written vertically from bottom to top and was not as prominent as before. Unfortunately, the new logo damaged Arnell, PepsiCo, and Tropicana's reputation.

Reactions to the New Logo

Customers' reactions were near unanimous when Tropicana's redesigned juice carton hit the shelves in January 2009. They hated it. Customers said the new design was "ugly," "stupid," and "a generic bargain brand" (Elliott, 2009, para. 5). One writer explained: "Consumers were confused by this new look that made the brand seem to be cheap, as Tropicana had always been perceived as a premium brand" (Marion, 2015, para. 15). In contrast to premium, the new logo fit in with the "low-range" store brands. The ordinary look of the package also soured shoppers (Marion, 2015). One customer wrote, "Do any of these package-design people actually shop for orange juice? … Because I do, and the new cartons stink" (Elliott, 2009, para. 6). When scanning the coolers, the new logo simply didn't stand out. If customers have trouble locating the product, then they will not buy it. As one writer remarked, "Consumers have to be able to *understand* what you're doing" (Edwards, 2009, para. 6). Customers also yearned for the old logo. One customer explained his emotional connection with the old design: "The old Tropicana package was a welcome presence in this household. It was familiar, cheerful, good hearted" (McCracken, 2009, para. 15). He continued: "But who cares about the old package? Who cares about the American consumer? Pepsi [the parent company] has an idea!" (para. 16). News articles about the new logo were overwhelmingly negative.

The media reacted with equal vigor. One critic and customer wrote the following scathing commentary on not just the design but also Arnell's mentality about the design process:

> It's not about you. It's not what you think is hip and happening. It's not about cool. It's not about New York City or … breathtaking mastery of the design vocabulary, or breakthroughs that reinvent the brand. It's about Americans at their breakfast table. How can this have escaped you? (McCracken, 2009, para. 21–22)

Tropicana's and Arnell's troubles grew quickly in large part because of the efficiency of social media. Complaints and opinions quickly went viral. Peter Shankman, a public relations specialist, commented on the potential advantages of social media to test ideas with customers in relation to Tropicana's woes. Shankman remarked,

"I can post something [on Twitter] and in a minute get feedback from 700 people around the world, giving me their real opinions" (Elliot, 2009, para. 15). The strength of customers' and critics' backlash, thus was partially a reaction against the decision-making process Tropicana and Arnell followed to create and roll out the new logo. PepsiCo, Tropicana, or Arnell overlooked the advantage of focus groups or other ways to gather customers' opinions to test perceptions about the redesigned logo. Instead, the new logo was based upon Arnell's conceptual thinking and went straight to market.

Peter Arnell's Explanation

The criticism of Arnell's work was swift. To respond, he held a press conference to explain his rationale. His explanation, however, only made matters worse. The YouTube channel, *Ad Age*, posted a video of Peter Arnell's comments:

> We thought it would be very, very important to take this brand and bring it or evolve it into a more current or modern state. ... Emotionally, it's still very, very difficult to, and it still remains difficult, for everyone to grasp the importance of that change because it's so dramatic. But, of course, historically, we always show the outside of the orange. What was fascinating was that we had never shown the product called the juice. ("Peter Arnell," 2009)

To some listeners, he sounded overly intellectual and out of touch. A writer from *CBS News* reacted as follows:

> Well, this is the problem, isn't it? Does orange juice really need to "evolve" into a "modern state"? Of course not. It just needs to be cold and fresh and taste strongly of oranges. But this is lost on Arnell. ... "Historically"? Seriously? This is OJ, not sociology 101. (Edwards, 2009, para. 5)

Companies and outside consulting firms all handle decisions like new logos, new products, and other changes in various ways. Some companies solicit outside opinions before finalizing decisions, and other companies make the decisions on their own and hope for the best.

For instance, Yahoo changed its 18-year-old logo in a way that contrasts with Tropicana's process in important ways. The first difference was that Yahoo surveyed its 12,000 employees to ask if it was indeed the right time for a new logo (Peterson, 2013). The survey showed that 87% of employees were ready to retire the old logo. Next, Yahoo's in-house design team made artistic choices aimed at modernizing the new logo. They played with various fonts and looks until they created lots of options. This step, the creative process of design itself, was relatively similar to Arnell's creative process. That is, the designers played with different ideas and developed some favorites. Finally, Yahoo laid out all of the potential new logos before its employees. The company used a "hot or not" type application to let employees compare the old logo with the new options side-by-side. Yahoo's logic made sense. Just because employees are ready to part ways with the old logo, "that doesn't guarantee people will like the replacement" (Peterson, 2013, para. 11). Of all the choices offered to employees over a month-long period, only the logo shown to employees on Day 10 received more votes than the old logo. In fact, Day 10 was many times more popular than the next several choices combined. Not surprisingly, Yahoo knew they had a winner. The new logo went over relatively well with the public and critics but was not acceptable to everyone (Hof, 2013). No new logo is. Unlike Tropicana, however, Yahoo's critics shrugged their shoulders at the new design and moved on. Tropicana and Arnell skipped the crucial stop of soliciting feedback and made their decision in a vacuum. While each company has the freedom to handle changes their own way, Yahoo—a beleaguered company in many other ways—provides a successful approach for handling a new logo.

Tropicana Reverses Course

Criticism grew over time instead of subsiding. About a month after the new packaging hit the shelves, PepsiCo's leaders announced that they would go back to the old Tropicana logo. Neil Campbell, president of Tropicana in North America, explained: "We underestimated the deep emotional bond" customers had with the old design (Elliott, 2009, para. 19). He continued, "Those consumers are very important to us, so we responded" (Elliott, 2009, para. 19). Campbell admitted the need to communicate with customers more effectively: "For companies that put consumers at the center of what they do, it's a good thing" (Elliott, 2009, para. 16). In fact, Campbell announced plans to reach out to every single customer who contacted Tropicana to explain their plan to go back to the original packaging. Perhaps more concerning to Tropicana than complaints was the sharp drop in sales. As the expression goes, customers "voted with their feet." When the new carton hit the shelves, sales dropped 20% for the month for a loss of an estimated $30 million (Zmuda, 2009). According to one source, Tropicana paid Arnell another $35 million for the rebranding campaign, an estimate that likely includes the associated advertisement campaign to promote the redesigned carton.

A quick reversal like Tropicana's is uncommon. Normally, companies stick with a change of direction even if it results in some negative feedback and a small dip in short-term sales, as is often the case. The reaction to Tropicana's change was so strong, however, the company had little choice but to abandon its plan. This hurt the reputation of everybody involved. A beverage industry insider stated about the logo change, "It's a black eye when you have to backtrack that quickly" (Zmuda, 2009, para. 9). The failed rebranding is cited as one of the biggest failures in recent memory (Hardy, 2013). In fact, although he claimed to have "moved on," Arnell's concerns about the failed campaign lingered. He told a *Newsweek* writer, "I can't believe that for the rest of my life I'm going to be known as Peter 'Tropicana' Arnell" (Lyons, 2009, para. 17). As for Arnell, he left his own firm two years later amid a divorce from his wife who ran the firm with him. He has since reemerged and is rebuilding his career in the branding and marketing world.

Questions:

- Nobody doubts Peter Arnell's artistic genius. Nevertheless, why didn't Tropicana's top-down approach to their new logo decision and rollout work?
- If you had been running Tropicana, how would you have handled this situation from the start?

Pushing a Dangerous Drug: The Case of Merck Pharmaceutical's Medication, Vioxx

From 1999 to 2004, over 25 million patients took a wildly popular pain medication called Vioxx, an anti-inflammatory pain medication that competed with common off-the-shelf drugs like ibuprofen, naproxen (i.e., Aleve), and more powerful prescription-dose competitors like Celebrex. At the time, Vioxx alone was bringing in revenue of up to $2.5 billion each year. Merck, the company who made and sold it, was a top-five pharmaceutical company with total revenue of over $20 billion a year (Merck, 2004). The manufacturer was, in many ways, a picture of success. Merck was spending hundreds of millions of dollars to produce new medications that, the company claimed, were superior to existing choices. It claimed that Vioxx was safer than alternative medications because it reduced the risks for stomach irritation and bleeding.

For years leading up to the sale of Vioxx, Merck worked diligently to establish a good reputation. The company's CEO at the time quoted George W. Merck, son of the company's founder: "Medicine is for people, not profit" (Gilmartin, 2002, para. 4). Merck's marketing slogan was "putting patients first." The company widely promoted the good works it did around the globe including an active vaccine campaign to cure a disease called River Blindness. The company website stated, "We seek to maintain high ethical standards and a culture that values honesty, integrity and transparency in all that we do. Company decisions are driven by what is right for patients" (cited in Lyon & Ulmer, 2009, p. 351). These stated values and priorities, however, did not align with what many patients experienced. The longer Vioxx was on the market, the more safety issues became apparent. Critics in the medical community began to question Merck's sincerity about prioritizing patients' health. For years, Merck responded defensively. Then, in 2004, the company recalled Vioxx from the market amid a groundswell of scrutiny from the medical community claiming the drug drastically increased the risks of heart attacks up to 500% ("Food and Drug," 2001). This case examines the way Merck continued to push Vioxx in top-down fashion despite the medical community's findings, the company's own data about the medication, and thousands of patient health issues associated with the drug.

Playing with Data

Behind the scenes, both the safety problems with Vioxx and the way Merck responded to the feedback became obvious almost immediately. As early as 2000, the first full year the drug was available, Merck produced a pamphlet (Merck, 2000) that handpicked and pooled data from several unrelated, short-term studies to make Vioxx look safer than it was. The pamphlet was designed to "set the record straight with your physicians regarding the cardiovascular profile of Vioxx" (Merck, 2000, p. 1). Instead of providing a comprehensive profile, the pamphlet omitted data from longer-term studies that revealed increased cardiovascular risks. Long-term data was available but deliberately left out of the pamphlet. The Food and Drug Administration (FDA) warned Merck not to use the pamphlet because the data was misleading to doctors (FDA, 2001). According to the FDA (2001), a longer-term study on Vioxx called VIGOR showed that the drug increased the risk of heart attack "five times higher" (p. 10) than the comparison drug in the study. Merck claimed the opposite, that Vioxx was perfectly safe and put out a press release about the study claiming it "confirms [a] favorable cardiovascular safety profile of Vioxx" (Merck, 2001a, p. 4). Merck stated that the VIGOR study did not, in fact, show an increase of heart attacks for Vioxx patients. Furthermore, its executives insisted that the data reflected a previously unnoticed "cardioprotective" benefit of naproxen, the comparison drug, and not a safety problem with Vioxx (Scolnick, 2005, p. 6). The company ignored the FDA's criticisms and continued to market the drug aggressively.

Merck also hired researchers who manipulated the data they reported to make Vioxx look much safer than it was. The *New England Journal of Medicine* published Merck's VIGOR study but later learned that important data had been deleted before it was submitted to the journal. The journal's editors later condemned the omission of these data, which rendered the "calculation and conclusions of the article incorrect" and misleading (Curfman, Morrissey, & Drazen, 2006, p. 2813). In a similar instance, Merck researchers were again accused of changing unfavorable data before submitting studies for publication. In one named "Advantage," (Lisse et al., 2003) a number of patient deaths were initially categorized as heart attacks but later changed to an unknown cause of death. Dr. Eliav Barr, a Merck scientist, emailed a colleague about one such patient's death: "[T]he clinical scenario [for the patient's death] is likely to be MI [heart attack]" (Berenson, 2005, para. 24). A Merck vice president for clinical research responded: "I would prefer [it to be categorized as an] unknown cause of death so we don't raise concerns" (Berenson, 2005, para. 25). These changes to published data ensured that the reported cardiovascular risks of Vioxx in journal articles were not statistically significant and would not attract as much scrutiny from physicians. Merck, thus, disregarded these early warnings in their own data, and Vioxx continued to grow in popularity.

Dodging Physician Questions

Similarly, Merck ignored physicians' relevant health-related concerns and questions during sales person encounters. Most of the $500 million Merck spent on marketing the drug was aimed at convincing physicians that Vioxx was the safest, most effective pain drug on the market. The year Vioxx hit the shelves, the company CEO (Gilmartin, 1999) wrote the following about the company's commitment to honest communication:

> Lives depend not only on the quality of our products and services, but also on the quality of the information we provide. … Information … must be useful, accurate, supported by scientific evidence where relevant, and presented honestly, fairly and by proper means. (p. 6)

In contrast to this statement, however, Merck did not train its pharmaceutical sales representatives with the principle of providing honest information in mind.

As criticism about the Merck-sponsored VIGOR study grew in the medical community, Merck instructed its sales reps to answer physicians' questions as follows:

> You may not discuss or respond to any questions about VIGOR. … [if asked by a doctor] QUESTION: I heard that VIOXX has a higher rate of MI [heart attack] than naproxen. Why was that? ANSWER: Doctor … because the study is not on the label, I cannot discuss the details with you. (Merck, 2001b, pp. 13–14)

Merck created a policy (i.e., "because the study is not on the label, I cannot discuss the details with you") that forbade its own sales reps to discuss the VIGOR study. However, the company encouraged sales reps to discuss freely other hand-picked data that was also not on the label.

In time, physicians began to talk to each other about Vioxx at medical conferences and through their professional networks. The number of reported heart attacks continued to grow. In a now well-known training document that Merck called "Dodge Ball Vioxx" ("Dodge Ball Vioxx," n.d.), sales reps are literally told to "dodge" concerns such as these:

- "I am concerned about the cardiovascular effects of Vioxx?"
- "Vioxx cannot be used for longer than five days when treating acute pain?"
- "I use Celebrex. I'm concerned about the safety profile of Vioxx?" (pp. 5, 8–9)

At the top of each page, a large graphically enhanced font says "Dodge Ball." The training document concludes in one-inch-high capital letters, "DODGE!" The questions reflected the growing concern about Vioxx's cardiovascular risks but Merck labels these questions as sales "obstacles" rather than treating them as legitimate medical inquiries. When faced with questions like these, sales reps were told to say convincingly, "Dr., let me say that based upon all of the data that are available, Merck stands behind the overall efficacy and safety profile of VIOXX" (Merck, 2003, p. 203).

Rather than listen to physicians' concerns, sales reps were trained to use "driving discussion words" ("Captivating the Customer," n.d., p. 5) to steer the conversation toward a sale. For example, they were told to lace their conversation with phrases like "Quality of life *plummets*," "*Unnecessary* pain/cost," "The *shocking* truth is," "The *staggering* statistic is," "The *immense* pain causes," "This is a critical time to," "The *solid experience* offers," "The *respected* leader in scientific outcomes," "High performance … Has *won* the *respect* of …" (p. 6, emphases in original). The training materials did not connect these phrases with any information or data about Vioxx. Instead, the company simply trained sales reps to use these phrases to "drive" the discussion and get the physician to agree to prescribe more Vioxx.

Silencing Critics

Over time, some physicians became more vocal critics of Vioxx. Some voiced their concerns at medical conferences. Again, rather than consider the feedback, Merck retaliated. For example, Lee Simon, a physician at a medical center in Boston, publicly mentioned "data showing [that] Vioxx might be associated with a risk of blood pressure and swelling" (Mathews & Martinez, 2004, p. A10). In the scope of treatments, side effects like these are not uncommon for many medications. Nevertheless, not long after making this statement, Dr. Simon received a phone call from Merck's medical director complaining about what he said. Dr. Simon reported, "I was shocked that there was a phone call made [to me] like that. … The company was attempting to suppress a discussion about this data" (Mathews & Martinez, 2004, p. A10). In a similar instance, Dr. Gurkirpal Singh from Stanford University's School of Medicine, a former supporter of Vioxx, was harassed when he publicly expressed his growing safety concerns about the lack of data:

> I asked Merck repeatedly for more data, including information on high blood pressure and heart failure rates. When I was unable to obtain this data after multiple requests, I added a slide to my presentations that showed a man-- representing the missing data-- hiding under a blanket. … I was warned that if I continued in this fashion, there would be serious consequences for me. I was told that Dr. Louis Sherwood, a Merck senior vice president and a former chief of medicine at a medical school, had extensive contacts within academia and could make life very difficult for me at Stanford and outside. ("Senate Finance Committee," 2004, pp. 368–370)

The Merck vice president then called several of Dr. Singh's supervisors at Stanford to complain. One, James Fries, explained: "I don't usually receive phone calls on Saturday at home from representatives of drug companies" (Prakash, 2005b, para. 3). Soon after the call, the vice president emailed a fellow executive to discuss the pressure he put on Dr. Singh's supervisor: "Fries and I discussed getting Singh to stop making the outrageous comments he has in the past few months. … I will keep the pressure on and get others at Stanford to help" (Prakash, 2005b, para. 8). In an another email to a Merck executive, the vice president advised the executive to "Tell Singh that we've told his boss about his Merck-bashing … [and] should it continue, further action will be necessary (don't define it)" (Prakash, 2005b, para. 9). One assumption is that Merck executives and scientists pushed a medication while deliberately hiding its acute risks. However, perhaps some of the individuals supported Vioxx due to the hazy thinking of financially-induced denial. At least some individuals at Merck acknowledged safety concerns. One was Heather Robertson, a Merck employee, who emailed executives involved in Dr. Singh's situation and cautiously broached the topic of safety: "Dr. Singh … reports product information that is not favorable to Merck … and although we may not like to hear about it, his information is scientifically accurate" (Prakash, 2005a, para. 41). Unfortunately, executives ignored her comments and insisted people like Singh were simply "Anti-Merck."

Withdrawal and Aftermath

Merck ignored the criticisms about Vioxx for years. By 2004, however, growing consensus in the medical community became too much to brush aside. Merck recalled Vioxx. Unfortunately, much of the damage was already done. Though estimates vary, between 29,000 and 60,000 patients likely died while taking the drug (see "Ethics: Medical Whistleblowers," 2005). Family members of the deceased patients sued Merck for billions of dollars in class-action lawsuits. The CEO resigned in 2005. Investors lost complete confidence in Merck. Company stock steadily sank from $90 per share when Vioxx was released to a low of $27 per share amid the growing crisis and recall. Though it has taken many years, Merck has since recovered from this crisis financially.

Questions:

- What were the costs of Merck's unbalanced, top-down communication approach regarding Vioxx?
- What would you do to make sure this did not happen again at Merck?

Chapter Discussion Questions

- How did these top-down communication norms shape these organizations' effectiveness?
- How did this communication approach influence their reputations?
- Why do you believe these organizations pushed their messages downward with such confidence at the expense of gathering upward communication? How could they have handled their communication processes differently?

Key Terms

- Top-down communication
- Organizational hierarchy

- Chain of command
- Downward messages
- Psychological contract
- Latent dissent
- Upward distortion

References

Athanassiades, J. C. (1973). The distortion of upward communication in organizations. *Academy of Management Journal, 16*, 207–226.

Baron, R. A. (1996). "La Vie En Rose" revisited: Contrasting perceptions of informal upward feedback among managers and subordinates. *Management Communication Quarterly, 9*, 338–349.

Bisel, R. S., Messersmith, A. S., & Kelley, K. M. (2012). Supervisor-subordinate communication: Hierarchical mum effect meets organizational learning. *Journal of Business Communication, 49*, 128–147.

Burris, E. (2012). The risks and rewards of speaking up: Managerial responses to employee voice. *Academy of Management Journal, 55*, 851–875.

Detert, J. R., & Burris, E. R. (2007). Leadership behavior and employee voice: Is the door really open? *Academy of Management Journal, 50*, 869–884.

Detert, J. R., & Edmondson, A. C. (2011). Implicit voice theories: taken-for-granted rules of self-censorship at work. *Academy of Management Journal, 54*, 461–488.

Gao, L., Janssen, O., & Shi, K. (2011). Leader trust and employee voice: The moderating role of empowering leader behaviors. *Leadership Quarterly, 22*, 787–798.

Kassing, J. W. (2002). Speaking up: Identifying employee dissent strategies. *Management Communication Quarterly, 16*, 187–209.

Kassing, J. W., & Avtgis, T. A. (1999). Examining the relationship between organizational dissent and aggressive communication. *Management Communication Quarterly, 13*, 100–115.

Krone, K. J. (1992). A comparison of organizational, structural, and relationship effects on subordinates' upward influence choices. *Communication Quarterly, 40*, 1–15.

Lyon, A. & Mirivel, J. (2011). Reconstructing Merck's practical theory of communication: The ethics of pharmaceutical sales representative-physician encounters. *Communication Monographs, 78*, 53–72.

Milliken, F., Morrison, E., & Hewlin, P. (2003). An exploratory study of employee silence: Issues that employees don't communicate upward and why. *Journal of Management Studies, 40*, 1453–1476.

Tourish, D., & Pinnington, A. (2002). Transformational leadership, corporate cultism and the spirituality paradigm: An unholy trinity in the workplace? *Human Relations, 55*, 147–172.

Tourish, D., & Robson, P. (2003). Critical upward feedback in organisations: Processes, problems and implications for communication management. *Journal of Communication Management, 8*, 150–167.

NASA References

Beaumont, P. (2003, February 2). NASA chiefs "repeatedly ignored" safety warnings. *The Guardian*. Retrieved from http://www.theguardian.com/science/2003/feb/02/spaceexploration.usnews3

Bergin, C. (2007). Remembering the mistakes of Challenger. *NASA Spaceflight*. Retrieved from http://www.nasaspaceflight.com/2007/01/remembering-the-mistakes-of-challenger/

Berkes, H. (2012, February 12). Remembering Roger Boisjoly: He tried to stop shuttle Challenger launch. *NPR*. Retrieved from http://www.npr.org/sections/thetwo-way/2012/02/06/146490064/remembering-roger-boisjoly-he-tried-to-stop-shuttle-challenger-launch

Boffey, P. M. (1986, April 4). NASA official says shuttle program had major flaws. *New York Times*. Retrieved from http://www.nytimes.com/1986/04/04/us/nasa-official-says-shuttle-program-had-major-flaws.html?pagewanted=all

Hafiz, Y. (2014, July 19). The Moon communion of Buzz Aldrin that NASA didn't want to broadcast. *The Huffington Post*. Retrieved November 11, 2015 from http://www.huffingtonpost.com/2014/07/19/moon-communion-buzz-aldrin_n_5600648.html

Hale, W. (January 13, 2013). After ten years: Working on the wrong problem. *Wayne Hale's Blog*. Retrieved from https://waynehale.wordpress.com/2013/01/13/after-ten-years-working-on-the-wrong-problem/

Rogers Commission Report. (1986). *Report of the Presidential Commission on the Space Shuttle Challenger accident*. Washington, DC: U.S. Government Printing Office.

United States, & Godwin, R. (2003). *Columbia accident investigation board: Report*. Burlington, ON: Apogee Books.

Wright, J. C., Kunkel, D., Marites, P., & Huston, A. C. (1989). How children reacted to televised coverage of the space shuttle disaster. *Journal of Communication, 39*, 27–45.

Netflix References

An explanation and some reflections. (2011, September 18). *Blog post from Reed Hastings on Netflix.com*. Retrieved from http://blog.netflix.com/2011/09/explanation-and-some-reflections.html

DVDs will be staying at netflix.com. (2011, October 10). *Hastings' blog post on Netflix.com*. Retrieved from http://blog.netflix.com/2011/10/dvds-will-be-staying-at-netflixcom.html

Goldman, A. (2011, October 23). Reed Hastings knows he messed up. *New York Times*. Retrieved from http://www.nytimes.com/2011/10/23/magazine/talk-reed-hastings-knows-he-messed-up.html

Lang, B. (2011, September 19). Netflix's Qwikster announcement leaves subscribers angry and analysts cold. *The Wrap*. Retrieved from http://www.thewrap.com/netflixs-qwikster-announcement-leaves-subscribers-angry-and-analysts-cold-31112

Sandoval, G. (2012, October 3). "Netflixed" author talks Hastings' glory, hubris, white lies. *C/Net*. Retrieved from http://www.cnet.com/news/netflixed-author-talks-hastings-glory-hubris-white-lies-q-a

Stelter, B. (2011, October 10). Netflix, in reversal, will keep its services together. *New York Times.* Retrieved from http://mediadecoder.blogs.nytimes.com/2011/10/10/netflix-abandons-plan-to-rent-dvds-on-qwikster/

Stempel, J. (2013, August 21). U.S. judge dismisses Netflix shareholder lawsuit over streaming. *Reuters.* Retrieved from http://www.reuters.com/article/2013/08/21/us-netflix-lawsuit-idUSBRE97K0S820130821

Wingfield, N., & Stelter, B. (2011, October 24). How Netflix lost 800,000 members, and good will. *New York Times.* Retrieved from http://www.nytimes.com/2011/10/25/technology/netflix-lost-800000-members-with-price-rise-and-split-plan.html

Tropicana References

Company overview of De Tomaso Automobili S.p.A.: Peter Arnell [executive profile]. (n.d.). *Bloomberg.* Retrieved August 11, 2015 from http://www.bloomberg.com/research/stocks/private/person.asp?personId=7468735&privcapId=79714785

Edwards, J. (2009). Arnell's "explanation" of failed Tropicana design resembles his nonsensical Pepsi document. *CBS News.* Retrieved from http://www.cbsnews.com/news/arnells-explanation-of-failed-tropicana-design-resembles-his-nonsensical-pepsi-document

Elliott, S. (2009, February 22). Tropicana discovers some buyers are passionate about packaging. *New York Times.* Retrieved from http://www.nytimes.com/2009/02/23/business/media/23adcol.html?_r=0

Hardy, T. (2013). 10 Rebranding failures and how much they cost. *Canny.* Retrieved from http://www.canny-creative.com/2013/10/10-rebranding-failures-how-much-they-cost/

Hof, R. (2013, September 5). Yahoo's new logo fails to impress—but people are talking about it! *Forbes.* Retrieved from http://www.forbes.com/sites/roberthof/2013/09/05/yahoos-new-logo-fails-to-impress-but-people-are-talking-about-it/

Lyons, D. (2009). The crazy genius of brand guru Peter Arnell. *Newsweek.* Retrieved from http://www.newsweek.com/crazy-genius-brand-guru-peter-arnell-76137

Marion (2015, May 21). What to learn from Tropicana's packaging redesign failure? *The Branding Journal.* Retrieved from http://www.thebrandingjournal.com/2015/05/what-to-learn-from-tropicanas-packaging-redesign-failure

McCracken, G. (2009, April 21). Tropicana: When CCOS go wrong. *Culturedby.* Retrieved from http://cultureby.com/2009/04/tropicana-when-ccos-go-wrong.html

Obnoxious Boston fan. (2014). Top 10 Super Bowl ads of all time. *Boston.com.* Retrieved from http://www.boston.com/sports/blogs/obnoxiousbostonfan/2014/01/top_10_super_bowl_tv_ads_ever_video.html

Peter Arnell explains failed Tropicana design [video]. (2009, February 26). *Ad Age.* Retrieved from https://www.youtube.com/watch?v=WJ4yF4F74vc

Peterson, T. (2013, September 5). How Yahoo picked a new look for an 18-year-old brand. *Advertising Age.* Retrieved from http://adage.com/article/digital/yahoo-picked-a-18-year-brand/243986/

Zmuda, N. (2009). Tropicana line's sales plunge 20% post-rebranding. *Advertising Age.* Retrieved from http://adage.com/article/news/tropicana-line-s-sales-plunge-20-post-rebranding/135735/

Merck References

Berenson, A. (2005, April 24). Evidence in Vioxx suits shows intervention by Merck officials. *New York Times*, p. 1.

Captivating the customer. (n.d.). [Training manual]. *Merck*. Retrieved September 12, 2005, from http://oversight.house.gov/index.php?option=com_content&view=article&id=2238&catid=44:legislation

Curfman, G. D., Morrissey, S., & Drazen, J. M. (2006). Expression of concern reaffirmed. *New England Journal of Medicine, 354*, 1193.

Dodge ball Vioxx. (n.d.). *Merck*. Retrieved from https://industrydocuments.library.ucsf.edu/docs/#id=nghw0217

Ethics: Medical whistleblowers speak out. (2005, June 24). *Drug Week*, p. 364. Retrieved from http://www.newsrx.com/newsletters/Drug-Week.html

Food and Drug Administration. (2001, February 8). FDA advisory committee briefing document: NDA 21-042, s007: VIOXX gastrointestinal safety. Retrieved from http://www.fda.gov/ohrms/dockets/ac/01/briefing/3677b2_03_med.pdf

Gilmartin, R. (1999). Code of conduct [Booklet]. Retrieved from http://www.merck.com/about/conduct.html

Gilmartin, R. (2002). The awards for alumni achievement. *President and Fellows of Harvard College*. Retrieved from http://www.hbs.edu/news/releases/AAA/gilmartin.html

Lisse, J. R., Perlman, M., Johansson, G., Shoemaker, J. R., Schechtman, J., Skalky, C. S., … Geba, G. P.; ADVANTAGE Study Group. (2003). Gastrointestinal tolerability and effectiveness of rofecoxib versus naproxen in the treatment of osteoarthritis: A randomized, controlled trial. *Annals of Internal Medicine, 139*, 539–546.

Lyon, A. (2007). "Putting Patients First": Systematically distorted communication and Merck's marketing of Vioxx. *Journal of Applied Communication Research, 35*, 376–398.

Lyon, A., & Ulmer, Robert R. (2009). Ethics in "Big Pharma": Communicating the risks of medicine. In: J. Keyton & P. Sockley-Zalabak (Eds.), *Case studies for organizational communication* (3rd ed.). Los Angeles, CA: Roxbury.

Mathews, A. W., & Martinez, B. (2004, November 1). E-mails suggest Merck knew Vioxx's dangers at early stage. *Wall Street Journal*, pp. A1, A10, A11.

Merck. (2000, April 28). Bulletin for VIOXX: New resource: Cardiovascular Card [Memo]. *Merck*. Retrieved from http://www.democrats.reform.house.gov/features/vioxx/documents.asp

Merck. (2001a, May 24). Bulletin for VIOXX: Action required: Revised response to *New York Times* article [Memo]. *Merck*. Retrieved from http://www.democrats.reform.house.gov/features/vioxx/documents.asp

Merck. (2001b). Project offensive meeting agenda & content: Representative meeting [Memo]. *Merck*. Retrieved from http://www.democrats.reform.house.gov/features/vioxx/documents.asp

Merck. (2004). Annual review. Retrieved from http://phx.corporate-ir.net/phoenix.zhtml?c=73184&p=irol-reportsannual

Prakash, S. (2005a, June 9). Part 1: Documents suggest Merck tried to censor Vioxx critics. *National Public Radio*. Retrieved from http://www.npr.org/templates/story/story.php?storyid=4696609

Prakash, S. (2005b, June 9). Part 2: Documents suggest Merck tried to censor Vioxx critics. *National Public Radio*. Retrieved from http://www.npr.org/templates/story/story.php?storyid=4696711

Scolnick, E. M. (2005, March 21). Vioxx: A scientific review. Retrieved from http://www.merck.com/newsroom/vioxx_withdrawal/

Senate Finance Committee Hearing. (2004, November 18). U.S. Senator Charles E. Grassley (R-IA) holds hearing on FDA, Merck, and Vioxx: Putting patient safety first, part 1. *Congressional Quarterly*.

5

Upward Communication and Case Studies

It's easy to get a bit insulated at the top, so you have to pursue honest feedback, even to the point of being uncomfortable.

—Ed Rust, CEO, State Farm Insurance (Jones, 2009, para. 17)

As previous chapters showed, traditional organizational structures were built to pass information from the top down. Few ensure that consistently high-quality information flows up the ladder to decision makers. Without good upward communication, leaders can make "out of touch," costly decisions. Even military personnel can make poor choices without the latest intelligence from the front lines. For organizational settings, I use the term ***intel*** to describe high quality and intelligently gathered information from clients, employees, and front-line supervisors about routine issues they face. This chapter, thus, explores the nature and value of routine upward communication. First, an introduction provides the nature and challenges of upward communication. Then four case studies illustrate upward feedback with varying degrees of success: FinancialCo, Nalgene, Domino's, and Nestlé Purina.

Upward Communication as a Leadership Responsibility

Managers believe they do a much better job gathering upward feedback than do their followers (Baron, 1996). This is due to common but ineffective practices of gathering feedback such as an ***open-door policy***. In theory, it is meant to communicate a supervisor's willingness to literally open his or her office door and listen to another person's ideas. This phrase sounds like an invitation but does not consistently produce the desired result. Morrison and Milliken's (2000) research showed, for example, that leaders' actions often discourage employees from approaching them; they do not actively ask for input and respond negatively to employees who offer it. Typically, only individuals in a supervisor's in-group have the courage to bring the boss feedback that results in a lopsided perspective. Consequently, the phrase "open-door policy" sounds polite but does not translate well to employees. After all, have you ever heard a manager announce that he or she had a "closed-door policy"? Leaders may not realize they are sending a mixed message.

The ***suggestion box*** is another largely ineffective tool for gathering upward feedback. In the US, for example, suggestion boxes generate only 1% of the suggestions compared to Japan (Dijk & Ende, 2002). The overwhelming majority of employees simply do not use them. The reasons are not surprising. Employees often wonder what exactly happens to the suggestions once they put them in the dusty receptacle? A student in class once said, "It used to be my job to empty the suggestion box at one of my first jobs." I excitedly replied, "Did you sort through them and figure out what to do with each idea?" He chuckled and replied, "I said it was my job to 'empty' the suggestion box. I was the janitor." The president of the company literally told him to throw out anything in the suggestion box each week. Systems like suggestion boxes can work—as shown in Japan—but only if employees believe their suggestions are considered seriously (Fairbank, Spangler, & Williams, 2002).

Similarly, many organizations now make efforts to use email or online surveys to gather feedback. Online surveys have great potential. However, some readers may wonder how genuine or effective these attempts are. As a customer, for example, have you ever experienced marketing messages disguised as feedback requests? A caller, website, or email may ask, "Do you have time for a brief survey?" These fill-out-a-survey requests sound like thinly veiled attempts to gather our personal information for future marketing, not a serious attempt at listening. Employees can experience the same feeling if they do not think anybody is listening. Feedback from informal open-door policies, suggestion boxes, and even online surveys are not typically effective. The methods themselves are not inherently flawed. In practice, however, these efforts do not gather the intel organizations need for high-quality decision making. In the end, only members of the leader's inner circle or chronic complainers are brave enough to share feedback, and even that is likely to lead to a skewed picture of organizational reality.

Thus, some of the most common practices for gathering upward communication are also the least credible and least effective. The difficulties that inhibit upward communication are easy to find in everyday life, and research on the topic goes back for decades (e.g., Athanassiades, 1973; Roberts & O'Reilly, 1974). The reasons are simple. They each (a) put the responsibility on the employee or customer to complain, approach a supervisor, etc. and (b) are often not taken seriously by organizations. I agree with Seeger and Ulmer (2003) who argued that being informed is part of leaders' ***communication-based responsibilities***. They explained that leaders have a special responsibility "to communicate and model appropriate organizational values, to be informed about organizational operations, and to create conditions that allow for the recognition, communication, and resolution of problems" (pp. 79–80). Employees or customers should not have to fight to be heard. To fortify organizations' overall health, communication systems should be designed to gather, interpret, and respond to organizational issues (Kassing, 2002; Pacanowsky, 1988). Organizational leaders are responsible for creating and using such systems to consistently produce high-quality upward feedback so they do not become misinformed or "out of touch."

A Consultative Approach

Upward feedback has traditionally been gathered informally to various degrees of effectiveness. *In Search of Excellence*, Peters and Waterman's popular book (1982), describes a leadership approach coined ***managing by wandering around*** or MBWA. The practice calls for leaders to get out of their offices and wander around to touch base with various departments. MBWA leaders schedule blocks of time to drop in unannounced. The practice establishes a norm of leadership presence, creates accessibility for the average worker, and provides direct observation. In one instance, Peters and Waterman describe a CEO who regularly wore an apron and grilled burgers for the front-line supervisors and employees on the floor of the factory warehouse to break down communication barriers. Simple questions like "How's it going?" lead to very different responses in the boardroom than they do while grilling burgers. The CEO found that his version of MBWA gave him a much clearer idea about the organization's status.

At its heart, MBWA takes a consultative approach to leadership whereby the leader solicits important information key decision-makers need from people spread throughout the organization's structure. Rather than claiming an "open-door policy" that puts the burden on the follower, the consultative leader seeks feedback about decisions from followers. Similar to Likert's (1961) concept of supportive relationships, a consultative relationship pursues good information from the people who have first-hand experiences to help make genuinely informed decisions. Colin Powell, for instance, was an accomplished General who understood the importance of encouraging upward feedback. In his autobiography, *My American Journey* (Powell & Persico, 1995), he explained that the more he advanced in rank, the less his subordinates disagreed. He developed a strategy to address this. When new subordinates arrived at his office, he walked them over to a small round table where they sat so close that their knees occasionally touched. Powell made small talk and deliberately disagreed with whomever he was speaking. Most individuals initially changed their opinions to align with his. Powell would eventually find an argument, any argument, the other person could not agree with until the two could have an open discussion and showed his appreciation for their willingness to disagree. From his view, a follower who was not willing to speak his or her true opinion was not much help.

The key to a consultative approach, like any suggestion system, is that employees believe the organization values their input, considers it, and includes the employees' point of view in decisions. If organizations gather opinions for the sake of appearances alone, people will see through this ruse. To foster a credible process, the organization must follow through on the feedback. Further, efforts such as MBWA and Colin Powell's approach embody admirable priorities but do not go far enough in gathering an adequate cross-section of opinions. Organizations must provide consistent and clear opportunities for members' contributions. Kassing and Avtgis (1999) refer to this as "articulated dissent [that] involves expressing dissent openly and clearly within organizations to audiences that can effectively influence organizational adjustment" (p. 102). An effective ***dedicated channel for upward communication*** consistently seeks feedback and demonstrates that employees and customers are organizational priorities. An effective upward communication channel should also be easy to access and use.

In addition to dedicated channels, organizations must prepare to handle constructive criticism smoothly. Even gentle criticism can unhinge some individuals. As Gao, Janssen, and Shi (2011) stated, employees who give suggestions "run the risk of being opposed by their leaders who usually feel a sense of ownership towards the current framework of thoughts and practices" (p. 794). This sense of ownership about the status quo can make people defensive and dismissive. Organizational supervisors would benefit from ongoing training to understand, interpret, and respond to upward feedback, especially when it challenges the dominant organizational perspective. For this reason, Kassing (2001) suggests that organizations train "supervisors to be receptive, open, and responsive to employee dissent … [to] encourage not only the immediate [employees] to express future concerns but also … signal enduring receptiveness to entire workgroups" (p. 461). That is, even if an individual categorically disagrees with the feedback he or she hears, the leader must project and embody a general disposition of openness, willingness, and interest in it. If not, employees will quickly conclude, "The boss doesn't really care." Organizations should look for opportunities to put suggestions into practice when possible. Detert and Burris (2007) explain that ***managerial openness*** is perhaps the best way to encourage employees to speak up: "Managerial openness refers to subordinates' perceptions that their boss listens to them, is interested in their ideas, gives fair consideration to the ideas presented, and at least sometimes takes action to address the matter raised" (p. 871). Training and coaching helps leaders respond in helpful ways.

Ultimately, upward channels help leaders make better decisions. From an ethical standpoint, they allow organizations to make informed decisions with the most utility. The perspective of ***utilitarianism***, which is credited to John Stuart Mill (1806–1873), an English philosopher, upholds the standard that the best and ethical decisions are those that create or promote *the greatest good for the greatest number of people*. To make the best decisions for the entire organization, we should accurately evaluate their anticipated costs and benefits. But conducting a thorough ***cost-benefit analysis*** is difficult when only considering the opinions of those closest to the decision makers or chronic complainers. A robust cost-benefit analysis will consider the views of the full range of stakeholders to ensure high quality intel, especially those who will be most influenced by the decision. Since employees and front-line supervisors typically comprise the vast majority of people in organizations, these groups must have reliable ways to channel their ideas upward. Otherwise, decisions may do the opposite and have the greatest benefit for the few people making them and little benefit to the organization's success. Asking for feedback takes courage because doing so may require people to change their minds and directions.

Why Seeking Upward Communication takes Courage

Asking for bottom-up communication takes courage. Consider the following understandable reasons we may hesitate to pursue honest feedback.

- ***Fear of handing decision-making power over to followers.*** Some people do not like to seek feedback because they think it takes them "out of the driver's seat." If the followers are steering the ship, then what use is the captain? However, listening and thoughtfully considering followers' feedback does not mean giving up decision-making responsibilities. When gathering upward feedback, leaders retain the decision-making role and are ultimately responsible for the outcomes. Gathering information helps organizations make the best decisions possible.

- ***Concern the upward feedback will be self-serving.*** Some leaders rightfully believe that seeking upward feedback will result in feedback meant to benefit employees alone but not the organization. This is a legitimate concern. Organizations must be prepared for some self-interested requests when asking for feedback and define guidelines thoughtfully.
- ***Concern that employees will bring up an issue that can't be solved.*** Organizations cannot resolve every request, criticism, and issue to 100% satisfaction. Thankfully, people understand this. Gathering upward feedback is not a "people-pleasing" process but, rather, a powerful way to make the organization better. Employees will gain confidence in the process when they see even a portion of their concerns addressed.
- ***Discouragement from negative feedback.*** Gathering upward feedback is not always going to be a touchy-feely "hug fest." Listening to some level of venting comes with the job description but can get taxing. Individuals responsible for gathering feedback can guide the process to move past mere negativity and use feedback to generate possible solutions.
- ***Feeling personally attacked.*** People often need the most courage when handling criticism that feels personal. If a follower does not like an organizational practice, the manager who established it may feel personally attacked. If feedback catches a leader by surprise, he or she may feel criticized for not recognizing the issue first. Nevertheless, when organizations provide consistent upward communication opportunities, leaders can become a crucial part of the solution rather than feeling like the target of employees' pent-up frustrations.

Benefits of Upward Feedback

Despite the understandable hesitancies of asking for bottom-up communication, feedback has many untapped benefits. A reliable system fosters commitment, employee voice, and satisfaction.

- ***Commitment.*** Employees become more committed to their organizations when they participate in a consistent process of upward communication. Farndale, Van Ruiten, Kelliher, and Hope-Hailey (2011) found "[e]mployees who believe they have the opportunity to voice their opinions regarding proposed changes to a higher level in the organization and believe that they can influence the decision making show higher commitment to the organization" (p. 123). When organizations take employees' views seriously, employees' feelings of obligation increase.

- ***Employee voice.*** As mentioned, employees routinely edit their messages to superiors to show themselves in a positive light and reduce risks. This skewed intel can harm organizations. A good upward feedback encourages ***employee voice,*** a term that refers to the ability to "have a say regarding work activities and decision making issues within the organization in which they work" (Wilkinson & Fay, 2011, p. 65). It allows for genuine employee engagement, participation, involvement, and empowerment, that "to improve[s] organizational functioning [and is] critical to performance" (Detert & Burris, 2007, p. 869) rather than distorted intel that contributes to blind spots.
- ***Satisfaction.*** Holland, Pyman, Cooper, and Teicher (2011) showed that "direct voice" was a primary contributor to employee satisfaction. Specifically, employees who had regular meetings with managers and the opportunity to speak up reported higher job satisfaction, were more efficient, and were more effective performers than employees who did not have these opportunities. Employees with a variety of direct voice opportunities reported even higher satisfaction than those with isolated opportunities. Holland et al.'s research on direct voice showed that employees want to speak for themselves rather than have an advocate speak for them.

Many issues clearly exist that complicate organizations' effectiveness in seeking and processing upward feedback. However, some pursue input aggressively. The cases below look at four organizations that listened to their employees and customers with various degrees of success. While some aspects of the cases that follow portray less-than-ideal outcomes, each provides lessons to be learned.

Upward Communication Case Studies

FinancialCo Struggles to Understand Why their Best Supervisors Do Not Want to Apply for a Management Team Opening

FinancialCo* (a pseudonym) is an investment firm headquartered in the western US with well over 1,000 employees. The company advises and manages individuals' and corporate investments such as mutual funds, stocks, and bonds. It employs many frontline customer service employees to field calls, handle questions, and resolve customer issues. Numerous supervisors work daily with these frontline employees. A team of six to eight mid-level managers, one of whom is the leader, oversees these supervisors. In terms of leadership style and culture, FinancialCo is located in a city with a reputation that is relatively informal compared to the "intense" reputation of New York or Boston. Its leadership prides itself for having friendly, supportive relationships with employee-level members. For example, top executives decided to put employees' desks around the perimeter of each floor against the windows instead of giving managers the best views of the beautifully landscaped grounds. In contrast, managers' average-sized offices were located near the center of each floor near the bathrooms and had no windows. The company's leaders made gestures like this to give employees preferred seating but also to send the broader message that the company cared about its people. FinancialCo also promoted employees from within to supervisory and management team openings as often as possible. Despite this employee-friendly design, one particular management team faced an issue. Their best employees did not want to become supervisors, and their best supervisors were not interested in applying for management positions. As the case shows, these managers struggled to understand and disagreed on how to address the issue.

An Issue Emerges

A management team led by "Heather" (a pseudonym) had historically performed well for the company. Lately, however, the team was experiencing more issues than others at the company. Over time, the relational distance grew between Heather's team and the supervisors and employees below them. This divide became more obvious in three related escalating incidents. Each time, the situations involved the way the management team interviewed employees and supervisors for promotions. In the first instance, Heather's team conducted an internal search to fill some supervisor-level openings. Following these interviews, some of their best employees gave Heather and her team a great deal of negative feedback about how the managers interacted with candidates during the interview process. In written feedback, employees described the leadership team as "unnecessarily intimidating," "unkind," and "adversarial." The feedback was consistent enough that FinancialCo's leaders above Heather became concerned about her team. Heather's team, too, was surprised by the feedback. From their view, they were just acting normally. They had little clue as to why employees found them unkind or adversarial. Still, the managers attempted to soften their image to build better relationships and were confident that they had done so. The second instance came in the next round of interviews for supervisor openings about six months later which resulted in similar feedback. Again, the managers above Heather became concerned. After all, the executives at FinancialCo took pride in the supportive communication style they had established with employees. They didn't like to hear complaints about a mid-level manager's poor dynamic with employees. The continued feedback and the executives' attention motivated Heather and her team to soften their approach and attempt to become even more engaged and supportive of the employees they led.

About six months later, however, Heather's team experienced the third and most serious situation. They had an opening on their own team and needed to hire a new manager to join them. When they made the announcement, they confidently encouraged all of their supervisors to apply. They waited a few weeks to allow supervisors time to submit their résumés, but just as the interviews were scheduled to begin, troubling signs surfaced. Heather received more negative feedback about the team and herself through the company's informal network. She did not want to reveal her source but felt it was important to share the feedback at the management team's upcoming weekly meeting. In past meetings, Heather was relatively relaxed and composed. Before this meeting, however, she paced the halls and spoke nervously to a few people nearby who were not on her team. "This is going to be a big deal," "We have a problem we're going to be dealing with today," "This won't be a typical meeting." She waited until the entire management team was in the meeting room making small talk before going in herself. She then entered with a serious expression on her face, closed the door behind her, and walked to her seat at the head of the table without saying a word. After a long pause, she announced, "I have something to say and I'm just going to say it." The team members leaned in to listen with focused attention. She stated the following in dramatic fashion:

> As you know, we're about to start interviews for the management opening. I have heard from a credible source that our top three supervisors are not interested in applying for the position. The supervisors do not want to talk to us directly about why they don't want to apply. But, for various reasons, they do not want to be part of the team.

The team peppered Heather with questions, but she provided only little bits of information at a time. While the criticism had a degree of variety, it pointed in the same direction as feedback from the past. The managers, including Heather, Bill, Paula, Mary, Mike, and Ted, were unnecessarily harsh. Nobody wanted to be around them, much less join their management team.

Employees and Supervisors' Perceptions and Managers' Interpretations

For about the next 90 minutes, Heather and her team discussed the feedback. The following exchange shows a representative piece of the meeting.

Heather stated, "Definitely we've had feedback that people don't get a very inviting feeling when we interview them. I think, though, we shored that up last time we interviewed employees for the supervisor opening, right?"

Some of the other team members tilted their heads and exchanged glances to signal some doubt about Heather's opinion but nobody spoke up at first.

Heather continued, "I think we're very, for the most part, inviting."

After another long pause, Bill seemed to agree, "Didn't we shore it up?"

Paula implied that she didn't agree by saying to Heather, "You scared Tom [an employee who had applied for a supervisor opening]."

Heather reached around to her own back and nonverbally acted as if she had been stabbed by Paula's words, "Okay, ouch. Okay, ouch over here."

The team members, however, did not laugh.

Mary reinforced Paula's point, "They were all scared though. It wasn't just Tom."

As the discussion progressed, it was clear that at least some of the team members did not believe the team had addressed the past concerns sufficiently about their perceived intimidation. Only Heather and Bill indicated a belief that the team had fixed or "shored up" their approach.

The discussion continued. Heather explained what she thought was a possible explanation for the team's negative reputation:

> I do think we've had our game faces on. You know, we haven't been the most happiest, perkiest, friendliest people out on the floor lately. You know, I take a lot of this work seriously. When I walk through a pod of people I probably don't say "Hi!" Perhaps I don't smile a whole lot.

Mike, who had remained mostly silent to this point, replied:

> You know, even if employees' and supervisors' beliefs are not reality in our view, the negative feedback is in some way the perception that's out there. Even if it's completely false, even if we believe the perception is wrong, we still need to do something differently to address it.

Mike's comment sunk in for a moment, but Heather did not react visibly. After a long pause, Heather moved to another point without acknowledging Mike's suggestion. On the one hand, it was clear that the group was technically discussing the feedback. On the other hand, it was not clear yet if Heather and the team were taking the feedback seriously enough to change their approach as Mike suggested they should.

Over the course of the meeting, two patterns of interaction became obvious, primarily involving Heather. First, Heather listed an item of feedback that she had heard through her unnamed contact, and then she quickly discounted the legitimacy of the feedback. She said, for example, "Another thing I've heard is that they think we don't value diversity. Well, I think we *do* value diversity." In another moment she commented, "Another criticism is that we only want people who are just like us. Yeah, that's true. Okay. We want people who share a core set of values." Heather seemed unaware or unconcerned about the dissonance or potential inconsistencies of her statements. In another instance, Heather listed behaviors that she claimed the team did not do very well and used the word "we" repeatedly to signal a collective criticism. It became clear, however, that while Heather was using the word "we," she was mainly speaking about her own personal behaviors. For instance, she stated, "We don't really spend social time with our people very much." Perhaps tired of being lumped in with Heather, this time Ted replied calmly, "I do." Heather ignored his comment and continued her list. "We don't really tell them enough they're doing a good job." Ted again replied, "I do." Heather snapped angrily at Ted, "Okay, whatever, Freak!" A long awkward silenced followed Heather's insult. Ted did not reply, and, in fact, did not speak for the rest of the meeting. After a few moments, Heather continued her pattern of listing an item of feedback and then discounting it. The second pattern involved joking. Heather joked when a criticism from her source or those in the room was aimed undeniably at her. She did this clearly when she replied to Paula's earlier comment in the exchange above. She joked, "Okay, ouch. Ouch over here," as she pretended to be stabbed in the back. She also spoke jokingly at her own expense in numerous instances. She said, for example, "I guess I'm the witch!" and laughed at a criticism about her cold demeanor. The others in the group did not laugh along with her. Her defensive and joking tone of voice indicated she was mainly dismissing or deflecting each individual piece of feedback instead of seeing the broader pattern that established her poor reputation.

Conclusion and Aftermath

As the meeting wore on, the team discussed the supervisors' feedback for most of a scheduled two-hour meeting. Eventually, the discussion petered out. In the last thirty minutes, the team gradually transitioned into their normal meeting agenda

Questions:

- What could these managers have done to collect and process upward feedback more effectively?
- How could the company use upward feedback to its advantage in the future?

by revisiting some old business and giving routine updates about the status of various projects. Importantly, neither Heather nor any other team member said anything about plans to follow up with the three top performing supervisors or Heather's unnamed source. Further, the group discussed no plan of action to tackle their declining reputation. Mike's earlier point about making changes even if the team believed the perceptions about them were wrong also did not resurface later in the meeting. Unfortunately, the team did little more than discuss the issue and drop it, which may be the same way they "shored it up last time." The team's poor reputation endured, and company executives became more serious about Heather's questionable leadership skills. Within a year of this incident, she was moved laterally to another mid-level position but one that had no supervisory responsibilities.

*This case study was developed from a previously unpublished paper. In this study, a small team of researchers videotaped two two-hour management meetings with the participants' permission. We were first given access to the organization and then an upper-level leader suggested that we focus our attention on this particular team. We also interacted with the managers on the team before and after the meetings and had several hours of informal participant-observation in the organization. The case focuses mainly on the second of the two meetings.

Customer Outcry and Nalgene's "BPAfree" Water Bottle Campaign

The average American drinks up to 30 gallons of bottled water each year (Gleick, 2013). In fact, the United States drinks more bottled water than any other nation in the world (King, 2008). It's a growing billion-dollar industry. To keep disposable plastic water bottles out of landfills, many consumers now use reusable water bottles. Nalgene is the top reusable water-bottle brand. Historically, Nalgene targeted hikers, campers, and outdoorsy customers. Unlike competitors, however, Nalgene successfully crossed over into the more general consumer market as bottled water consumption took off. Its bottles are now widely used on college campuses, by corporate America, and in the baby bottle market. While drinking water is good for our health, the plastic water bottles they come in have a bad reputation. Many plastics, for instance, have potential risks. In fact, one study (Yang, Yaniger, Jordan, Klein, & Bittner, 2011) showed "almost all commercially available plastic products ... leached chemicals" (p. 989). One such chemical is bisphenol A (BPA), perhaps the most well known ingredient in some plastics. This case looks at the way Nalgene responded when public perception about BPA turned sour. As the case shows, Nalgene reacted cleverly to the growing mistrust in its core product.

BPA's Use and Potential Risk

For years, BPA was a key and relatively non-controversial ingredient in Nalgene's bottles, at least to the general public. The company enjoyed a positive reputation primarily for its water bottles' near indestructibility. Numerous loyal customers, for instance, have uploaded lighthearted YouTube videos putting their Nalgene bottles through any number of strength tests and even outright attempts to destroy them. With a twinkle in their eye, customers slam the bottles on concrete, hit them with hammers, and even run over them with lawn mowers. While not indestructible, they are extremely tough. BPA was one of the chemicals that made bottles extraordinarily hard, durable, and able to withstand extremely high and low temperatures. They can hold boiling water without softening, which is ideal for hikers and campers who may decide to boil water in the wilderness and then store the purified water for later use. Nalgene's bottles rate a 10 out of 10 for impact resistance. Compared to most disposable water bottles, its bottles seem to last forever. In 2007, however, the Canadian government began running tests on BPA over concerns that it was leeching or "migrating" into the water people were drinking. Canadian health advocates feared that BPA had a harmful "hormone-mimicking" effect (Frasher, 2008, para. 1). A Canadian newspaper claimed, "The hormonal effects of BPA have been so extreme in lab rats that males have been turned into females" (Frasher, 2008, para. 8). Public statements about BPA became alarming very quickly. Tony Clement, Canada's health minister, suggested that BPA should be in the same category as asbestos, lead, and mercury (Frasher, 2008). Clement's position is serious, indeed, since asbestos exposure can be deadly. Similarly, both mercury and lead are highly toxic heavy metals. When ingested, they can cause loss of vision, hearing, and speech as well as comas, seizures, and even death. Canada's primary concern was that BPA was used in baby bottles and infant-formula containers. The chemical's potential risks for babies were particularly concerning because of their natural health vulnerability and the potential for lifelong harm.

In the US, public concern about BPA peaked in 2008 when on April 9 the *Today Show* on *NBC* aired a segment warning viewers of its dangers (Kraft & Raz, 2014). The segment showed various people drinking out of Nalgene water bottles as the reporter discussed the hazards of BPA. At one point, a workout instructor stated in a disappointed tone, "I thought these were safe" (Kosinski, 2008). *Today Show* host Matt Lauer mentioned Nalgene bottles by name and interviewed a doctor from the Mount Sinai Center for Children's Health who stated firmly that Nalgene bottles and those like them "are not safe for use across the board." As the two spoke, a graphic showed "DO NOT USE" in red capital letters and Matt Lauer read from his notes:

> A Center for Disease Control study detected BPA … in the urine of 95% of adults sampled. Scientists have measured BPA in the blood of pregnant women, in umbilical cord blood, and in placentas all at levels demonstrated in animals to alter development. Now, that's a very alarming fact, isn't it? (Kosinski, 2008)

To this, the expert stated, "Unfortunately, there's no level of exposure that has been identified as being safe and children and women of childbearing age are especially susceptible" (Kosinski, 2008). The segment suggested both checking the labels on plastic and using glass containers. With coverage like this, not surprisingly customers of all ages began to fear BPA for adults and babies alike. One writer called the situation a "public relations nightmare" (Esposito, 2008, para. 1) for companies like Nalgene. After all, BPA was the key ingredient in the company's only product. An analyst in the plastics industry commented on his surprise at the public's widespread anxiety: "This [BPA] issue has gotten more traction than I thought it would" among adult consumers (Esposito, 2008, para. 24). The fallout threatened Nalgene's entire business.

Industry Experts' Point of View

Many plastics experts who were familiar with the scientific studies on BPA, however, debated the reports in the media. They claimed, in fact, the actual scientific results on BPA's effects on humans were not nearly as alarming as news coverage like the *Today Show* made it sound. The early reports from Canadian health advocates broadcast the potential risks on humans were being announced almost simultaneously with data-driven industry reports that showed the opposite. Steven G. Hentges, executive director of Polycarbonate/BPA Global Group of the American Chemistry Council, stated the following: "There is no evidence to prove the low-dosage hypothesis [for humans]. After thousands of tests, the science just doesn't support it" (Stafford, 2008, para. 12). A spokesperson for the American Chemistry Council put the scientific results on the rat studies in perspective when comparing the potential exposure to humans:

> [T]he potential migration [leeching] of BPA into food is extremely low, generally less than 5 parts per billion under conditions typical for uses of polycarbonate products. At this level, a consumer would have to ingest more than 1,300 pounds of food and beverages in contact with polycarbonate every day for an entire lifetime to exceed the safe level of BPA set by the U.S. Environmental Protection Agency. Consequently, human exposure to BPA from polycarbonate plastics is minimal and poses no known health risk. (Esposito, 2008, para. 11–12)

Individuals and organizations on both sides of the BPA controversy debated for some time. The pro-BPA camp consisted of mainly plastics scientists who argued that, while the studies on rats themselves were valid, the rats' exposure was thousands of times higher than any human would ever realistically encounter. The anti-BPA side argued that the possible effects of BPA on humans "cannot be dismissed." Further, they argued, while definitive studies on humans had not been done yet, BPA did show up in dangerous levels unexpectedly in samples from concerning places like umbilical cord fluid, as mentioned on the *Today Show*. By connecting the dots, the anti-BPA advocates convinced the public that BPA was a major health concern.

Nalgene's "BPA Free" Campaign and Hearing Customers' and Retailers' Feedback

Interestingly, while many players in the plastics industry debated these issues, Nalgene's leaders did not. Nalgene's public comments on BPA were surprisingly scarce. Instead, even though their customers' beliefs about BPA were based upon potentially incomplete and sensational news reports, Nalgene took their customers' opinions seriously, often hearing about them through retail store managers. For instance, the manager of an outdoor gear store in Connecticut commented, "We actually ended up pulling [Nalgene bottles] off the shelves here. … Not really because we believe too strongly that there's a huge health risk, but more because of what our customers were asking for" (King, 2008, para. 4). Jingesh Shah, an analyst who followed the BPA issue, commented, "If regulators have concerns about a product, they do testing. But if a retailer sees that a product has a negative perception, they just pull it. There's no phase out period" (Esposito, 2008, para. 30). In the midst of Nalgene's public relations nightmare, other companies acted quickly to promote their glass and stainless steel bottles as safe alternatives to plastic water bottles. Instead of joining the debate, defending its key product, or undermining the use of glass or stainless steel, however, Nalgene listened to its customers and provided them with what they wanted.

Just one day after the *Today Show* segment on the dangers of BPA, Nalgene announced its new line of "bpafree" products. Eric Hansen, the company's Outdoor Senior Marketing Director, stated the following:

> We've never been about one style of bottle or one type of material. We offer more than eight different product lines in seven different materials, the largest bottle offering on the market today. Consumers can now use the information available through Nalgene Choice to easily find the perfect bottle that fits their needs, from our classic bottles to the newest Everyday Tritan options. (Hockensmith, 2008, para. 8–9)

The "Tritan" option Hansen mentions is the key chemical ingredient that Nalgene used to replace BPA. Like BPA, Tritan makes the plastic incredibly hard and virtually indestructible. According to nalgenechoice.com, the site that Hansen mentioned in his statement, the new bottles rate a 10 out of 10 for impact resistance. Rather than debate alongside industry experts or attempt to "correct" the public's perception with an information-driven marketing campaign, thus, Hansen's position was cleverly simple: *for those who want "bpafree," we've got you covered. Visit our website.* The announcement was well-timed and came as concerns about BPA reached a fever pitch. The company's website further spells out the "Anatomy of Nalgene" in ways that underscore the bottles' safety: "Nalgene bottles are molded from 100% virgin resin with nothing but FDA compliant colors added. The finished products are tested according to the requirements of the US FDA for food and beverage contact as published in chapter 21 of the Code of the Federal Register section 1580" (Nalgene.com/anatomy, 2015, para. 3). The company listened to its customers' health concerns rather than defend itself against negative perceptions. As a result, the company bounced back before the issue ballooned into a full-blown crisis.

The success of Nalgene's "bpafree" campaign was so successful it makes Nalgene's choice to do so look obvious in retrospect. In the midst of the decision process, however, no one can tell the future. As mentioned, some people described Nalgene's situation as a "public relations nightmare" (Esposito, 2008, para. 1). Hugely popular shows like the *Today Show* were directly telling customers never to use Nalgene bottles and stating directly that they were "not safe for use across the board." Some customers at the time planned to sue Nalgene for not disclosing risks. The context was surely blurrier at the time than it is in hindsight. Nalgene had to weigh the numerous costs of changing directions that included potential government regulation, competitors' reactions, existing consumer sensitivities, the economic costs of changing the production process of their water bottles, and the unpredictability of customers' future choices (Kraft & Raz, 2014). Changing the company's core product is difficult. No one could predict whether customers would forgive, forget, and buy Nalgene bottles again. Because of the company's choices, however, that's exactly what customers did almost instantly.

Nalgene's response was so swift and so well timed, it prompts the question, how did Nalgene find a solution to the BPA perception problem so quickly? Behind the scenes, the plastics community was knee deep in studying and trying to understand the potential risks of BPA long before the general public had ever heard of BPA. Experts in the industry know far more about their products than the advocates who appeared on TV. Thus, while many in the industry believed it was safe, Nalgene looked at the very real possibility that BPA might not be a viable option in the future. As such, they considered potential substitute chemical ingredients even before the groundswell of the anti-BPA messages took hold. In essence, the early industry uncertainty about BPA prompted Nalgene to tinker with its product. The notion for making bottles with Tritan instead of BPA was already in the Nalgene decision-making pipeline. With the help of retail store managers and their core customers' feedback, Nalgene accelerated its Tritan bottles and branded them "bpafree" to capitalize on public perception. With one slogan, Nalgene positioned its product as the solution rather than the problem.

Is BPA Dangerous?

BPA is now perhaps the most studied plastic ingredient of all time. Determining the relatively safety or risks of BPA is clearly beyond the scope of this case study. Groups on both sides of the BPA debate hold fast to their opinions. Individuals and groups who are most deeply embedded in the science do not believe the results demonstrate it is unsafe. From 2009 to 2013, for instance, an FDA subcommittee reviewed fresh studies on BPA, its potential hazards, and its relative tendency to migrate from plastic. In 2014, the FDA's final update (Abraham, 2014) concluded that no adjustments to the existing government regulations on BPA were needed in the allowable amounts of BPA in food and beverages (i.e., parts per billion). This report concluded that earlier studies detecting BPA in unexpected amounts in unexpected places (e.g., umbilical cord fluid, etc.) were most likely due to contamination in the laboratory, which is filled with equipment and testing materials also containing BPA. A researcher involved in the FDA's study, Justin Teeguarden, discussed the problems that contamination causes during an interview on *National Public Radio:* "Contamination [in the lab] is a common problem. We observed it in our own study, but because we were monitoring for it, we were able to overcome that particular problem" (Hamilton, 2012, para. 15).

Interestingly, in the newest studies, people who were tested ingested a diet of food and liquid contained and stored in BPA containers but showed no evidence that BPA was in their system. Teeguarden said that if any BPA was present, then it was "in amounts that are below our limit of detection" (Hamilton, 2012, para. 10). Further, the early study on rats, another concern for health advocates, had little relevance for two reasons: (a) the amounts the rats ingested was exaggerated over 1000x, and (b) additional research showed that humans are not affected by BPA the same way rodents are. These follow-up studies were not intended to prove that BPA is safe but, instead, to test the claim BPA was dangerous, which the studies did not demonstrate.

In 2012 and in response to public outcry, the FDA banned BPA in baby bottles and sippy cups, but did so largely to quell public outcry. In fact, the American Chemistry Council, whose conclusions were the same as the FDA's, requested the ban on infant products simply as a way to move past the issue. Michael Taylor from the FDA indicates that the FDA has not changed its position on BPA despite the ban: "[The FDA] has been looking hard at BPA for a long time, and based on all the evidence, we continue to support its safe use" (Tavernise, 2012, para. 5). In contrast, health advocates who are against BPA continue to lobby against its use. Health advocates' position is consistent with the public's perception. Store shelves are still stocked with entire sections dedicated to "BPA free" products. Meanwhile, Nalgene remains out of the debate and has continued to grow and reach new heights of success. In 2014, the company teamed up with Michelle Obama for the Partnership for a Healthier America's "Drink Up" campaign, which encourages Americans to drink more water.

Questions:

- Nalgene did not debate health advocates on TV or try to change the public's opinion about BPA. Do you think the company should have fought negative perceptions?
- How did Nalgene use retail store managers' and customers' feedback to its advantage? Did their approach surprise you?

Domino's Finally Listens to Customer Complaints

Domino's Pizza was founded in 1960 in Michigan with just one store. The company gained fame by introducing its 30-minute-delivery-or-you-get-it-free guarantee in the early 1970s. By the late 1970s, the chain grew to over 200 franchise store locations and opened thousands of locations worldwide in the decades to come. Though the company eventually dropped its 30-minute guarantee over safe driving concerns, the name Domino's became synonymous with fast home delivery. By 2015, Domino's ballooned to almost 12,000 stores worldwide, making it the world's largest pizza chain ("Domino's Pizza," n.d.). Domino's became so successful that most other pizza chains and even local "mom and pop" pizza restaurants now offer fast delivery to compete with Domino's. Unfortunately, while Domino's reputation for speedy delivery remains intact, the chain never established a strong positive reputation for the taste of its pizza as the pizza giant grew. As Domino's CEO (Craig, 2014) later put it, "We were the 30-minute guys. We were the delivery guys who were going to get a pizza to you that's OK, but we're going to get it to you quickly. And that just stopped working at one point" (para. 10). The organization could no longer compete simply because it delivered its pizza fast; virtually everybody delivered pizza fast. Domino's sales remained flat for several years leading up to 2009 and some US locations were forced to close due to lack of sales (Domino's, 2013). Domino's stock price sunk approximately 90% to $3 per share by the end of 2008 from a high of over $33 per share just two years earlier, a far greater drop than the rest of the stock market at the time. This all changed, however, in 2009 when Domino's took aggressive steps to reinvent its pizza and reconnect with customers. This case looks at the bold and clever process Domino's used to listen to its customers.

Incoming CEO Makes Changes

In 2007, at the near depths of the company's financial troubles, Domino's promoted Patrick Doyle to the position of president. Doyle was promoted from within the company and brought a fresh perspective to the upper levels of leadership not seen before at the company. Doyle recognized that Domino's had an issue with the perceived quality of its core product and stated, "There comes a time when you know you've got to make a change" ("Pizza Turnaround," 2009). Doyle hired a marketing consulting firm to run focus groups and find ways to finally listen to its customers. The focus group facilitators asked direct questions about Domino's most glaring weakness: taste. Domino's released customers' brutally honest opinions in their heavily viewed 2009 promotional video, Pizza Turnaround (2009). Customers said the pizza was "Flavorless," "Mass produced, boring, bland pizza," "Worst excuse for pizza I've ever had," and "Microwave pizza is far superior." One particularly feisty customer said, "It's pizza. Where's the love? How hard [is it?] It's bread, sauce, cheese, and fresh ingredients. It doesn't feel like there's much love in Domino's pizza." Three dominant themes surfaced in the feedback: (a) the crust tastes like cardboard, (b) the sauce tastes like ketchup, and (c) the cheese is flavorless. Clearly, that's the whole pizza. To drive the point home, Domino's leaders printed, circulated, and posted customer comments on the walls of the Ann Arbor Michigan headquarters' kitchen to remind the leadership team about the unavoidable perceptions the company faced.

Domino's Reaction to the Bad News

Domino's leaders at various levels reacted to the feedback in a visibly unsettled way. Brandon Solano, Domino's head chef, stated, "You know, when you first hear it, it's shocking." Another chef responded, "This hits you right in the heart. This is what we've done, this is what *I've* done for 25 years now." The point of Domino's focus groups, however, were not simply to record customers' low opinions of the company's pizza. The leaders wanted to change things for the better. Doyle, the company's president, stated about the feedback, "You can either use negative comments to get you down or you can use them to excite you and energize your process to make it a better pizza. We did the latter." Karen Kaiser, Domino's marketing director, explained the scope of the change, "You can't just add a little salt or add a little something to the recipe. We basically had to start over." She continued, "We listened to our consumers and they want us to be better and we want them to be happier. We want people to love our pizza." Meredith Baker, product manager, drove the point home, "Most companies hide the criticism they're getting and we actually faced it head on." The company's chefs responded by experimenting with ten crust types, sixteen sauces, and dozens of cheeses.

Domino's then did something even more courageous and risky. The head chefs took their new pizza back out to the same focus customers who hated the original recipe. The interactions, which appear to be genuine and unannounced visits ("We Delivered," 2009), happened at each of the customer's front door. At first, the customers each seemed a little embarrassed that they had spoken so directly about their low opinion of the pizza. One customer, Saul, originally said in the focus group, "To me, Domino's tastes low quality and forgettable." At the door, he was surprised when the chefs arrived and asked him if he had indeed made that comment. He replied, "I didn't know you were listening but I was being truthful." The chefs then offered a slice of the new pizza. He took a piece and said before biting, "I'm telling you how it is. This is the real thing right now." He took a bite and after a long pause said, "First thing off the bat, it does not taste like Domino's pizza the way I know Domino's. I'm in. I'm in, guys." At another doorstep, Adrianne, the customer who originally asked pointedly, "Where's the love?" tasted the pizza and replied, "Wow. Thank you. Thanks for making a great pizza, finally." Other customers voiced their appreciation that the company actually listened to their opinions. For instance, another customer, Claudia, said during her encounter, "I didn't know I would be facing the head chef ... I'm so really impressed that you took it seriously. I can't believe you listened." To be sure, Domino's took maximum advantage of this process for marketing purposes. Further, some people might dismiss Domino's focus groups and the massive advertising campaign that followed as *mere* marketing. Nevertheless, the company continued to pursue customer feedback long after this ad campaign ended and still does to this day.

In other words, "Domino's Pizza Turnaround" was not a one-time gimmick. The company started a "show us your pizza" campaign not long after it launched its new recipe. The campaign asked customers to submit photos of their pizza directly to the company, particularly photos of pizzas that were not delivered up to the customers' expectations. Customers submitted over 25,000 photos. The company used this feedback to push for higher levels of consistency and quality throughout the pizza chain. Since then, the company also moved decisively into social media and online videos to open direct lines of communication from customers to receive ongoing feedback. True to form, unlike some companies, Domino's leaves even the rudest comments on its social media channels. While no company can satisfy the individual whims and changing preferences of each customer, Domino's demonstrates the effective use of these channels to listen to customers' common concerns.

Results and Media Coverage

The Domino's Pizza Turnaround campaign was successful by every measure. In the first quarter of 2010, the first time Domino's change of approach could have show up on the books, the company reported a "historic same-store-sales gains, up 14.3%," one of the largest sales increases ever for the fast-food industry (Domino's, 2010, para. 1). Sales continue to climb each year since the change. Domino's stock also has climbed steadily since leaders started listening to customers and was up from $3 per share in 2008 to an incredible $60 per share as of 2013. Domino's innovative marketing campaign was covered by numerous media outlets and has received virtually unanimous praise for its bold approach even years later. One writer (Toporek, 2011), for instance, summed up Domino's message as "we stunk; now we don't" and that no-spin message "told the truth" and "resonated with customers" (para. 15, 16, and 18). The pizza chain is growing again not simply because it gets the pizza there quickly. It is recovering lost customers and earning new ones because of the quality of its core product.

Since the turnaround, Patrick Doyle has been promoted to CEO. He is a frequent guest on news and talk shows to talk about Domino's radical transformation from a large but sleepy pizza chain with a questionable reputation to one that is taking risks and connecting with customers. In 2013, Doyle was interviewed about the company's continued success on CBS News' *This Morning* show (Domino's, 2013). He was asked, "Most companies don't like to hear their customers saying bad things and then [Domino's] put it on the air for everybody to hear. Why did you think that was a good idea?" Doyle responded, "The marketing world has changed so much. There's a relationship now that is two way and it didn't used to be like that. … You have to be willing to listen to people and to understand their perceptions of you and you've got to make real changes." Domino's focus groups and resulting marketing campaign showed that people are not just hungry for pizza, but also want companies to listen.

Questions:

- What did Domino's put at risk by admitting its pizza was not very good?
- How did the company use overwhelmingly negative feedback to its advantage?

Great for Pets and People: Nestlé Purina Relies on Employee Feedback to Shape the Company

Americans love their pets and they feed them well. Approximately a third to half of American households own a cat or dog ("Pet Statistics," n.d.). Purina is one of the nation's largest pet food companies. Its classic logo, a small red and white checkerboard, has been a familiar site to most pet owners over the past several decades. Purina's roots go back over a hundred years, but in 2001, it was purchased by Nestlé, one of the largest food companies in the world. It is now named Nestlé Purina and its headquarters are in St. Louis, Missouri. The company manufactures and/or sells various pet food brands such as Alpo, Fancy Feast, Mighty Dog as well as brands that use the Purina name like Purina Dog Chow, Purina Cat

Chow, and Purina ONE among others. In America, pet owners spend an incredible amount of money on their pets. Purina alone sells over $11 billion worth of pet food and related products each year ("Top Pet Food Companies," n.d.). The company employs over 7,000 people in 13 states. The company encourages employees to bring their pets to work.

Interestingly, in the last several years the company is becoming known for more than just pet food or its pet-friendly policies. Purina is one of the best places to work in the country according to its employees. In 2016, Purina was awarded a prestigious World at Work seal of distinction for "employee engagement" and "work-life effectiveness" ("Nestlé Purina Petcare Receives," 2016) and has won many local employment awards in St. Louis. Even more impressive, the company has been ranked in the top ten for Glassdoor's employee choice award for numerous consecutive years. This case explores how an otherwise low-key company in a traditional industry became one of the most desirable places to work in the nation.

Purina and Glassdoor

Glassdoor, featured elsewhere in this book, is an online company that provides a wide range of information on organizations across the country since 2007. Like many online career-related companies, Glassdoor lists position openings, related career information, and provides other resources for job seekers. Most importantly, it provides employee-generated reviews about their employers. The site lists typical salaries, benefits, CEO approval ratings, and pro-and-con reviews about the various companies. The goal of Glassdoor is to "provide a realistic sense of what's behind many U.S. corporations" (Nestle, 2014, para. 4). The site allows past and current employees to post information about their positions and companies anonymously, by job title, and/or by name. Purina has enjoyed incredible employee ratings for years running and placed in the top 10 from 2013 through 2015. Its peak was #3 in 2014 ("Purina Shoots," 2015). Over 600 employees have posted feedback about Purina. Employees give the company an overall score of 4.3 out of five and 93% of employees would recommend the company to a friend looking for a job (Nestlé Purina, 2016). The company also receives consistent marks across the five primary categories that Glassdoor rates quantitatively: Culture and values, 4.4; work-life balance 4.1; senior management 4.1; compensation and benefits, 4.1, and career opportunities, 4.1. Employees also respect the company's senior leaders. Its CEO received a 94% approval rating. To put these numbers in context, Purina outdoes numerous iconic companies like Apple, Microsoft, Coca-Cola, Hershey, and most others. It is only until we reach Glassdoor scores at the level of Google (4.4) and Facebook (4.5) that Purina finds its peers.

How is it that a pet food company became a "hot" employer that competes with and even out performs many of the nation's most desirable employers? According to company leaders, they listen to their employees' opinions, especially those posted on Glassdoor. Steve Degnan, Purina's Chief Human Resources Officer, explained.

> We're monitoring these comments all the time. Our monthly reports to the leadership team include a full extract of the latest Glassdoor reviews. To me that's an instantaneous pulse survey of the whole company; it's a great thing to share with leadership. (Freeman, 2014, para. 10)

In addition to periodic internal surveys, the public online display of employees' scores and comments get the company's attention. Purina representatives routinely reply to employees' posts with clarification and/or gratitude. This sends the message to employees that somebody is actually reading and paying attention to their concerns.

One major issue, for instance, surfaced in employees' opinions about work-life balance. The company now scores well in this category overall at 4.1 out of 5 but the current scores reflects changes the company made based on employee feedback. In the qualitative comments employee's offered, 161 reviews mentioned that the company handled employees' work-life balance well but 46 reviews mentioned it as an area that needed improvement. Numerous other comments mentioned the "long hours" and the stress this can cause. When asked about the work-life balance criticism, Degnan replied, "We're hearing it, we're taking it seriously" (Freeman, 2014, para. 11). In response, the company initiated training for managers to establish a better work-life balance in their departments and launched a video campaign within the company that featured thirty visible Purina leaders acknowledging the problem and suggesting some concrete ways to fix it. Part of the problem, however, was vacation time. The company noticed a backlog of unused time off because few employees actually used all of their available paid vacation days. Degnan stated, "We're monitoring it closely as a leadership team. The CEO is on this. He takes it seriously and therefore the leadership team does too. We take pride in our culture, so anything that could erode [it] becomes alarming to us" (Freeman, 2014, para. 18). Purina leaders saw positive results from their actions.

Following the training, 40% of employees on an internal survey reported, "yes, their department head had addressed the issue with them and was beginning to take some steps to deal with it" (Freeman, 2014, para. 16). In addition to the changes the company asked its managers to make, "An even larger percentage [of employees] said that they personally started to work on the issue themselves and were taking more control" of their schedules (para. 16). When Purina fixes problems like this, leaders know it is doing more than just listening to its current employees. Degnen reflected, "We're really cognizant of [work-life balance] and want to use that as a competitive advantage in order to attract the best talent. I think that it is a big issue for people in managing their careers and those who might consider working for us" (Freeman, 2014, para. 14). Purina consistently follows a simple process of gathering data from Glassdoor and internal measures and it fixes the most pressing issues.

Another issue, for instance, was the desire for more career advancement. The company's data showed that while some employees felt good about their career options, other employees were not so optimistic about their future prospects at the company. Purina now invests more time, energy, and money in helping employees prepare for and see the opportunities. Each year, for instance, company leaders "spend one to three days talking to large groups of employees about where they'd like to go in the company and how they can get there" (Freeman, 2014, para. 24). The company also invested in "process and an evolving set of tools available online in our career development center where employees can access information, testimonials, videos and documents about a[n available] position or [other] department in the company" to help inform employees about opportunities within the company (Freeman, 2014, para. 21). Each employee also meets with his or her supervisor to discuss personal goals at the company and where he or she would like to take their career in the coming year. The company spends an average of $2,400 per employee for training and development each year (Brain, 2013). In contrast, the Association for Talent Development estimates that the average manufacturing organization spends just $530 and organizations across all industries average $1,200 per year (Miller, 2014). While other companies use these types of pro-employee practices, it is important to mention that many of Purina's employees are not coming from Ivy League schools and the company is not in employment hotspots like Silicon Valley. Purina is an old company located in the mid-South and situated in a traditional food processing and manufacturing industry. Many employees have only a high-school education. Employees like this—similar to those at the Amazon warehouse, Foxconn factories, and the Jim Beam plant—do not typically have the ear of the company CEOs and do not normally see this level of attention and care.

Employees' Point of View and Results

A central feature of Glassdoor is the qualitative comments section of employee feedback. Employees post their opinions, both positive and negative. As noted above, some employees point out problems and make suggestions that are critical. When employees say something harsh, the company does not blame them. Its leaders get to work. About this, Degnen said, "There's no recrimination [for negative comments] … When we see a comment that might indicate a problem, we find out what happened and solve the problem. That's the circle of information you need to keep things healthy" (Freeman, 2014, para. 2). Employees know Purina is listening. A forklift operator posted in December 2015, "They listen and follow through with employee suggestions if it is beneficial to the company and they are willing to try new ideas if you have good ones. Love this CAREER" ("Nestlé Purina," 2016). Another employee in December 2015 described the executive team as "down to earth and meets with employees on a regular basis, which diminishes the so called 'corporate' cloud'" ("Nestlé Purina," 2016). This same employee described his or her fellow co-workers as having "a high work ethic" and supporting a "fun, energetic, and friendly atmosphere."

An anonymous ten-year veteran employee in December 2015 described the overall arc of his or her career at the company as follows:

> In my time with the company, I have held roles in our retail arm, our sales division, our category development department, and marketing. The fact that I have been encouraged to work across so many functions illustrates Nestlé Purina's commitment to continued learning, the emphasis they place on developing people, and the value they place on bringing diversity of thought into their various departments. Along the way, I have encountered amazing learning opportunities, was allowed to fail (which is a good thing!), and have worked with some truly amazing people who are passionate about the company, pets, and keeping our culture one that is truly the envy of everyone I know. Getting to bring my dog to work is also pretty awesome!

A concern on most employees' minds lately is the direction of the company as it moves forward with Nestlé. According to several comments on Glassdoor, Nestlé has brought a more bureaucratic approach to Purina. In November 2015, one manager put it in these words, "Purina is slowly being taken over more and more by Nestlé and losing some of the 'smaller' feelings and atmosphere that used to exist" ("Nestlé Purina," 2016). A related issue is the company's slow speed of adapting to a changing marketplace. Employees sometimes made comments about too much "red tape," that the company was "slow to adapt," "Not as fast and nimble as we would like," and that leaders must "Find a way to turn a massive ship faster" ("Nestlé Purina," 2016). It is interesting that employees do not go to Glassdoor simply to praise or vent strictly in terms of their own short-term desires. Many comments, such as these, want the company as an entire enterprise to remain a strong and competitive company that is also a great place to work. The comments seldom get petty.

Purina's employees offer the feedback but company leaders take responsibility for listening. Degnen stated, "I always come back to leadership behaviors on these things. The most important thing is how people think, talk, work and act and how they behave towards each other. I think that's the secret of this place" (Freeman, 2014, para. 24). The company's CEO weighed in with similar sentiments after ranking third in the country.

> Being recognized is a great honor, and ranking third best in the nation is icing on the cake. ... I'm particularly proud of this award because it's based entirely on the feedback of associates who posted reviews on Nestlé Purina's Glassdoor page. This is a company with an outstanding culture and great work environment that includes bringing our pets to work.

When discussing Purina and award-winning companies like it, Glassdoor's CEO and Founder, Robert Hohman, said, "The best investment is in communication. Anything you read on Glassdoor about your company should not be a surprise; it should instead underscore the areas where your company excels and any areas that could be improved" (Freeman, 2014, para. 5). Companies like Purina who seek feedback tend to do well on many levels. One final measure is annual employee turnover. Purina boasts a turnover rate of just 5% annually compared to an average in the manufacturing industry of 34% and a national average of 15% (Brain, 2013; "Survey Research Yields Data," n.d.).

Questions:

- In contrast to an "open-door policy," why does Purina's use of Glassdoor and internal surveys work so well?
- How can employees tell Purina's leaders are sincere in their desire to hear employees' voices?

Chapter Discussion Questions

- What did these organizations put at risk by asking for feedback? To what extent do you believe it required courage?
- What if the feedback these companies received was even worse? Would asking for upward communication still be a good idea?

- How did soliciting upward feedback help these organizations apply a *utilitarian* ethic? In other words, how did gathering good intel help them make decisions that would *promote the greatest good for the greatest number of people*?

Key Terms

- Intel
- Open-door policy
- Suggestion box
- Communication-based responsibilities
- Managing by wandering around
- Consultative leaders
- Dedicated upward communication channel
- Managerial openness
- Utilitarianism
- Cost-benefit analysis
- Employee voice

References

Athanassiades, J. C. (1973). The distortion of upward communication in organizations. *Academy of Management Journal, 16*, 207–226.

Baron, R. A. (1996). “La Vie En Rose” revisited: Contrasting perceptions of informal upward feedback among managers and subordinates. *Management Communication Quarterly, 9*, 338–349.

Detert, J. R., & Burris, E. R. (2007). Leadership behavior and employee voice: Is the door really open? *Academy of Management Journal, 50*, 869–884.

Dijk, C. V., & Ende, J. V. D. (2002). Suggestion systems: Transferring employees’ creativity into practicable ideas. *R & D Management, 32*, 387–395.

Fairbank, J., Spangler, W., & Williams, S. D. (2002). Motivating creativity through a computer-mediated employee suggestion management system. *Behavior & Information Technology, 22*, 305–314.

Farndale, E., Van Ruiten, J., Kelliher, C., & Hope-Hailey, V. (2011). The influence of perceived employee voice on organizational commitment: An exchange perspective. *Human Resource Management, 50*, 113–129.

Gao, L., Janssen, O., & Shi, K. (2011). Leader trust and employee voice: The moderating role of empowering leader behaviors. *Leadership Quarterly, 22*, 787–798.

Holland, P., Pyman, A., Cooper, B. K., & Teicher, J. (2011). Employee voice and job satisfaction in Australia: The centrality of direct voice. *Human Resource Management, 50*, 95–111.

Jones, D. (2009, December 9). What is a CEO's secret to longevity? *USA Today*. Retrieved from http://usatoday30.usatoday.com/MONEY/usaedition/2009-12-28-ceolongevity28_CV_U.htm

Kassing, J. W. (2001). From the looks of things: Assessing perceptions of organizational dissenters. *Management Communication Quarterly, 14*, 442–470.

Kassing, J. W. (2002). Speaking up: Identifying employee dissent strategies. *Management Communication Quarterly, 16*, 187–209.

Kassing, J. W., & Avtgis, T. A. (1999). Examining the relationship between organizational dissent and aggressive communication. *Management Communication Quarterly, 13*, 100–115.

Likert, R. (1961). *New patterns of management*. New York, NY: McGraw-Hill.

Morrison, E. W., & Milliken, F. J. (2000). Organizational silence: A barrier to change and development in a pluralistic world. *Academy of Management Review, 25*, 705–725.

Pacanowsky, M. E. (1988). Communication and the empowering organization. In J. A. Anderson (Ed.), *Communication Yearbook, 11* (pp. 356–379). Newbury Park, CA: Sage.

Peters, T., & Waterman, R. (1982). *In search of excellence*. New York, NY: Harper & Row.

Powell, C., & Persico, J. (1995). *My American Journey*. New York, NY: Ballantine Books.

Roberts, C. H., & O'Reilly, C. A. (1974). Failures in upward communication: Three possible culprits. *Academy of Management, 17*, 205–215.

Seeger, M. W., & Ulmer, R. R. (2003). Explaining Enron: Communication and leadership responsibility. *Management Communication Quarterly, 17*, 58–84.

Wilkinson, A., & Fay, C. (2011). Guest editors' note: New times for employee voice? *Human Resource Management, 50*, 65–74.

Nalgene References

Abraham, S. A., et al. (2014). Updated review of literature and data on Bisphenol A. [Memorandum] from the *Department of Health & Human Services*. Retrieved from http://www.fda.gov/Food/FoodborneIllnessContaminants/ChemicalContaminants/ucm166145.htm

Frasher, J. (2008, April 23). It's the "beginning of the end" for bisphenol-A. *Yukon News*, p. 21.

Gleick, P. (2013, April 25). Bottled water sales: The shocking reality [blog]. Retrieved from http://scienceblogs.com/significantfigures/index.php/2013/04/25/bottled-water-sales-the-shocking-reality

Hamilton, J. (2012). How much BPA exposure is dangerous? [Interview] *National Public Radio*. Retrieved from http://www.npr.org/2012/03/30/149668771/how-much-bpa-exposure-is-dangerous

Hockensmith, D. (2008, April 14). Firms adopt BPA-free bottles. *Plastics News*, p. 3.

Kosinski, M. (April 9, 2008). Consumer alert: How save are plastic bottles? *Today Show, NBC*. Retrieved from http://safemama.com/2008/04/09/bpa-in-plastics-featured-on-today-show

Stafford, S. (2008, April 22). Plastic danger report refuted. *Berkshire Eagle*. Retrieved from http://www.berkshireeagle.com

Tavernise, S. (2012, July 7). F.D.A. makes it official: BPA can't be used in baby bottles and cups. *New York Times*. Retrieved from http://www.nytimes.com/2012/07/18/science/fda-bans-bpa-from-baby-bottles-and-sippy-cups.html?_r=0

Yang, C. Z., Yaniger, S. I., Jordan, V. C., Klein, D. J., & Bittner, G. D. (2011). Most plastic products release estrogenic chemicals: A potential health problem that can be solved. *Environmental Health Perspectives, 119*, 989–996.

Domino's References

Craig, V. (2014, April 4). Deep dish: Domino's CEO talks turnaround success. *Fox Business*. Retrieved from http://www.foxbusiness.com/business-leaders/2014/04/09/deep-dish-dominos-ceo-talks-turnaround-success

Domino's CEO talks corporate, GOP rebrand: "Be willing to listen." (2013, May 31). *CBS This Morning*. Retrieved from http://www.cbsnews.com/videos/dominos-ceo-talks-corporate-gop-rebrand-be-willing-to-listen/

Domino's Pizza, Inc. (n.d.). *Yahoo*. Retrieved from http://finance.yahoo.com/q/pr?s=DPZ

"The pizza turnaround" Documentary [video]. (2009). Retrieved from pizzaturnaround.com on October 12, 2015.

Toporek, A. (2011, June 6). Eleven reasons Domino's turnaround campaign worked. *SpinSucks*. Retrieved from http://spinsucks.com/communication/eleven-reasons-dominos-turnaround-campaign-worked

We delivered. (2009). *Dominos*. Retrieved from. Retrieved from https://www.youtube.com/watch?v=czyu-EUwQsQ

York, E. B. (2010, May 4). Domino's reports 14% same-store-sales hike for first quarter. *AdAge*. Retrieved from http://adage.com/article/news/domino-s-reports-14-store-sales-hike-quarter/143682

Purina References

Brain, S. (2013, March 15). Nestlé Purina PetCare best places to work winner: Large companies. *St. Louis Business Journal*. Retrieved from http://www.bizjournals.com/stlouis/print-edition/2013/03/15/nestle-purina-petcare---best-places-to.html

Freeman, C. (2014, December 19). Listening, responding to employee concerns boosts Nestlé Purina to top of Glassdoor list. *Bureau of National affairs (NBA)*. Retrieved from http://www.bna.com/listening-responding-employee-n17179921191/

Miller, L. (2014, November 8). 2014 state of the industry report: Spending on employee training remains a priority. *Association for Talent Development*. Retrieved from https://www.td.org/Publications/Magazines/TD/TD-Archive/2014/11/2014-State-of-the-Industry-Report-Spending-on-Employee-Training-Remains-a-Priority

Nestlé Purina PetCare receives WorldatWork Work-Life 2016 Seal of Distinction. (2016). *Purina.com*. Retrieved from http://newscenter.purina.com/worldatworkseal

Nestlé Purina PetCare reviews. (2016, January). *Glassdoor.* Retrieved January 12, 2016 from https://www.glassdoor.com/Reviews/Nestl%C3%A9-Purina-PetCare-Reviews-E14081.htm

Nestlé Purina ranks again on Glassdoor's best places to work list. (2014, December). *Nestlépurina.com.* Retrieved from https://www.nestlepurinacareers.com/blog/whats-new-at-purina/glassdoor-best-places-to-work/

Pet statistics. (n.d.). *American Society for the Prevention of Cruelty to Animals.* Retrieved from https://www.aspca.org/animal-homelessness/shelter-intake-and-surrender/pet-statistics

Purina shoots up to Glassdoor's #3: "Best place to work". (2015, January 8). *Purina.com.* Retrieved from https://www.purina.com/meet-purina/about-us/purina-shoots-up-to-glassdoors-3-best-place-to-work

Survey research yields data on employee turnover. (n.d.). *National Business Research Institute.* Retrieved from https://www.nbrii.com/employee-survey-white-papers/survey-research-yields-data-on-employee-turnover

Top pet food companies. (n.d.). *Petfoodindustry.com.* Retrieved from http://www.petfoodindustry.com/directories/211-top-pet-food-companies

6

Tips, Tools, and Resources to Move from Top-Down to Upward Communication

Is your organization actively seeking feedback? As Kassing (2002) showed, if people are not given this opportunity, they will still communicate their point of view but in less productive ways. Alternatively, employees are more committed, satisfied, efficient, and effective when they are regularly asked for their input (Farndale, Van Ruiten, Kelliher, & Hope-Hailey, 2011; Holland, Pyman, Cooper, & Teicher, 2011). The case studies in the previous chapter underscore the benefits of gathering feedback from customers as well. In short, regularly seeking input is one of the best investments of time and energy organizations can make. This chapter provides some first-step suggestions for building upward communication.

Mindset Minute: Is Your Organization Open to Feedback?

For some readers, the problem goes deeper than the lack of dedicated upward communication channels. We must examine our unspoken beliefs to gauge our openness to feedback. At least three related mindsets shape our reluctance to embracing input. The first is what I call the *royalty mindset.* These leaders believe themselves to be superior to those "below" them. Followers serve them rather than the organization. Have you ever worked for a boss who acts as if he or she "owns" you, as if you are a servant who can't say no? Have you ever met an executive who seemed overly concerned about his or her persona or celebrity image? Second is the *people-are-stupid mindset* that believes most people are stupid and should be treated as such. An individual with this attitude typically shows his or her impatience and exasperation with others. The third is a *defensive mindset.* If somebody criticizes even a minor aspect of a person's work, the individual feels unfairly and personally attacked and fights back or shuts down in response. Do any of these mindsets remind you of yourself? See Boxes 6.1 and 6.2. A person with any of these will not be particularly motivated to ask for upward feedback to help make better decisions.

Box 6.1. Top-Downward Communication Cues.

When somebody says ...	**It can send the message ...**
I have an open-door policy.	The burden to speak up is on you.
You have a right to your opinion.	You should have kept quiet.
I want to be empowering but ...	I'm not going to empower you.
You'll get used to it.	We're stuck in a top-down context.

Ideal Leadership Conditions to Help Subordinates Speak Up

Courageous organizations want their people to speak up. They will be better off if employees feel free to offer important feedback. Without encouragement, however, most will remain silent. Organizations can establish the ideal conditions to get upward feedback flowing in three main ways.

High-quality relationship. First, organizations must create high-quality working relationships between supervisors and employees to ensure upward feedback. Kassing's (2000) research shows that subordinates see their relationship with their supervisors as "high quality" when the leader engages in open and direct communication, involves followers in decisions, and engages in mutual opinion sharing in conversations. Similarly, Detert and Burris (2007) found that managers' openness was the key determinant that encouraged subordinates to speak up. Further, Gao, Janssen, and Shi (2011) found that leaders increase the likelihood of employee voice by establishing trusting and empowering relationships. In general, thus, those who regularly engage and encourage employees to get involved in decisions will likely receive upward communication. This can start with the basic habit and attitude of Managing by Wandering Around

(MBWA) (Peters & Waterman, 1982) mentioned in Chapter 5, but can clearly be developed into a more systematic approach and dedicated channels of upward communication.

Motivating rationale. Second, organizations should provide employees with a motivating rationale to speak up. That is, when an organization's leaders explain the importance of getting things right, employees ask more questions and voice concerns. Edmondson's (2003) Harvard Business School study on hospital operating room teams suggested leadership behaviors for helping employees speak up. One main reason operating team members (e.g., nurses) were more likely to speak up was the leader (e.g., surgeons) provided a clear motivating rationale for a new practice (e.g., it will help patients recover faster and go home earlier). When team members heard surgeons signal the importance of using the new technology effectively, for example, they asked questions and spoke up more frequently to make sure they were equipped to adopt the new system successfully. When we know an outcome matters, we will care enough to communicate upward to make sure we do the job well. In contrast, when some surgeons did not explain the importance or benefits of the new system, those nurses did not believe the hospital was truly committed to new changes and did not speak up.

Reduce risks. Third, employees need to feel that speaking up is safe. On a daily basis, they must believe "that engaging in risky behaviors like *voice* will not lead to personal harm" (Detert & Burris, 2007, p. 871). Organizations can increase the ease of speaking up in a variety of ways. For instance, Edmondson's (2003) study on operating room teams found that effective surgeons created ease by consistently downplaying power differences between themselves and the team members in four key ways (see p. 1439):

1. Leaders made a point of taking action on others' input
2. Leaders communicated that team members were just as important as the team leader
3. Leaders communicated a sense of humility, for instance, by mentioning their own limits and shortcomings
4. Leaders under-reacted, rather than overreacted, to team members' errors

Team leaders who communicated this way reduced the perceived power differences between themselves and the rest of the team, and employees believed success or failure would result from a collective effort where their contributions mattered. Of course, the most important part of establishing these ideal conditions for upward feedback is to maintain them in the midst of hearing difficult feedback.

Box 6.2. Upward Communication Cues.

When somebody says ...	It can send the message ...
Would you please send me that in an email?	I want to get that feedback in writing.
Let's put that on the agenda for our next meeting.	Let's get even more upward feedback.
I'd like your input on something.	I really do want your input.
And how could we accomplish that?	I'm taking your idea seriously.

Dedicated Channels for Upward Communication

Organizations should approach bottom-up communication as routinely as they do top-down communication. If leaders want better intel, they must weave upward communication into the fabric of the organization's culture and processes. Further, the wrong attitude can undermine even the slickest and most well-designed upward-feedback system. The end goal, for instance, cannot be to make people feel appreciated. When it comes to upward feedback, I agree with Larkin and Larkin's claim (1994) that "communication should have one goal: improve performance" (p. xi). That means leaders must instill effective ways of gathering intel to make the best possible decisions. Organizations should consider adding some of the following dedicated upward communication channels to ensure that high-quality information gets to the right people. A ***dedicated upward communication channel*** provides a consistent pathway to move representative feedback up the chain of command without the usual upward distortions.

Surveys

Quantitative surveys can be an effective way to gather feedback, but they must be done correctly. Surveys should be used to gather opinions from the largest groups such as customers and employees. We need to hear from a cross-section to get an accurate sense of groups' opinions. While no hard-and-fast rules exist, leaders can feel more confident that results are trustworthy when response rates are high. I once conducted a survey for a client with a high response rate of over 80%. We were all confident that the results captured the mood of the moment. However, a response rate of even 20% can be effective (Visser, Krosnick,

Marquette, & Curtin, 1996). Organizations should aim for higher rates in smaller organizations so participants with disparate opinions do not sway the overall averages too much.

Importantly, not all surveys are equally effective. Most employee-morale and organizational-climate surveys reveal how employees feel but provide little guidance for making concrete improvements. Larkin and Larkin (1994) explained the three fatal flaws of surveys. First, "they become a fishing expedition" (p. 134) because the leaders are not quite sure what they are looking for. Second, surveys also often ask too many questions and numerous data points but provide no guidance for improving scores. Third, nothing happens after the survey. Organizational leaders look at the results and say "Hmmm, that's interesting," file the survey, and conduct another one a year later. In contrast, Nestlé Purina's use of Glassdoor.com's straightforward data works well because leaders discuss the results regularly and make helpful changes in response.

As Larkin and Larkin (1994) also pointed out, surveys must be simplified to four or five questions that focus on key issues, and leaders must know ahead of time what action they will take once they receive the results. Some surveys are even shorter. Larkin and Larkin (1994, p. 135) gave the following example of a one-question survey: "The company cafeteria offers good value for the money." They offer a ten-point scale for employees' responses. The authors argued that leaders should agree on planned responses and offered a sample of the following three:

- If the average score is 7 or above, then the leaders announce a two-year contract extension with the existing caterers.
- If the score ranges between 4 and 7, the leaders move to a temporary contract, give the caterer time to adjust, and repeat the survey one year later.
- If the average is below 4, leaders announce that the caterer's contract is suspended, and the organization will begin a search for a new contractor.

Clearly, surveys like this are designed to help organizations *take action* and get beyond the "Hmmm, interesting" responses prompted by most academic instruments. In contrast, academic or scholarly surveys are designed to *learn about* workplace complexities and seek sophisticated and nuanced understandings of issues. I agree with Larkin and Larkin on this point. Where organizational performance is concerned, surveys should be simple and lead to concrete action steps. Additionally, organizations do not have to hire outside consulting firms to gather this input. Free services like Glassdoor.com and SurveyMonkey.com provide quick and easy ways to solicit input.

Focus Groups

Focus groups are excellent ways to gather upward feedback from customers, employees, and front-line supervisors. Like the ones Domino's used to learn customers' true opinions, focus-group interviews pull together target participants. According to Krueger and Casey (2000), "For some individuals, self-disclosure comes easily—it is natural and comfortable. But, for others, it is difficult or uncomfortable and requires trust, effort, and courage" (pp. 7–8). Focus groups help people speak up and make sense of their own opinion in mutually influential, social ways just as in everyday life.

Why focus groups? I suggest focus groups alone or in addition to traditional survey questions for a variety of reasons. First, they provide qualitative data including reasons, explanations, and details that formed participants' opinions. Most organizations rely mainly on quantitative data. Market analyses, employee climate surveys, and customer satisfaction surveys generally provide scores or statistics. Most numerical scores, however, leave readers wondering *why* respondents rated an item high or low. Compare the following quantitative and qualitative answers from Rabøl, McPhail, Østergaard, Andersen, and Mogensen (2012, p. 132):

> Quantitative: "How would you rate communication on your team?
> Answer: 6 (out of 10)"
>
> Qualitative: After being asked, "When does [the hospital] team communication function less well?" a nurse explained, "We have two separate chart systems. They should match but they do not always do that. There are observations and orders in the wrong place. I have the overview and [the doctor] goes to see the patients. We supply the [missing] information."

To make better decisions, organizations need to know exactly what is occurring. Qualitative responses provide this clarity. Second, focus groups provide a good balance of information-rich data and efficiency of data collection. As Morgan (1997) explains, they have "a reputation for being quick and easy" (p. 13) for the amount of concentrated data they provide on a focused topic. The richness of this data provides a precise understanding of problems and a starting point for potential solutions.

Running focus groups. Though they can be relatively quick and easy, focus groups have to be done well to produce high-quality intel. First, the process should be led by an experienced focus-group leader, sometimes called a "researcher" or facilitator. Ideally, organizations should consider hiring a professional who has no stake in the outcomes. A trusted, objective member from another part of the organization can also play this role. The researcher performs several jobs in the focus group: "moderator, observer, and eventual analyst" of participants' comments (Krueger & Casey, 2000, p. 11). Importantly, individuals who have some connection to the leader, project, product, service, and so on should not be involved in leading focus groups because they will have difficultly performing the role in an unbiased manner.

The researcher must then assemble the right groups to interview. These normally have six to eight participants so each person has the opportunity to contribute without competing for airtime. Normally, the leader will run three to four groups for each type of participant (Krueger & Casey, 2000). For instance, if an organization is planning to interview both customers and employees, the researcher should schedule three to four groups of each type (i.e., six to eight groups total). The goal is to reach the point of saturation in the data or the point where each group repeats the same key ideas. Participants should be homogeneous because "group members' similarities create a safe communicative environment" (Favero & Heath, 2012, p. 339). For instance, you should not mix and match types of people (e.g., mixing employees into groups with supervisors). Favero and Heath (2012) looked at work/life balance issues faced by women in a certain age range. A focus group that included both single working moms and married moms who worked by choice would likely produce a wide range of potentially conflicting opinions that would be difficult to interpret. To maintain the similarity of the participants, they narrowed their criteria further and "selected career women from dual-career families who chose to work outside the home" (p. 339). In contrast, single mothers who had little choice but to work outside the home would likely describe their own work-life balance concerns in a different but equally important way.

Lastly, the researcher must design the focus group interview so as to gather and later analyze the best data possible. For example, questions should not attempt to influence the groups' opinions. Questions such as "Don't you think …?" or "Do you have a problem with the way he handled …" imply the researcher's preferences and may dissuade participants from their initial opinions. Instead, the researcher should ask clear and simple open-ended questions. The focus group should be run for a predetermined amount of time, such as 90 minutes to two hours. The researcher should also videotape and then transcribe the discussion. For academic focus groups, researchers generally transcribe all comments word-for-word. On the practical side, the researcher can transcribe comments pertaining to the questions. In such cases, providing a brief summary of participants' comments, particularly when the conclusions appear rather straight-forward, is justifiable (Stewart & Shamdasani, 1990).

The analysis and written report must be systematic and fair. The findings can be passed directly up to decision makers to avoid the upward distortions that pass up the favorable news and leave out the unfavorable. The full report typically includes representative or exemplar comments from participants' main themes rather than displaying all the data. As shown in the Domino's case (e.g., "Crust tastes like cardboard"), nothing is so compelling and instructive as hearing participants' comments verbatim. If used well, focus group interviews can be a powerful way to ensure that high-quality feedback from customers, employees, and front-line supervisors makes its way directly to the highest decision-making levels in the organization.

Monthly Skip-Level Meetings with Front-Line Supervisors

Skip-level meetings, which involve a high-level leader skipping over one or more levels of managers to talk to front-line supervisors, play an important role in upward feedback. As Larkin and Larkin (1994) show, front-line supervisors are the best group to focus on to improve organizational performance. I once consulted with an already successful and still growing hotel and spa. The general manager, who was the highest ranking leader in the hotel, met monthly with his front-line supervisors to get informed on issues, listen to suggestions, and solve problems. He told me, "Oftentimes, the supervisors had issues with other departments. The kitchen needed better coordination with reservations. The spa needed better communication with reservations. By the end of most meetings, they've worked it all out and, I simply have to support the agreed upon action steps." In most cases, the general manager simply facilitated the discussion and affirmed new agreements among the supervisors. Without skip-level meetings, supervisors lacked the forum and influence to make these changes on their own. At other times, the leader will need to step in and commit time, resources, and decision-making power to make needed changes. While the rest of the economy struggled, the hotel and spa grew rapidly because the hotel's and restaurant's reputations soared under this manager. Skip-level meetings alone will not necessarily lead to good upward feedback, however. Detert and Edmondson (2011) suggest that organizational members may hesitate to speak up in such meetings if they feel their comments might be perceived as criticizing their immediate supervisor. One or two skip-level meetings will not instantly undo self-censorship learned over the years. As with any other tools discussed here, these meetings must be done in conjunction with creating and maintaining ideal communication conditions over the long run.

Monthly One-to-One Meetings with Direct Reports Dedicated to Upward Communication

In some industries, managers meet weekly or bi-weekly one-on-one and face-to-face with their direct reports. In others, meetings are less frequent. Supervisors should strive to dedicate at least one out of every four meetings to upward communication. Most followers credit their supervisors for asking questions like, "How are things going with you?" or "Is there anything I can help you with?" at almost every meeting. In contrast, however, an upward-communication meeting should be entirely dedicated to gathering intel. The issues leaders ask about will vary across time and industries, but in general the meeting should include at least three main agenda items:

- Follow up on the action items from the previous feedback meeting.
- Prepare questions aimed to bring issues to the surface, even those about the supervisor's effectiveness.
- Next steps or action items the supervisor will take as a follow-up to the meeting.

This basic format will ensure that the leader actively seeks out feedback and follows up. Meetings like this put the burden of being informed where it belongs, on the leader.

Supervisors' Opinion Reports

One of the most effective dedicated channels for upward communication is the supervisors' opinion report (Larkin & Larkin, 1994), which is meant to be "an unbiased listing of supervisors' dominant worries" (p. 7). It can be particularly helpful when the CEO or top leader can ask supervisors to offer their opinions on a specific current issue. Alternatively, the leader can open with a prompt such as the following: "What is one thing you've noticed you wish you had the authority to change that would make your department more effective or more efficient? Explain what this change would involve." Larkin and Larkin specify that reports are particularly helpful for potential changes. These should be (a) limited to just one paragraph, (b) anonymous, and (c) shared with all "supervisors, managers in charge of the change, and, most importantly, the CEO" (p. 7). Larkin and Larkin state firmly, based upon their decades' worth of consulting with Fortune 500 companies, "Unless the report goes to the CEO, these supervisors' concerns will never be addressed" (p. 7). For streamlined administration of these reports, a person with strong administrative skills acting in a human resources capacity can collect the opinion reports via email, remove any identifying information, and sort the responses into dominant themes.

The "Magic" Legal Pad

The last tool is the "magic" legal pad because it the simplest possible solution and has the highest potential return on investment. Many organizations spend a great deal of money on computer software to collect feedback, generate reports, etc. In many cases, a simple handwritten list will do the job much more quickly and effectively. Imagine how effective a customer call center could become, for example, if each phone representative kept nothing more than a legal pad next to his or her phone. Each time a customer called with a question, complaint, or request, the employee simply started a list for each issue and put hash marks next to each item every time a customer called about that issue. Instead of continuing to handle each call in isolation, those pages could be passed on to the supervisor at the end of each shift or week. He or she would distill the various items into the call centers' top priorities: the most common questions, complaints, and requests. Supervisors would then be equipped with up-to-the-minute intel for their next supervisor opinion report, skip-level meeting, or one-on-one meeting with their manager. In a less-than-ideal situation, they could minimally train their own people to respond more effectively to customers' top concerns. The "magic" pad is clearly not magic but is symbolic of any number of free and simple ways to solicit input.

Conclusion

It doesn't take a sophisticated or expensive knowledge-management system to get results. In fact, the dedicated channels and methods for upward communication mentioned in this chapter are all straight forward, practical, and relatively inexpensive and are suggested first-steps. The key to improving organizations is pursuing feedback free from upward distortions in order to make better decisions.

Still, asking for potentially negative feedback takes courage. Most people are hesitant because they are afraid of what they will hear. As the previous chapter's case studies show, upward communication is crucial for organizational effectiveness. The two self-assessment tools below (Boxes 6.3 and 6.4) will help you gauge your level of openness to feedback.

Box 6.3. Self Evaluation for Soliciting Feedback?

What is Your Comfort Level Soliciting Feedback?

Check any of the following topics about which you currently ask for regular feedback.

_____ Food or restaurant choices for lunches or special gatherings
_____ Office furniture or layout decisions
_____ Dress code
_____ Work scheduling
_____ Potential product or service quality improvements
_____ Ways to expand the organization's reach
_____ The organization's new logo
_____ The training and orientation experience
_____ Company policy
_____ Hiring decisions
_____ Peer evaluation of co-workers
_____ Budget priorities
_____ Termination decisions
_____ Evaluation of your personal strengths and development areas

Point of Reflection: How many items did you check off? How would you rate your current norms about gathering upward feedback?

Box 6.4. A Self Evaluation for Willingness to Communicate Upward Feedback.

A Self Evaluation: Willingness to Communicate Upward Feedback

Researchers have known for decades that many people change messages to sound better before they pass them up the chain of command (e.g., Athanassiades, 1973). Would you? How would you handle these messages if you were expected to pass them up to your decision-making boss? For each message, check the response that comes closest to how you would actually handle this situation.

1. The results from the employee satisfaction survey you are in charge of show that employees do not trust the senior executives.
   _____ Pass the message up as is
   _____ Pass the message up but add my own opinion
   _____ Pass the message up but explain the flaws in their opinions
   _____ Pass only what you see as potentially positive parts of the message up
   _____ Avoid passing it up if possible

2. A lot of customers have been complaining about a new service in which your boss had great hope.
   _____ Pass the message up as is
   _____ Pass the message up but add my own opinion
   _____ Pass the message up but explain the possible flaws in their opinions
   _____ Pass only what you see as potentially positive parts of the message up
   _____ Avoid passing it up if possible

3. Employees have told you they do not want a new computer system unless (a) they have some input into choosing it, and (b) they get trained adequately before the new system goes into use. The last system took months to learn and hurt productivity. You're not sure if your boss knows any of this.
   _____ Pass the message up as is
   _____ Pass the message up but add my own opinion
   _____ Pass the message up but explain the possible flaws in their opinions
   _____ Pass only what you see as potentially positive parts of the message up
   _____ Avoid passing it up if possible

4. Most of the front-line supervisors you manage all have the same issue. Some of their best employees have resigned recently because they feel the new compensation structure, which was initiated by the CEO, makes it even harder to earn bonuses even though the company is still making a steady profit and the company's costs have remained the same.
   _____ Pass the message up as is
   _____ Pass the message up but add my own opinion
   _____ Pass the message up but explain the flaws in their opinions
   _____ Pass only what you see as potentially positive parts of the message up
   _____ Avoid passing it up if possible

5. Your organization recently launched a new marketing strategy. Most of your employees don't see how it relates to what your organization actually does and don't feel confident answering customer questions about it. Your boss helped design the marketing campaign.
   _____ Pass the message up as is
   _____ Pass the message up but add my own opinion

_____ Pass the message up but explain the flaws in their opinions
_____ Pass only what you see as potentially positive parts of the message up
_____ Avoid passing it up if possible

Results: Based upon your answers, how willing are you to pass feedback up the chain of command as is?

References

Detert, J. R., & Burris, E. R. (2007). Leadership behavior and employee voice: Is the door really open? *Academy of Management Journal, 50*, 869–884.

Detert, J. R., & Edmondson, A. C. (2011). Implicit voice theories: taken-for-granted rules of self-censorship at work. *Academy of Management Journal, 54*, 461–488.

Edmondson, A. C. (2003). Speaking up in the operating room: How team leaders promote learning in interdisciplinary action teams. *Journal of Management Studies, 40*, 1419–1452.

Farndale, E., Van Ruiten, J., Kelliher, C., & Hope-Hailey, V. (2011). The influence of perceived employee voice on organizational commitment: An exchange perspective. *Human Resource Management, 50*, 113–129.

Favero, L. W., & Heath, R. G. (2012). Generational perspectives in the workplace: Interpreting the discourses that constitute women's struggle to balance work and life. *Journal of Business Communication, 49*, 332–356.

Gao, L., Janssen, O., & Shi, K. (2011). Leader trust and employee voice: The moderating role of empowering leader behaviors. *Leadership Quarterly, 22*, 787–798.

Holland, P., Pyman, A., Cooper, B. K., & Teicher, J. (2011). Employee voice and job satisfaction in Australia: The centrality of direct voice. *Human Resource Management, 50*, 95–111.

Kassing, J. W. (2002). Speaking up: Identifying employee dissent strategies. *Management Communication Quarterly, 16*, 187–209.

Kassing, J. W. (2000). Investigating the relationship between superior-subordinate relationship quality and employee dissent. *Communication Research Reports, 17*, 58–70.

Krueger, R. A., & Casey, M. A. (2000). *Focus groups: A practical guide for applied research* (3rd ed.). Thousand Oaks, CA: Sage.

Larkin, T. J., & Larkin, S. (1994). *Communicating change: How to win employee support for new business directions.* New York, NY: McGraw-Hill.

Morgan, D. L. (1997). *Focus groups as qualitative research* (2nd ed.). Thousand Oaks, CA: Sage.

Rabøl, L. I., McPhail, M. A., Østergaard, D., Andersen, H. B., & Mogensen, T. (2012). Promoters and barriers in hospital team communication. A focus group study. *Journal of Communication in Healthcare, 5*, 129–139.

Stewart, D. W., & Shamdasani, P. N. (1990). *Focus groups: Theory and practice.* Newbury Park, CA: Sage.

Visser, P. S., Krosnick, J. A., Marquette, J., & Curtin, M. (1996). Mail surveys for election forecasting? An evaluation of the Colombia dispatch poll. *Public Opinion Quarterly, 60*, 181–227.

Part III

Moving from Secretive to Transparent Communication

7

Secretive Communication and Case Studies

It's not the crime that gets you. It's the cover up.

—*Journalism Saying*

From the 1990s to the 2000s, Penn State's athletic department ignored reports that a football staff member was sexually abusing young boys he brought to campus. The abuse continued for decades even after some leaders knew about it. When enough victims finally stepped forward and the issue went public, the head coach was fired, the football team was stripped of its titles, the college was fined over $60 million, and the team was ineligible for title games for four years. Unfortunately, the past fifteen years of front-page headlines announced a seemingly endless string of scandals from the nation's largest organizations. As Redding (1996) points out, "The preponderance of everyday problems that plague all organizations are ... problems that are patently ethical or moral in nature" (p. 18). No organization is immune to difficulties or the temptation to hide them (Mesmer-Magnus & Viswesvaran, 2005). What separates organizations that prosper, however, is how they respond when non-routine and potentially damaging issues emerge (Ulmer, Sellnow, & Seeger, 2010). Organizations practice secretive communication within their walls that frequently makes their problems worse. This chapter first explores secretive communication and the trouble it can create. Second, four case studies show organizations that struggled with it: GlaxoSmithKline, the Boy Scouts, University of North Carolina at Chapel Hill, and General Motors.

The Trouble with Secrecy

A secretive approach to communication starts at the top. Leaders set the tone. Employees adapt. As Keenen (2000) argues, "Upper-level managers [in particular] set the ethical climate and culture for employees at lower levels and throughout the organization" (p. 203). Stan Lee, the superhero comic book writer, often said through his characters, "With great power comes great responsibility." One of leaders' primary responsibilities is to discuss potential wrongdoing by supervisors, peers, and/or subordinates. Unfortunately, many organizations become their own worst enemies by keeping quiet. Consider the damage ***secrecy*** or ***closed communication*** can cause:

- Numerous banks and government-sponsored lenders caused the biggest housing "bubble" and economic crisis since the Great Depression. In the early 2000s, lenders approved mortgages they knew some borrowers could not afford. This led to an unsustainable sharp rise in home prices. When this bubble burst, the consequences rippled through every part of the economy. Sadly, decision-makers knew these choices exposed the banks to unprecedented levels of risk but did not correct their unwise and sometimes-illegal practices.
- The Securities and Exchange Commission (SEC) ignored credible tips that Wall Street CEO Bernie Madoff was running a $12 billion Ponzi scheme that stole money from investors. By the time Madoff's son turned him in, the scam cost investors an astounding $65 billion. Madoff will now spend the rest of his life in jail.
- British Petroleum (BP) and Transocean cut financial corners and ignored their own failed tests on the integrity of a key oil pipe on BP's Deep Water Horizon oilrig. Despite known safety concerns, leaders instructed employees to continue operations. The decision resulted in the deadly explosion of thc oil platform, the worst oil spill in history, unprecedented environmental and economic damage, and over $60 billion in lawsuits and cleanup costs in the Gulf of Mexico.

As is often the case, these examples show that insiders knew something was wrong but were not willing to stop it. They kept quiet about early warning signs and prevented others from speaking openly. As Rogers (1987) explained, "When communication is closed, organizations do not identify their problems until they become crises" (p. 60). Clearly, problems like these do not simply go away when we ignore them. They grow.

An error does not become a mistake unless you refuse to correct it. (Orlando Battista, Scientist & Author)

Pressure for Secrecy Multiplies Problems

Many employees experience pressure to be secretive. Some organizational cultures become so tight-lipped that chronic incompetence, errors, or moral wrongdoing become normal, accepted, and even defended. For instance, could twisted sports locker-room norms (e.g., "What happens in the locker room, stays in the locker room") have contributed to Penn State's coaching staff's inability to confront ongoing sexual abuse of minors in its own showers? When issues like this finally come to light, outsiders can hardly believe people inside the organization did little or nothing to stop the wrongdoing. It would be unwise to dismiss all of the people involved in these scandals as bad or evil. I suspect that many people surrounding the primary wrongdoers were sickened by what they witnessed but still said nothing because they were caught in a dysfunctional system.

Mum effect. Even ordinary moral and good-natured people still feel numerous pressures to keep silent. Milliken, Morrison, and Hewlin (2003) found that 85% of professionals and managers admitted to staying silent about at least some of their important concerns. The ***mum effect*** describes our "reluctance or failure to deliver negative information … [it describes] keeping silent, or mum, about undesirable messages" (Marler, Mckee, Cox, Simmering, & Allen, 2012, p. 98). It usually involves significant, hard-to-discuss issues. According to Marler et al. (2012), it embodies various activities such as "some manner of delaying, distorting, or altogether avoiding delivering negative information" (p. 99). Most people find it even more difficult to discuss issues that have a moral or ethical component compared to issues that have practical or technical components. It would be much easier, for instance, for most people to confront a fellow employee about missing an important deadline than about missing money from an expense account.

When we face potentially moral wrongdoing, the territory feels unfamiliar and our steps look unclear. The ***moral mum effect*** is like a code of silence about potential wrongdoing. The term means "workers' tendency to avoid describing behavior in ethical terms in order to preserve others' face" (Bisel, Kelley, Ploeger, & Messersmith, 2011, p. 156). Bisel et al. ask us, for instance, to imagine the pressure organizational members might feel when attempting to refuse an unethical request such as deliberately over-billing a client. The authors explained: "Denying a request by labeling it unethical may [amplify the] risk [of] job security" (p. 155). Transparency takes courage because we put our own and others' credibility, careers, and professional relationships at risk. Additionally, many of us generally like our co-workers and realize they have families who count on them. For these reasons and others, our vision gets fuzzy. We may view our silence as "sticking by our friends," a positive act. People who maintain secrecy about even obvious moral failings may falsely believe they are "protecting the company" (Lyon, 2007). To make matters worse, Bisel et al. warn that our silence can legitimize and normalize unethical requests. Within a dysfunctional culture, activities like shredding official documents, lying, or deleting key data can appear like the behavior of a loyal employee. See Box 7.1 for common problems.

Box 7.1. Common Moral Mum Effect Problems.

Check the box to the left of any of the following common issues you would be most willing to discuss openly. About which issues would you be tempted to stay mum?

- ❑ Bullying, mistreatment
- ❑ Unethical billing practices
- ❑ Deceptive marketing
- ❑ Accounting fraud
- ❑ Data manipulation
- ❑ Negligence
- ❑ Sexual harassment, abuse
- ❑ Sexism, racism, etc.
- ❑ Product defect or issue
- ❑ Harmful product or service
- ❑ Alcohol or drug abuse
- ❑ Stealing from the organization
- ❑ Personal gain at the expense of the organization
- ❑ Abuse of one's position
- ❑ Chronic incompetence
- ❑ Critical errors
- ❑ Unsafe working conditions
- ❑ Environmental harm
- ❑ Illegal business practice

Whistleblowing. The pressure to remain silent will not work on everyone. Consider the context for Enron's whistleblower discussed in Chapter 1. The leaders of this large energy company enforced secrecy. Its executives told Wall Street stock analysts that the company's method to make money was a "black box," a phrase leaders used that contained secrets they would not reveal to stock analysts (Mclean & Elkind, 2003). Enron's attitude was, you just have to "trust us." Its executives hid behind this black-box explanation while committing accounting fraud, insider trading, and numerous other illegal business practices and made it very difficult for other executives to talk about these taboo issues. Nevertheless, Sherron Watkins (Swartz & Watkins, 2004), an Enron executive, had the courage to confront in writing Ken Lay, Enron's Chairman, about what she saw as massive accounting irregularities. She became known as Enron's "whistleblower." Eventually *somebody* spoke up.

When an issue is too important to ignore, employees and leaders typically discuss the problem openly with peers and/or superiors first. If this does not work, they may decide to blow the whistle to stop the wrongdoing. As Johnson, Sellnow, Seeger, Barrett, and Hasbargen (2004) explain, "Whistle-blowing involves an individual with some level of unique or inside knowledge using public communication to bring attention to some perceived wrongdoing or problem" (p. 353). Near and Miceli (1985) state that a ***whistleblower*** is a person who discloses "illegal, immoral or illegitimate practices under the control of their employers" (p. 4) to an individual or organization that can potentially do something about it. Would-be whistleblowers usually begin by discussing issues with the people around them, as did Watkins from Enron, but are often silenced. They may then engage in ***internal whistleblowing*** by going outside of the normal chain of command, for instance, by calling an established hotline (Kaptein, 2011). If they are still not satisfied, ***external whistleblowing*** is frequently the next step whereby the person reports the problem to an outside person or entity such as the media, governmental agency, or professional organization (Kaptein, 2011).

John Kopchinski, a sales representative for Pfizer, a large pharmaceutical company, eventually blew the whistle on the company's illegal activities. The company began marketing its painkiller drug, Bextra, for off-label conditions. "Off-label marketing" is a dangerous and illegal practice because it recommends medications to patients for conditions not legally approved for the drug. At first, Kopchinski complained to Pfizer executives about the aggressive off-label marketing of its drugs. They dismissed his concerns and soon fired him. By then, however, Kopchinski had gathered enough evidence to prompt a federal investigation. When asked why he decided to blow the whistle, he replied, "You have to live with yourself when you look at yourself in the mirror" (Hensley, 2009, para. 4). Pfizer eventually paid over $2.3 billion in civil and criminal fines and were forced to stop off-label marketing.

The resistance and ***retaliation*** whistleblowers experience demonstrates the level of pressure organizational insiders face to practice secrecy. Even though Kopchinski likely saved patients' lives and forced the company to correct an illegal practice, people at Pfizer did not see him the way the public did. Organizational insiders see whistleblowers like Kopchinski as tattle-talers, snitches, rats, or traitors (Grant, 2002). Even when whistleblowers uncover major moral failings, insiders still attack them with vitriol, attempt to discredit them, and often do all they can to ruin the whistleblowers' lives (Johnson et al., 2004). Though whistleblowers ultimately save many companies, they often lose professional credibility, friends, and their jobs in the process. Not surprisingly, the overwhelming majority of organizational members prefer to stay quiet when they see something wrong.

Despite insiders' attempts to discredit them, whistleblowers usually fit an otherwise admiral profile. As Mesmer-Magnus and Viswesvaran (2005) explain, in contrast to employees who remain quiet despite direct knowledge of wrongdoing, whistleblowers have better job performance, have higher education levels, hold supervisory or higher-level positions, and score higher on moral-reasoning tests. Before blowing the whistle, they are considered ideal employees. Whistleblowers also feel that part of their responsibility and obligation is to report wrongdoing more so than non-whistleblowers. Kopchinski from Pfizer fits this profile. He was educated at the prestigious West Point Academy, was a Gulf War veteran, and worked for Pfizer for 11 years. He drew on his past experience when making the decision to go public. "In the Army, I was expected to protect people at all costs," he said. "At Pfizer, I was expected to increase profits at all costs, even when sales meant endangering lives. I couldn't do that" (Berkrot, 2009, para. 6, 7). Out of the thousands of employees, only Kopchinski and several unnamed employees spoke up.

People outside of the organization usually see whistleblowers more favorably than insiders. Grant (2002) characterizes whistleblowers' image as "saints of secular culture" (p. 393) because they protect the public from harmful activities and put themselves at great professional risk. Despite the inside pressure for secrecy, whistleblowing decreases the chances of wrongdoing in the future, plays an important monitoring function for emerging risks, and can help organizations become healthy again (Johnson et al., 2004; Kaptein, 2011). Most organizational members are not eager to blow the whistle. Instead, 81% of employees prefer to discuss issues directly with a supervisor, and 52% prefer to handle issues directly with the party in question (Kaptein, 2011). This is good news. People prefer to discuss problems within the walls of the organization rather than go public. Leaders at all levels, thus, must listen and handle these discussions thoughtfully so blowing the whistle is not necessary.

In sum, as Box 7.2 shows, keeping secrets is difficult today. Further, as the examples of Penn State, the banking industry, and Bernie Madoff show, cover-ups that come to light in the information age do so in spectacular fashion. So far, this chapter shows the enormous pressure organizational members face to keep quiet about non-routine issues that can hurt their organization's effectiveness and even long-term existence. The cases that follow demonstrate the particular ways a secretive approach shaped the outcomes of these difficulties.

Box 7.2. Can We Really Keep Secrets Anymore?

Transparent conversations are more important than ever. Almost all problems will come to light eventually if they are not confronted early. Technology, like tiny memory chips, can be easily concealed. Preventing evidence of illegal, unethical, or inappropriate practices from "leaving the building" is not possible. Further, employees can use YouTube, blogs, Twitter, Facebook and other emerging social media to disperse information to thousands of contacts with the click of a button. Information about corporate wrongdoing regularly goes "viral." Even more striking, organizations like Wikileaks and others' sole purpose is to leak government and corporate misconduct to the global public. In this context, organizations must be both courageous and wise. The old strategy of "deny, deny, deny" won't help. By addressing the issues honestly, directly, and immediately, insiders will not feel the need to go public.

Cases of Secretive Communication

Cheryl Eckard Blows the Whistle at GlaxoSmithKline

GlaxoSmithKline (GSK) is one of the top five pharmaceutical companies in the world with annual sales of $45 billion ("Factbox," 2010; "Global," 2010). Its website (gsk.com) publishes its slogan, "Do more, feel better, live longer." Some of its most well-known drugs are Avandia for diabetes, Paxil for depression, Zantac for acid reflux, and Nicorette and Nicoderm for smoking cessation. Headquartered in London, England, GSK has offices and manufacturing plants all over the world and employs over 97,000 people. The community of Cidra, Puerto Rico, hosts one of GSK's facilities. It manufactures 20 different drugs and employs 900 people. In 2001 and 2002, however, the Food and Drug Administration (FDA) investigated the Cidra plant and found numerous significant violations. It issued an official warning letter to GSK leaders, who vowed to fix the plant's problems. They sent Cheryl Eckard, a long-time and trusted employee, and her team to Cidra to evaluate the progress of those changes. This case examines how Eckard, the Cindra plant, and Eckard's supervisors responded to the problems identified by the FDA's investigation and Eckard's team.

Eckard's Investigation

While Cheryl Eckard served as GSK's Manager of Global Quality Assurance, her main responsibilities were to inspect GSK facilities to ensure the medications had the proper ingredients, strength, and purity. From 1992 through 2003, Eckard led successful international investigation teams and coordinated GKS and FDA efforts for quality assurance. When she arrived at Cidra, thus, Eckard and her team had lots of experience. As expected, they found numerous problems cited by the FDA but also identified additional problems the federal agency had not noticed. These problems included medication mix-ups; uncalibrated machines; hundreds of improperly executed steps in manufacturing, sorting, packaging, and processes; and flawed data-review procedures designed to maintain quality. Consequently, some medicines were tainted with bacteria, some were too weak or too strong, and some were mislabeled entirely.

The scale of the problems shocked Eckard. She explained later in an interview on CBS's show, *60 Minutes*, "All the systems were broken. The facility was broken. The equipment was broken. The processes were broken. It was the worst thing I had run across in my career" (Pelley, 2011). An antibacterial ointment called Bactroban, for example, was supposed to be mixed in a sealed tank to ensure the medicine's purity and prevent any outside contamination. Instead, Eckard witnessed employees "opening up the lid and they were sticking their body into the tank and scraping it with a paddle" (Pelley, 2011). She also noticed that different kinds of drugs were being put in the same bottle. An antidepressant, for instance, was put in packages for the diabetes drug. When she saw the extent of the problem, she notified company leaders. She explained, "I contacted the Vice President of Quality for North America and told him that he needed to shut down the factory and call the FDA. I urged him to stop the trucks that were leaving the docks that day" (Pelley, 2011). Eckard recalled a story she later relayed to her boss about a customer's trip to the pharmacy that she believed was a result of the broken Cindra plant:

> A grandmother came in to pick up this little [8-year-old] boy's prescription. In front of the pharmacist, she opened up the bottle, she tore off the induction seal, looked at it and became upset. She said, "I knew it. His medicine has always been yellow but last month it was pink and he's been so sick." (Pelley, 2011)

The pink version of Paxil carried 250% the dosage of the boy's normal yellow pill. Eckard's team investigated the incident and took their findings about the mix-up at the manufacturing plant to her supervisors approximately five months after she initially urged them to take action to fix the plant.

Eckard's superiors, however, did not react how she expected. GSK quickly denied any errors at Cidra. Representatives from that plant told the FDA, "given the current process controls in place, it was highly unlikely that [the boy's medication mix up] occurred on our premises" (Case, 2008, p. 49). She reflected on GSK's response: "We all knew. They all knew it was real" (Pelley, 2011). Instead, plant managers theorized, without providing any evidence, the mix-up must have happened after the medications left the plant. Beyond the manufacturing problems at Cidra, Eckard's team gathered enough information to convince her that GSK was "divert[ing] reject drug product from the Cidra plant to black markets in Latin America" (Case, 2008, p. 3). The further her investigation went, the more dysfunction she revealed.

GSK's Response

Eckard soon realized that GSK executives were not taking any meaningful action and managers at the Cidra plant had taken almost no steps to fix the problem. When she returned to the plant a few months later to evaluate the facility's progress, the on-site leaders lied about fixing the problems. Eckard found their attempts to deceive her upsetting and described the pressure plant managers put on her:

> The VP of manufacturing at the factory pulled me aside and said, "We can all tell that you've been crying. You come here every day and you're eyes are swollen. So I want to ask you to stop that." And I said to him, "You know, I do cry ... and what I don't understand is why I'm the only one. Why aren't you crying?" (Pelley, 2011)

Despite the plant's numerous failed inspections and blatant attempts to cover up wrongdoing, Cidra and GSK leaders still did nothing to change. The plant continued to ship tainted, sub-par, and mixed-up medication for months.

After months of pushing her superiors to take genuine action, most of the higher-level executives simply stopped communicating with her. At the height of her concern and frustration, Eckard sent the following voicemail to several high-ranking executives:

> This is not easy for me but you have an opportunity to bring about what the company taught me, that I am a change agent. That it is my job to bring accelerated, sustainable change. That is what I will do and I am trying to do it through you. ... I have been here for a long time. I have never been in trouble. I have never caused trouble. I'm loyal to the company. I work here. I wish you no harm. I wish the company no harm. I have seen a decline, a cancer that has continued to grow. If you want the company to stay healthy, if you want patients to stay healthy, something has to be done. Something difficult, but something major has to happen. We have been negligent. We have lied to the FDA. We have lied to ourselves. (Extra, 2011)

Her supervisors ignored the message. Instead of listening to her warnings, the executives bypassed Eckard and took control of her Cidra inspection team.

Eckard Blows the Whistle

After eight months of investigation and attempts to persuade executives, Eckard made her final stand. She told her bosses she "would not participate in a cover-up of the quality assurance and compliance problems" (Case, 2008, p. 40). She sent a complete report to seven high-ranking leaders at GSK outlining the numerous issues at the plant. She warned GSK leaders that if the FDA were aware of the full extent of the plant's issues, the government would likely shut down the factory. Within a few weeks in mid-May, 2003, leaders told Eckard GSK was downsizing and encouraged her to take a "redundancy package" and leave the company voluntarily. She refused. A few weeks after, a vice president at the company "formally presented the redundancy package to her, took her security badge, and escorted her from the premises" (Case, 2008, p. 45). Despite her best efforts, Eckard could not get GSK executives to listen to her warnings.

Soon after being fired, Eckard turned over all the information she had showed GSK leaders to the FDA. The agency quickly seized all medications at the factory and shut it down permanently. Eckard and the FDA cooperated in a lawsuit against GSK. Company leaders ultimately pleaded guilty to knowingly distributing tainted drugs. Two of GSK's biggest customers are Medicaid and Medicare, government healthcare programs for the poor and elderly. As such, the government ordered GSK to pay fines totaling $750 million. Officials and experts condemned GSK once the company's activities were brought to light. Carmen Ortiz, U. S. Attorney for Massachusetts, the state where the legal proceedings took place, said after the court's decision, "We will not tolerate corporate attempts to profit at the expense of the ill and needy in our society. … The fine is significantly higher than the profits that were made by the company" (Howe, 2010, para. 7). Dr. Jeremy Avord, a professor of medicine at the Harvard Medical School and leading expert on pharmaceuticals, offered his perspective: "Just because something [like manufacturing medicine] is complicated doesn't mean it is okay to get it wrong. … We expect in exchange for these high prices, the companies are going to actually manage their manufacturing processes carefully" (Pelley, 2011). While GSK treated Eckard as if she had done something wrong, the public condemned the company's actions.

Aftermath for GSK and Eckard

Under current law, whistleblowers like Eckard are entitled to up to 20% of the fines levied by the government. Eckard's portion of GSK fines came to $96 million. When asked about critics who presume Eckard was financially motivated, she explained her true motivation: "I hope and I pray that their mothers, and their brothers, and their children have safer medicine today than they had before I filed that lawsuit" (Pelley, 2011). She said on the courthouse steps at the completion of the case, "This is not something that I ever wanted to do … It's difficult to survive this financially, emotionally. You lose all of your friends because all of your friends are the people you have at work" (Howe, 2010, para. 4). She continued, "You have to believe in your heart that this is the right thing. … In my case, I was very, very concerned about patient safety" (Howe, 2010, para. 10).

Company leaders admitted guilt and now claim to have fixed GSK issues. GSK released a statement:

> We regret that we operated the Cidra facility in a manner that was inconsistent with current good manufacturing practice requirements. … Our commitment to compliance … is demonstrated by the fact that we have not received an FDA warning letter at any plant since the Cidra facility was cited in July 2002. (Howe, 2010, para. 8)

A spokesperson elaborated on GSK's response: "We spend $600 million a year making sure our plants and equipment are state-of-the-art. … The company was very disappointed that this occurred. We regret that this occurred, but we've learned from it" (Pelley, 2011). Though company leaders expressed "regret" in this incident, GSK's tendency toward wrongdoing and secrecy does not appear to be isolated to this incident. As recently as 2012 in an unrelated incident, company leaders pleaded guilty to off-label marketing, bribing physicians to prescribe its medications, and failing to report data about drugs' safety concerns to the FDA (Thomas & Schmidt, 2012). As in Eckard's case, whistleblowers inside GSK informed the government about these crimes. Fines tied to that case alone will cost GSK over $3 billion.

Questions:

- To what extent did hiding the company's problems help or hurt it?
- Why do you believe company leaders treated Eckard as if she was misbehaving when she tried to fix the Cidra plant's problems?

Hiding Sexual Abuse in the Boy Scouts of America

"Johnny's" parents signed him up for the Boy Scouts of America (BSA) when he was eight years old. Like many others, they chose the iconic Boy Scouts to teach him important skills like first aid, swimming, camping, cooking, and community citizenship. What Johnny's parents did not know when they made their decision, however, was that BSA had a long undisclosed history of its leaders sexually abusing young boys in their care. BSA was founded in 1910 with the purpose of providing an "educational program for boys and young adults to build character, to train in the responsibilities of participating in citizenship, and to develop personal fitness" ("About," n.d., para. 1). The organization provides programs for boys from seven years old up to age twenty-one. Adult male Scout leaders make up most of BSA's leadership who interact directly with the boys during weekly meetings and other activities. BSA has worked hard over the decades to present itself as a wholesome organization that represents all that is good about traditional America. Clearly, the Boy Scouts has provided a great experience to the overwhelming majority of its young members. Unfortunately, this does not undo the fact that the organization worked hard at keeping a disturbing trend of sexual abuse out of the public eye. This case looks at how deep the problem was and how the organization essentially covered up a pattern of abuse.

Lawsuits and "Perversion Files"

Over the years and in the midst of teaching boys first aid, camping, and other valuable skills, some parents had accused specific Scout leaders of sexually abusing their sons. In response, BSA handled each incident quietly on a case-by-case basis for decades and the organization escaped public scrutiny on the issue. However, in the 1990s Patrick Boyle, an author and *Washington Times* reporter, wrote a series of articles on the sexual abuse leading up to his book (1994) entitled *Scout's Honor: Sexual Abuse in America's Most Trusted Institution.* The allegations and evidence in the book shocked many people who defended the Boy Scouts as a valuable and upright organization. The book also inspired others to investigate the organization further, particularly the claim that BSA had kept secret but detailed records of sexual abuse as far back as World War II. Internally, BSA called this database the Ineligible Volunteer Files. As a result of a sexual abuse lawsuit in 2012, the Oregon Supreme Court ordered the release of a portion of what is now referred to in the press as BSA's "perversion files" or database containing information on adult Boy Scout leaders' incidents of sexual abuse of boys in its care (Goodale, 2012). The *Los Angeles Times* assembled the most comprehensive and interactive version of the database currently available to the public (see www.latimes.com/local/boyscouts).

BSA's own records confirm the shocking extent of the abuse. The "perversion files" track cases of confirmed or suspected abuse from 1947 until January 2005. The database contains information from the organization's 20,000 pages of confidential files on approximately 5,000 men and a few women who perpetrated the abuse. While BSA kept detailed records for its own purposes, its leaders seldom reported these crimes to the police. In a sample of approximately 500 reports from 1970 to 1991, for instance, 80% of these incidents were never reported to police (Bartkewicz, 2012b). Accused or confirmed abusers were merely put on internal BSA probation but were not asked to leave the organization immediately. Eventually, some abusers were asked to "resign" rather than being expelled. BSA also allowed the abusers to lie about their dismissal and offer whatever reason they preferred for their departure. One abuser, for instance, claimed "extensive travel" requirements led to his resignation while another cited his "chronic brain dysfunction" as his reason. Further, leaders assured the abusers via letter, "We are making no accusations and will not release this information to anyone, so our action in no way will affect your standing in the community" (Bartkewicz, 2012b, para. 8). BSA was essentially ensuring that the abusers would not be held accountable for past abuse. However, BSA's main goal was not necessarily to help pedophiles maintain their personal standing in the community but, rather, to safeguard the organization's reputation against the notion that sexual abuse might be occurring in the Scouts.

According to BSA's own data, the decision to keep quiet about the abuse had unintended consequences. The hands-off approach actually worsened the problem. Without a show of force from leaders, the number of internal files on abuse skyrocketed over 1,000% from the early to the late 1980s ("Tracking Decades," 2013). Further, at least 40% of perpetrators abused more than one confirmed victim. Many abused an astounding 10–20 or more boys before being asked to resign (Bartkewicz, 2012a, para. 8). BSA protected the abusers so thoroughly that 125 perpetrators were either dismissed or resigned and then rejoined BSA and became Scout leaders after the organization intended to "blacklist" them. In one case, a Minnesota man went to jail for sexual abuse but returned to BSA to lead his troop again when he was released. In another, an Indiana Scout Master was convicted of abusing a 14-year-old boy but nevertheless led two more Scout troops from 1971 to 1988 and eventually confessed to abusing over 100 additional boys during that time. BSA leaders' concealment and inaction allowed this pattern of disturbing abuse to grow. It is important to state the overwhelming majority of Scout leaders were not sexual predators, and most boys were safe while participating in the Scouts. Nevertheless, the BSA organization created an environment that protected abusers and its own reputation, thereby allowing more abuse to occur.

BSA Leaders' Response

During the ongoing lawsuits, BSA was forced to release its "perversion files." When it did, the organization issued an apology and explained how it planned to prevent abuse in the future. One version of BSA's apology reads as follows:

> The Boy Scouts of America believes even a single instance of abuse is unacceptable, and we regret there have been times when the BSA's best efforts to protect children were insufficient. For that we are very sorry and extend our deepest sympathies to victims. (Bartkewicz, 2012a, para. 10)

From one perspective, the apology marks a beginning in that BSA acknowledges abuse from some of its Scout leaders, something it denied for decades. From another perspective, BSA's statements do not accept full responsibility and may indicate continued secrecy.

First, the statement does not acknowledge leaders' failure to confront widespread and repetitive abuse in the past. In fact, the statement characterizes the BSA's approach as the organization's "best efforts" even though a procedure as simple as reporting abuse to police was not BSA's standard protocol. It only required the mandatory reporting of abuse to the police as of 2011.

Second, BSA's apology positions the abuse as if it occurred in the distant past. Another line from BSA's online apology, credited directly to Wayne Perry, BSA's President, reads, "While it is difficult to understand or explain individuals' actions from many decades ago, today [BSA] is a leader among youth serving organizations in preventing child abuse" (Perry, n.d., para. 1). Perry's use of the phrase, "from many decades ago," ignores recent abuse. According to its own files, the organization was still tracking abuse cases as recently as January 2004 to January 2005. Additionally, the claim that BSA is now a "leader" in prevention is baseless. BSA provides no evidence that its culture has changed and no research by which BSA compared its organization to others.

Third, BSA continues to defend its secretive approach for handling abusers even after the growth of abuse became clear. One BSA statement reads, "The sole purpose of the [perversion] files is to prevent those deemed ineligible from registering as Scout leaders" ("Know the Facts," n.d., para. 7). Despite this statement, BSA's secretive approach to handling these files did not prevent abuse even by repeat offenders nor did the files slow the increase of future abuse by other Scout leaders.

Fourth, and perhaps most disturbing, to this day BSA has not initiated action to root out sexual abusers. Regarding the lawsuits surrounding the release of these files, for instance, BSA leaders' internal response or investigation was virtually non-existent. The organization made no efforts to systemically and definitively rid the organization of abusers once and for all. People who followed the issue were not impressed by BSA's response. Tim Kasnoff, an attorney who won a past law suit against the BSA for sexual abuse, noted, "they are still in denial, and this is eroding their credibility" (Goodale, 2012, para. 11). Kasnoff contrasts BSA's internal response with Penn State's realization that just one member of its athletic staff was accused of abuse: "[At Penn State] you had only a single individual, and the institution's response was to bring in the former head of the FBI … to investigate and clean house" (para. 10). The former FBI chief essentially turned Penn State upside down, conducted hundreds of interviews with staff and victims, and "brought every bit of evidence to light" (para. 10). Penn State's decisive action, Kassnoff stated, "while painful, … has sent a clear message. The Boy Scouts have not done anything like this to send a clear message to parents" (para. 11). In contrast, BSA attempted to minimize the perception of harm done by its abusers, released information about abuse only when a court forced it to do so, and then issued unsupported statements that the decades-long problem of abuse in BSA was now solved. No BSA executives were fired. No local Scout leaders were dismissed. Nobody, it seems, has been held accountable. From the outside, BSA appears to be handling its internal processes just as quietly as it has in the past.

Final Reflections

BSA's internal documents show that throughout its history the organization tolerated the sexual abuse of its young boys. Instead of protecting victims, leaders protected abusers from prosecution to safeguard the organization's reputation. Its approach both (a) prevented parents from making an informed choice about enrolling their sons in the organization, and (b) perpetuated an organizational culture that allowed the abuse to grow. Perhaps most disturbing is that the leaders as far back as 1947 were fully aware of the widespread abuse but kept parents and even other Scout leaders in the dark. Each new BSA President adopted a similar hands-off approach to handling thousands of egregious crimes. Despite decades'

Questions:

- To what extent do you believe the Boy Scout's approach to sexual abusers contributed to the problem?
- In your opinion, what would be an ideal organizational response to a problem like this?

worth of opportunities to take decisive, transparent action, not a single leader has had the courage to speak up with force. The situation would never had escalated to such unsettling levels had the first BSA leader to encounter these issues taken initiative, involved the police, made a public example of the abuser, and conducted a thorough and transparent investigation throughout BSA's ranks. Given current leaders' understated and guarded response, it is difficult to disagree with critics who are still not convinced that BSA may not be a safe place for their sons*.

**Author's note:* I participated briefly in the Boy Scouts as a youth. My time in the organization was positive. I learned lots of skills, was mentored by caring adults, and made some friends. I did not experience, witness, or hear about anything inappropriate.

Academic Fraud at University of North Carolina at Chapel Hill: Exposure of a Shadow Curriculum for Student Athletes

College sports is a big business. Many large college teams televise games, recruit major sponsors, and sell tens of thousands of tickets. With millions of dollars pouring in, not surprisingly, debates about whether or not college athletes should be paid are common on campuses across the country. The standard argument against paying them is that they already get compensated through athletic scholarships that amount to a free college education. After all, the argument goes, "when we say, 'student-athlete' that means they are 'students' first." However, an investigation at the University of North Carolina at Chapel Hill (UNC) revealed that many of its student athletes were not, in fact, receiving a legitimate education. Instead, they were being funneled into bogus "paper classes" for which they received full credit and high grades for doing almost nothing. From 1993 to 2011, UNC had a "shadow curriculum" (Culpepper, 2014) to help student athletes boost their overall grade-point average and remain eligible to play. During this 18-year period, over 3,100 students took these classes. The investigation was particularly shocking because UNC is a large, nationally known, public university with a reputation for an intense research focus. This case looks at how this fraudulent practice was developed and how it continued for so long in an institution known for academic rigor.

What an Investigation Showed

Allegations about the "shadow curriculum" gained national attention in 2012 when a UNC employee spoke to the press (Kane, 2012). In 2014, UNC hired Kenneth Wainstein, a former attorney for the FBI and the Department of Justice, to investigate the allegations. The report (Wainstein, Jay, & Kukowski, 2014) released several months later showed that UNC's system of "paper classes" emerged in the early 1990s and was known by a network of select administrators, teachers, athletic staff, academic counselors, and student athletes. A central figure in the investigation was Deborah Crowder, a UNC alum. In 1979, Crowder became the secretary and then administrator for the Department of African and Afro-American Studies (AFAM). As a non-teaching employee, her role was strictly administrative. In 1992, however, the AFAM department put a new chair in charge, Dr. Julius Nyang'oro. He had a comparatively hands-off approach to leadership and "was willing to delegate substantial authority to Crowder" (p. 1). In this looser, more "permissive environment" (p. 1), Crowder hatched a plan to help student athletes earn high grades with no effort.

To do so, she designed classes that were offered as independent studies to students she selected. The classes required only a final paper. Unlike traditional independent studies, however, students had no interaction with any faculty member. Though she was not a teacher, Crowder graded the papers and entered the final grades without faculty oversight. The grades were generous with mostly A's and high B's. Dr. Nyang'oro, the department chair, had full knowledge and approval of this system. In time, the number of paper classes grew to over 300 independent studies per semester. In the late 1990s, Crowder restructured the independent studies so that the paper classes were registered as large lecture courses to draw less attention. The approach, however, stayed the same. The "classes" did not meet and involved no quizzes or tests, no reading, no presentations, and no interaction with any faculty members. In essence, they only existed as a line on students' official transcripts but did not exist in reality.

These classes were clearly geared toward struggling athletes. Of the students in these courses, "47.4% were student-athletes, even though student-athletes make up just over 4%" (Wainstein et al., 2014, p. 3) of the entire student body. The courses were especially popular for students "who played the 'revenue' sports of football and men's basketball" (Wainstein et al., 2014, p. 2). Fifty percent played football, 12% played men's basketball, 6% played women's basketball, and 30% were Olympic athletes and other sports. Grades awarded were well above students' normal performance. Athletes' grades in paper courses averaged a 3.55, approximately 90%, while the average student athletes' GPA in genuine courses in the major was 2.84, approximately 82%. To make matters worse, the papers the students handed in as their only assignment were often plagiarized or incoherent. The investigation (Wainstein et al., 2014) showed that "a significant proportion of the papers submitted in these classes included large amounts of copied sentences and paragraphs. In a number of cases, students submitted papers with original introductions and conclusions, but with copied "'fluff' text in between" (p. 4). In some instances, the academic counselors who supported athletes at UNC even drafted portions of the papers students submitted for grades.

Crowder's Motivation and Support

Neither Crowder, the department secretary, nor Nyang'oro, the department chair, sought out to commit academic fraud, at least from their view. To them, "helping" to keep all players eligible was one obvious way to help teams win games. Crowder was a Tar Heels sports fan through-and-through. She even missed work after disappointing losses from UNC's men's basketball team. Further, the investigation concluded that Crowder and Nyang'oro may have been motivated by a sense of "compassion" for the students. Crowder attended UNC years earlier, and as a student, she felt unsupported because the faculty focused instead on "the best and the brightest" (Wainstein et al., 2014, p. 1). Wainstein's (2014) report concluded Crowder felt "it was her duty to lend a helping hand to struggling students, and in particular to that subset of student athletes who came to campus without adequate academic preparation for Chapel Hill's demanding curriculum" (p. 1). When Nyang'oro became the chair of the department, he too felt compassion for struggling student athletes and approved of Crowder's system for the sham courses.

The scope of UNC employees' involvement in the shadow curriculum goes well beyond Crowder and Nyang'oro. Student athletes are supported by the Academic Support Program for Student Athletes (ASPSA) at UNC and other colleges. The investigation at UNC found that "a number of ASPSA counselors had a complete understanding of the characteristics of these paper classes" (p. 64). Counselors steered student athletes to them, and in some instances the counselor "took it upon himself or herself to select and register a player for a paper class without even asking the player" (p. 66). They even suggested the grades that Crowder should enter to make sure UNC's GPA requirements were satisfied. When Crowder retired in 2009, the shadow curriculum began to break down. These academic counselors grew concerned and informed the coaching staff that student athletes would no longer have access to classes "that met degree requirements in which [the football players] didn't go to class … didn't take notes [or] have to stay awake … didn't have to meet with professors [and] didn't have to pay attention or necessarily engage with the material" (p. 4). The ASPSA counselors asked Nyang'oro to continue offering the classes, which indicates they were full partners in the paper class system.

The report (Wainstein et al., 2014) also concluded that some coaches and senior members of the athletic staff and ASPSA were aware of paper classes and how the system worked, but may have "made a conscious effort not to learn the specifics about the paper classes" (p. 66). Evidence indicates at least some on the coaching staff became uncomfortable after realizing the full extent of the issue. One example is basketball coach Roy Williams who was hired in 2003. Over time, he expressed concern that such a high percentage of his players, 10 of 15 players on the 2005 roster, were majoring in African and Afro-American Studies. To Williams, "it looked like the players were being steered into that major, and after a year or two on the job he asked … to make sure that basketball and ASPSA personnel were not steering players to the AFAM Department" (p. 73). In the years that followed, the number of Williams' players majoring in AFAM declined until they reached insignificant levels by 2009.

Further, at least three other faculty members knew about the paper classes and looked the other way. Some supervisory administrators knew or at least should have known as well. For example, an administrator knew that Nyang'oro was listed for as many as 300 independent studies a year, an impossible feat. However, "She never asked how he or his small department could possibly teach 300 different independent studies in a single year and never challenged him on the quality of instruction these students were or were not receiving in these independent studies" (p. 5). Instead, the administrator made the "inexplicable decision" (p. 5) to not look into the issue further. The shadow curriculum continued for years without interruption until Crowder retired.

The extent of the problem at UNC came to light when a former reading specialist spoke out to the local press. Mary Willingham gave an interview to *The News and Observer* (Kane, 2012) after leaving her position as reading specialist but while she was still an employee at UNC. *The News and Observer* described what Willingham experienced:

> Numerous football and basketball players came to the university with academic histories that showed them incapable of doing college-level work, especially at one of the nation's top public universities. Diagnostic tests administered by the university confirmed their lack of preparedness and also identified learning disabilities that would need extensive

> remediation to put them on a successful academic path. Some athletes told Willingham they had never read a book or written a paragraph, but they were placed in no-show classes that required a 20-page paper and came away with grades of B or better. (para. 8–9)

After speaking with the press, Willingham was demoted and given extra work. She claimed that "university officials verbally attacked" (Ganim, 2014, para. 7) her when she gave another interview to CNN about national college literacy rates. In May of 2014, she resigned from her position at the college because it had become an intolerable hostile work environment. She claims that leaders did not focus on fixing the problem when she brought the issue to light, but "Instead they are attacking my character. That is not leadership" (Ganim, 2014, para. 12).

College Sports' Worst Kept Secret

Few people act surprised when hearing about colleges cutting corners for student athletes. Still, UNC's troubles rise above the rest. In the wake of this scandal, UNC's chancellor announced a series of policies, initiatives, and oversight mechanisms "to ensure academic irregularities do not, and will not, happen again on our campus" ("Our Commitment," 2014, para. 1). When taking a long view of the scandal, it looks as though UNC leaders swept the issue under the rug whenever it came up. From demoting and berating Mary Willingham, to a senior administrator ignoring the consistent listing of hundreds of independent studies, to coaches denying any knowledge whatsoever about paper classes, leaders refused to take the issue seriously. As such, bad feelings about the fraudulent practice continue to linger. A *Chronicle of Higher Education* article called it the "scandal that won't die" (Stripline, 2014). Gerald Gurney, a professor from Oklahoma University who studies academic fraud, stated, "UNC is the mother of all academic fraud violations. … I have no doubt that the scale of the North Carolina case constitutes the most significant academic fraud case in the NCAA" (Ganim, 2014, para. 17). Part of the issue was that leaders at UNC knew about the paper classes years earlier. UNC commissioned a 2012 investigation that concluded only Crowder and Nyang'oro were involved, and no coaches, academic counselors, or administrators had any knowledge about or involvement in steering student athletes to those courses (Stripline, 2014). The follow up investigation revealed that the scandal went much deeper than two UNC employees.

In fact, numerous internal committees and groups looked at student athletes and the AFAM department following Crowder's retirement in 2009 but did not raise serious concerns about what turned out to be a systemic problem. Wainstein's 2014 investigation undermined the credibility of these earlier reports.

For instance, the lead investigator of the 2012 report framed the issue as having little to do with keeping student athletes eligible. The author of the report stated directly, "This was not an athletics scandal. … This was an academic scandal" (Stripling, 2014, para. 20). UNC leaders and their investigators appeared unwilling to look closely at their nationally ranked athletic program. Jay M. Smith, a history professor at UNC, stated his frustration: "They didn't want to dig deeper to find the motor of the academic scandal, and it's for that reason that here we are, four years later [after Crowder retired] and still asking questions" (Stripline, 2014, para. 17). The question remains, is UNC finally getting serious about holding student athletes to the same standards as the school's other students?

The ripple effect from Wainstein's report continues. In an interesting twist, former UNC student athletes have filed a class action lawsuit against the school for "failing to fulfill their stated missions of educating athletes" (Wolverton, 2015, para. 1). Michael Carrier, who teaches law at Rutgers University called the lawsuit "ambitious" in part because "College athletes know what they're getting into, and they know there are going to be some corners cut" (Strauss, 2015, para. 10). While a successful lawsuit may not be likely, clearly many of UNC's student athletes did not receive a legitimate education while playing for the Tar Heels, and their prospects for playing professionally are slim. Only 1.2% of NCAA men's basketball players and 1.7% of men's football players play professionally after college (Manfred, 2012). Shadow curriculums and paper courses won't help the overwhelming majority of student athletes' long-term career prospects. UNC is perhaps the biggest-name school involved in academic fraud but is certainly not alone. The National Collegiate Athletic Association (NCAA) is investigating allegations of academic misconduct involving athletes at 20 colleges (Wolverton, 2015). Willingham summed up the unfairness to student athletes concisely: "[W]e bring these kids to college, and they make money for us without getting a real education" (Wolverton, 2014, para. 8).

Questions:

- Many people at UNC looked the other way. How did this shape the collective attitude toward the shadow curriculum at UNC over time?
- Why are organizations like UNC willing to keep quiet about ethical issues that can harm their good reputations?

GM's Ignition Switch Investigation Reveals a Culture of Inaction

General Motors (GM) is an auto-industry giant. Based in Detroit, Michigan, GM has historically been the world's largest auto manufacturer. In its early days, the company made well-known brands like Chevrolet, Cadillac, and Buick. By the 21st century, the company has grown so large that it now employs over 200,000 people on six continents and sells dozens of auto brands throughout the world ("Our Company," n.d.). Despite its long history of growth and success, GM's reputation has been severely tarnished in recent years and experienced deep financial problems even before the US economy crashed in 2008 (Basu, 2014). Subsequently, GM filed briefly for bankruptcy and took a government "bailout" of over $50 billion in taxpayer money (Healey, 2013). Around this time, it scrapped some of its well-known brands like Saturn and Pontiac (Basu, 2014). The company slipped into a leadership tailspin, cycling through five different CEOs since 2009, at a feverish pace. In 2014, Mary Barra took the wheel. The most troubling issue for GM in recent years, however, involved something rather small: a faulty ignition switch. For over 10 years, some of GM's ignition switches on popular models Chevy Cobalt and Saturn Ion unexpectedly moved from the "run" position to the "accessories" position ("How GM," 2014). Most people put little thought into their vehicle's ignition switch unless they had trouble starting their cars. Still, this seemingly minor technical issue had disastrous results.

In the early 1990s, many customers complained that the ignition switches in some small GM models felt stiff and took too much effort to turn ("How GM," 2014). They thought the rough ignition made the cars feel "cheap." With this feedback, GM engineers set out to make an ignition that turned more smoothly to make it "feel like it was a European sports car or something" ("How GM," 2014, para. 4). This feeling was meant to "give drivers the impression that they were better designed" ("How GM," 2014, para. 2). Rather than a genuinely improved ignition, however, the redesign loosened the ignition switch too much. The resulting ignition turned when it should not have and was prone to rotating back out of position, which killed the engine and most electrical functions including the airbags and power steering. The unintended turning could result from something as minor as touching or bumping the keys with the driver's knee or even from the weight of a few keys on the ring. These faulty ignitions were installed in hundreds of thousands of cars and contributed to at least 13 deaths and 50 accidents. Unfortunately, this issue persisted for many years and was not publicized. The company did not do a recall or warn customers sufficiently about the faulty switches even though many employees and executives knew about the problem and the growing list of associated accidents and deaths. This case looks at what the people at GM knew, when they knew it, and what they did about it.

New CEO Orders a Full Investigation

After the resignation of a veteran CEO in 2009 and a series of three short-term CEOs from 2009 to 2014, GM announced that company veteran Mary Barra would be the company's new leader. She took over in mid-January and learned of the ignition switch issue about two weeks later. By February, GM announced widespread recalls. Barra also announced that she had hired former prosecuting attorney, Anton Valukas, to conduct a complete investigation into the matter. While it was underway, Barra testified before Congress and vowed to be completely transparent:

> This is an extraordinary situation. It involved vehicles we no longer make, but it came to light on my watch and I'm responsible for resolving it. When we have answers, we will be fully transparent with you, with our regulators, and with our customers. (GM CEO, 2014)

By June 2014, Valukas completed his investigation. He interviewed 230 key witnesses from GM, looked at emails, hard drives, hard copies of documents, and so on to compile his findings that were then released to the public. When the report came out, Barra seemed embarrassed for GM: "the report is extremely thorough, brutally tough and deeply troubling. … it is enormously painful to have our shortcomings laid out so vividly. I was deeply saddened and disturbed as I read the report" ("GM CEO," 2014, para. 8). She apologized and vowed to fix the problem and the company's culture.

GM's Knowledge about the Ignition Switch Flaw

The design of the faulty ignition goes back many years. In the late 1990s, GM patented the ignition. It was "designed to be cheaper, less prone to failure and less apt to catch fire than previous switches" ("How GM," 2014, para. 15). When testing prototypes, however, the switch worked poorly and did not meet GM standards for the amount of force needed to rotate it. Testers discovered the defect as early as 2001 when testing the Saturn Ion in 2001 (Basu, 2014; Warren, 2014). Despite this data, GM engineer Ray Degiorgio approved the new switch in 2002 for use in the Ion ("How GM," 2014). Customer complaints for this model started immediately. Rather than fix the issue, GM approved the same ignition in the Chevy Cobalt in 2004. Customers kept complaining. A significant issue in the decision-making process at GM was that engineers did not label the ignition switch issue as a "safety" problem. Instead, they called it a "customer satisfaction" issue and viewed the ignition as "annoying but not particularly problematic" ("How GM," 2014, para. 22). Valukas, who wrote the report investigating GM's handling of the issue, wrote, "The decision not to categorize the problem as a safety issue directly impacted the level of urgency with which the problem was addressed and the effort to resolve it" ("How GM," 2014, para. 9). Employees treated complaints about the ignition like any other satisfaction complaint.

While GM insiders dragged their feet, reports of fatal accidents involving the Saturn Ion and Chevy Cobalt started adding up. In 2005, a 16-year-old Maryland girl crashed into a tree and died when her car turned off and the airbags failed to deploy on impact (Basu, 2014). In 2007, a reported four fatal crashes occurred involving both the Saturn Ion and Chevy Cobalt where the airbags did not work. In 2010, 29-year-old Brooke Melton crashed and died when her ignition malfunctioned. Numerous families of crash victims sued and settled quietly with GM during this period. Clearly, GM knew about these crashes and hundreds of other complaints but took almost no action to fix the ignition switch. From 2001 to 2014, GM decision-makers closest to the problem discussed several possible fixes but in each case ultimately rejected the solutions. At the end of January 2014, Mary Barra took over as CEO and learned for the first time the full extent of the safety issues related to the ignition switches (Valukas, 2014). Two weeks later, GM finally announced a recall of all affected models more than a decade after GM engineers knew the ignition switch was faulty.

Complications and the Long Delayed Recall

Though GM engineers and many leaders knew the ignition was causing accidents and deaths, the company resisted making changes. Early on, Ray Degiorgio, the engineer closest to the ignition switch issue, instructed others at GM not to make the change because, he claimed, "it is close to impossible to modify the present [and 'fragile'] ignition switch" without causing "mechanical and/or electrical problems" (Naughton, Plungis, & Higgins, 2014, para. 18). In 2006, GM approved a design change and began using the new part in cars but did not change the part number. This made it appear even to GM employees that the new ignition was the same as the old ignition. Consumer-safety advocate, Joan Claybrook, commented on this change: "sign[ing] off on changes to the part, that's a good thing. The problem is why the part number wasn't also changed. … Some are concerned that by not changing the part number, that was an attempt to cover up that there was a problem" (Naughton et al., 2014, para. 15). By keeping the part number the same, GM did not raise suspicions and avoided a recall. Not changing the part number also caused great confusion when later trying to diagnose the "root cause" for the ignition problem and the exact models and years of cars that had faulty switches.

Several potential fixes existed along the way that could have facilitated a recall, but still GM took no action. For instance, by 2007, managers knew of one such potential solution that would have involved just a few minutes of labor and a part that cost a mere 57 cents (Durbin & Krisher, 2014). Still, the company decided not to recall the cars. In total, CEO Barra estimated that doing the recall in 2007 would have cost GM $100 million for the entire recall at the time, a fraction of the eventual monetary costs to GM. Despite known issues and with possible solutions in hand, GM did little with its data about defects, accidents, and deaths. Frank Borris, the head of the National Highway Traffic Safety Administration's Office of Investigation stated, "The general perception is that GM is slow to communicate, slow to act, and, at times, requires additional effort of ODI that we do not feel is necessary with some of your [auto industry] peers" (Shepardson, Henkel, & Burden, 2014, para. 3). Maryann Keller, an auto industry analyst and author of two books on GM, speculated about why GM failed to take action: "The question is: Why didn't they act? … Was it in their best interest not to do it? Were their careers going to be side-tracked if they did? Was their boss' career going to be side-tracked?" (Naughton et al., 2014, para. 7). The Valukas report gave the strong impression that GM insiders were looking out for their own careers and company profits while ignoring the dangers to drivers.

The Valukas report also revealed troubling cultural features at GM. Some employees reported a general "reluctance to raise issues or concerns in GM's culture" (Valukas, 2014, p. 252). The report shows that the "culture, atmosphere, and supervisors may have discouraged individuals from raising safety concerns" (p. 252). Supervisors warned employees with specific statements such as "never put anything above the company" and "never put the company at risk" (pp. 252–253). Not surprisingly, employees who knew the most about the ignition issues "did not elevate the issue to their superiors" (p. 253). When employees did bring various problems to supervisors, they frequently experienced "push-back" from managers. The "common thread [or practice] was to hold more meetings and refer the matter to additional groups or committees" (p. 253) instead of taking action or adequately informing supervising executives. Importantly, GM's culture of avoidance was not the work of some isolated executives. GM formally trained employees to avoid the use of certain words and phrases when corresponding within GM. For instance, employees were told to avoid the word "problem" and to use "issue, condition, matter" instead; replace "safety" with "has potential safety implications"; and avoid "defect" and say "does not perform to design" (Valukas, 2014, p. 254). GM also followed an unofficial practice of not taking notes at safety meetings to avoid possible scrutiny in the future. Because of this, "determining the identity of any actual decision-maker was virtually impenetrable. No single person owned any decision" (p. 255). The result was a culture filled with committees, sub-committees, and *ad hoc* committees with almost no record of who belonged on the committees or what they discussed and decided.

Action at Last

When the Valukas report reached the CEO in June of 2014, she took action to fix GM. Barra fired 15 employees who worked closely on the ignition switch issue (Bennett & Ramsey, 2014). The Valukas report did not find direct evidence of a deliberate cover up. Instead, the investigation showed a network of employees who were simply unwilling to handle the problem aggressively in GM's culture of neglect. GM set aside a $600 million compensation fund for lawsuit settlements with victims' families ("General Motors," 2015). Unfortunately, the ignition switch recall triggered a variety of other recalls that cost GM over $3 billion and involved an astounding 12 million vehicles ("General Motors," 2015). This was a 3,000% increase over what a recall would have cost the company years earlier when they first proposed a viable solution. Additionally, the initial report of 13 deaths was drastically underestimated. By May 2015, GM compensation fund approved the 100th death claim for settlement ("General Motors," 2015). Clearly, this far exceeds the original estimates of 13 deaths the company stated. Further, dozens more death claims and hundreds of additional accidents are still under review by GM. In total, over 4,300 death and accident claims have been filed against GM related to the faulty ignition switches ("General Motors," 2015). In 2015 while still under Mary Barra's leadership, however, GM received some welcomed good news. Its auto sales in almost every category were up noticeably, and investor confidence has risen even as some of its competitors' sales have struggled.

Questions:

- What about GM's culture prompted engineers and decision-makers to let a small, fixable problem balloon into a large, costly problem?
- If you had been in charge, what communication processes would you have put in place to make sure issues like this received the attention they deserved?

Chapter Discussion Questions

- How did keeping secrets and/or ignoring small problems contribute to the organizations' troubles?
- What do you believe was driving these organizations to camouflage their internal problems? Did it help them to do so?
- How did the practice of secrecy shape these organizations' cultures?

Key Terms

- Secrecy
- Closed communication
- Mum effect
- Moral mum effect
- Whistleblower
- Internal whistleblowing
- External whistleblowing
- Retaliation

References

Berkrot, B. (2009, September 2). Pfizer whistleblower's ordeal reaps big rewards. Retrieved from http://www.reuters.com/article/2009/09/02/us-pfizer-whistleblower-idUSN021592920090902

Bisel, R. S., Kelley, K. M., Ploeger, N. A., & Messersmith, J. (2011). Workers' moral mum effect: On facework and unethical behavior in the workplace. *Communication Studies, 62*, 153–170.

Grant, C. (2002). Whistle blowers: Saints of secular culture. *Journal of Business Ethics, 39*, 391–399.

Hensley, S. (2009, September 3). Pfizer whistleblower tells his Bextra story. *National Public Radio*. Retrieved from http://www.npr.org/blogs/health/2009/09/pfizer_whistleblower_tells_his.html

Johnson, C. E., Sellnow, T. L., Seeger, M. W., Barrett, M. S., & Hasbargen, K. C. (2004). Blowing the whistle on Fen-Phen. *Journal of Business Communication, 41*, 350–369.

Kaptein, M. (2011). From inaction to external whistleblowing: The influence of the ethical culture of organizations on employee responses to observed wrongdoing. *Journal of Business Ethics, 98*, 513–530.

Keenen, J. P. (2000). Blowing the whistle on less serious forms of fraud: A study of executives and managers. *Employee Responsibilities and Rights Journal, 12*, 199–217.

Lyon, A. (2007). "Putting patients first": Systematically distorted communication and Merck's marketing of Vioxx. *Journal of Applied Communication Research, 35*, 376–398.

Marler, L. E., McKee, D., Cox, S., Simmering, M., & Allen, D. (2012). Don't make me the bad guy: Organizational norms, self-monitoring, and the mum effect. *Journal of Managerial Issues, 24*, 97–116.

McLean, B., & Elkind, P. (2003). *The smartest guys in the room: The amazing rise and scandalous fall of Enron.* London: Portfolio.

Mesmer-Magnus, J. R., & Viswesvaran, C. (2005). Whistle-blowing in organizations: An examination of correlates of whistle-blowing intentions, actions, and retaliation. *Journal of Business Ethics, 62*, 277–297.

Milliken, F. J., Morrison, E. W., & Hewlin, P. F. (2003). An exploratory study of employee silence: Issues that employees don't communicate upward and why. *Journal of Management Studies, 40*, 1453–1476.

Near, J. P., & Miceli, M. P. (1985). Organizational dissidence: The case of whistleblowing. *Journal of Business Ethics, 4*, 1–16.

Redding, W. C. (1996). When will we wake up? In: J. S. Jaksa & M. S. Pritchard (Eds.), *Responsible communication: Ethical issues in business, industry, and the professions* (pp. 17–40). Cresskill, NJ: Hampton Press.

Rogers, D. P. (1987). Development of a measure of perceived communication openness. *Journal of Business Communication, 24*, 53–61.

Swartz, M., & Watkins, S. (2004). *Power failure: The inside story of the collapse of Enron.* New York, NY: Doubleday.

Ulmer, R. R., Sellnow, T. L., & Seeger, M. W. (2010). *Effective crisis communication: Moving from crisis to opportunity.* Thousand Oaks, CA: Sage.

GlaxoSmithKline References

Case NO.: C.A. No: 04 CV10375. (2008). [Lawsuit against GlaxoSmithKline]. Retrieved from http://www.taf.org/eckardcomplaint3.pdf

Extra: Phone call to Glaxo. (2011, January 2). *60 Minutes.* Retrieved from https://www.youtube.com/watch?v=M91B2E-VNG4

FACTBOX: The 20 largest pharmaceutical companies. (2010, March 26). Reuters [electronic version]. Retrieved from http://www.reuters.com/article/2010/03/26/pharmaceutical-mergers-idUSN2612865020100326

The Global 2000. (2010). *Forbes* [electronic version] Retrieved from http://www.forbes.com/lists/2010/18/global-2000-10_The-Global 2000_Sales_2.html

Howe, P. (2010, October 26). Whistleblower wins 96 million in GlaxoSmithKline case. Retrieved from http://www.necn.com/pages/landing?blockID=339520

Pelley, S. (2011, January 2). Bad medicine: The Glaxo case. *60 Minutes.* Retrieved from http://www.cbsnews.com/videos/bad-medicine-the-glaxo-case

Thomas, K., & Schmidt, M. S. (2012, July 2). Glaxo agrees to pay $3 billion in fraud settlement. *New York Times.* Retrieved from http://www.nytimes.com/2012/07/03/business/glaxosmithkline-agrees-to-pay-3-billion-in-fraud-settlement.html?_r=0

Boy Scouts References

About the BSA. (n.d.). Retrieved from http://www.scouting.org/About.aspx

Bartkewicz, A. (2012a, August 5). Boy Scouts' "perversion files" didn't stop some sex offenders from preying on kids again. *New York Daily News*. Retrieved from http://www.nydailynews.com/news/national/boy-scouts-perversion-files-didn-stop-sex-offenders-preying-kids-article-1.1129444#ixzz38IsOfFpz

Bartkewicz, A. (2012b, September 16). Boy Scouts covered up sex abuse allegations in hundreds of cases, "perversion files" show. *New York Daily News*. Retrieved from http://www.nydailynews.com/news/national/boy-scouts-covered-sex-abuse-allegations-hundreds-cases-perversion-files-show-article-1.1160825

Boyle, P. (1994). *Scout's honor: Sexual abuse in America's most trusted institution*. Rocklin, CA: Prima.

Goodale, B. (2012, October 10). Boy Scouts child abuse files: Can the organization withstand their release? *MinnPost*. Retrieved July 23, 2014 from http://www.minnpost.com/christian-science-monitor/2012/10/boy-scouts-child-abuse-files-can-organization-withstand-their-rele.

Know the facts: BSA Ineligible Volunteer Files. (n.d.). Retrieved July 23, 2014 from http://www.scouting.org/BSAYouthProtection/BSA_Communications/Ineligible_Volunteer_Files.aspx

Perry, W. (n.d.). Boy Scouts of America Statement on Ineligible Volunteer Files. Retrieved July 23, 2014 from http://www.scouting.org/sitecore/content/BSAYouthProtection/BSA_Communications/IVFileStatement.aspx

Tracking decades of allegations in the Boy Scouts. (2013, January 3). *Los Angeles Times*. Retrieved July 23, 2014 from http://spreadsheets.latimes.com/boyscouts-cases/.

UNC References

Culpepper, C. (2014, October 22). Wainstein probe implicates over 3,000 students in University of North Carolina academic scandal. *Washington Post*. Retrieved from https://www.washingtonpost.com/news/sports/wp/2014/10/22/wainstein-probe-implicates-over-3000-students-in-university-of-north-carolina-academic-scandal/

Ganim, S. (2014, July 1). Whistle-blower in University of North Carolina paper class case files lawsuit. *CNN*. Retrieved from http://www.cnn.com/2014/07/01/us/university-north-carolina-paper-class-lawsuit/

Independent inquiry press conference [press release]. (2014, October 22). Retrieved from http://carolinacommitment.unc.edu/updates/press-release-regarding-2014-independent-inquiry-press-conference/

Kane, D. (2012, November 17). UNC tolerated cheating, says insider Mary Willingham. *The News & Observer*. Retrieved from http://www.newsobserver.com/news/local/education/unc-scandal/article15573761.html

Our commitment: Taking action and moving forward together. (2014). *University of North Carolina at Chapel Hill*. Retrieved from http://carolinacommitment.unc.edu/

Strauss, B. (2015, January 22). Claiming academic fraud, ex-athletes sue North Carolina and N.C.A.A. *New York Times.* Retrieved from http://www.nytimes.com/2015/01/23/sports/former-athletes-sue-north-carolina-over-academic-fraud.html?_r=0

Stripling, J. (2014, September 8). At Chapel Hill, a scandal that won't die. *The Chronicle of Higher Education.*

Wainstein, K. L., Jay, A. J., & Kukowski, C. D. (2014, October 16). *Investigation of irregular classes in the Department of African and Afro-American Studies at the University of North Carolina at Chapel Hill.* New York, NY: Cadwalader, Wickersham & Taft.

Wolverton, B. (2014, September 8). A whistle-blower spurs self-scrutiny in college sports. *The Chronicle of Higher Education.* Retrieved from http://chronicle.com/article/A-Whistle-Blower-Spurs-/148669/

Wolverton, B. (2015, January 21). NCAA says it's investigating academic fraud at 20 colleges. *The Chronicle of Higher Education.* Retrieved from http://www.chronicle.com/article/NCAA-Says-It-s-Investigating/151315/

GM References

Basu, T. (2014, March 31). Timeline: A history of GM's ignition switch defect. *National Public Radio.* Retrieved from http://www.npr.org/2014/03/31/297158876/timeline-a-history-of-gms-ignition-switch-defect

Bennett, J., & Ramsey, M. (2014, June 5). GM fires 15 employees over recall failures. *Wall Street Journal.* Retrieved from http://www.wsj.com/articles/gm-ceo-probe-found-pattern-of-incompetence-1401973966

Durbin, D., & Krisher, T., (2014, April 1). Thirteen GM traffic deaths are tied to a 57-cent part. *St. Louis Post-Dispatch.* Retrieved from http://www.stltoday.com/business/local/thirteen-gm-traffic-deaths-are-tied-to-a--cent/article_afe8f97b-34c5-52ea-87ea-46dec9c61d27.html

General Motors under fire as ignition switch death toll hits 100. (2015, May 20). *The Irish Times*, p. 8.

GM's Barra: Will be transparent as we investigate. (2014). *CNBC Videos.* Retrieved from http://news.yahoo.com/video/gms-barra-transparent-investigate-205100760.html

GM CEO Barra: Will be fully transparent when we have answers [Video testimony to Congress]. (2014, April 1). Retrieved from http://video.cnbc.com/gallery/?video=3000263370

Healey, J. R. (2013, December 10). Government sells last of its GM shares. *USA Today.* Retrieved from http://www.usatoday.com/story/money/cars/2013/12/09/government-treasury-gm-general-motors-tarp-bailout-exit-sale/3925515/

How GM employees didn't view "switch from hell" as a safety issue despite decade of clues (2014, June 6). *Guelphmercury.com.* Retrieved from http://www.guelphmercury.com/news-story/4564541-how-gm-employees-didn-t-view-switch-from-hell-as-a-safety-issue-despite-decade-of-clues/

Naughton, K., Plungis, J., & Higgins, T. (2014, April 11). Documents show GM slow to respond to safety concerns. *Bloomberg.* Retrieved from http://www.bloomberg.com/news/articles/2014-04-11/sidelined-gm-engineer-signed-off-on-ignition-work-around

Our company [GM website]. (n.d.). General motors. Retrieved from http://www.gm.com/company/aboutGM/our_company.html

Shepardson, D., Henkel, K., & Burden, M. (2014, April 11). GM criticized as "slow to act" by feds in 2013. *The Detroit News.* Retrieved from http://www.detroitnews.com/article/20140411/AUTO0103/304110091#ixzz3pzTqkT99

Valukas, A. R. (2014). Report to the board of directors of the General Motors Company regarding ignition switch recalls. *New York Times.* Retrieved from http://www.nytimes.com/interactive/2014/06/05/business/06gm-report-doc.html?_r=0

Warren, Z. (2014, March). General Motors reveals it knew about ignition switch issues in 2001. *Inside Counsel.* Retrieved from http://www.insidecounsel.com/2014/03/13/general-motors-reveals-it-knew-about-ignition-swit

8

Transparent Communication and Case Studies

Bad news does not improve with age.

—*Dan Amos, CEO of Aflac*

Transparent communication allows organizations to identify and resolve issues in the initial stages before they get out of control. As the previous chapter shows, once they grow larger, resolving them becomes difficult. This chapter argues that, as soon as potential problems surface, organizations should practice transparent communication within their walls. A model for transparent communication inside organizations provides a conceptual foundation to achieve this goal. In the four case studies here, transparency played a central role: Massachusetts General Hospital, Taco Bell, JetBlue, and Texas Health Presbyterian Hospital.

The Importance of Transparent Communication

The term "***transparency***" has various meanings. As Rawlins (2009) states, "Simply put, transparency is the opposite of secrecy" (p. 73). People use the term widely and loosely in journalism and politics. Regarding organizations, existing writings come mainly through the areas of corporate social responsibility and public relations (e.g., Christianson, 2002; Christianson & Langer, 2009). These conceptualizations of transparency commonly emphasize the need for organizational insiders to provide important information to outsiders (Florini, 2007). Its general hope is to reduce fraud, corruption, risk, and the abuse of power (Nadesan, 2013). Clearly, transparency should be a top organizational priority. Despite its potential benefits, however, many practical barriers and challenges discourage organizations from communicating forthrightly with the public (DeTienne & Lewis, 2005). As the previous chapter explains, many of these pressures start inside of already dysfunctional organizations. Therefore, this chapter explores the norms and practices necessary behind closed doors to jumpstart transparent communication. As Nadesan (2013) explained, transparency is a "fundamentally communication phenomenon" (p. 252). If organizational insiders cannot communicate troublesome issues honestly among themselves, little hope exists for them to communicate transparently with the public or government regulators.

A Model of Internal Transparent Communication

Research on internal transparent communication for organizations is still a developing area. My simple model of its practices (see Figure 8.1) enables both internal and external stakeholders by interweaving three overlapping views of transparent communication: (a) openness, (b) candid conversations, and (c) information sharing.

Openness

An important component of transparency is openness, which has two interconnected halves. One is the use of transparent processes. May (2013), for instance, states that open or "[t]ransparent organizations have clear and visible governance, mission, policies, procedures, and guidelines" (p. 26). Overt rules help maintain a system of checks and balances so no particular individual takes unfair advantage of a situation. ***Organizational openness*** seeks visible processes through which information flows freely. Karl Weick was an instrumental voice in laying groundwork regarding organizational studies about openness. For Weick (1990), it fundamentally helps organizations identify wrong assumptions. To guard against a skewed version of reality, Weick (1990) states, "It is largely through [the] open exchange of messages, independent verification, and redundancy, that the false hypothesis can be detected" (p. 583). Communication processes that address troubling issues should happen in plain sight to make sure people understand them from multiple angles. Similarly, Rogers (1987) explained, "When communication is open, organizations are able to identify their problems before they get out of hand" (p. 60). In the best interest of the organization's health and effectiveness, thus, its structure must publicize activities and encourage information sharing between and among organizational members. If information is only shared on a "need-to-know basis," it will be difficult for organizations to identify incorrect assumptions and reach their full potential. Transparent processes are an essential component of organizational openness.

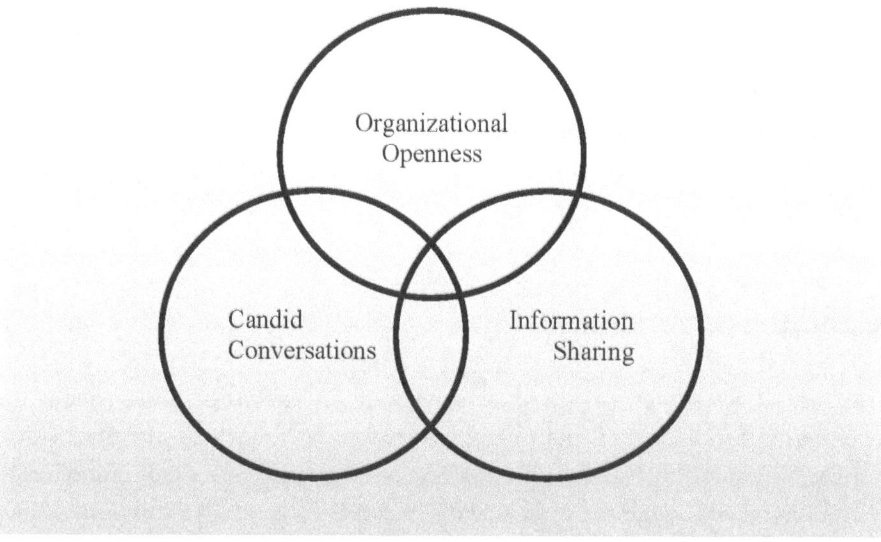

Figure 8.1. Transparent Communication Model.

The other half is ***disclosure***. This type, Rogers (1987) explains, "is a vehicle for handling non-routine and negative information. … It does not include routine orders, instructions, or reports. It does include the bad, the unusual, the exception, and the novel" (p. 60). Though we should discuss non-routine events, virtually any communication event is suitable for disclosure. Conversations in meetings, small groups, and one-on-one are all ideal occasions for communication about issues of concern. Weick (1990) argues that organizations ought to demand this type of disclosure from all members about potential problems and states, "Part of any job requirement must be the necessity for talk. Strong, silent types housed in systems with norms favoring taciturnity can stimulate unreliable performance" (p. 589). We should, therefore, create norms in our environments that encourage rather than discourage open communication.

The goal, Weick explained, is to avoid the communication phenomena of ***pluralistic ignorance***, a contributor to initial stages of crises that result from keeping quiet. Weick (1990) explained its presence in the following mindset: "I am puzzled by what is going on, but I assume that no one else is, especially because they have more experience, more seniority, higher rank" (p. 588). People often keep quiet when they notice something odd because they assume it is only odd to them. When people finally speak their mind, their reaction is, "You too? I thought I was the only one who didn't know what was going on" (Weick,

1990, p. 590). Organizational members at all levels, therefore, should disclose their views preemptively. The longer problems linger, the greater the likelihood they will damage organizations. In contrast to secrecy, "openness is positively correlated with organizational performance" (Rogers, 1987, p. 53). We do not serve our organization's long-term interests when we close our mouths because we believe somebody else's opinion might be different or an issue might be sensitive.

Candid Conversations

The second component of the transparency model is ***candor***. This extends the expectation for disclosure about organizational issues to include more individual topics. Organizational members at all levels must engage in frank, honest conversations, even though the topic may be sensitive at times. As Antonioni (2006) defined it, "To be candid means to be open, straightforward, and sincere in our expression, sharing what we think without evasion and without being rude" (p. 25). Some authors argue that the inability to be candid with colleagues is a key sign of a dysfunctional team (Lencioni, 2002). In contrast, candid conversations are one of the ways organizations and leaders build high-trust cultures (Whipple, 2009). The best method to encourage candor, of course, is to model it. We all make large and small errors. When we do, it's best to be transparent about our own blunders. We should also be candid about emerging issues around us. This sometimes means delivering corrective feedback to others. An underperforming team member, for example, may need to hear about how his or her poor work is hurting the team and change. For this reason, candor should go hand in hand with respect, kindness, and care. When done well, candid conversations point the interaction in a supportive direction and allow the other person a safe space to be honest also. While difficult, these build trusting relationships and effective organizations over time (May, 2013).

"Transparency" or the buzzword "candor" should clearly not be used as an excuse to be hurtful or make unnecessary personal comments. This approach is a misuse of the term. Conversations should be woven with the threads of sincerity, openness, and respect in equal parts. For instance, readers may have heard people make extremely rude comments but excuse their discourtesy with a flippant phrase such as "I'm just being honest." Candor creates a vulnerability that we must handle carefully. We must want the best for other people involved and ultimately encourage improvement in a supportive way. As such, we must learn to hold back comments that cut too deeply.

Remember not only to say the right thing in the right place, but far more difficult still, to leave unsaid the wrong thing at the tempting moment. (Ben Franklin, founding father, author, and political theorist)

Information Sharing

The third component of transparent communication is providing balanced information to support others' decision-making. This starts by communicating with those inside the organization and ultimately extends to the external stakeholders the organization serves. Nilsen (1974), for instance, provides a powerful ethical standard to appeal to when calling for greater transparency. He stated that communication should support free and informed choices about important issues, a standard he calls ***significant choice***. Communicators have an obligation to provide information to allow listeners to make "well-reasoned decisions" (Ulmer & Sellnow, 1997, p. 216). This type of transparency is particularly important in organizations where members are constantly expected to persuade other members. Most proposals, marketing strategies, and public relations campaigns are persuasive in nature. Professionals must constantly "pitch" our ideas or "make our case" for funding, approval, and participation in desired projects. In such situations, we may be tempted to tell only the side of the story that favors us. Because of this, Nilsen (1974) explains, "When we communicate to influence the attitudes, beliefs and actions of others," communicators should be evaluated to the degree they support the "free, informed, and critical choice on matters of significance in [the listeners'] lives" (p. 46). This means sharing information that supports the overall effectiveness of our organizations, not just our individual, departmental, or team's interests.

Organizational members have a responsibility to communicate transparently with internal and external stakeholders. Individuals, organizations, and society's interests are best served when communication provides "adequate information, diversity of views, and knowledge of alternative choices and their possible consequences" (Lyon, 2007, p. 18). Nilsen suggests informed decisions also require (a) knowledge about possible short- and long-term consequences as well as alternative options, and (b) an awareness of the motives of the people who want to influence us, including the goals they seek and the values they serve (see p. 45). In practice, for example, if a medication has certain health risks, the manufacturer, and, in turn, physicians should disclose those risks in an unambiguous fashion. Patients should hear about a range of alternatives regarding their associated risks and benefits as well as any financial or resource ties the physician has to the drug companies involved (Lyon & Ricci, 2012). Transparent information sharing allows listeners to make genuinely informed choices.

To many, Nilsen's view is the gold standard for transparent information sharing, but some critics claim his standards are too high. He replies to critics as follows (1974):

> [I am attempting] to do justice to the concept of man as a being of dignity and intrinsic worth, with a capacity for rational choice. If at times the principles sound unrealistic or idealistic, let the reader ask himself whether he could ask less and still remain consistent in his conception of man. Let the reader ask whether other men's (sic) wants and needs are as legitimate as his own. If others have the same capacities, the same title to dignity, how else could one talk and still maintain one's integrity? (p. 19)

A key aspect of courageous communication is high standards for organizations. Nilsen provides a clear ethical guidepost for expecting adequate information to make high-quality choices. This three-part model of transparency brings together existing threads of research to paint a well-rounded view of an open communication process. Transparency, however, takes practice.

Responding to Crisis Transparently

Emerging crises test organizations' willingness and ability to communicate transparently. For instance, spokespeople who are not willing to speak transparently within the walls of the organization seldom can do so during a full-blown crisis (Lyon, 2007). For decades, research on crisis has demonstrated the advantages of communicating transparently and various ways organizations respond to escalating issues. When a crisis goes public, Benoit (1997) described how leaders engage in *denying* and *shifting the blame* to another party, claiming that the organization was *provoked* by an outsider, maintaining that leaders *did not know* about an issue, casting the crisis as a random *accident*, claiming *good intentions* despite bad results, *attacking and discrediting* the accuser of the wrongdoing, and attempting to *minimize* the perception of harm done. In limited instances when the organization is truly not to blame, these strategies may work. They aim to move the attention off the organization to the responsible party. This is appropriate because it leads to a greater degree of truth. However, if the organization or one of its members is to blame, these strategies should clearly not be used. They will only amplify the crisis. Lance Armstrong, for instance, lied about using performance-enhancing drugs for years, pressured others to lie, and attacked the reputation of those who accused him of "doping." When the truth finally came out, he suffered a great deal more than other top athletes who admitted the truth when accused of drug use. The results in cases like this are predictable.

In contrast, some leaders handle crises much more transparently with great success. Benoit (1997) describes these strategies as *apologizing* (*i.e., mortification*), financially *compensating* any victims or parties negatively affected, and taking *corrective action* to make sure the problem does not recur in the future. For example, Schwan's has been providing fine frozen food delivered right to each customer's doors with great success since the 1950s. In 1994, the company's sterling reputation was threatened by an emerging salmonella outbreak among its ice cream customers (Sellnow, Ulmer, & Snider, 1998). Schwan's leaders instantly accepted responsibility and fixed the problem in their process, apologized face to face to every ice cream customer, paid for all medical costs for salmonella testing and treatment, and reached financial settlements with families most affected. The company's business bounced back quickly and customers rewarded the company's honest approach with their continued loyalty. Almost without exception, organizations that come clean and take action sooner rather than later restore their operations much more quickly than organizations that try to cover up the truth.

Mistakes are always forgivable if one has the courage to admit them. (Bruce Lee)

Transparent Communication Takes Courage

Transparent communication aims to reduce fraud, corruption, risk, and power abuse but requires a great deal of courage. If we imagine ourselves in the midst of an ethically pressured situation, we may wish somebody else were handling the issue instead of us. Our desire to remaining loyal to our colleagues and the organization might tempt us to rationalize keeping silent. People who feel guilty will probably attack us in response. Further, the more serious the wrongdoing, the more potential exists for us to be discredited, fired, and punished.

It takes courage to overcome these pressures even though the alternatives are clear. When we keep silent, dysfunction thrives, and organizations cause their own crises.

Though transparent communication is difficult, it brings rewards. Personally, it provides a clear conscience. Adam Smith, an economist and moral philosopher, once pondered, "What can be added to the happiness of a man who is healthy, out of debt, and has a clear conscience?" Our truthfulness and openness also demonstrate our character and establish our credibility (Weiner, 2006), primary currencies in professional life. Once we lose credibility, we relinquish our ability to lead. Transparent conversations cultivate smoother, more trusting relationships with our colleagues (Whipple, 2009). At any organizational level, transparency strengthens companies' long-term reputations by helping to identify and correct mistakes promptly.

In the case studies below, transparent communication plays a central role, sometimes behind the walls of the organization and at other times more publicly. The cases also show, while positive outcomes are not guaranteed, transparent communication is perhaps the best approach to getting an organization back on track when trouble surfaces.

Cases Involving Transparent Communication

Wrong-Site Surgery at Massachusetts General Hospital

In 2010, 65-year-old patient "Marie" checked into the hospital for a trigger-finger release operation. Unfortunately, her surgeon botched the procedure. The surgery took place at Massachusetts General Hospital (MGH), one of the nation's top hospitals and ranked #2 behind Maryland's highly regarded John's Hopkins Hospital (Leonard, 2013). Founded in 1811, MGH has a long tradition of excellence as Harvard Medical School's main teaching hospital. Its outstanding reputation attracts some of the most renowned specialists in the nation. Dr. David Ring, an Associate Professor at Harvard Medical School and orthopedic surgeon at MGH, specializes in surgery on the hands and arms and performed the wrong surgery on Marie. He has published hundreds of journal articles and five textbooks on the subject. In 2013, he was appointed as the new chief of Hand and Upper Extremity Service in MGH (David, 2013). He is, by every measure, a leader in his organization at the peak of his professional career. However, Dr. Ring and other surgeons like him around the world currently work in hospital contexts that are increasingly concerned about "wrong-site surgery." This case looks at the contextual pressures surrounding Marie's mistaken surgery and how Dr. Ring responded when he realized he had made a terrible error.

Wrong Site Surgery and Marie

Wrong-site surgery occurs when a doctor operates on the wrong part of the patient and is more common that most patients realize. In fact, 21% of surgeons admit to operating on the wrong site at least once. According to a 2009 survey (Wong et al., 2009), these mistakes happen in various ways:

- Approximately 59% of these involved the wrong side (i.e., left vs. right)
- 23% were done on another site (e.g., the correct hand but the wrong finger)
- 14% were the wrong procedure (e.g., trigger finger instead of carpal tunnel)
- 5% were performed on the wrong patient

Since wrong site surgeries have increased over the past two decades, the medical community has adopted a series of safety checks to reduce these mistakes. In 1994, for instance, Canada began a program called "Operate Through Your Initials" whereby doctors would write their initials on the exact site of intended incision with a marker before the patient ever enters the operating room (Wong, Lewis, Herndon, Martin, & Brooks, 2009). In 1998, surgeons in the U. S. started a similar campaign called "Sign Your Site." Additionally, in 2007, numerous surgery associations agreed to use universal safety protocols to ensure proper care, most importantly, the use of a "time out." In sum, "The guidelines recommend that the time-out include the surgeon, anesthesiologist, nurse, and patient and that just before induction of anesthesia, all participants agree on the patient's identification, the operation type, and the correct surgical site" (Ring, Herndon, & Meyer, 2010, para. 18). Ideally, these time outs act as pauses and verifications to avoid a wrong-site mistake. They are supposed to act as a virtual stop sign whereby everything comes to a momentary halt to ensure that everybody in the room agrees before moving forward. Hospital conditions, however, are not always ideal, and these protocols do not always prevent errors.

The patient in this case, Marie, suffered from "trigger finger." The term describes the painful locking or hitching of a finger that makes it difficult to extend fully. When the affected finger releases, it snaps open like the sudden release of a gun's trigger after firing. Marie arrived at MGH for surgery on her left ring finger. However, Dr. Ring mistakenly performed a carpal tunnel release surgery on her hand.

Dr. Ring's Mistake

Dr. Ring was slated to perform six surgeries, a busy day by any measure. He had three large surgeries and then three hand surgeries. Marie was his sixth patient. The first two hand surgeries were for carpal tunnel syndrome and Marie's was a trigger finger release surgery. Despite knowing this ahead of time, Dr. Ring later recalled, "My mindset at the start of the day was, 'I have three big procedures' that I have specifically planned and prepared for and a few 'carpal tunnels' to perform today" (Ring et al., 2010, para. 6). Following his first carpal tunnel procedure, Dr. Ring, who speaks both English and Spanish, was asked to help translate during Marie's preoperative preparation since she only spoke Spanish. Surgeons do not normally play this role, but the hospital was short-staffed. During this preparation, Dr. Ring noticed that the correct arm was marked for surgery in accordance with hospital protocol. He discussed the patient's condition and "confirmed a persistent trigger finger of the left ring finger" (Ring et al., 2010, para. 8). He then left Marie and performed his second carpal tunnel procedure of the day while her nurse completed the preoperative preparations.

In addition to Dr. Ring's six surgeries, the stress level in the surgery unit was high. Because several other surgeons were running behind schedule, Marie had to be moved to another operating room. The nurse who performed Marie's preoperative assessment, however, was not moved to the new operating room with her. Instead, another nurse took over. This move caused an additional delay and the loss of specific knowledge about what had occurred while the first nurse worked with Marie. While this patient was being moved, Dr. Ring visited with one of the two previous carpal tunnel patients who complained about intense pain and discomfort following the surgery. Dr. Ring explained.

> Although I was able to help put her at ease, the encounter was very emotional, producing in me both the cognitive and physiological aspects of anxiety, as well as a resolve to do everything possible to prevent such an unpleasant experience for future patients. … I recall privately counseling myself that the next operation would be "the best carpal tunnel release that I have ever performed." (Ring et al., 2010, para. 10)

By the time he entered Marie's operating room, her arm had already been washed in preparation for surgery. Because of this, the site marking had been wiped off. He also noticed that a tourniquet was missing from the inventory of supplies needed for surgery. He asked the nurse to get one, and she left the room briefly to do so. This caused the nurse to fall behind on her paperwork and took her attention off of the patient. Dr. Ring then spoke to the patient in Spanish, which the nurse "mistook as a time-out, and as a consequence, no formal time-out took place before the procedure was begun" (Ring et al., 2010, para. 11). In other words, Dr. Ring assumed the nurse took a time out before he arrived in the room. In turn, the nurse assumed that Dr. Ring was taking the time out with the patient while speaking Spanish. At that point, Dr. Ring admits plainly, "I performed a carpal-tunnel release on this patient, rather than a trigger-finger release" (Ring et al., 2010, para. 12).

Dr. Ring's Response

Dr. Ring did not realize his mistake until after the surgery. He reported the following:

> About 15 minutes later, while I was in my office dictating the report of the operation, I realized that I had performed the wrong procedure. I immediately informed the staff and then went straight to the patient and personally informed her of the error. I apologized and explained that I could perform the correct procedure if she wanted me to do so. She agreed and I reassembled the staff. During the preparations for the correct procedure, I filed a safety report and notified the hospital's risk manager of the error and the rectification. I then performed a trigger-finger release, without complication. (Ring et al., 2010, para. 12)

After the patient recovered and went home, Dr. Ring called Marie's son several times to apologize and arrange follow-up care. Dr. Ring informed her son that all fees would be waived in accordance with MGH's policies. A few days after the incident, Marie's son told Dr. Ring that she "had lost faith in [him] and would not return" (Ring et al., 2010, para. 13). Marie continued her postoperative follow-up with a community clinic. The hospital negotiated a financial settlement not long after the surgery.

To his credit, Dr. Ring did not hide, deny, or blame others for his mistake. Instead, he wrote and published the incident as a case study in the *Case Records of the Massachusetts General Hospital.* He hoped his admission would stimulate a discussion about wrong-site surgery among fellow surgeons and nurses. The case was also published in the November 11, 2010 issue of the *New England Journal of Medicine* where he explained his goals plainly: "By publishing this case, we hope to encourage health care practitioners to discuss such events, investigate them fully, disclose them quickly and clearly to patients and their families, care for the providers involved, and use these learning opportunities to reduce the risk for future patients" (Ring et al., 2010, para. 30). He emphasized the importance of following universal protocols strictly and described how familiarity with a task can tempt a person to stretch the rules: "For example, a stop sign is a clear signal to stop a motor vehicle completely and look in both directions before proceeding" (para. 22). Using the stop sign metaphor for the time out policy, he described his participation as Marie's translator during preoperative preparation in addition to his discussion with her just prior to surgery as an ineffective "rolling stop." The *New York Times,* ABC News and other media outlets covered Dr. Ring's public apology and drew attention to efforts that reduce wrong-site surgery.

Responses to Dr. Ring's Openness

In addition to mainstream press coverage, surgeons from North America, Europe, and Asia posted their praise on the *New England Journal of Medicine's* comments section following the article:

- Please let me express my respect and my admiration to Dr. Ring who had the courage to disclose his case of medical error to a wide public in order to let us learn from the mistakes that happened to his patient. In the light of today's mentality of our profession of "always being perfect and never showing weakness," Dr. Ring for me represents honesty, openness, professionalism and courage. (Kiss, 2010)
- You must have a lot of courage … to publish this article. Thanks for your transparency and honesty, … A very solid example for others to follow. (Gibson, 2010)
- It takes courage and candor from the authors and I believe it can be hugely helpful to read such full and frank accounts and analysis of these desperately upsetting incidents. (Mann, 2010)

Dr. Ring's admissions and explanation have no doubt helped other physicians do the same. Ultimately, a published case like Dr. Ring's will help patients receive better care. In fact, numerous subsequent journal articles cite Dr. Ring's case study and encourage change. A positive follow up "Letter to Editor" in the *New England Journal of Medicine* made additional suggestions for reducing wrong site surgeries. Another physician commended Dr. Ring for avoiding the typical behaviors after a mistake like this: "He did not call the risk manager, the hospital lawyer or an administrator to ask what to do, or to get permission to do what he thought was right. Dr. Ring did the right thing for the right reason" (Glantz, 2010). Importantly, Dr. Ring's promotion as the chief of his department came after this incident. Had he chosen to handle his error secretly, his rise in leadership would have been questionable.

Questions:

- Why did Dr. Ring's response require courage?
- To what extent did Dr. Ring's transparency help or hurt his career? Why?

Got a Beef with Taco Bell?: "Thank You for Suing Us"

In 2006, 39 customers in New Jersey and Long Island suffered from E. coli poisoning after eating tainted lettuce at Taco Bell (McFadden, 2006). In 2010,

155 people became sick from salmonella-tainted Taco Bell food (Morran, 2010). In both cases, health experts believe that the contamination originated when suppliers of Taco Bell's raw products such as lettuce and tomatoes sold the tainted food to Taco Bell locations. On the one hand, the restaurant's response in both cases was timely and effective at stopping further illnesses. On the other, company leaders handled these issues quietly and did little publicly to reassure customers and restore the company's image.

In 1962, long before these controversies, Glen Bell opened his first Taco Bell restaurant in Southern California. Today, the chain includes almost 6,000 locations in the US that specialize in tacos, burritos, nachos, and quesadillas. To compete against fast-food giants like McDonald's and Burger King, a Taco Bell advertising slogan throughout the 2000s urged customers to "Think Outside the Bun." The chain crafted a reputation for selling fast food at low prices with numerous menu items starting under one dollar. While the chain is popular, its low prices, description as "fast food," and food-borne illness incidents have not established a strong reputation of the food's quality. In 2011, Taco Bell faced another challenge, an accusation of not using enough beef in its tacos to technically label the filler as beef. The way the company responded this time, however, differed from the past. Instead of handling the issue quietly, Taco Bell approached the controversy in a straight-forward fashion and provided the company a needed boost in public perception. This case looks at how the restaurant chain used direct and open communication to settle a controversy quickly.

Lawsuit: It's Not Beef

In January 2011, Taco Bell faced a striking attack on the quality of its food. A California woman hired an Alabama-based law firm, Beasley Allen, to file a lawsuit against Taco Bell "alleging that the fast-food chain's seasoned beef wasn't beefy enough to be called beef" (Barclay, 2011, para. 1). Lawyers claimed that they and/or their client had conducted laboratory tests that showed definitively that Taco Bell's beef recipe contained less than 35% beef. By USDA standards, a recipe must include at last 40% actual meat to be called "beef." The lawsuit alleged the remaining portion was filling. Timothy Blood, an attorney from the firm, stated that his client wanted Taco Bell to "simply tell the truth" (Hutchison & Moisse, 2011, para. 12). The lawsuit grabbed national headlines in newspapers and on television, and some accepted the allegation as fact. For instance, one stated, "Taco Bell Sued Over Meat That's Just 35 Percent Beef" (Taco, 2011b). The media drew lots of negative attention to Taco Bell, perhaps because it resonated with past issues for the company. The lawsuit did not seek financial compensation but, rather, that the company be honest in its marketing and communication with the public. Dee Miles, another attorney from the firm, stated, "We are asking that they stop saying that they are selling beef" (Taco, 2011b).

Taco Bell's Transparent Response

Unlike leaders' understated food-borne illness responses in 2006 and 2010, Taco Bell responded publicly and swiftly to these allegations. President and CEO Craig Creed said about the lawsuit's claim of 35% beef: "Their number is so wrong, it's ludicrous" (Smith, 2011, para. 7). The company did not handle the lawsuit quietly as most organizations do when being sued. In fact, in the next few months, the company vigorously defended the quality of its beef and used the potential crisis as an opportunity to inform the public about the exact contents of its recipe. In a video posted to the company's YouTube channel, Creed explained that beef made up 88% of the company's taco meat recipe.

> I want you to know the truth about our food. Our beef is 100% USDA inspected, just like the quality beef you buy in the supermarket and prepare in your home. We then season it in our unique recipe of seasonings, water, spices, and other ingredients to provide Taco Bell's signature taste and texture. Think of it when you're making chili. You add your own recipe of seasoning and spices to give the beef flavor and texture. Otherwise, it would just taste like unseasoned ground beef. (Creed, 2011a)

The video and accompanying press releases emphasized the comparison of Taco Bell's approach to the way people cook at home, "when you make chili, meatloaf or meatballs, you add your own recipe of seasoning and spices" (Creed, 2011b, para. 4). Taco Bell's beef, the company explained, is not only 100% USDA inspected: it also "passes our 20 [internal] quality checkpoints" ("Real Employees," 2011, para. 3). The videos, press releases, and interviews all reminded customers that Taco Bell's now not-so-secret recipe was available for all to see on the company's website.

The company spent between $3 to 4 million on a marketing campaign brazenly entitled, "Thank You for Suing Us" (Barclay, 2011). The primary ad continues, "The claims made against Taco Bell and our seasoned beef are absolutely false" ("Taco Bell Asks," 2011a, para. 3). The company placed full-page ads in the nation's top newspapers such as *New York Times, Wall Street Journal, USA Today,*

Boston Globe, *Chicago Tribune*, *Los Angeles Times*, and many others that showed ingredients and their relative proportion (Creed, 2011b):

> Our recipe for seasoned beef includes ingredients you'd find in your home or in the supermarket aisle today:
>
> - 88% USDA-inspected quality beef
> - 3–5% water for moisture
> - 3–5% spices (including salt, chili pepper, onion powder, tomato powder, sugar, garlic powder, cocoa powder and a proprietary blend of Mexican spices and natural flavors)
> - 3–5% oats, starch, sugar, yeast, citric acid, and other ingredients that contribute to the quality of our product. (para. 4)

Additionally, in response to the claim that Taco Bell used "meat filling," the company stated plainly, "Our seasoned beef contains no 'extenders' to add volume, as some might use" (Creed, 2011b, para. 6). Taco Bell was as open as possible about its recipe and let consumers know exactly what they were buying.

Lawsuit Withdrawn

In response to Taco Bell, the law firm that filed the class action suit was unable to produce any lab tests it had claimed it possessed that showed Taco Bell's meat recipe only contained 35% beef. No lab test results nor any mention of a specific lab were ever mentioned publicly by the law firm or its client. Not surprisingly, approximately three months after the initial news, the firm voluntarily and quietly withdrew its lawsuit. Taco Bell, however, was not as quiet. The company followed the law firm's withdrawal with another national ad campaign to reinforce its central message. The headline read, "Would it kill you to say you're sorry?" The press release accompanying the ad campaign read, "We stand behind the quality of every single one of our ingredients, including our seasoned beef, and we want consumers to know that we didn't change our marketing or product because we've always been completely transparent" ("Taco Bell Asks," 2011a, para. 2). The company made sure readers knew the law firm had dropped its suit voluntarily and emphasized its point with a list of statements: "No changes to our products or ingredients. No changes to our advertising. No money exchanged. No settlement agreement" ("Taco Bell Asks," 2011a, para. 8). The ad closed with the following text: "As for the lawyers who brought this suit: You got it wrong, and you're probably feeling pretty bad right about now. But you know what always helps? Saying to everyone, 'I'm sorry.' C'mon, you can do it!" ("Taco Bell Asks," 2011a, para. 11, 12). Of course, it is unlikely that Taco Bell's leaders expected an apology. Instead, the company used the lawsuit withdrawal as another opportunity to remind the public, in dramatic fashion, that Taco Bell was telling customers the truth.

Transparency Pays

Today, Taco Bell serves more customers than ever, over 2 billion per year. Whether or not one chooses to eat at Taco Bell in the future, it is difficult to deny the company turned a potential crisis into an opportunity that strengthened its reputation by providing information to its customers that was once proprietary. Taco Bell's marketing never claimed to have the best product in the fast food industry. It simply communicated openly about its product's ingredients. The company's quick, confident ads and online videos signaled to customers and the law firm that Taco Bell could indeed verify the truthfulness of its recipe. Creed, Taco Bell's CEO, stated plainly after the law firm dropped the suit, "[W]e want consumers to know that we didn't change our marketing or product because we've always been completely transparent" (Taco, 2011a, para. 2). The potential crisis also did not hurt Taco Bell in any significant way financially. On the contrary, Taco Bell's approach built confidence in the organization. For example, its stock price dipped slightly from $50 per share to $46 per share when the lawsuit hit the national headlines but bounced back when Taco Bell released the details of its recipe. It continued to rise throughout the company's "thank you for suing us" ad campaign. A year after the lawsuit was withdrawn, its stock moved above $70 per share, an astounding 40% increase in one year.

Questions:

- Taco Bell shared its once secret recipe to respond to criticism. Do you believe this level of openness was necessary in this situation?
- Why do you think the public and investors responded so positively to Taco Bell's transparency?

Valentine's Day on the Tarmac: JetBlue's Response to Disproportionate Delays and Cancellations

In early 1999, David Neeleman announced his plans to start a new airline, JetBlue. Within a year, the airline reached amazing success with over $100 million in revenue ("Our Company," 2015). Competing in the airline industry is difficult for even established companies. The field is crowded and most airlines look for ways to cut costs in every way possible (e.g., extra bag fees, smaller seats, fees to simply change seats, etc.). In contrast, JetBlue's goal was simple: "To bring humanity back to airline travel." Thus, despite positioning itself as a low-cost airline, JetBlue provides leather seats, a TV screen for each seat, Sirius satellite radio, and other unexpected amenities. Flight attendants are also personable and enthusiastic. Headquartered in Queens, New York, its earliest flight routes went to already-popular destinations such as NYC to Florida, NYC to Las Vegas, etc. Throughout the early 2000s, the airline added more planes and routes.

JetBlue built the airline on customer loyalty by treating people right. The company has won numerous industry awards including JD Power & Associates' award for "customer satisfaction among low-cost carriers" each year from 2006 through 2015 ("Our Company," 2015) as well as winning the overall customer satisfaction award in 2005 when competing head-to-head with major airlines such as American, United, and Delta. Customers were not the only people happy with JetBlue. In 2015, *Forbes* ranked it #19 on the list of the nations' 500 best places to work. Its stellar reputation helped JetBlue grow very quickly. However, for its founder and CEO, David Neeleman, the runway hasn't always been smooth. On February 14, 2007, a major winter storm hit the North Eastern US. New York City airports such as John F. Kennedy (JFK) experienced a significant ice storm that virtually halted flights out of the airport. Unfortunately, many of JetBlue's routes departed and returned to JFK. Only 17 of its 156 scheduled flights departed that day before all remaining flights were canceled (Hanna, 2008). Those had a domino effect on the airline at other airports resulting in a total of 250 cancellations that day. While most airlines bounced back quickly from the ice storm's cancellations, JetBlue did not. It was criticized for botching its response to the storm. This case examines the relative transparency with which the company handled the incident that damaged its reputation.

Valentine's Day on the Tarmac at JFK

Valentine's Day was anything but romantic for hundreds of passengers flying out of JFK in 2007. Several flights made it out on the morning of February 14, but the airport was then closed for takeoffs. However, many flights were already boarded and had pushed back from the gates while awaiting take off. These planes were essentially stuck on the tarmac. A *New York Post* article explained the issue: "Empty jets were frozen to the ground, blocking the gates to inbound flights. Departing flights that did escape were unable to get airborne because conditions suddenly changed—and their gates had been filled by other airplanes" (Olshan, 2007, para. 2). Some in-bound passengers were stranded on the plane without a gate for six to eight hours after landing. Departing flights were also stranded.

One such plane, flight 755, was stranded for an astounding 10.5 hours on the runway and gained the most media attention. Flights headed to places like Aruba, Cancun, and Pheonix were filled with initially optimistic vacationers and newlyweds. The fact that passengers were stranded on Valentine's Day heightened their frustrations and sharpened the media's emotional angle on the incident.

Conditions on the grounded planes deteriorated throughout the day. Food and water ran low quickly. One passenger later said, "They had nothing but pretzels and peanuts to give people, and soft drinks" (Olshan, 2007, para. 10). The lines for the bathrooms were long, and the planes' cabins developed a foul odor, and the toilets were overfilled (Pearlman, 2007). One passenger said, "[T]hey had to open the door every 20 minutes just so we could get fresh air" (Olshan, 2007, para. 16). It was a miserable scene. One passenger suffered a panic attack and locked herself in the bathroom for an hour. Perhaps worst of all, the pilots and crew offered little to no information to the passengers about exactly how long they would be stranded. Because of FAA regulations, the crew could not simply open the door, let people deplane themselves, and walk. One passenger remarked, "You gotta realize the frustration—you can look out the window and you can see, there's the gate, if you let us off the plane we can walk there" (Olshan, 2007, para. 13). Rudy Maxa, a travel writer and frequent media guest, commented on the psychological aspects of a situation like JetBlue's stranded passengers' "flying rage" compared to "road rage" when things go wrong: "You have no control [on a plane]. … some people are afraid of flying, because they have no control. They feel they have control of their car, even if they are [stuck] in [snow] drifts" (Conan, 2007, para. 16). JetBlue's long-standing "no cancellations" policy normally assured passengers that they would reach their destination, but in this case it backfired. In the end, the airline canceled all of the stranded flights leaving JFK that day and eventually deplaned all of the passengers.

Unfortunately for the growing airlines and its fliers, the problem was far from over. It took several days until February 20th before the airline was departing 100% of its flights. Passengers might forgive the airline for an extraordinary delay or isolated cancellations. What was more confusing was why JetBlue continued to cancel up to 25% of flights per day almost a week after the ice storm. By the end of the worst week in the airline's history, "over 131,000 [JetBlue] customers [had been] affected by the cancellations, delays, and diversions" (Hanna, 2008, para. 11). JetBlue's historically wonderful reputation made the wave of delays and cancellations even more surprising. Airline industry analysts and media pundits were baffled by how long it took the airline to bounce back. Customers were obviously livid. One customer stranded on Valentine's Day started a blog about the experience that invited fellow passengers to contribute. They posted their videos from the ordeal, and the blog quickly gained media attention.

JetBlue's Response

In many ways, Neeleman's response to the fiasco was effective. He was apologetic, explained exactly what went wrong, and announced steps to make sure the airline didn't repeat its mistake. In the days immediately after February 14, he made numerous media appearances to apologize and attempt to restore customer confidence in the airline. He made appearances on shows like *Late Night with David Letterman* and the *Today Show*. He gave interviews to *New York Times* and *National Public Radio* (NPR). He told *New York Times* he was "humiliated and mortified" (Bailey, 2007, para. 1). Neeleman was in full damage-control mode. Clearly, Neeleman knew the company's reputation for treating customers well was on the line. He Told Matt Lauer on the *Today Show*, "This [storm] affected us to our core and we are determined to not only become better in the future but to put in place processes [to make sure] that it never happens again. … It's not what happens to you [as a company], it's how you react to it and our reaction is going to be unbelievable" (Costello, 2007). In the public's clamor to see somebody fired over the incident, Neeleman stated that he would not fire anybody:

> Accountability rests with the CEO. Even though I wasn't responsible for that particular part of the operation, that's where I spent three days and sleepless nights. And, I know what failed, what can be fixed … and we will be better than any other airline. (Costello, 2007)

For Neeleman's, this experience was a learning experience that would ultimately make JetBlue stronger.

Neeleman also explained in detail the company's weaknesses that made effects of the ice storm last for so long. He said it was operating on a "shoestring communications system" and "an undersized reservation system" (Bailey, para. 2). The ice storm left employees out of position. Neeleman said, "I had flight attendants sitting in hotel rooms for three days who couldn't get a hold of us. I had pilots e-mailing me saying, 'I'm available, what do I do?'" (Bailey, 2007, para. 6). The part of the airline responsible for finding available pilots and crew to point them to their next flight was significantly undersized for a company that had grown as quickly as JetBlue:

> We had a weakness in our system. … [The storm] displaced over 1,000 people, our flight crew members. As they tried to put that back together again, they didn't get it done. Not because [our scheduling people] are not good or we didn't have the system [in place] but we were just overwhelmed by it. (Costello, 2007)

The airline vowed to fix this problem by hiring 300–400% more people to work on scheduling to address the company's growth. Indeed, the company began training additional people to help with scheduling just days after February 14, even before all of its flights were back to normal.

In addition to beefing up the behind-the-scenes operations, Neeleman also announced several pro-passenger policies. The primary reassurance was JetBlue's "Passenger Bill of Rights" ("JetBlue," 2007). This commitment was a centerpiece of Neeleman's media tour and explained that the airline would compensate passengers with specific amounts of money for various types of departure and arrival delays. The amounts were in writing as a self-imposed penalty on the company for not delivering reliable service. For example, a 90-minute to two-hour departure delay would result in an automatic credit of $25 per passenger. Fliers would not even have to request the credit. Two- to three-hour delays resulted in a $50 credit for every customer. In contrast, most airlines do not make a similar offer for delays. Most passengers must argue with the airline individually for any compensation, even for canceled flights. Perhaps most importantly, the Bill of Rights states that planes will not be permitted "to remain on the tarmac for more than three hours" (JetBlue, 2007, p. 1). Travel writer Rudy Maxa praised JetBlue's response in a radio interview on *NPR*. He reminded listeners that many major airlines such as American and Northwest have stranded passengers on the tarmac almost all day in the past and did not respond as well as JetBlue:

> I will say that Jet Blue, actually, is the first airline I've seen, to apologize, you know, within 24 hours—to grovel, to give back the people's money and offer them a free trip. I mean, Northwest [airlines] stonewalled nine years ago when [long delays] all started as if, you know, what, who, me, nobody's here, not us. (Conan, 2007, para. 47)

In contrast, JetBlue applied the Bill of Rights retroactively for all customers affected by the ice storm. This one move alone cost the airline over $30 million (Costello, 2007; Hanna, 2008). The self-imposed penalties were meant to help customers and reassure the public, investors, and media that future weather issues would be one-day events.

Behind the Scenes Tension and Aftermath

While Neeleman's media appearances and statements seemed to hit all the right notes, his less public interactions did not. For instance, he met with Genevieve McCaw, the passenger who started a blog about being stranded on Valentine's Day.

McCaw spoke to the press: "I felt like he was dismissive, and it was insulting" (Pearlman, 2007, para. 10). McGraw left the meeting commenting more on his demeanor than the substance of the conversation: "he seemed to get agitated, really short and speaking over me" (Pearlman, 2007, para. 12). A writer from the influential magazine *FastCompany* interviewed Neeleman and noticed a similar tone. The writer described Neeleman in the interview as "burdened, testy, exhausted" (Slater, 2007, para. 1). Clearly, the sustained pressure was getting to Neeleman. During the interview, he expressed frustration that the media was focusing undue attention on JetBlue but letting other airlines off the hook: "You're overdoing it. Delta screwed people for two days, and we did it for three and a half, okay? So go ask Delta what they did about it. Why don't you grill them?" The reporter wrote in response, "Because Delta is not JetBlue. Neither is American [Airlines]. The fact that those airlines stranded customers during the storm isn't surprising. They simply met the public's low expectations. JetBlue is an airline that aspires to be better" (Slater, 2007, para. 7). About fifty minutes into the interview, Neeleman snapped, "Look, I haven't slept in three weeks … I'm tired of talking. Emotionally, I am done … I just want to go out and run the company" (Slater, 2007, para. 1). The reporter also credits Neeleman for apologizing unexpectedly a few minutes later for snapping at him.

Without question, Neeleman's media blitz and the promised changes helped turn JetBlue's immediate crisis around. Other storms hit with little effect on JetBlue. For instance, another ice storm shut down JFK on March 16. A top executive at JetBlue explained that the next day "we had a flight completion factor of 98%. I'm very proud of that" (Reed, 2007, para. 13). Nevertheless, the Valentine's Day ice storm revealed much deeper issues than its inability to handle bad weather. The airline was struggling with its growth, and behind-the-scene changes were already happening. The company's inability to respond well to an ice storm simply revealed that its systems and operations were inadequate to sustain the airline's growth. An analyst who follows the airline industry commented after the ice storm that the airline now "knows it has to make some changes if it wants to be around long term … [and go] from a scrappy start-up to a more mature carrier" (Reed, 2007, para. 7). Even though Neeleman promised that nobody would be fired over the Valentine's Day crisis, most top executives were replaced in the months that followed. The new leaders put entirely new systems in place and built the company's capacity to keep up with its growth. In other words, these firings were not to punish the

Questions:

- How would you rate Neeleman's response to JetBlue's crisis?
- Given Neeleman's high level of transparency, why do you believe he ultimately lost his job? Is there anything he could have done differently to keep his job?

former executives but to acquire different skill sets needed to help the airline get to the next level. Entrepreneurial leadership needed to conceptualize, inspire, and start a brand new kind of company are not necessarily those needed to manage, maintain, and grow a company on a day-to-day basis. In the end, David Neeleman was removed as CEO a few months after the crisis had passed and was given a role as a non-executive chairman of the company. He later left this post and started a new airline, Azul, now the third largest airline in Brazil, where he was born (Sciaudone & Almeida, 2015).

Treating "Patient Zero" for Ebola at Texas Health Presbyterian Hospital: Mistakes, Apologies, and Changes

In 2014, a massive Ebola outbreak swept through West Africa in countries like Liberia, Sierra Leone, and Guinea. It began in early 2014 and spread to tens of thousands of people. By the end of 2014, the epidemic was the largest in history with over 11,000 confirmed deaths from Ebola in six countries (CDC, 2015c). Media in the US began to take notice as the virus spread, particularly when the infections spread to faith-based healthcare volunteers from the US. In August 2014, Dr. Kent Brantly with Samaritan's Purse, for instance, was flown back from Liberia for treatment. At the time, some people publicly criticized the decision to bring the physician, and thus, the virus, to the US. Donald Trump, for example, received media attention for repeatedly tweeting opposition. Trump tweeted, "The U.S. cannot allow EBOLA infected people back. People that go to far away places to help out are great-but must suffer the consequences!" (Bailey, 2014, para. 12). In October 2014, some people's worst fears appeared to be coming true when a confirmed case of Ebola was reported at Texas Health Presbyterian Hospital in Dallas. The patient, Thomas Duncan, was evaluated, quickly misdiagnosed, and released by the hospital even though he told them he had recently traveled from Liberia and displayed typical early-stage Ebola symptoms. He returned to the hospital two days later and was admitted but died on October 8th after a week and a half of hospitalization. Duncan became known as "patient zero" or the first case diagnosed in the US. The hospital fell under close scrutiny because his misdiagnosis may have increased the likelihood of his death. Further, healthcare workers at the hospital were treating a patient who they did not know had Ebola, and the hospital's protocols for handling Ebola were not clear and consistent. Unfortunately, two nurses contracted the virus while treating Duncan. Many people blame the hospital for numerous mistakes and the inconsistent communication from hospital leaders. This case explores those early missteps as well as the hospital's level of transparency during and following the crisis.

What Is Ebola?

Ebola is still a mysterious virus. According to the Centers for Disease Control (CDC), Ebola is a virus "first discovered in 1976 near the Ebola River" in an area of Africa now called the Congo (CDC, 2015a, para. 3). The deadly virus often spreads among animal carriers, such as fruit bats and monkeys, who may infect humans. It spreads among infected humans through direct contact with bodily fluids such as "urine, saliva, sweat, feces, vomit, breast milk, and semen" as well as through sharing needles and syringes infected with the virus (CDC, 2015c, para. 2). Like many viruses, Ebola often spreads when these bodily fluids inadvertently come in contact with an individual's broken skin, eyes, nose, or mouth (e.g., shaking an infected person's hand and later scratching one's own eye). It cannot, however, be transmitted through the air. Healthcare workers as well as family members caring for infected patients are at the highest risk for contracting the virus. In its early stages, Ebola is difficult to detect because symptoms, such as fever and headache, are common to many viruses. Within several days, patients exhibit more acute symptoms such as muscle pain, diarrhea, vomiting, and unexplained bleeding or bruising (CDC, 2015b). Currently, no approved vaccine or medicine is available to treat Ebola directly. Most patients who recover do so largely based upon patients' own immune system and timely treatment of the symptoms (i.e., providing intravenous fluids, maintaining an oxygen supply, etc.). Unfortunately, approximately 50% or more of Ebola patients die. Only experimental or "investigative" drugs such as "Brincidofovir" are currently available to treat the virus (Varga, 2014, p. 3), but these are not widely available. Testing on vaccines continues but is in the early stages.

Texas Health Presbyterian Hospital's Misdiagnosis of Patient Zero

Texas Health Presbyterian Hospital (THPH) opened in 1966 on the site of a former orphanage. Both the orphanage and the hospital were directly connected to a Presbyterian church in the area ("History," 2015). Over the next several decades, THPH grew to a facility with almost 900 beds and 1,200 physicians. At around 10:30 p.m. on September 25, 2014, Thomas Duncan arrived at THPH's emergency room. Duncan, 42, was on his first trip to the US. He lived in Liberia full time and came to visit friends and family in the Dallas area. When admitted, he had a temperature of 101.1°F and complained to his nurse about "abdominal pain, dizziness, nausea and headache" ("Notable Elements," 2014, p. 1). At this point, Duncan's symptoms were still common to many viruses and did not indicate that he had Ebola specifically. Among other questions, his nurse asked him about his travel history and noted that he travelled "from Africa 9/20/14," five days prior. At the time, the information did not strike the nurse as particularly relevant, and she did not tell the physician about it directly, as prompted by the hospital's protocol and Centers for Disease Control guidelines. Instead, she recorded the information into the hospital's Electronic Health Record in routine fashion along with the other information she gathered about Duncan.

When he met with a physician an hour later, he told the physician that he was a "local resident," that "he had not been in contact with sick people, and that he had not experienced nausea, vomiting or diarrhea" ("Notable Elements," 2014, p. 2). The Electronic Health Record shows that the physician accessed various data about Duncan throughout his treatment but did not indicate the physician directly viewed Duncan's travel history. Over the next two hours, Duncan's temperature spiked to 103°F but returned to 101°F. At 3:37 a.m. on September 26, his physician recorded, "patient is feeling better and comfortable with going home" ("Notable Elements," 2014, p. 2). The physician discharged Duncan with a diagnosis of abdominal pain and a sinus infection. He told Duncan to take his medication, drink plenty of fluids, and return if he experienced increased pain, vomiting, a higher fever, or any other symptoms. It is important to note that Duncan was released despite telling a hospital employee directly about his recent travel from Africa and that this information was not relayed face-to-face to his physician. According to hospital protocol, it should have been. Further, the physician should have asked more specific questions about his recent travel. Duncan returned to the hospital two days later on September 28 by ambulance, was almost immediately identified as a potential Ebola patient, and the hospital notified the CDC. The hospital began aggressive treatment and Duncan was the first Ebola patient to receive the experimental drug Brincidofovir. Unfortunately, Duncan died on October 8, 2014.

Hospital Leaders Send Mixed Messages and Admit Mistakes

The first few days of Thomas Duncan's admission and treatment were confusing for all involved. The hospital was in unknown territory treating Ebola and scrambled to figure out how the patient was initially misdiagnosed and sent home. In the confusion, the hospital released conflicting reports. Initially, it stated that a problem with its Electronic Health Records (EHR) system prevented Duncan's physician adequate access to his travel history. A few days later and while Duncan was still alive, the hospital reversed that statement and explained, "[T]he patient's travel history was documented and available to the full care team in the electronic health record" (Fernandez, Shear, & Goodnough, 2014, para. 4). Leaders later apologized more fully for the mistake. Dr. Daniel Varga, the Chief Clinical Officer and a Senior Executive Vice President, stated, "[I]n our effort to communicate to the public quickly and transparently, we inadvertently provided some information that was inaccurate and had to be corrected. No doubt that was unsettling to a community that was already concerned and confused" (Varga, 2014, pp. 1–2). He also offered his heartfelt apology publicly about Duncan's death as he spoke to a congressional house committee via satellite video feed:

> It's hard for me to put into words how we felt when our patient Thomas Eric Duncan lost his struggle with Ebola on October 8. It was devastating to the nurses, doctors, and team who tried so hard to save his life. We keep his family in our thoughts and prayers. Unfortunately, in our initial treatment of Mr. Duncan, despite our best intentions and a highly skilled medical team, we made mistakes. We did not correctly diagnose his symptoms as those of Ebola. We are deeply sorry. (Varga, 2014, p. 1)

In addition to his apology, he disclosed the exact points at which Duncan's travel history fell through the communicative cracks and their failure to take proper action. The hospital concluded that "communication [from the hospital to employees about Ebola] is critical but it is no substitute for training" (Varga, 2014, p. 4) workers exactly how to enact the new protocols. In short, the hospital admitted it had not adequately prepared the staff. Among the changes were steps to make sure that future incoming patients' travel history was recorded immediately and displayed more prominently in the Electronic Health Record for all to see. High-risk patients' initial interview questions were also changed to gather more specific information about potential Ebola exposure. Further, hospital staff would be required to attend all training related to treating Ebola patients. In the past, the hospital offered such training, but it was not mandatory.

Nurses Test Positive for Ebola Amid Confusing Protocols

At some point during his treatment, two hospital nurses who were caring for Duncan contracted the Ebola virus. Nina Pham, a nurse who had extensive contact with Duncan on multiple occasions, tested positive for the Ebola virus on Saturday, October 11, after getting a fever the day before. At first, Dr. Tom Friedman from the CDC sounded like he was indirectly blaming the nurse at a news conference: "At some point, there was a breach in protocol, and that breach in protocol resulted in this infection … protocols work. … But we know that even a single lapse or breach can result in infection" (Cohen, Almasy, & Yan, 2014, para. 9). Pham's lawyer responded on her behalf: "Nina said, 'What do I do? What do I wear?' and her nurse manager printed out a piece of paper from the CDC, and that is the sum total of the training this young lady received. … She wasn't given the proper equipment, and she wasn't taught how to put it on and take it off" (Pérez-Peña, 2015, para. 8). The protective gear the hospital initially issued nurses left portions of their necks exposed to potential contact. Nurses were told to cover their necks with medical tape to cover exposed areas, but it is not clear whether or not all nurses complied. The nurses were concerned that the tape would harm their skin upon removal, which could make a potential contamination more likely. The hospital quickly replaced that gear with more adequate protective clothing and equipment.

Nurses in Dallas and indeed across the country complained that their respective hospitals did not adequately train them to handle Ebola patients either. A spokesperson for a national nurses union stated, "The protocols that should have been in place [for healthcare workers interacting with Ebola patients] in Dallas were not in place, and that those protocols are not in place anywhere in the United States as far as we can tell" (Shoichet, 2014, para. 2). The Ebola training for nurses was not mandatory at the time and not treated as more relevant than the hundreds of other training seminars nurses are invited to attend. Even the act of removing protective garments and gear after treating a patient is a meticulous process that requires thorough training. One misstep can result in coming in direct contact with the virus.

On October 13, a second nurse, Amber Vinson, who also gave care to Duncan, was undergoing self-monitoring of potential Ebola symptoms as the CDC had instructed (Levs & Yan, 2015). She took her own temperature 99.5°F and tested positive for Ebola the next day. Vinson and all who treated Duncan had been instructed by the CDC not to fly on commercial flights. After taking her temperature, Vinson boarded a plane from Cleveland to Dallas potentially exposing 132 other Frontier Airline passengers. She had flown from Dallas to Cleveland three days earlier. Both Vinson and Pham recovered from the Ebola Virus in about two weeks, likely because they monitored their own temperatures numerous times daily as instructed by the CDC and hospital officials. As result, they were each quickly placed in isolated units, and care started without delay. The nurses were the only two cases of Ebola that were transmitted in the US.

Virus Contained in US, Continues in Africa

In the US, the Ebola virus was quickly contained. Texas Health Presbyterian Hospital clearly made mistakes, especially in the first few days of interacting with Duncan. The hospital's mere notification of the staff about updated CDC guidelines was not an adequate preparation for handling actual Ebola patients. Nevertheless, the hospital's openness about its mistakes early on likely helped it and other hospitals and healthcare professions in the nation make quick adjustments to prepare for additional US Ebola cases. In the days that followed Duncan's admission and treatment, officials quickly admitted their mistakes publicly. Leaders held regular press conferences, spoke publicly to Congress, and communicated daily with the CDC to make sure they were following protocols correctly. These changes and training clearly worked as the virus did not spread beyond the two nurses who likely made contact with the virus before the hospital adapted to the CDC's Ebola protocols. Further, the hospital quickly reached a legal settlement with Duncan's family only a month after his death. His family's lawyer described the hospital's interaction throughout the settlement negotiations as "cooperative" and added, "This settlement is as good if not better than the family might have received if they went to court" (Silverstein, 2014, para. 5).

Questions:

- Are you satisfied with THPH leaders' level of transparency about the hospital's mistakes?
- What do you recommend they do to improve their communication in the future?

Nina Pham, the first nurse to contract the virus, praised the hospital staff as "best team of doctors and nurses in the world" but later filed a lawsuit in 2015 against the hospital calling for even greater transparency about behind-the-scenes hospital preparedness. She stated, "I'm facing a number of issues with regard to my health and my career, and the lawsuit provides a way to address them. But more importantly, it will help uncover the truth of what happened, and educate all healthcare providers and administrators about ways to be better prepared for the next public health emergency" (Hennessy-Fiske, 2015, para. 6). The investigation into exactly how Pham came into contact was incomplete as of this writing. Meanwhile, the number of total cases in West African countries continued to climb throughout 2016. Healthcare workers there, who are often volunteers, remain at the greatest risk.

Chapter Discussion Questions

- How did transparency ultimately help these organizations? In what ways did their responses require courage?

- How do you believe the transparency shown in these cases will likely shape their organizational cultures in the future? Do you believe the outcome would have changed had they taken a secretive approach?
- To what extent do these organizations support employees' and customers' need to make a significant choice about the organization?

Key Terms

- Transparency
- Organizational openness
- Disclosure
- Pluralistic ignorance
- Candor
- Significant choice

References

Antonioni, D. (2006). Practicing candor. *Industrial Management, January/February*, 24–30.

Benoit, W. L. (1997). Image repair discourse and crisis communication. *Public Relations Review, 23*, 177–186.

Christianson, L. T. (2002). Corporate communication: The challenge of transparency. *Corporate Communications: An International Journal, 7*, 162–168.

Christianson, L. T., & Langer, R. (2009). Public relations and the strategic use of transparency: Consistency, hypocrisy, and corporate change. In: R. L. Heath, E. Toth, & D. Waymer (Eds.), *Rhetorical and critical approaches to public relations II* (pp. 129–153). Hillsdale, NY: Routledge.

DeTienne, K., & Lewis, L. (2005). The pragmatic and ethical barriers to corporate social responsibility disclosure: The Nike case. *Journal of Business Ethics, 82*, 391–406.

Florini, A. (2007). The battle over transparency. In A. Florini (Ed.), *The right to know: Transparency for an open world* (pp. 1–18). New York, NY: Columbia University Press.

Lencioni, P. (2002). *The five dysfunctions of a team: A leadership fable.* San Francisco, CA: Jossey-Bass.

Lyon, A. (2007). "Putting Patients First": Systematically distorted communication and Merck's marketing of Vioxx. *Journal of Applied Communication Research, 35*, 376–398.

Lyon, A., & Ricci, M. (2012). The case of Wyeth, DesignWrite, and Premarin: The ethics of ghost-writing medical journal articles. In: Steve May (Ed.), *Case studies in organizational communication: Ethical perspectives and practices* (2nd ed., pp. 197–206). Thousand Oaks, CA: Sage.

May, S. (2013). *Case studies in organizational communication: Ethical perspectives and practices* (2nd ed.). Thousand Oaks, CA: Sage.

Nadesan, H. (2013). Transparency and neo-liberal logics of corporate economic and social responsibility. In: Ø. Inlen, J. Bartlett, & S. May (Eds.), *The handbook of communication and corporate social responsibility* (pp. 252–275). West Sussex: Wiley-Blackwell.

Nilsen, T. R. (1974). *Ethics of speech communication* (2nd ed.). Indianapolis, IN: Bobbs-Merrill.

Rawlins, B. (2009). Give the emperor a mirror: Toward developing a stakeholder measurement of organizational transparency. *Journal of Public Relations Research, 21*, 71–99.

Rogers, D. P. (1987). Development of a measure of perceived communication openness. *Journal of Business Communication, 24*, 53–61.

Sellnow, T. L., Ulmer, R. R., & Snider, M. (1998). The compatibility of corrective action in organizational crisis communication. *Communication Quarterly, 46*, 60–74.

Ulmer, R. R., & Sellnow, T. L. (1997). Strategic ambiguity and the ethic of significant choice in the tobacco industry's crisis communication. *Communication Studies, 48*, 215–233.

Weick, K. E. (1990). The vulnerable system: An analysis of the Tenerife air disaster. *Journal of Management, 16*, 571–593.

Weiner, A. (2006). *So smart but. ...: How intelligent people lose credibility and how they can get it back.* San Francisco, CA: Jossey-Bass.

Whipple, R. T. (2009). *Leading with trust is like sailing downwind.* Provo, UT: Executive Excellence Publishing.

Massachusetts General Hospital References

David Ring named as new chief of the Hand and Upper Extremity Service. (2013). [Internal hospital news release]. Retrieved from http://www.massgeneral.org/ortho/news/newsarticle.aspx?id=4251

Gibson, J. (2010, November 11). Lemonade from a lemon [comments section of *NEJM's* online version]. Retrieved November 15, 2013 from http://www.nejm.org/doi/full/10.1056/NEJMcpc1007085#t=comments.

Glantz, L. (2010, November 12). Fine example of ethical behavior. [comments section of *NEJM's* online version]. Retrieved November 15, 2013 from http://www.nejm.org/doi/full/10.1056/NEJMcpc1007085#t=comments.

Kiss, G. (2010, November 13). A professional example of high standards. [comment on *NEJM's* online version]. Retrieved November 15, 2013 from http://www.nejm.org/doi/full/10.1056/NEJMcpc1007085#t=comments.

Leonard, K. (2013). Best hospitals 2013–14: Overview and honor roll. *U.S. News and World Report.* Retrieved from http://health.usnews.com/health-news/best-hospitals/articles/2013/07/16/best-hospitals-2013-14-overview-and-honor-roll

Mann, R. (2010, November 11). Courageous and helpful [comments section of *NEJM's* online version] Retrieved November 15, 2013 from http://www.nejm.org/doi/full/10.1056/NEJMcpc1007085#t=comments.

Ring, D. C., Herndon, J. H., & Meyer, G. S. (2010). Case 34-2010: A 65-year-old woman with an incorrect operation on the left hand. *New England Journal of Medicine, 363*, 1950–1957.

Wong, D. A., Herndon, J. H., Canale, S. T., Brooks, R. L., Hunt, T. R., Epps, H. R., ... Johanson, N. A. (2009). Medical errors in orthopaedics: Results of an AAOS member survey. *Journal of Bone Joint Surgery of (A), 91*, 547–557.

Wong, D. A., Lewis, B., Herndon, J., Martin, C., & Brooks R. (2009). Patient safety in North America: beyond "operate through your initials" and "sign your site." *Journal of Bone Joint Surgery of (A), 91*, 1534–1541.

Taco Bell References

Barclay, E. (2011). With lawsuit over, Taco Bell's mystery meat is a mystery no longer. *National Public Radio.* Retrieved from http://www.npr.org/blogs/health/2011/04/22/135539926/with-lawsuit-over-taco-bells-mystery-meat-is-a-mystery-no-longer

Creed, C. (2011a). Taco Bell: Of course we use real beef [Public relations video]. Retrieved July 23, 2014 from http://www.youtube.com/watch?v=ah05FEWcJWM.

Creed, C. (2011b). Updated class action lawsuit statement. [Press release]. Retrieved from http://www.tacobell.com/Company/newsreleases/UPDATED_CLASS_ACTION_LAWSUIT_STATEMENT_2011

Dawson, K. (2011). Lawsuit filed over Taco Bell's meat. *Indiana Public Media.* Retrieved from http://indianapublicmedia.org/eartheats/lawsuit-filled-taco-bells-meat/

Hutchison, C., & Moisse, K. (2011). Taco bell fights "Where's the Beef" lawsuit. *ABCnews.com.* Retrieved from http://abcnews.go.com/Health/Wellness/taco-bell-defends-beef-legal-action/story?id=12785818

McFadden, R. D. (2006). E. Coli sickens 39 in New Jersey and New York. *New York Times.* Retrieved from http://www.nytimes.com/2006/12/05/nyregion/05coli.html?pagewanted=all&_r=0

Morran, C. (2010). Taco Bell sued over salmonella outbreak. *Consumerist.* Retrieved July 23, 2014 from http://consumerist.com/2010/08/09/taco-bell-sued-over-salmonella-outbreak/.

Real employees, real seasoned beef, unreal offer. (2011). [Press release]. Retrieved from http://www.tacobell.com/Company/newsreleases/REAL_SEASONED_BEEF_UNREAL_OFFER_2011

Smith, A. (2011). Taco Bell: "Thanks for suing us." *CNN.com.* Retrieved from http://money.cnn.com/2011/01/28/news/companies/taco_bell_beef/

Taco Bell asks attorneys; Would it kill you to say you're sorry? (2011a). [Press release]. Retrieved from http://pwrnewmedia.com/2011/taco_bell/beef_grade/index.html

Taco Bell Sued over meat that's just 35 percent beef. (2011b). *Foxnews.com.* Retrieved from http://www.foxnews.com/health/2011/01/25/wheres-beef-taco-bell-sued-ingredients

JetBlue References

Bailey, J. (2007, February 19). JetBlue's C.E.O. Is "mortified" after fliers are stranded. *New York Times.* Retrieved from http://www.nytimes.com/2007/02/19/business/19jetblue.html?pagewanted=all&_r=0

Conan, N. (2007, February 19). Delays, passengers and a bill of rights. *NPR.* Retrieved from http://www.npr.org/templates/story/story.php?storyId=7488530

Costello, T. (2007). Jet Blues. After the storm: Back in the air. *Today Show, NBC*. Retrieved from https://www.youtube.com/watch?v=1V2ff3easYc

Hanna, J. (2008). JetBlue's Valentine's day crisis. *Working Knowledge*. Retrieved from http://hbswk.hbs.edu/item/5880.html

JetBlue Airlines' customer bill of rights. (2007, April 15). *Jetblue.com*. Retrieved from http://www.jetblue.com/p/about/ourcompany/promise/Bill_Of_Rights.pdf

Neeleman, D. (2007). Our promise to you [video]. *On JetBlueCorpComm*. Retrieved from https://www.youtube.com/watch?v=-r_PIg7EAUw

Olshan, J. (2007, February 15). 10 hrs. On JetGlue. *New York Post*. Retrieved from http://nypost.com/2007/02/15/10-hrs-on-jetglue

Our company: History. (2015). *Jetblue.com*. Retrieved from http://www.jetblue.com/about/ourcompany/history.aspx

Pearlman, T. (2007, March 9). JetBlue "hostage" unhappy with CEO. *Oakland Tribune*. Retrieved from http://www.insidebayarea.com/dailyreview/localnews/ci_5394009

Reed, D. (2007, February 26). Airline again forced to cancel hundreds of flights. *USAToday.com*. Retrieved from http://usatoday30.usatoday.com/travel/flights/2007-02-26-flight-delay-usat_x.htm

Sciaudone, C., & Almeida, H. (2015, May 17). Azul founder Neeleman submits bid to acquire TAP Portugal. *Bloomberg*. Retrieved from http://skift.com/2015/05/17/azul-founder-neeleman-submits-bid-to-acquire-tap-portugal

Slater, C. (2007, May). Lessons from the tarmac. *Fastcompany*. Retrieved from http://www.fastcompany.com/59573/lessons-tarmac

Texas Health Presbyterian Hospital References

Bailey, S. P. (2014, September 8). Ann Coulter, Donald Trump Ebola comments prompt Christian backlash. *Huffington Post*. Retrieved from http://www.huffingtonpost.com/2014/08/08/ann-coulter-ebola_n_5662698.html

CDC. (2015a). About Ebola virus disease. Retrieved from http://www.cdc.gov/vhf/ebola/about.html

CDC. (2015b). Signs and symptoms. Retrieved from http://www.cdc.gov/vhf/ebola/symptoms/index.html

CDC. (2015c). Transmission. Retrieved from http://www.cdc.gov/vhf/ebola/transmission/index.html

Cohen, E., Almasy, S., & Yan, H. (2014). Texas nurse who had worn protective gear tests positive for Ebola. *CNN.com*. Retrieved from http://www.cnn.com/2014/10/12/health/ebola/index.html

Fernandez, M., Shear, M. D., & Goodnough, A. (2014). Dallas hospital alters account, raising questions on Ebola case. [Electronic version]. *New York Times*. Retrieved from http://www.nytimes.com/2014/10/04/us/containing-ebola-cdc-troops-west-africa.html?_r=0

Hennessy-Fiske, M. (2015, March 3). Nina Pham, Dallas nurse who survived Ebola, sues hospital. *Los Angeles Times*. Retrieved from http://www.latimes.com/nation/la-na-nina-pham-sues-hospital-ebola-20150302-story.html

History. (2015). Texas Health Presbyterian Hospital. [website]. Retrieved May 1, 2015 from https://www.texashealth.org/dallas/Pages/History.aspx.

Levs, J., & Yan, H. (2015, October 15). CDC: U.S. health worker with Ebola should not have flown on commercial jet. *CNN.com*. Retrieved from http://www.cnn.com/2014/10/15/health/texas-ebola-outbreak/index.html

Notable elements of Mr. Duncan's initial emergency department visit (2014, October 16). *House Energy and Commerce Committee*. Retrieved from http://energycommerce.house.gov/sites/republicans.energycommerce.house.gov/files/Hearings/OI/20141016/Timeline2.pdf

Shoichet, C. (2014, October 15). Nurses' union slams Texas hospital for lack of Ebola protocol. *CNN.com*. Retrieved from http://www.cnn.com/2014/10/15/health/texas-ebola-nurses-union-claims/index.html

Silverstein, E. (2014, November 19). Thomas Eric Duncan's family reaches settlement with Dallas hospital after Ebola death. *Inside Counsel*. Retrieved from http://www.insidecounsel.com/2014/11/19/thomas-eric-duncans-family-reaches-settlement-with

9 Tips, Tools, and Resources to Move from Secrecy to Transparency

As with tips, tools, and resources in Chapters 3 and 6, this one provides additional strategies to communicate more transparently amid organizational pressure to keep quiet. It also offers face-attentive ways, suggests strategies for overcoming the moral mum effect, and explores the dynamics of apologizing and forgiving in professional settings.

Crafting Difficult Messages and the Role of Face

One of the main forces preventing us from speaking about controversial issues is our desire to help others maintain or save face. Words like "face" and "honor" are not currently as common in US and European workplaces as they are in other parts of the world, such as Japan (e.g., Tanaka, 2011). Nevertheless, we are aware of our own and others' reputations during interactions. As Bisel, Messersmith, and Kelley (2012) define it, "Face refers to the public self-image each of us claim for ourselves" (p. 131). Most of us want to be seen in a positive light. Bisel et al. explain the desire to be free from imposition and maintain an esteemed face are attributes common to all human beings. We all have a basic "desire for approval and acceptance from others" (Erbert & Floyd, 2004, p. 255). Consequently, most of us adjust our language or do "facework" when approaching others. As Bisel et al. (2011) define it, "Face*work* is any attempt to counter, to mend, or to mitigate the effect of face threatening actions" (p. 155) by softening or shaping our language. Below are three ways to craft difficult messages that preserve other people's face.

Helping others Maintain Face

Our conversational approach matters. Researchers (e.g., Brown & Levinson, 1987; Dunleavy et al., 2008; Erbert & Floyd, 2004, etc.) categorize five strategies of delivering potential face-threatening communication, known as "face-threatening acts" (FTA). They move roughly from most severe to least.

- ***Bald-on-record***. The speaker makes no attempt to soften a message or help the other person maintain face (e.g., "Your direction is wrong.").
- ***Positive politeness***. The speaker shapes the message to minimize threats to the person's face by appealing to the listener's otherwise positive qualities and emphasizing the mutual desires of both parties (e.g., "You're a great leader and you normally lead us in the right direction. I think this particular decision would not be your best.").
- ***Negative politeness***. This strategy reduces the perceived imposition the message causes the listener and minimizes face threat (e.g., "If we made just a few small changes, I think this will be headed in the right direction. It won't take long to tweak.").
- ***Off-the-record***. A message is never stated directly but only implied. A listener could interpret these indirect messages in a variety of ways.
- ***Forgo the FTA***. The speaker does not share the message with the potential listener. This non-message has arguably no impact on the listener's face.

Our conversational messages may not fit neatly into these categories, but these terms can be useful reference points from which to shape potentially difficult messages in less face-threatening ways.

Notice how the employee and leader in the following brief dialogue help each other save face about not meeting a deadline. The *positive* and *negative politeness* phrases are italicized.

Employee: *I realize you're very busy.* I wanted to talk about something. *It will only take a moment.*

Leader: *It's no problem at all. I have the time.*

Employee: *You've probably already figured this out but* I wanted to bring something to your attention. *Your deadlines are usually spot on and very reasonable.* And, the team is working hard on the project. But now that we're underway, I don't think that deadline is attainable.

Leader: I've gotten the sense that you might be behind. Tell me more.
Employee: There are more moving parts on this than usual. *Normally, I'd say a deadline like this is doable.* On this particular project, *if it's not too much trouble,* I think the deadline needs to be adjusted *just by about a week or two* to get it right.
Leader: I hear you. *I'm glad you brought this to my attention.* Let me take a look at the pending projects on the calendar and *I'll see what I can do.*
Employee: *I appreciate that you took the time to listen.*

The employee's face-attentive messages position the leader in an esteemed position. The leader, too, makes it easy for the employee to share his or her message. He signals that it is perfectly reasonable to sit down and talk about the issue and even thanks the employee for participating in the conversation.

Use of Stories for Challenging Topics

Direct advice confronts people with their shortcomings. Harrison and Barlow (2009) discuss how narratives communicate advice *indirectly.* Few methods resonate as well as a timely, well-told, non-face-threatening story. In professional settings, we can choose from endless success stories, cautionary tales, and recountings of tricky situations. For problematic issues, stories should be concise. A complete one can be told in as little as 30 seconds or less. The following three-point template can help structure a quick story.

- **Beginning:** Includes the people, time, and place involved
- **Middle:** Includes the most relevant actions or decisions in the story
- **Ending:** Includes the resolution of the events

The moral of the story is the sometimes-unspoken fourth point in the format. Most listeners will quickly connect the dots: "If somebody is being bullied, we should do something about it." Stories are also safe ways to introduce problem areas because they don't point the finger at anybody. They empower all listeners to become part of the solution: "We're not going to let that happen here!"

A story fitted to the circumstance is an effective way to introduce a touchy subject. Bisel et al. (2011), for instance, suggest that leaders relate their own past shortcomings or courageous moments.

> We recommend that managers look for opportunities to tell and retell instances of their own unethical behavior as well as the heroism of labeling behavior as unethical. [e.g.,

> using organizational technology for personal use, etc.]. … Managerial narratives about how these actions are committed, raised to the level of mindful inspection by talk, and then ceased or remedied will produce positive organizational culturing. (pp. 165–166)

Stories are a powerful way to help others feel normal and free to share negative information (e.g., Keenen, 2000). We make it much easier for others to bring up their concerns when we smoothly discuss our own mistakes or how we handled missteps.

Talking in Problem-Solution Format

A third way to bring up touchy subjects is to appeal to the facts of the situation and suggest a solution. According to research by Kassing (2005, 2002), employees see these two related strategies as the most credible:

- ***Solution presentation*** by "providing solutions to address the dissent triggering issue rather than or in addition to evidence." (2002, p. 196)
- ***Direct-factual appeal*** by "supporting dissent claim with factual information derived from some combination of physical evidence, knowledge of organizational policies and practices, and personal work experience." (2002, p. 196)

Similarly, Weiner (2006) suggested that professionals gain credibility when they communicate difficult messages in problem-solution order with evidence and in a minimum amount of time. The following template (Box 9.1) is modeled after Weiner's (2006, p. 28) while keeping Kassing's (2002, 2005) findings in mind. A communicator can use the talking points to deliver a challenging message in about 30 seconds.

Each point should use only one or two sentences. Here's an example of how this would look following Weiner's (2006) points.

> *[Problem]* We've heard some concerning feedback about Burt Johnson. He has been reporting some questionable travel expenses that go far beyond what the other managers spend on a typical business trip. *[Consequences]* Of course, it might be an innocent mistake. Either way, it's upsetting some people who travel with him and he's draining funds we'll need later in the year. *[Solution]* I suggest we meet with him privately, go over his last three reimbursement requests and clarify the policy before it goes any further. *[Action]* If you agree, I can schedule a meeting with him before his trip next week.

People sometimes have trouble boiling down difficult issues into succinct statements. The payoff is worth it. As Weiner (2006) shows, crisp messages create the impression that we are prepared and assertive, even if we feel nervous.

Box 9.1. Problem-Solution Talking Points.

Name the problem that could hurt the company if it is not addressed.

Suggested ways to start this statement

- "I've become uncomfortable with the high levels of ..."
- "We've heard some concerning feedback about ..."
- "I wanted to bring something to your attention that I'm concerned is hurting us."

Show the consequences, evidence, and reasons for how it's bad for business in the long run if it is not addressed.

Suggested ways to start this statement

- "It's creating a bad impression with customers."
- "This is costing us ____________ every day we don't address it."
- "It's hurting morale and productivity."

Suggest a solution.

Suggested ways to start this statement

- "We should [insert action] before this gets out of hand."
- "Here's what I think we should do ..."
- "It's time to ..."

Offer to take the first step of the solution.

Suggested ways to start this statement

- "If you agree, then what I'd like to do is ..."
- "Here's what I'm *personally* willing to do at this point ..."
- "The first step of my plan is to ..."

Mindset Minute: Are You Committed to Transparency?

The most important prerequisite for transparent communication is the right mindset that avoids secrecy. If we have a habit of being "tight lipped" about problems, we likely buy into such sayings as "loose lips sink ships." Thus, if our commitment to transparency is not deeply entrenched, tools, tips, and resources alone will not overcome the fear, anxiety, and other emotions driving our silence. If we acknowledge

Box 9.2. Statements That Signal a Secretive Mindset.

When people say ...	They might mean ...
"Let's keep this between us."	This is a secret.
"It's business. What can you do?"	We have to accept wrong activities.
"It happens throughout the industry."	If others are doing it, it's acceptable.
"If you want to play with the big boys, this is how the game is played."	To get ahead, you have to do things that are wrong.

that transparent communication is preferable, the best way to develop a deeper commitment and mindset is through practice. I suggest three ways.

First, we should be role models for transparent communication when we respond to minor issues. You can, for instance, look for opportunities where you did not deliver 100% on a project. Publicize your small blunders. You could say at a meeting, "We're a week late. We weren't able to accomplish everything we'd hoped. That said, I'm thankful we did, in fact, launch our project and make it over the finish line." Leaders who practice this habit for small gaffes find it easier to discuss larger mistakes.

Second, we can ask questions rather than make decisive statements. If you feel uneasy in a given situation, others probably do as well. You could ask, "How do you all feel about promoting John given his past character issues?" Questions create conversational space to talk about potential problems in a less face-threatening way compared to stating a direct opinion.

Third, we should encourage others' transparency outright. You could say, for example, "Sharron, I appreciate all the details and transparency you've provided. You've kept us in the loop throughout this difficult issue." This signals to the communicator and to anybody in earshot that disclosure and openness are ideal. Take every opportunity to say, "I appreciate your honesty." See Boxes 9.2 and 9.4 to gauge your mindset by the statements you make.

Ways to Overcome the Moral Mum Effect

As Chapter 7 explains, people often avoid discussing ethically questionable behaviors as described by the moral mum effect. We tend not to talk about underlying issues that can harm our organizations the most. Three practical ways to start these important conversations are powerful questions, coupling issues, and an outsider's perspective.

Moral and ethical questions. To discuss the taboo topic is to use morally evaluative labels. In US society, we find labels disempowering and even harsh. However, we can harness their power to pinpoint behaviors that will harm the organization, its members, and/or its clients. Thus, labeling wrong behavior is sometimes necessary. Labels such as ethical/unethical, right/wrong, good/bad, etc. destabilize cultural norms and cast harmful behavior as normal (Bisel et al., 2011). Labels like "wrong," for example, provide an alternative value with which to make sense of behavior that we might otherwise tolerate. The easiest path into a discussion like this is by posing a question that interjects a moral dimension into the discussion. Bisel et al. (2011) suggest the following sample questions "as a template that should be adjusted to particular situations to facilitate difficult conversations" (p. 165):

- Remember we did X and later found it was less-than-ethical? How might this situation be similar?
- What piece of information might lead an outsider to believe that our actions appear morally wrong?
- Let's say that we would be deemed solely responsible for the consequences of any unethical behavior in the workgroup. How does that change our view of this decision/action/request?

Questions like these will likely unsettle some people because few discuss them with ease. However, once we pose a question, others will find it hard to ignore. Had insiders asked questions like these at the Boy Scouts, GM, and the University of North Carolina at Chapel Hill, for instance, leaders could have addressed problems years earlier. Further, we are simply asking a question, not accusing or pointing the finger at any particular individual. Once asked, others will likely offer their opinions.

Coupling issues. The second way to break the moral mum effect is through coupling two issues: *operational* and *moral* concerns. People are much more comfortable discussing task, functional, or operational issues such as "We can't because we'll lose money" (Bisel et al., 2011, p. 57). Operational language keeps messages concrete and can be used as an opening to discuss deeper issues. By coupling moral and operational issues, we also add breadth to the discussion and increase the chances of being taken seriously. Weiner (2006) explained, "Your understanding of the breadth of an issue is reflected in all of the reasons you feel the way you do about it" (p. 19). When addressing a controversial subject, we should lead with (a) the operational justifications either for or against a direction and follow with (b) the moral/ethical reasons. Here is a sample of what it might sound like at a meeting:

> Peer: We have had some quality control issues with our production line, but I think we have to push ahead anyway. If we don't, we may miss our window of opportunity.
>
> You: I think we should not move forward until we are 100% sure the quality control issues have been fixed. Two reasons. [*Operational Reason*] One, we risk a failed launch and will lose money if we ship a product that is clearly inferior to the competitors'. [*Moral*] Two, the quality control issues you mentioned really come down to the safety of our product. We're not doing right by our customers if we sell them a potentially dangerous product. It's not good business.

By keeping operational reasons in the discussion, we have demonstrated our commitment to the "hard-nosed," concrete aspects of the decision, thereby avoiding the role of "the ethics guy." Further, while labeling a practice as good or bad has its place, it's not always necessary to use the words "ethical" or "unethical." Words and phrases like "good business," "doing right," "safety," and "dangerous" introduce a moral yardstick and vocabulary that is now available to everybody at the meeting.

Outsider's perspective. A third way to break through the moral mum effect is by pulling a hypothetical outsider's perspective into the discussion. At one time or another, we suffer from myopia. The asbestos (Heath, 1990), tobacco (Ulmer & Sellnow, 1997), and pharmaceutical industries (Lyon, 2007; Lyon & Ricci, 2012) were and still are plagued by short-term, narrow, and inward-looking views. They all made decisions without consideration for the long-term consequences on the health of their organizations. A veteran public relations consultant I know said that he often confronted his clients with what he called the "front-page" question. This is a common tactic in professional settings to get people to see issues from an outsider's view. Clients would call my friend in when problems surfaced and they needed his help to "spin" the story. They rarely wanted to address the deeper issues.

At some point in the process he'd ask them a version of this pointed question: "If you knew that tomorrow this issue landed on the front page of all the major newspapers, how do you think people would react? Would you be proud of the company's actions?" The clients usually moved beyond the self-justifying rationalizations and saw their activities in the inevitable light of society's broader standards. Instead of a fictitious reputation-damaging headline such as "Local CEO Protected Sexual Harassers," my friend guided them to imagine a new headline like, "Local CEO Fires Vice President for Sexual Harassment."

In addition to the actual front-page question, here are some sample questions and statements that take the same aim and can be tailored to your specific situation and style:

Box 9.3. Just How Transparent Should We Be?

Some leaders today are pushing transparency into formerly taboo areas to improve their organizations' health. Whole Foods, a dominant health food store chain, publicizes employees' and executives' salaries within the organizations (Clark, 2006). Any employee or executive can consult the Whole Food's salary book to see how much money people make. Similarly, Joel Gascoigne, the CEO of Buffer, a growing social media company, stresses openness at every turn (Bishop, 2013). All of Buffer's members know exactly what fellow members earn. Gascoigne believes Buffer's transparency builds trust and helps recruit new talent. Sharing information about salaries is only one way some organizations show how far they will go to promote transparency.

At the same time, "transparency" does not mean we should talk about all matters openly. It is obviously not necessary to know everything about everybody. Some topics, especially about people's private lives and personal information, should be off limits (e.g., past employment difficulties, issues at home, political or other beliefs, etc.). Human resource departments today must diligently follow the law regarding personal privacy, particularly around organizational members' health. Neither leaders nor employees should use labels like "transparency" or "openness" to justify gossip or other irresponsible communication.

- "I'm imagining how this will look to an outsider. That's how our actions will be judged if we do this."
- "We made a mistake. People will find out. We have to own up to and fix it."
- "There's a high likelihood that this will blow up in our faces if we go forward. We will be the ones on the hook when people find out."

Pointed communication like this awakens people and forces them to take an outsider's perspective. Clearly, we cannot be 100% transparent about every issue (See Box 9.3)

Box 9.4. Statements That Signal a Transparent Mindset.

When people say …	**They might mean …**
"Let's get the issues out on the table."	Open communication will help.
"We shouldn't have to constantly push to get information."	Transparency is everybody's responsibility.
"I'd like to clear the air on this topic."	We need to be more candid.
"Our process needs to be above board and above reproach."	We should use a full-disclosure process as we move forward.

Forgiveness at Work

What do we do when people admit their faults? Can forgiveness play a role in professional settings? Most of us understand the nature of forgiveness in personal or romantic relationships. If somebody transgresses (e.g., makes a mistake, hurts the other person's feelings, etc.), people often work toward apology and forgiveness as ideal relational goals (Merolla, 2008). Forgiveness is a key step in restoring the relationship to full health. In the same way, some researchers have shown the importance for forgiveness in organizational life. Caldwell and Dixon (2010) describe it as a sign of a noble, compassionate, and effective leader. They define it as the decision to "accept and to look past the faults of another and to reconcile a relationship despite a perceived betrayal" (p. 93) or other failures.

The application of this concept in professional settings is relatively recent. Forgiveness in professional settings can "serve the organization for the better" (Fehr & Gelfand, 2012, p. 682) by restoring damaged relationships and freeing members at all levels to move forward. In contrast, refusing to admit mistakes and/or holding grudges takes time and energy away from more important matters. This does not mean that we must forgive every professional error or make forgiveness part of our organization's official procedure. Some people may act in self-interest to the consistent harm of others. Instead of a policy, organizational members can add forgiveness to their list of cultural ways to respond to most errors, particularly when the "offender" comes clean. I agree with Fehr and Gelfand (2012): "forgiveness climates must emerge gradually and genuinely from social contexts, leaders, and an organization's core values" (p. 682), rather than from organizational rules or policies.

In most ways, forgiveness at work is similar to forgiveness in other contexts with its two overarching steps. First, in professional and organizational settings it usually involves a person who recognizes that he or she made an error in his or her tasks, responsibilities, or professional relationships and demonstrates some level of remorse. The individual may overtly apologize (e.g., "I'm sorry I screwed this up") or express regret less directly (e.g., "I feel terrible about that"). This shows both empathy for those negatively affected by the error and signals a restorative change in the individual's attitude and likely future action. Dr. Ring from Massachusetts General Hospital, for instance, immediately apologized to his patient for performing the wrong surgery on her hand and followed up by telephone a few days later to do so again. The apology did not undo his mistakes but made it easier on everybody involved to move forward with dignity and avoid future mistakes.

Simply admitting a mistake does not necessarily constitute an apology, just an admission of guilt. Pete Rose, for instance, played for the Cincinnati Reds for most of his 23 years in professional baseball. He was an outstanding, Hall-of-Fame-Caliber player. Unfortunately, he was accused of illegally gambling on Reds games while he was a player and, later, the team's manager. As part of his punishment, he was banned from baseball and labeled as ineligible for the sport's prestigious Hall of Fame. For years, he refused to admit guilt. Rose finally came clean in his book *My Prison Without Bars* (Rose & Hill, 2004) but did so without remorse. His tone was defensive and unapologetic. Not surprisingly, his lifetime ban continued. We may hesitate to accept somebody's apology if we get the impression it is not sincere or is a partial apology (e.g., I'm sorry *you* are upset). When people apologize genuinely, they accept ownership of the mistake. The *Admitting Mistakes Template* below (Box 9.5) may have helped Pete Rose regain eligibility for the Hall of Fame. You can use it to begin a transparent conversation about your own shortcomings large and small.

Box 9.5. Admitting Mistakes Template.

Own the mistake:

- "This was my mistake …"
- "This one is on me …"
- "I'm responsible …"

↓

Apologize

- "I apologize for the confusion this caused …"
- "I'm sorry this created more work for everybody …"
- "Please accept my apology …"

Say what you'll do to fix it (now or in the future)

- "I'll make sure I have it double-checked by the next deadline …"
- "I've cleared my calendar today to deal with this …"
- "It won't happen again. I'm meeting with Chuck today to hammer out a better way to handle this next time around …"

Follow through with actions

- Once you've said the above, others will evaluate you by your behavior.

In the second step of forgiveness, the individuals who were negatively affected can offer forgiveness. When a person remorsefully admits his or her wrongdoing, forgiveness can be given directly (e.g., "All is forgiven.") or less clearly (e.g., "It's alright."). Forgiveness does not change an individual's level of responsibility or mean that a person is off the hook. The person who made the initial mistake is usually responsible for making it right. Forgiveness simply cleans the slate and helps the offender "regain self-esteem and restores the ability of people to work together comfortably" (Caldwell & Dixon, 2010 p. 93). Forgiveness rinses the relationship of baggage and provides organizations a powerful way to move forward.

Conclusion

The foregoing tips, tools, and resources provide ways to put transparent communication into practice one courageous step at time. As the Roman Emperor Hadrian once said about pursuing Rome's ambitious construction, "Brick by brick, my citizens. Brick by brick." Similarly, transparent communication is a necessary, foundational practice for healthy organizations. The openness survey below may be a useful tool to gauge the extent to which your colleagues see you as a transparent communicator (Box 9.6).

Box 9.6. Openness Survey.

Openness Survey

To evaluate communication openness, the following survey was adapted from Spillan and Mino's (2001) research. If you are feeling courageous, ask six to eight people to fill it out anonymously. Photocopy the instructions and questions, explain briefly why you want their feedback, and arrange a way to receive them back anonymously within 24 to 48 hours.

Instructions: Answer each item by circling a score from 1 to 10 *(10 is highest)* about the person who gave you this survey. Arrange to return it to them in the next 24–48 hours.

1. Asks me for my opinion(s)
   1 2 3 4 5 6 7 8 9 10
2. Listens to new ideas that I may have
   1 2 3 4 5 6 7 8 9 10
3. Follows up on my opinions or suggestions
   1 2 3 4 5 6 7 8 9 10

4. Listens to complaints I may have
   1 2 3 4 5 6 7 8 9 10
5. Listens to bad news that I may have
   1 2 3 4 5 6 7 8 9 10
6. Acts on complaints or criticisms I provide
   1 2 3 4 5 6 7 8 9 10

References

Bisel, R. S., Kelley, K. M., Ploeger, N. A., & Messersmith, J. (2011). Workers' moral mum effect: On facework and unethical behavior in the workplace. *Communication Studies, 62*, 153–170.

Bisel, R. S., Messersmith, A. S., & Kelley, M. (2012). Supervisor-subordinate communication: Hierarchical mum effect meets organizational learning. *Journal of Business Communication, 49*, 128–147.

Bishop, K. (2013). How much?! Breaking the workplace taboo. [Electronic copy]. *CNBC.com.* Retrieved from http://finance.yahoo.com/news/earn-much-breaking-workplace-taboo-083600785.html

Brown, P., & Levinson, S. C. (1987). *Politeness: Some universals in language usage.* Cambridge: Cambridge University Press.

Caldwell, C., & Dixon, R. D. (2010). Love, forgiveness, and trust: Critical values of the modern leader. *Journal of Business Ethics, 93*, 91–101.

Clark, H. (2006). Whole foods: Spinning CEO pay. *Forbes*. Retrieved from http://www.forbes.com/2006/04/20/john-mackey-pay_cx_hc_06ceo_0420wholefoods.html

Dunleavy, K. N., Martin, M. M., Brann, M., Booth-Butterfield, M., Myers, S. A., & Weber, K. (2008). Student nagging behavior in the college classroom. *Communication Education, 57*, 1–19.

Erbert, L. A., & Floyd, K. (2004). Affectionate expressions as face-threatening acts: Receiver assessments. *Communication Studies, 55*, 254–270.

Fehr, R., & Gelfand, M. J. (2012). The forgiving organization: A multilevel model of forgiveness at work. *Academy of Management Review, 37*, 664–688.

Harrison, S., & Barlow, J. (2009). Politeness strategies and advice-giving in an online arthritis workshop. *Journal of Politeness Research, 5*, 93–111.

Heath, R. L. (1990). Effects of internal rhetoric on management of response to external issues: How corporate culture failed the asbestos industry. *Journal of Applied Communication Research, 18*, 153–167.

Kassing, J. W. (2002). Speaking up: Identifying employees' upward dissent strategies. *Management Communication Quarterly, 16*, 187–209.

Kassing, J. W. (2005). Speaking up competently: A comparison of perceived competence in upward dissent strategies. *Communication Research Reports, 22*, 227–234.

Keenen, J. P. (2000). Blowing the whistle on less serious forms of fraud: A study of executives and managers. *Employee Responsibilities and Rights Journal, 12*, 199–217.

Lyon, A. (2007). "Putting patients first": Systematically distorted communication and Merck's marketing of Vioxx. *Journal of Applied Communication Research, 35*, 376–398.

Lyon, A., & Ricci, M. (2012). The case of Wyeth, Design Write, and Premarin: The ethics of ghost-writing medical journal articles. In: Steve May (Ed.), *Case studies in organizational communication: Ethical perspectives and practices* (2nd ed., pp. 197–206). Thousand Oaks, CA: Sage.

Merolla, A. J. (2008). Communicating forgiveness in friendships and dating relationships. *Communication Studies, 59*, 114–131.

Rose, P., & Hill, R. (2004). *My prison without bars*. Emmaus, PA: Rodale.

Spillan, J. E., & Mino, M. (2001). Special peers' perceived use of communication openness and functional communication skills in specific organizational contexts. *Communication Research Reports, 18*, 53–66.

Tanaka, H. (2011). Politeness in a Japanese intra-organisational meeting honorifics and socio-dialectal code switching. *Journal of Asian Pacific Communication, 21*, 60–76.

Ulmer, R. R., & Sellnow, T. L. (1997). Strategic ambiguity and the ethic of significant choice in the tobacco industry's crisis communication. *Communication Studies, 48*, 215–233.

Weiner, A. (2006). *So smart but. ..: How intelligent people lose credibility and how they can get it back.* San Francisco, CA: Jossey-Bass.

Part IV

Moving from Impersonal to Engaging Communication

10 Impersonal Communication and Case Studies

Do we even know what rudeness is any more? Can I just pick up a magazine and put it in front of your face and read it while you're talking? Is that okay?

—*Jerry Seinfeld, speaking about cell phones*

Most people in professional settings experience impersonal communication. NBC's show *The Office* centers on a small paper supply company called Dunder Mifflin that competes with the "big box" office supply chain stores. In one episode, "The Salesmen," characters Dwight and Jim, drive to pitch their services to a potential client who prefers to do business with a big chain store because of the low prices. To show the contrast between Dunder Mifflin and large competitors, Dwight says, "May I borrow your phone?" He puts the call on the speaker without explanation, gets routed through a big competitor's automated phone system, and is put on hold. Jim continues to tell the client about Dunder Mifflin. During a pause in Jim's pitch, Dwight looks at the phone speaker and says to the manager, "This is one of those big guys. I've been on hold this whole time." At that moment, Jim calls Dunder Mifflin's office and a cheerful employee instantly answers. Jim hangs up and explains the superior service and personal touch his company offers. The difference between doing business with big or small companies may resonate with readers' experiences. This chapter looks at the growing reality of impersonal communication in the workplace first, by exploring its foundations, and, second, by presenting four case studies that fostered impersonal communication: Amazon, Comcast, Abercrombie & Fitch, and AOL.

Impersonal Communication and The Forces Encouraging It

We all know what impersonal communication feels like from experience. It lacks the irreplaceable human characteristics of warmth, emotion, and connection shared verbally and nonverbally. Quite often in organizational life, we play specific roles that define the boundaries of our interactions. If we let them, these roles can limit how we engage others to varying degrees. A business website describes ***impersonal communication*** as follows:

- A type of communication or interaction that is based specifically on social roles, such as communication between a sales representative and a potential customer. The manner of communication is informal and superficial, covering topics necessary to instigate a sale or similar transaction. (Impersonal, n.d. para. 1)

Communication within these roles can feel mechanical and too goal-driven to allow genuine connection. The organization is counting on us to perform our tasks.

At the same time, leaders and employees alike may be consenting to unhelpful norms about their communication approach. Consider, for example, the social distance many new supervisors feel they must establish with employees. This interpersonal distance does not help supervisors or organizations reach their goals. Teven (2007, 2010) showed that supervisors who communicated with nonverbal immediacy received high ratings from subordinates, but supervisors who communicated impersonally received low ratings from them. Those who did not display nonverbal immediacy were rated "lower in competence, trustworthiness, and goodwill" (Teven, 2010, p. 79). In general, employees will not respond well or work hard for supervisors who are not willing to connect with them. Interestingly, supervisors who communicated ***immediacy*** by using warm nonverbal displays (e.g., eye contact, smiling, etc.) but who also communicated their power over employees (e.g., "Because I'm the boss and I say so") (p. 75) were also rated low in competence, trustworthiness, and goodwill. In other words, superficial warmth toward others will not work. Employees must know that supervisors' nonverbal immediacy reflects a genuine, positive regard that goes deeper.

Personal communication styles aside, a variety of forces in modern-day life converge to encourage impersonal-communication dynamics in organizations. To be more efficient, we now work with and alongside computers and machines all day. As customers, we use ATM machines more often than human bank tellers.

We purchase anything from clothing, medicine, and even food online. Factory workers use forklifts and robotic arms for heavy loads. Employees and leaders at most levels work almost seamlessly with various types of computer software. In popular culture, some say we've entered the age of the "cyborg" because we are constantly linked to technology. Bian and Leung (2014), for example, found that ***cellphone addictions*** contributed to a variety of undesirable outcomes such as: "(a) disregard of harmful consequences; (b) preoccupation; (c) inability to control craving; (d) productivity loss, and (e) feeling anxious and lost" (p. 171). Despite these negative results, people continue to adopt new technologies at a record pace.

Certainly, many technologies have made our work more efficient, but at a price. They are changing the way we view the human communication process and even people. Workplaces can be so automated with spreadsheets, statistics, and other types of data that they eclipse the way we see people. At the root level, organizations often represent individuals as simple numbers and aggregated data. Even in our personal lives on social media, people seem to compete for how many "friends" or "followers" they have amassed. Does this shift in mindset diminish how we view each other and, thus, interact? If we are not mindful, these layers of technology, automation, and data keep person-to-person communication at arm's length. Technology has a high potential to ***depersonalize*** our relationships with co-workers and clients alike, if we let it. Technology, however, is not the primary reason for this problem. In the 21st century, other more enduring pressures precede it.

The Drive for Efficiency

The ***drive for efficiency*** is deeply embedded in organizational thinking. Producing-more-for-less is not inherently bad. Technology can speed up processes in helpful ways. However, some schools of thought can become almost religious about the "cheaper, better, faster" efficiency mantra. Systems and people can only be spread so thin until they become unreliable, cost more money than they save, and frustrate everybody involved (e.g., drop in customer satisfaction, lower employee morale, decreased productivity, turnover, etc.). An unfettered drive for efficiency can make us see people as the problem. In the 1992 film, *The Player*, Tim Robbins plays a studio executive who wants to make high-quality movies that also make a profit. A fellow studio executive who is only interested in cutting costs suggests, "I'm just saying there's time and money to be saved" if the studio eliminated screenplay writers from film making. Robbins' character replies sarcastically, "If we could just get rid of these actors and directors, maybe we've got something here." The unbridled drive for efficiency undercuts the importance of people and encourages us to see others not as full human beings but as resources or obstacles. Readers may have noticed, for example, the difficulty of speaking with a live person when contacting an organization, as did Dwight from *The Office* in the story that opened this chapter. Many systems are now designed to minimize human interaction. This mindset can depersonalize work and objectify employees and even customers.

Objectification of Employees

Researchers and managers have ***objectified employees*** to some degree since the earliest days of organizational studies. The well-known father of scientific management, Frederick Taylor, a mechanical engineer, essentially viewed people as mechanical instruments within the larger organizational machine. Thinkers like Taylor created the earliest factories as large apparatuses with rules, policies, procedures, and steps to guide every process. This early approach boosted productivity at the time, but many organizations have inherited Taylor's thinking without fully considering its negative consequences. At least three lingering tendencies from this era put modern-day organizations at a disadvantage.

1. ***Managers think, employees do.*** As Braverman (1998) explains, far too many work designs separate the intellectual side of work (e.g., creation, design, modification, evaluation, improvements, etc.) with its execution (e.g., assembly, production, delivery, etc.). As Taylor (1947) put it, "to work according to scientific laws, the management must take over and perform much of the work which is now left to the men" (p. 26); that is, take over the creation, design, modifications, etc. Employees, in other words, should leave the thinking to the managers and only perform mundane tasks. This philosophy deprives organizations of the untapped intelligence and potential of its employees.
2. ***Deskilling employees through repetitive motion.*** Even today, work is broken into tiny parts that are easy to perform. Taylor (1947) conducted and encouraged time-and-motion studies whereby the manager's role was "timing [employees] with a stop watch" (p. 48) during each step and tasks in any given work process. While it is easy to train and therefore replace employees when their job description is narrow and repetitive (Braverman, 1998), in the long run, this contributes to a de-skilled employee pool. Many organizations today complain about the lack of

qualified applicants and expertise needed for organizations to compete. How can organizations perform at the highest levels if they simultaneously de-skill their employees?

3. ***No talking allowed.*** As an extension of the first two tensions, managers of yesteryear discouraged communication between employees while working. In most case, the "no talking" rule was likely unofficial and simply viewed as not working hard. My grandfather, for example, worked in textile mills throughout his life in New England. He explained that factories were loud, the work was dangerous, and talking was a risky distraction. Still, not allowing employees to speak borders on inhumane treatment. Some prisons, in fact, use communication deprivation as a form of punishment that has been characterized as torture (Gawande, 2009). We have come a long way since the earliest factories. However, many managers and organizations today perceive casual conversations and small talk as "goofing off." Ironically, these same organizations list communication as the most important skill for employees. Further, lack of communication skills among new employees and job applicants frustrates many leaders (Caliendo, 2013).

When combined, these three overlapping dispositions cast employees as objects more than whole human beings. Unfortunately, many organizations today cling to these tendencies long past their expiration date. If we accept an impersonal, objectified view of people, we will treat them as such all the more. We may start to see them as mere obstacles that hinder or instruments to advance the pursuit of our professional goals. Have you ever worked at an organization that didn't seem to care about its people? As customers, have you ever been treated like you were inconveniencing the organization?

I-It Communication: The Root of Impersonal Communication

The root of impersonal communication goes even deeper still than the early factories. It comes, perhaps, from human nature itself. Martin Buber (1947, 1970), a communication philosopher, would likely align impersonal communication with his view of *I-It* communication and relationships. In its simplest form, ***I-It communication*** is monologue that occurs between ourselves (i.e., "I"), who we see as the center of the conversation, and the other person (i.e., "It"), who we see as separate from us. We see the *It* as an object, instrument, or resource. *I-It* describes a relationship between non-equals. As Holba (2008) explains, *I-It* communicative moments "remain a form of functional communication" (p. 497) but do not engage the other individual in a genuine or personal way. If we view others through *I-It* glasses, people hardly merit the fullness of our care, compassion, and attention. This mindset shapes what Holba (2008) describes as encounters that "can feel empty and flat, often causing human beings to feel a sense of homelessness, loneliness, or emptiness" (Holba, 2008, p. 497). For this reason, Buber describes *I-It* communication as a monologue. The "I" cares about, focuses on, and thus speaks in terms of a person's own interests but has little regard for the "It" receiver in the conversation. Admittedly, avoiding *I-It* communication in moments of high stress, when multi-tasking, and in brief repetitive interactions is difficult. The challenge today is to design work processes that make *I-It* communication less likely.

Further, *I-It* conversations are not always easy to spot. They can sound truly unidirectional and include a pattern of turn taking between communicators, that is, what appears to be a back-and-forth, equal exchange. In many cases, this form of a conversation simply camouflages an *I-It* mindset. Buber (1947) calls this a "monologue disguised as dialogue" (p. 22). Readers may have sensed an *I-It* disposition in conversations with others. Have you ever had somebody who communicated in friendly ways and yet seemed to steer a conversation toward his or her goals? Many organizations train their employees to view others as *It* (e.g., revenue sources, sales volume, etc.) but simultaneously teach salespeople to mimic genuine, dialogic communication while covertly driving the discussion in a predetermined direction (e.g., Lyon & Mirivel, 2011). These conversations may bounce back and forth and appear socially supportive, but most people can feel a shift in the conversation, that moment when the other person is pursuing his or her interests and cares little about ours. It feels like the other person looks at our face and sees "$" rather than us. Thus, the *I-It* mindset is temporarily hidden beneath a disguised monologue but usually reveals itself soon enough. In the aforementioned business explanation of impersonal communication—"informal and superficial, covering topic necessary to instigate a sale or similar transaction"—(Impersonal, n.d. para. 1) we see the imprint of an *I-It* mindset.

Dehumanization at Work

Forging deeper into the issue, research on ***dehumanization*** explains the way in-group members see those in the out-group. This research intersects with

Buber's *I-It* sensibilities as well as objectification in organizations. As Mirivel (2012) explained, "To dehumanize someone, by definition, is to deprive them of their humanity. ... Unfortunately, dehumanizing practices occur everywhere. Insults and name-calling are salient examples of dehumanization" (p. 10). We often label, categorize, and put others in boxes we mistakenly believe to be natural and legitimate classifications. According to Leyens et al. (2001), we see our in-group members as possessing the best human characteristics or "essence" and see out-group members as perhaps possessing this human essence but to a lesser degree. Our in-group includes people who we see as "one of us" and the out-group as the "other." Viki et al. (2006) found that people consistently assigned human-associated words with their in-group and sub-human and animal terms to out-group members and suggested it is "possible that people who view out-groups as less human than the in-group may support the ill treatment of such groups or may at least fail to empathize with their suffering" (p. 769). From a strictly rational standpoint, if we don't see others as fully human, then we do not necessarily believe they deserve humane treatment.

Organizations frequently use labels to characterize customers and employees, perhaps without realizing the implications. For example, the airline industry describes difficult passengers as "irates" (e.g., "We have an 'irate' in seat 5a") and baggage handlers as "throwers." The National Guard forces referred to protesters in Baltimore, Maryland, in 2015 as "enemy forces" (Starr, 2015, para. 1). We may hear certain groups within our own organization referred to in disparaging ways (e.g., accountants are "bean counters," lawyers are "ambulance chasers," etc.). Labeling out-group members can lead to unequal and harsh treatment toward them. We see other evidence of dehumanization today in workplace bullying, hazing, sexual harassment, harsh treatment, and so on. Organizations must be aware of the labels they use for people and groups. Divisions in thought shape our interactions.

In sum, the temptation for more technology, pressure for efficiency, and our view of people all shape the way we treat others. These impersonal communication practices can seep into most areas of organizations and make them less effective. In some situations, we cannot avoid routine, impersonal interactions, and superficial exchanges with others. For instance, my garbage collector would not likely appreciate my hailing him down from the truck every Tuesday at 5:30 a.m. to chat. Sometimes, we just need to get on with our routine. The case studies below show numerous instances of impersonal communication practices that in some instances took a harmful turn.

Cases Involving Impersonal Communication

Things are Heating Up and Cooling Down at an Amazon.com Warehouse

Amazon.com is the world's largest online retail store. With over $60 billion in annual sales and climbing, Amazon is the e-commerce equivalent of brick-and-mortar retail giants like Walmart ("Knowledge," 2013). In the mid-1990s, Amazon CEO, Jeff Bezos, started the company by specializing in selling books. Through acquisitions and partnerships over the years, Amazon now offers a full range of retail products it will deliver right to your door. Its corporate headquarters are in Seattle, WA but for any given order, the company ships products from one of dozens of massive warehouses located across the country, often near airports. This decentralized design allows the company to deliver to each region in a timely fashion. Each warehouse employs hundreds and sometimes thousands of workers who receive deliveries from suppliers; sort, store, and track merchandise; and process and ship products to fill in-coming orders. In 2011, an Amazon warehouse located in Breinigsville, Pennsylvania, was at the center of a controversy about treating its employees poorly. This case explores how the Amazon warehouse leaders handled two separate issues involving extremely hot and cold working conditions.

Summer Heat Controversy

Amazon's Breinigsville warehouse consists of two large buildings and employs over 1,600 workers from throughout the Lehigh Valley area including the nearby city of Allentown. In June and July of 2011, employees complained about high temperatures in the warehouse to an Occupational Safety and Health Administration's (OSHA) regional office. As its name suggests, OSHA is a federal agency that sets standards, inspects, and enforces workplace health and safety codes (www.osha.gov). In essence, OSHA provides checks and balances for companies regarding employees' safety and well-being. The heat was regularly exceeding 100 degrees and most areas of the warehouse were not air-conditioned. The temperature became even higher when warehouse leaders established a policy. Fearing theft, they kept the loading doors closed at all times, which virtually eliminated airflow. A site safety manager disclosed this information to OSHA in July, 2011 after employees' initial complaints that actual temperatures plus humidity sometimes produced a heat index between 108 and 112 degrees (Soper, 2015). A former employee claimed that the heat index reached 114 degrees on the ground floor of the receiving area.

Warehouse leaders knew about medical incidents but still did not open the bay doors to increase airflow. One employee stated, "Imagine if it's 98 degrees outside and you're in a warehouse with every single dock door closed" (Soper, 2015, para. 25). Instead, managers hired an ambulance company "to have ambulances and paramedics stationed at its two adjacent warehouses during five days of excessive heat in June and July" (Soper, 2015, para. 65). In contrast, no other warehouses in the Breingsville area needed ambulances during this period. Chris Peischl, the ambulance company's director of operations, stated "The majority of people we saw were heat-related. … We saw 20 to 30 people who cooled down, we helped hydrate them and they went back to work" (para. 67). The ambulances brought an additional 15 employees to hospitals. An employee who quit because of the summer heat and mandatory overtime stated, "I never felt like passing out in a warehouse and I never felt treated like a piece of crap in any other warehouse but this one. They can do that because there aren't any jobs in the area" (Soper, 2015, para. 4). Employees were not the only party to complain. An emergency room doctor contacted federal employees to report "an 'unsafe environment' [at the warehouse] after he treated several Amazon warehouse workers for heat-related problems" (Soper, 2015, para. 10). From the hospital's view, the number of people coming from one specific employer was medically unusual. In one complaint to OSHA, an employee explained that employees were also disciplined when they could not handle the heat (Employee Complaint 422732, 2011). The employee stated, "We have a six-point system where when you reach six points you get fired. People who were sent home early accrued 1.5 points for heat exhaustion that was at the hands of Amazon.com" (para. 1). Employees were passing out in the heat. Even pregnant employees were expected to continue working through the hottest days of the summer.

Working in Amazon's enormous warehouses is generally difficult even without the heat. Some employees walk between 7 and 15 miles per shift (Yarow, 2013). The physical demands, pace, and expectations for productivity are constant. Still, even when the heat was at its worst, leaders at the Breinigsville site did not adjust their expectations for productivity. *The Morning Call*, an area newspaper, interviewed 20 current and former Amazon employees about warehouse working conditions. In addition to the heat, a *Morning Call* reporter summarized what he'd heard:

> Employees were frequently reprimanded regarding their productivity and threatened with termination. … The consequences of not meeting work expectations were regularly on display, as employees lost their jobs and got escorted out of the warehouse. Such sights encouraged some workers to conceal pain and push through injury lest they get fired as well. (Soper, 2015, para. 8)

After hearing complaints and contacting warehouse leaders, an OSHA director (Soper, 2015) provided recommendations: (1) reduce the temperature and humidity, (2) provide hourly breaks, (3) communicate the actual heat index to employees regularly, (4) provide fans for each work station.

Amazon's Response

Warehouse leaders did not speak to the press directly after these stories surfaced. Instead, a spokesperson from Amazon's headquarters in Seattle, Michele Glisson, emailed a statement which was credited to the warehouse general manager, Vickie Mortimer: "The safety and welfare of our employees is our No. 1 priority at Amazon, and as the general manager, I take that responsibility seriously. … We go to great lengths to ensure a safe work environment, with activities that include free water, snacks, extra fans and cooled air during the summer" (Soper, 2015, para. 70). The statement paints a more favorable picture than employees' experienced. For instance, the "cooled air" the manager was referring to was only available in specific break rooms in the warehouse. Amazon's reply to OSHA similarly minimized employees' experiences and stated that only "15 of these 1,600 employees experienced heat-related symptoms" and that "6 of these employees were treated at a local ER for non-work related medical conditions triggered by the heat" (Soper, 2015, para. 43). These numbers, stated as fact, were much lower than the figures provided by the ambulance company that actually treated the employees.

The letter to OSHA then listed the warehouse's current policies and practices including a limited number of fans, bottled water, and the distribution of "cooling" bandanas. From employees' standpoint, these provisions obviously did not help enough. Only 5% of employees interviewed by *The Morning Call* described the current conditions in the warehouse as good. Prompted by employee complaints and instructions from OSHA, warehouse leaders took additional steps to improve working conditions. Amazon's letter to OSHA (Soper, 2015) indicated that the company had purchased additional fans, intended to install temporary air conditioners, and hired local Emergency Medical Technicians (EMTs) to work on site at the warehouse to respond to on-going concerns about warehouse temperatures. Further, managers removed any point deductions counted against employees who had to leave work because of the heat. One worker, however, explained that the additional changes such as fans did little to reduce the heat. He stated, it now felt like "working in a convection oven while blow-drying your hair" (Soper, 2015, para. 64).

It's Not All Hot Air

Despite leaders' claims that they addressed the heat and employees properly, this was not the only temperature-related incident at the warehouse. About six months prior to the extreme heat, employees were also subjected to extreme cold. On several days in November and December, 2010, the warehouses were evacuated when somebody in the warehouse triggered a false fire alarm. Managers believed that somebody was pulling fire alarms as a distraction to steal from the warehouse. In those instances, over 1,200 employees on the overnight shift evacuated the building and remained outside in 20 degrees for up to two hours before being allowed back in the building. They were not allowed to take their coats with them or stay in their cars to keep warm. A worker stated, "There were pregnant women, men and women in T-shirts and shorts. … I am absolutely disgusted with this company's practices and I do believe OSHA should visit this building and give them some sort of coaching on how to better handle the situation before there are more people suffering from hypothermia" (Soper, 2011, para. 44). Some managers, however, remained inside the building throughout the evacuations. On one such night, "six employees were taken by ambulance to a hospital for treatment, about 30 workers out of 1,200 that evacuated were allowed to board ambulances at the warehouse to get warm" (Soper, 2011, para. 13). Paul Grady, a 53-year-old employee, suffers from chronic joint pain and a heart condition, both of which make him particularly vulnerable in cold weather. After evacuating on one occasion, he explained his health conditions to managers and asked if he could stay inside with them to stay warm, but they refused. Grady stated, "They didn't care about anybody standing outside freezing because they knew they could replace us the next day if they had to" (Soper, 2011, para. 16). Recently and more tragically, two employees died on the job at an Amazon warehouse in New Jersey and Pennsylvania (Kellog, 2014). In one case, shelving collapsed and crushed a 52-year-old mother. In the other case, a 57-year-old grandfather was caught in a conveyor belt and dragged violently. In both cases, OSHA cited the warehouse for serious safety violations that contributed to these deaths. The problems at Amazon, however, are not isolated to the company's warehouses.

Life Beyond the Warehouse: Rumblings at Amazon's Corporate Headquarters

In 2015, another controversy surfaced. *New York Times* ran an unfavorable exposé about life at Amazon's corporate headquarters and CEO Jeff Bezos. Based on 100 interviews with current and former employees, the issue of employee treatment again drew the most criticism. An employee in the office used the term "purposeful Darwinism" to describe the company's cutthroat environment (Kantor & Streitfeld, 2015, para. 4). The story outlines the various ways managers and fellow employees look for reasons to get each other fired or cause them to quit. Life at Amazon headquarters was described as a "bruising" environment with "unreasonable expectations" leaders themselves boasted about (para. 3). A former employee who worked for two years as a book marketer described the toxic environment: "You walk out of a conference room and you'll see a grown man covering his face. Nearly every person I worked with, I saw cry at their desk" (Kantor & Streitfeld, 2015, para. 7).

Bezos has confessed in the past, "It's not easy to work here" (Kantor & Streitfeld, 2015, para. 25) but insisted that the culture displayed in *New York Times* "article doesn't describe the Amazon I know or the caring Amazonians I work with every day" (Cook, 2015, para. 3). While he personally does not offer an alternative description of life at Amazon and refused to be interviewed by the *New York Times*, he pointed to an employee's favorable account in LinkedIn. The employee, who worked at Amazon for 18 months when he wrote the essay, called the *New York Times* story biased and described his relatively normal and positive experience at the company. Other former employees then affirmed the original *New York Times* piece to various degrees. One former employee who took a position at Hewlett-Packard stated, "Amazon was the most toxic work environment I have ever seen" (Steitfeld & Kantor, 2015, para. 20). Another said, "I didn't see a whole lot of crying at desks. But I did see a lot of crying in bathrooms" (para. 15). Others offered a more moderate evaluation such as a current employee who was "surprised to see anyone saying they had no idea what they were signing

Questions:

- How do you think Amazon leaders view their employees? How is their view demonstrated through actions?
- What advice would you give Amazon for improving its culture?

up for. It was always clear to me" (para. 16). Debates like these are not easily settled. Ultimately, each employee past and present has his or her own perception of the work experience. Nevertheless, few if any people claim that Amazon is an amazing place to work and it has the distinction of having the second highest turnover rate of any Fortune 500 company, an embarrassing title to be sure (Giang, 2013). In this light, Amazon leaders and employees no doubt wish the debate did not focus entirely on questions about just how terrible life is at Amazon.

Interacting with Customers at Comcast: "We'd Like to Disconnect Please"

Comcast is the largest cable provider in the US and is headquartered in Philadelphia, PA. It owns many well-known TV brands including NBC, the Weather Channel, Universal Television, and many others. Comcast provides fully integrated communications services to its customers such as cable, Internet, phone, and related products. By all measures, the company is massive. It generates just under $70 billion per year, almost as much as Coca-Cola and McDonald's combined. In addition to being known for its size, Comcast also has a longstanding poor reputation. In 2010, comsumerist.com rated it as the "Worst Company in America" (Comcast, 2010). The company was a runner up in previous years. Comcast has been plagued by abysmally low customer satisfaction ratings for many years with scores typically in the 50% to 60% satisfaction range ("Benchmarks by Company," 2014). Its employees have been vocal about their dissatisfaction with the company. A blog entitled "Comcast must die" (comcastmustdie.blogspot.com) is filled with complaints and confessions of current and former Comcast employees. Not all comments are negative but most are. The most common way customers interact with Comcast is through one of the company's call centers.

One particularly frustrated customer recorded a conversation with one of Comcast's customer service representatives. Ryan Block, a well-known writer, critic, and technology guru, posted this call to soundcloud.com (Block, 2010). The recording gained instant media attention and became a source of embarrassment for Comcast as well as an illustration of an all-too-common experience for how customers often feel treated by companies. This case looks at the call as well as responses from the company and employees in light of the company's customer service training, policies, and culture.

The 18-Minute Call

In July 2014, Ryan Block's wife called Comcast to cancel their service. The couple was moving and decided to do business with a Comcast competitor when they moved to their new home. After a frustrating 10-minute conversation with a customer service representative who would not agree to disconnect service, Block's wife handed the phone to him. Block began recording the call at this point, which lasted another eight minutes. Below, the transcript shows the first two minutes and thirty seconds of the call.

Block: Ok, we'd like to disconnect. We'd like to disconnect please.

Comcast: Ok, so why don't you want the faster speed? Help me understand why you don't want faster Internet.

Block: Help me understand why you can't just disconnect us.

Comcast: Because my job is to have a conversation with you about keeping your service, about finding out why it is you're looking to cancel the service.

Block: I don't understand. Is this for?

Comcast: If you don't want to talk to me, you can definitely go into the Comcast store and disconnect your service there. You can kill two birds with one stone. You've got to return that cable card to the store anyway.

Block: We're actually going to just mail the cable card in, but if you can just please cancel our service, that would be great. That is all we want.

Comcast: We are actually not able to return a cable card by mail.

Block: Then I will send someone, like a TaskRabbit, to go return the cable card for us. I don't personally intend to go return the cable card. That's why we're probably not going to be cancelling in-store. So that's why I need you to cancel by phone. So can you cancel us by phone? The answer is yes, correct?

Comcast: It sounds like you don't want to go over this information with me. I mean, if you don't want to go over that information, ok, then that's the easiest way to get your account disconnected.

Block: I am declining to state why we are leaving Comcast, because I don't owe you an explanation. So if you can just please proceed to the next question, if you have to fill out your form, that's fine. Please proceed to the next question, and we will attempt to answer that if possible.

Comcast: So, I mean, being that we are the number one provider of Internet and TV service in the entire country, ok, why is it that you're not wanting to have the number one Internet rated service, number one-rated TV service available?

Block: I'm declining to state. We're switching providers. Can you please go to the next question?

Comcast: Ok, so what is it about Astound that's making you want to change to them?

Block:	I'm declining to state. Can you please go to the next question so we can cancel our service?
Comcast:	Ok, so, I mean, I'm just trying to figure here what it is about Comcast service that you're not liking, that you're not wanting to keep. I mean, why is it that you don't want to keep that service?
Block:	This phone call is a really actually amazing representative example of why I don't want to stay with Comcast. So can you please cancel our service?
Comcast:	Ok, but I'm trying to help you. Ok, you are not letting me help you by declining answers by doing all this. I'm trying to hear you.
Block:	The way you can help me is by disconnecting my service.
Comcast:	But how is that helping you, though?
Block:	Because that's what I want.

The call continues in much the same pattern for another six minutes. The customer, Ryan Block, requests repeatedly to have his service disconnected and the Comcast employee refuses to respond directly to his request. Block remains composed but becomes even firmer as the call wears on, "Is this like a joke? Are you punking us right now?" The call finally ends with the employee confirming that Block's service has been disconnected. The employee was either unwilling or unable to provide the customer a confirmation number upon request. Block later visited a Comcast store and confirmed that his service had actually been disconnected. Clearly, the employee was not aware that Block had been recording the conversation. However, customer service calls like this one open directly with the statement to the customer that the call may be recorded for training purposes.

Responses from Comcast and Its Employees

Block's recorded call was played over six million times on his soundcloud.com account and was covered in the media by numerous outlets. Even *Good Morning America* played a portion of the call and offered their commentary (Kim, 2014). The company released the following statement to the press in the days following the most intense media coverage:

> We are very embarrassed by the way our employee spoke with Mr. Block and are contacting him to personally apologize. The way in which our representative communicated with him is unacceptable and not consistent with how we train our customer service representatives. We are investigating this situation and will take quick action. While the overwhelming majority of our employees work very hard to do the right thing every day, we are using this very unfortunate experience to reinforce how important it is to always treat our customers with the utmost respect. (Kim, 2014, para. 6)

Around the same time, Comcast communicated internally a slightly different message to its call representatives. The company memo was leaked to the press by an employee.

> I have tremendous admiration for our Retention professionals, who make it easy for customers to choose to stay with Comcast. … If a customer is not fully aware of what the product offers, we ask the Retention agent to educate the customer and work with them to find the right solution. … The agent on this call did a lot of what we trained him and paid him—and thousands of other Retention agents—to do. He tried to save a customer, and that's important, but the act of saving a customer must always be handled with the utmost respect. (Watson cited in Morran, 2014, para. 12)

The public apology clearly labels the employee's approach "unacceptable" and "not consistent" with the company's training. Within company walls, however, Comcast leaders use a corporate vocabulary very differently from how customers would describe calls like this. Comcast sees cancellation calls as opportunities to "make it easy for customers to choose to stay with Comcast," "to educate the customer" and "to save" the customer. Moreover, though he may have gone a bit too far, Comcast explains that the employee essentially "did a lot of what we trained him and paid him" to do.

In the weeks following the call and apology, employees leaked other Comcast documents. One such set of documents were Comcast's training materials. These materials confirm what many customers and employees have complained about, "selling services is a required part of the job, even for employees doing tech support" (Hutchinson, 2014, para. 2). A large portion of the training materials is devoted to "solving" customers' problems by "selling" them additional services. The materials specify that employees have to follow certain steps including "overcome [customers'] objections" and "proactively close [the] sale" (cited in Hutchingson, 2014, para. 4). Thus, a customer may view his or her request to disconnect his or her services as routine and straightforward. To Comcast, however, every call is designed to sell and extract more revenue from customers. This clash of priorities sets the stage for potentially tense interactions.

Employees interviewed by the press about the recorded call generally agree. The employee went a bit too far but was doing so under the strain of Comcast's pressurized culture. A former Comcast call center representative said, "That rep, (may God have mercy on his soul) was doing exactly as he was told to do" (Quirk, 2014, para. 6). Another employee affirmed that calls like this are not unusual, "That now-famous [Block] call with the retention specialist is something I have seen [at Comcast] hundreds of times. We locked down the ability for most customer service reps to disconnect accounts. We queue the calls for customers looking to disconnect to a retention team" (Jeffries, 2014, para. 17). A former billing specialist at Comcast explained how he saw his job expectations change over his employment even for non-sales employees, "They were starting off with, 'just ask' … Then instead of 'just ask,' it was 'just ask again,' then 'engage the customer in a conversation,' then 'overcome their objections.'" (Jeffries, 2014, para. 12). Even though the billing specialist received high scores in resolving customers' issues, he was repeatedly reprimanded for low sales and eventually fired (Jeffries, 2014, para. 12, 13). Still another employee outlines Comcast's policy on pushing back against customers who wanted to disconnect their service, "We were coached that, regardless of wanting to cancel, or being declined after a pitch, we had to offer at least three rebuttals" (Jeffries, 2014, para. 26). Simply canceling a customer's service upon request went directly against how Comcast trains its employees.

Plainly put, employees get financially rewarded for "saves" and selling additional services and conversely penalized for the lack of sales and "disconnects" or calls resulting in cancelled service (Quirk, 2014). An employee confirmed that customer service representatives are only allowed a maximum of three disconnects per shift (Quirk, 2014). Employees with three or more disconnects for three shifts in a row "were shown the door" (Quirk, 2014, para. 9). Because of policies like these, call reps resort to communication tactics designed to make the conversation dissatisfying and avoid having the disconnect counted against them. For instance, call reps may attempt to drag out the call for so long that the customer simply hangs up. When they call back, they will likely get another call representative who disconnects the service. Additionally, the longer a rep drags out a call, the fewer calls, and thus fewer potential disconnects, the employee will have to face on any given shift. Reps may also suggest that the customer goes to a Comcast store in person to disconnect service. This arrangement discourages employees. A current employee explained how the company's policies spoiled what could have been a great job.

> I thought it'd be the job of a lifetime … I love the Internet, computers, and love helping people. I'd like to think I'm a really nice computer guy. … My hopes have slowly been diminished and crushed as requirements from "upper management" become more strict, and not on promoting people to work harder but discouraging [employees] from being helpful. (Bennett-Smith, 2012, para. 2, 4).

In short, according to Comcast's own employees, the company's pressurized culture and policies, in part, encourages employees to adopt an adversarial posture toward customers. Ryan Block's recorded call merely illustrates deeply embedded practices at Comcast that make interactions like this more likely.

Epilogue

It is possible, as Comcast's apology suggests, that difficult calls with Comcast like this one are isolated incidents. Nevertheless, as mentioned, Comcast's customer satisfaction ratings have been poor for years ("Benchmarks by Company," 2014). Further, other customers have published their own accounts of other frustrating experiences with Comcast customer service representatives. Numerous customers have posted their accounts of similar and very recent call experiences in the comments section of Block's (2010) original post. Similar dissatisfying experiences have been published elsewhere. Not long after this difficult cancellation call, another customer posted a video of his experience showing that he'd been on hold for over three hours until the customer service center finally closed (Brodkin, 2014). In another example, a customer service representative lied to a customer, telling him that Comcast was "mandated by law" to cap customers' data usage and therefore had to charge the customer for over usage (Brodkin, 2015a). In still another example, a customer service representative changed the customer's first name to "A—hole" on his bill (Brodkin, 2015b). The number of past and present employees willing to speak directly to the press about their discouraging experiences at Comcast does further damage to the company's already troubled reputation as a difficult place to work. Thus, despite Comcast's frequent apologies and explanations that the company does not condone this type of conduct from its employees, it appears as if the company itself has pressured employees in a variety of ways that normalize abrasive interactions with customers.

Questions:

- To what extent do you believe the phone rep was following the company's training vs. acting alone?
- Have you ever experienced phone calls with organizations that made you uncomfortable?

Abercrombie & Fitch's Objectification of Customers and Employees: An Old Interview Comes Back to Bite the Hip Retailer

The Abercrombie and Fitch (A&F) brand has been around for over a century. In its earliest days, the company sold clothing, high-end fishing gear, tents, and guns. It struggled and was all but non-existent during the 1970s and 1980s but was reinvented in the mid-1990s with a focus on the teen and young adult market. In this resurgent phase, it is headquartered in Columbus, OH and run by CEO Mike Jeffries until 2014. When he took over, he refocused the company mainly on clothing and an obsession with creating a "sexy and emotional experience" for A&F customers (Denizet-Lewis, 2006, para. 20). Jeffries pushed this envelope so far that the company has come under scrutiny for selling little more than a sexy image. For years, for example, many of the company's advertisements featured good-looking, fit young adults romping around wearing very little clothing at all. Further, live male models pose shirtless in the storefront windows of A&F's retail locations in major cities around the world. A&F stood out in an already looks-obsessed fashion industry. In 2006, Jeffries gave a candid, in-depth interview to *Salon* (Denizet-Lewis, 2006). The *Salon* writer spent two days with Jeffries and mingled with others at A&F headquarters. At the time, the article did not make many waves but was re-discovered in 2013 by *Business Insider* (Lutz, 2013) and rerun in various forms in multiple online magazines and news outlets. By 2013, both social media and the public's sensitivity to issues of bullying, racial issues, and sexual objectification were in full swing. Jeffries' earlier interview was revisited, reinterpreted, and translated by one online magazine's headline as "Abercrombie & Fitch CEO Explains Why He Hates Fat Chicks" (Levinson, 2013). The coverage of A&F was pointed, but was it fair? This case looks at how Jeffries characterized its customers and employees in objectifying ways.

The Interview

At the time of the *Salon* interview, Jeffries was 61 years old. Despite his age, he dressed in torn A&F jeans, flip flops, and a blue muscle polo. His hair is bleached blond, his teeth have been bleached, and he appears to have had cosmetic surgery. When asked by the interviewer about his bleached hair, he responded, "Dude, I'm not an old fart who wears his jeans up at his shoulders" (Denizet-Lewis, 2006, para. 1). Not surprisingly, Jeffries wants to embody the A&F brand. He is, after all, the leader of the company. When asked about the image he wants A&F to promote, it comes down to sex in its various forms. He stated bluntly, "[Sex is] almost everything. That's why we hire good-looking people in our stores. Because good-looking people attract other good-looking people, and we want to market to cool, good-looking people. We don't market to anyone other than that"

(Denizet-Lewis, 2006, para. 23). He continued to explain the rationale behind A&F's hiring and marketing approach:

> In every school there are the cool and popular kids, and then there are the not-so-cool kids. … Candidly, we go after the cool kids. We go after the attractive all-American kid with a great attitude and a lot of friends. A lot of people don't belong [in our clothes], and they can't belong. Are we exclusionary? Absolutely. Those companies that are in trouble are trying to target everybody: young, old, fat, skinny. But then you become totally vanilla. You don't alienate anybody [that way], but you don't excite anybody, either. (Denizet-Lewis, 2006, para. 24)

A&F exclusionary hiring practices resulted in a lawsuit a few years before Jeffries' interview. Jennifer Lu, an Asian-American college student in southern California, was once a sales person for A&F but was fired because of her race. After a corporate official visited the store and saw Lu, the executive "pointed to an Abercrombie poster and told our management at our store, 'You need to have more staff that looks like this.' And it was a white Caucasian male on that poster" (Leung, 2015, para. 8). Lu and several other employees were fired because they didn't fit A&F's image.

When asked about A&F's exclusionary hiring practices, which historically focused not just on good-looking people but almost entirely young, white employees, Jeffries responded:

> I don't think we were in any sense guilty of racism, but I think we just didn't work hard enough as a company to create more balance and diversity. And we have, and I think that's made us a better company. We have minority recruiters. And if you go into our stores you see great-looking kids of all races. (Denizet-Lewis, 2006, para. 35)

The *Salon* interviewer noted that during the two-day visit to A&F headquarters, "If looks could kill, everyone here would be dead. Jeffries' employees are young, painfully attractive" (Denizet-Lewis, 2006, para. 5). The interview triggered a number of concerns for readers, especially from 2013 forward. Additionally, A&F struggled with diversity issues long after Jeffries *Salon* interview despite his claim at the time that the company had created a diverse company.

A&F's Objectifying Policies, Practices, and Products

Jeffries' focus has always been honed in on a very narrow definition of the "right" look. In fact, the company has a controversial "look policy" that employees must "maintain a consistent level of dress and grooming that represents what people expect from [the brand]" (cited in Abercrombie, 2009, para. 1). In part, the policy specifies the following appearances expected of employees: They must, have "a clean, natural, classic hairstyle" (para. 2). Any make-up must "enhance natural features and create a fresh, natural appearance" (para. 2). Employees fingernails have to be "clean and presentable [and] should not extend more than one quarter-inch beyond the tip of the finger" (para. 3). Employees' facial hair is not allowed and banned and discreet tattoos are allowed but only if "they represent the Abercrombie" look (para. 5). The policy also specifies the exact way clothing must be worn with exact precision: "women's jeans should be cuffed at seven-eighths of an inch; the top three buttons of a denim shirt should be left undone" (cited in Abercrombie, 2013, para. 6). In practice, the company's look policy extends beyond the written word and gets applied in concerning ways as earlier lawsuits from employees demonstrate. The problem persisted even years later after A&F was sued numerous times. For example, two employees were fired for wearing religious headscarves (Bhasin & Fairchild, 2013). A&F later settled the lawsuit with the former employees. Another employee was not allowed to wear a small silver cross (Abercrombie, 2013). A third was relegated to the stockroom and not allowed to work with customers because she was an amputee and wore a partial prosthetic left forearm and hand (English, 2009). Even employees at the corporate offices must follow A&F's look policy despite the fact that they are far from the public eye.

A&F has also experienced scrutiny around some of the products they sell, mainly for over-sexualizing young females. For example, some T-shirts for young ladies read, "Who Needs a Brain When You Have These?" "Gentlemen Prefer Tig Ol' Bitties" and "Do I Make You Look Fat?" (Denizet-Lewis, 2006, para. 36). Another racially insensitive T-shirt read, "Wong Brothers Laundry Service—Two Wongs Can Make It White" (para. 38). The company also sold sexualized products for very young females such as padded bikini tops for 7-year-olds marketed as "the pushup triangle" (Shipman, 2011, para. 2). A few years earlier, it marketed 10-year-old female thong underwear with the words "wink, wink" and "eye candy" printed on the front side (Shipman, 2011, para. 10). When asked about the public reaction against marketing underwear like this for very young girls, Jeffries responded, "That was a bunch of bullshit … People said … that we were sexualizing little girls. But you know what? I still think those are cute underwear for little girls" (Denizet-Lewis, 2006, para. 22). Some would-be customers have also taken issue with the limited sizes A&F offers. The company only stocks women's sizes from XS to L and won't stock jeans above size 10. The average US woman wears size 14 jeans. The sizes are a bit more generous for men offering up to XXL for men. As one fashion writer speculates, the larger men's sizes are "probably to appeal to beefy football players and wrestlers" (Lutz, 2013, para. 9).

Apologies and Termination

Reactions to Jeffries' interview and the surrounding controversies gained momentum. Numerous celebrities spoke out, the press covered the developing story in an almost entirely negative light, and protesters even gathered in front of A&F's Ohio headquarters. Jeffries responded to the public's growing discontent:

> I want to address some of my comments that have been circulating from a 2006 interview. While I believe this 7 year old, resurrected quote has been taken out of context. … I sincerely regret that my choice of words was interpreted in a manner that has caused offense. A&F is an aspirational brand that, like most specialty apparel brands, targets its marketing at a particular segment of customers. However, we care about the broader communities in which we operate and are strongly committed to diversity and inclusion. We hire good people who share these values. We are completely opposed to any discrimination, bullying, derogatory characterizations or other anti-social behavior based on race, gender, body type or other individual characteristics. (Vultaggio, 2013, para. 3, 4)

For some, the apology was too little, too late. The public's outcry did not die down. In the days following his apology, a group of A&F executives met with the founder of Change.org, 18-year-old Benjamin O'Keefe who struggled with an eating disorder, in part, over his appearance insecurities. O'Keefe suggested a boycott of A&F until they stocked larger sizes. Following this meeting, A&F issued a second apology:

> We look forward to continuing this dialogue and taking concrete steps to demonstrate our commitment to anti-bullying in addition to our ongoing support of diversity and inclusion. We want to reiterate that we sincerely regret and apologize for any offense caused by comments we have made in the past which are contrary to these values. (Cited in Abercrombie, 2013, para. 8)

Despite these apologies, A&F's reputation continued to suffer. In response, the company added larger sizes. It also no longer markets in such overtly sexual ways. For instance, it no longer uses live topless male models in the front windows of its retail stores. The company also announced at the end of 2014 that Mike Jeffries, at 70 years old, was no longer going to be the company's CEO after the company lost money every quarter for almost three straight years (Rupp, 2014). As recently as 2015, A&F store

Questions:

- Do you believe Jeffries took his views about marketing and hiring too far? How would you change A&F if you were the CEO?
- How do you believe social media influenced the outcome of the case?

managers were still sending employees home and cutting their hours as a form of discipline when employees did not fit the company's "look policy." Employees filed a lawsuit against what they see as discriminatory policies (Babcock, 2015). Many customers and employees alike have lost their taste for the company's approach.

AOL's Public Embarrassment of Employees

In the early 1990s America Online (AOL) was a popular dial-up Internet, email, and content service provider. Its business model was common at the time; it offered its services for a flat monthly fee. In the 2000s, however, the number of its subscribers steadily declined as other competitors entered the marketplace. In response to its struggling subscription base, AOL shifted its focus from a subscription-reliant business model and offered many of the same services for free (e.g., email, Instant Messenger, AOL News, etc.) that were once available for paying customers only. It wanted to attract more users to increase advertising revenue. In 2009, its newly hired CEO, former Google executive Tim Armstrong, aggressively pursued a content-driven business model and looked for ways to provide interesting content, attract viewers, and, thus, generate more money by selling ads. Under Armstrong, AOL soon purchased a variety of websites, such as the already-popular online news source *Huffington Post* (Peters & Kopytoff, 2011). His leadership brought needed success to its content-driven business model often by buying out existing successful websites.

One was Patch.com, a news website that provides a mixture of local and national news in one place. Armstrong had founded it before joining AOL. Its users select from 600 local areas or "patches" rather than visiting an assortment of websites. By catering to the local news market, Patch employees could attract local advertisements, a still largely untapped market online. Once purchased by AOL, however, Patch struggled. At a particularly stressful juncture in 2013, Armstrong held a tense conference call with over 1,000 Patch employees listening. During its opening minutes, Armstrong publicly and spontaneously fired a Patch employee. This action was an unusual move in corporate America. The public firing over a seemingly minor issue prompted questions about Armstrong's ability to work well with others. About a year later, Armstrong also publicly embarrassed two employees at AOL who had delivered babies with serious medical issues that resulted in high healthcare bills. This case explores the reputational and leadership difficulties of Armstrong's insensitive leadership approach.

Conference Call to Patch Employees: The Firing and Reactions

Armstrong was excited about purchasing Patch, a company he founded, for AOL. However, it did not make a profit and was costing AOL dearly. In 2013, the day before the company-wide conference call, Armstrong told Wall Street analysts that AOL would be cutting the number of Patch websites from 900 to 600. This was not only a likely source of embarrassment for Armstrong but also meant the impending loss of jobs for many employees. Thus, employee morale was already suffering before the conference call, which was "supposed to be Armstrong's attempt to rally the troops" (Carlson, 2013b, para. 8). Instead, the call made matters worse. It involved a number of employees who were present in the room and another 1,000 listened in from their dispersed offices. One employee in the room with Armstrong was Abel Lenz, a creative director who, in part, worked on Patch's internal website. According to an employee, in this role "Lenz always took photos at Patch's all-hands meetings. He would later post them to Patch's internal news site" (Carlson, 2013a, para. 10). Following the controversial conference call, an insider leaked a 2-minute and 33-second segment of the opening moments of the call to a business blog, jimromenesko.com (Romenesko, 2013).

The leaked portion of the call provides Armstrong's opening remarks. A *Forbes'* writer (Adams, 2013) described Armstrong's tone as "defensive and threatening" (para. 7) to listening employees. Armstrong begins as follows:

> There's a couple of things I want you guys to realize and really think about and sink in. And if it doesn't sink in and you don't believe what I'm about to say, I'm going to ask you to leave Patch. And I don't mean that in a harsh way. (Romenesko, 2013)

For the next minute, Armstrong explained that he is accepting "full responsibility for anything that is not right at Patch," is not bothered by information that some employees have apparently leaked to the press about his handling of Patch, and will not be "changing directions" because of those leaks. During the opening minute of the call, he directly encourages uncommitted employees to resign. Next is the segment beginning at 1 minute and 45 seconds. In it, Armstong continues speaking to the entire staff about his concerns but then abruptly addresses and fires Abel Lenz:

> If you think what's going on right now is a joke, and you want to joke around about it, you should pick your stuff up and leave Patch today, and the reason is, and I'm going to be very specific about this, is Patch from an experience—*Abel, put that camera down right*

> *now! Abel, you're fired. Out!* [5 second pause]. If you guys think that AOL has not been committed to Patch, and won't stay committed to Patch, you're wrong. The company has spent hundreds of millions of dollars, the board of directors is committed, I'm committed, Bud is committed. (Romenesko, 2013)

The leaked portion of the call then stops. The conference call itself continued for one hour and forty minutes (Romenesko, 2013). A few minutes after the leaked portion of the call ended, an unnamed AOL employee relayed to a writer (Carlson, 2013a) that Armstrong told employees the internal leaks about Patch made the company seem like "loser-ville" (para. 6) to the press and added, "That's why Abel was fired. … We can't have people that are in the locker room giving the game plan away" (para. 6, 7). Getting fired is never easy; getting fired hastily in front of an entire company is an embarrassing experience for everybody involved. Numerous employees leaked the call and spoke to the press in the days following the firing to complain about Armstrong. For his part, Abel Lenz would not comment to the press about the incident. The blogger who originally posted the conference call also posted the photograph Lenz had snapped the moment before he was fired, and other sites republished it (Yarow, 2013). It showed Armstrong standing and speaking at a small podium with several employees in the background.

A few days later, Armstrong emailed a statement to AOL employees in which he provided the context for the firing and apologized for his handling of the situation:

> I am writing you to acknowledge the mistake I made last Friday during the Patch all-hands meeting when I publicly fired Abel Lenz. It was an emotional response at the start of a difficult discussion dealing with many people's careers and livelihoods. … We talk a lot about accountability and I am accountable for the way I handled the situation, and at a human level it was unfair to Abel. I've communicated to him directly and apologized for the way the matter was handled at the meeting. … Abel had been told previously not to record a confidential meeting, and he repeated that behavior on Friday, which drove my actions. (Gara, 2013, para. 4, 5)

Armstrong's account adds a layer of complexity if not conflicting information in at least three ways. First, he stated that by photographing him, Lenz was somehow "leaking" confidential corporate information. While it may be true that Armstrong told Lenz not to record confidential meetings, Lenz had photographed conference calls in the past for the company's internal website (Carlson, 2013a). In this instance, it is not clear how a simple photograph can somehow give "the game plan away," as Armstrong claimed. Second, just seconds earlier in the call, Armstrong states, "I don't care if people leak information." The timing of this statement and the abrupt firing of Lenz is ironic. Third, the conference call was being audio-recorded by somebody else anyway. Whatever his reasons, previous conversations between Armstrong and Lenz and some apparent in-the-moment misunderstanding led to this public firing.

The reaction to his behavior was strong despite his apology and explanation. In the readers' comments section of an article about the incident published by businessinsider.com (Carlson, 2013b), one reader named "Bensky" summed up many other readers' opinions:

> Of course you're not getting the whole story. However, the manner in which he fired him was the worst part of the story. I still think the guy is under too much stress for him, personally, to handle. This is the sound you hear when a guy finds himself in the middle of a jungle, loses it, and starts thrashing at the bushes with a machete to find a way out.

A staff writer for *Forbes* (Adams, 2013) said something similar: "It seems that Armstrong's [Patch] venture failed. But a leader should never take his own mistakes out on his employees. … he should work through those emotions with a friend, counselor or coach before dumping on his workforce" (Adams, 2013, para. 10). One incident like firing Abel Lenz does not mean much in isolation. However, it does prompt the question, *if this is how Armstrong treats people publicly, how might he treat them behind closed doors?* In the following months, AOL laid off hundreds of Patch employees and sold the company about five months after the leaked conference call.

Blame It on the Babies

About six months after firing Lenz, Armstrong announced a plan to change the way AOL contributed to or "matched" employee contributions to the company's 401k retirement program. Previously, it provided matching contributions each pay period. To help cut costs, Armstrong told employees and the press that the company would be matching employees' contributions at the end of the company's financial year. If employees were fired or quit the company before this time, they would not receive the matching contribution (Kaufman, 2014). When explaining why the company was making this change, Armstrong blamed the soaring cost of providing healthcare coverage to its employees. To make his point, he provided an example about the high cost of two AOL employees' newborn babies:

> We had two AOL-ers that had distressed babies that were born that we paid a million dollars each to make sure those babies were OK in general. And those are the things that add

> up into our benefits cost. So when we had the final decision about what benefits to cut because of the increased healthcare costs, we made the decision, and I made the decision, to basically change the 401(k) plan. (Fish, 2011, para. 17)

Armstrong's blame-it-on-the-babies comment did not sit well with AOL employees and the public.

One of the new mothers, the wife of an AOL employee indirectly mentioned by Armstrong, wrote an essay responding to Armstrong's point of view:

> Let's set aside the fact that Armstrong—who took home $12 million in pay in 2012—felt the need to announce a cut in employee benefits on the very day that he touted the best quarterly earnings in years. For me and my husband—who have been genuinely grateful for AOL's benefits, which are actually quite generous—the hardest thing to bear has been the whiff of judgment in Armstrong's statement, as if we selfishly gobbled up an obscenely large slice of the collective health care pie. … While he's at it, why not call out the women who got cancer? The parents of kids with asthma? These rank among the nation's most expensive medical conditions. … In other words, we experienced exactly the kind of unforeseeable, unpreventable medical crisis that any health plan is supposed to cover. Isn't that the whole point of health insurance? (Fei, 2014, para. 5, 6, 9)

In the days that followed, Armstrong reversed his decision to change AOL's retirement matching program. He told employees, "The leadership team and I listened to your feedback over the last week. We heard you on this topic. … we have decided to change the policy back to a per-pay-period matching contribution" (AOL, 2014, para. 3). He also made a private call to Deanna Fei, the new mother who wrote the essay calling Armstrong out, to apologize personally. Fei stated after the call, "His apology was heartfelt and I appreciated it and I do forgive him" (Fish, 2011, para. 22). Like the incident with Abel Lenz, Armstrong's apology after a seemingly spontaneous moment caused uproar at AOL and with the public.

Questions:

- Armstrong has helped AOL financially in some ways. Does this excuse or justify his impersonal approach for handling employees?
- If you were giving advice to Armstrong, what would you say about how he relates to people?

Reflections on Leadership

As one writer mentioned (Fish, 2011), if you look at AOL's financial decisions alone, Armstrong should be viewed as a capable leader. He took a struggling company, transitioned it to one that is making money again, and increased AOL's stock value. There is more to leading a company, however, than satisfying the stockholders. The same writer commented, "If your employees don't consider your company a place that they would recommend as a workplace, it is going to be difficult to attract the top notch talent required to take your business to the next level" (Fish, 2011, para. 1). In fact, since Armstrong took over, many executives closest to Armstrong have left AOL: "[T]hey have had a tremendous amount of turnover at the executive level, with two COOs, four advertising Presidents, four heads of Media, three CTOs, and four heads of PR. With turnover like this, you have to wonder if Armstrong's leadership techniques are wearing on the staff" (Fish, 2011, para. 25). This exodus signals that incidents like Abel Lenz's public firing and blaming babies for cutting costs on employees' retirement funds may not be isolated incidents.

Chapter Discussion Questions

- What commonalities do you see in the cases regarding how the organizations and/or leaders treated people?
- Treating people well costs nothing more than treating them harshly. Why, then, do organizations like these promote an impersonal approach when interacting with employees and customers?
- To what extent can these organizations change the way they communicate outwardly if they maintain an *I-It* mindset?

Key Terms

- Impersonal communication
- Immediacy
- Cell phone addictions
- Depersonalization
- Drive for efficiency
- Objectification of employees
- *I-It* communication
- Dehumanization

References

Bian, M., & Leung, L. (2014). Smartphone addiction: Linking loneliness, shyness, symptoms and patterns of use to social capital. *Media Asia, 41*, 159–176.

Braverman, H. (1998). *Labor and monopoly capital: The degradation of work in the twentieth century* (25th anniversary ed.). New York, NY: Monthly Review Press.

Buber, M. (1947). *Between man and man*. (R. G. Smith, Trans.). London: Routledge & Kegan Paul.

Buber, M. (1970). *I and Thou*. New York, NY: Charles Scribner's Sons.

Caliendo, K. (2013, November 14). Communication skills are lacking in the labor force. *CNBC*. Retrieved from http://www.moneynews.com/Economy/job-communication-skills-work-force/2013/11/14/id/536577#ixzz2mc8Z0gBx

Gawande, A. (2009, March 30). Hellhole: The United States holds tens of thousands of inmates in long-term solitary confinement. *New Yorker*. Retrieved from http://www.newyorker.com/reporting/2009/03/30/090330fa_fact_gawande

Holba, A. (2008). Revisiting Martin Buber's I-It: A rhetorical strategy. *Human Communication, 11*, 495–510.

Impersonal communication. (n.d.) *Business Dictionary*. Retrieved December 29, 2015 from http://www.businessdictionary.com/definition/impersonal-communication.html

Leyens, J. P., Rodriguez-Perez, A., Rodriguez-Torres, R., Gaunt, R., Paladino, M. P., Vaes, J., & Stea, P. D. (2001). Psychological essentialism and the differential attribution of uniquely human emotions to ingroups and outgroups. *European Journal of Social Psychology, 31*, 395–411.

Lyon, A., & Mirivel, J. (2011). Reconstructing Merck's practical theory of communication: The ethics of pharmaceutical sales representative-physician encounters. *Communication Monographs, 78*, 53–72.

Mirivel, J. C. (2012). Communication excellence: Embodying virtues in interpersonal communication. In: T. J. Socha & M. J. Pitts (Eds.), *The positive side of interpersonal communication* (pp. 57–72). New York, NY: Peter Lang.

Starr, B. (2015, April 17). Missouri National Guard's term for Ferguson protesters: "Enemy forces". *CNN*. Retrieved from http://www.cnn.com/2015/04/17/politics/missouri-national-guard-ferguson-protesters/

Taylor, F. W. (1947). *Scientific management (comprising Shop management, The principles of scientific management, & Testimony before the Special House Committee)*. New York, NY: Harper & Row.

Teven, J. J. (2007). Effects of supervisor social influence, nonverbal immediacy, and biological sex on subordinates' perceptions of job satisfaction, liking, and supervisor credibility. *Communication Quarterly, 55*, 155–177.

Teven, J. J. (2010). The effects of supervisor nonverbal immediacy and power use on employees' ratings of credibility and affect for the supervisor. *Human Communication, 13*, 69–85.

Viki, G. T., Winchester, L., Titshall, L., Chisango, T., Pina, A., & Russell, R. (2006). Beyond secondary emotions: The infrahumanization of outgroups using human-related and animal-related words. *Social Cognition, 24*, 753–775.

Amazon References

Cook, J. (2015, August 16). Full memo: Jeff Bezos responds to brutal *NYT* story, says it doesn't represent the Amazon he leads. *New York Times*. Retrieved from http://www.geekwire.com/2015/

full-memo-jeff-bezos-responds-to-cutting-nyt-expose-says-tolerance-for-lack-of-empathy-needs-to-be-zero

Employee complaint 422732. [complain to OSHA]. (2011). Retrieved from http://www.scribd.com/doc/65232030/OSHA-Complaints-About-Amazon#scribd

Giang, V. (2013, July 28). Ranking America's biggest companies by turnover rate. *Business Insider.* Retrieved from http://www.slate.com/blogs/business_insider/2013/07/28/turnover_rates_by_company_how_amazon_google_and_others_stack_up.html

Kantor, J., & Streitfeld, D. (2015, August 15). Inside Amazon: Wrestling big ideas in a bruising workplace. *New York Times.* Retrieved from http://www.nytimes.com/2015/08/16/technology/inside-amazon-wrestling-big-ideas-in-a-bruising-workplace.html?_r=0

Knowledge. (2013, November 11). In Amazon and Walmart's battle for dominance, who loses out? *Forbes.* Retrieved from http://www.forbes.com/sites/knowledgewharton/2013/11/14/242013/

Soper, S. (2011, November 6). Amazon workers left out in the cold. *The Morning Call.* Retrieved from http://www.mcall.com/news/local/amazon/mc-amazon-workers-left-out-in-the-cold-20120123,0,2487826,full.story

Soper, S. (2015, August 17). Inside Amazon's warehouse. *The Morning Call.* Retrieved from http://www.mcall.com/news/local/amazon/mc-allentown-amazon-complaints-20110917-story.html

Steitfeld, D., & Kantor, J. (2015, August 17). Jeff Bezos and Amazon employees join debate over its culture. *New York Times.* Retrieved from http://www.nytimes.com/2015/08/18/technology/amazon-bezos-workplace-management-practices.html

Yarow, J. (2013, February 8). An inside look at the pretty miserable working conditions at an Amazon warehouse. *Business Insider.* Retrieved from http://www.businessinsider.com/working-conditions-at-an-amazon-warehouse-2013-2

Comcast References

Benchmarks by company. (2014). *American customer satisfaction index* [webpage]. Retrieved June 29, 2015 from http://www.theacsi.org/index.php?option=com_content&view=article&id=149&catid=&Itemid=214&c=all&sort=Y2014

Bennett-Smith, M. (2012, September 19). Comcast employee tells world he hates his job in Reddit AMA post. *The Huffington Post.* Retrieved November 17, 2015 from http://www.huffingtonpost.com/2012/09/19/comcast-employee-tells-world-he-hates-his-job-reddit-ama_n_1897425.html.

Block, R. (2010). Comcastic service disconnection (recording starts 10 mins. Into call). *Soundcloud.* Retrieved November 17, 2015 from https://soundcloud.com/ryan-block-10/comcastic-service.

Brodkin, J. (2014, August 13). Here's another Comcast cancellation horror story, with video evidence. *Ars Technica.* Retrieved from http://arstechnica.com/business/2014/08/heres-another-comcast-cancellation-horror-story-with-video-evidence

Brodkin, J. (2015a, February 19). Comcast agent tells customer that data caps are "mandated by law." *Ars Technica.* Retrieved from http://arstechnica.com/business/2015/02/comcast-agent-tells-customer-that-data-caps-are-mandated-by-law/

Brodkin, J. (2015b, January 28). Comcast bill changes customer's first name to "A—hole." *Ars Technica*. Retrieved from http://arstechnica.com/business/2015/01/comcast-bill-changes-customers-first-name-to-ahole/

Comcast is crowned Consumerist.Com's 2010 "Worst Company in America". (2010). *PR Newswire*. Retrieved from http://www.prnewswire.com/news-releases/comcast-is-crowned-consumeristcoms-2010-worst-company-in-america-92097574.html

Hutchinson, L. (2014, August 19). Leaked Comcast employee metrics show what we figured: Sell or perish. *Ars Technica*. Retrieved from http://arstechnica.com/business/2014/08/leaked-comcast-employee-metrics-show-what-we-figured-sell-or-perish/

Jeffries, A. (2014, August 4). This is Comcast's internal handbook for talking customers out of canceling service. *The Verge*. Retrieved from http://www.theverge.com/2014/8/4/5967255/this-is-comcasts-internal-handbook-for-talking-customers-out-of

Kim, S. (2014, July 15). Comcast apologizes for "unacceptable" customer service call that won't end. *ABC News*. Retrieved from http://abcnews.go.com/Business/comcast-apologizes-unacceptable-customer-service-call-end/story?id=24567047

Quirk, M. B. (2014). Comcast employees say needy retention call is totally normal. *Consumerist.com*. Retrieved from http://consumerist.com/2014/07/16/comcast-employees-say-needy-retention-call-is-totally-normal

Abercrombie & Fitch References

Abercrombie & Fitch apology: Brand issues another mea culpa for CEO's past comments (2013, May 23). *Huffington Post*. Retrieved from http://www.huffingtonpost.com/2013/05/23/abercrombie-and-fitch-apology_n_3323668.html

Abercrombie & Fitch: The "look policy." (2009, June 24). *The Guardian*. Retrieved from http://www.theguardian.com/money/2009/jun/24/abercrombie-fitch-look-policy-discrimination

Babcock, G. (2015, July 22). Abercrombie & Fitch faces new lawsuit over employee "Look Policy." *Complex*. Retrieved from http://www.complex.com/style/2015/07/abercrombie-and-fitch-employee-look-policy-law-suit

Bhasin, K., & Fairchild, C. (2013, September 18). Abercrombie dress code enables discrimination, insiders say. *Huffington Post*. Retrieved from http://www.huffingtonpost.com/2013/09/18/abercrombie-dress-code_n_3943131.html

Denizet-Lewis, B. (2006, January 24). The man behind Abercrombie & Fitch. *Salon*. Retrieved from http://www.salon.com/2006/01/24/jeffries/

English, R. (2009, June 13). I was banished to the stockroom, says disabled shop girl now suing Abercrombie & Fitch for discrimination. *Daily Mail*. Retrieved from http://www.dailymail.co.uk/news/article-1192674/I-banished-stockroom-says-disabled-shop-girl-suing-Abercrombie--Fitch-discrimination.html

Leung, R. (2015, December 5). The look of Abercrombie & Fitch. CBS News. Retrieved from http://www.cbsnews.com/news/the-look-of-abercrombie-fitch-05-12-2003/

Levinson, S. (2013, May 3). Abercrombie & Fitch CEO explains why he hates fat chicks. *Elite Daily*. Retrieved from http://elitedaily.com/news/world/abercrombie-fitch-ceo-explains-why-he-hates-fat-chicks/

Lutz, A. (2013, May 3). Abercrombie & Fitch refuses to make clothes for large women. *Business Insider*. Retrieved from http://www.businessinsider.com/abercrombie-wants-thin-customers-2013-5

Rupp, L. (2014, December 9). Abercrombie CEO leaves chain after overseeing rise and fall. *Bloomberg*. Retrieved from http://www.bloomberg.com/news/articles/2014-12-09/abercrombie-fitch-ceo-mike-jeffries-to-step-down-immediately

Shipman, C. (2011, March 28). Padded bikini top for 7-year-olds draws parents' ire. *ABC News*. Retrieved from http://abcnews.go.com/US/abercrombie-fitch-padded-bikini-top-year-olds-parents/story?id=13236904

Vultaggio, M. (2013, May 16). Mike Jeffries, Abercrombie & Fitch CEO, apologizes for inflammatory comments in Facebook post. *International Business Times*. Retrieved from http://www.ibtimes.com/mike-jeffries-abercrombie-fitch-ceo-apologizes-inflammatory-comments-facebook-post-1265973

AOL References

Adams, S. (2013, August 14). AOL's Chief demonstrates the worst way to fire someone. *Forbes*. Retrieved from http://www.forbes.com/sites/susanadams/2013/08/14/aols-chief-demonstrates-the-worst-way-to-fire-someone/

AOL CEO reverses benefit cuts, apologizes for "distressed babies" comment. (2014, February 8). *Huffington Post*. Retrieved from http://www.huffingtonpost.com/2014/02/08/tim-armstrong-401k-cuts-aol-_n_4753148.html

Carlson, N. (2013a, August 9). AOL CEO Tim Armstrong fired this man in front of 1,000 coworkers. *Business Insider*. Retrieved from http://www.businessinsider.com/aol-ceo-tim-armstrong-appeared-to-fire-this-man-in-front-of-1000-coworkers-2013-8

Carlson, N. (2013b, August 12). Leaked audio: Listen to AOL CEO Tim Armstrong fire a Patch employee in front of 1,000 coworkers. *Business Insider*. Retrieved from http://www.businessinsider.com/leaked-audio-listen-to-aol-ceo-tim-armstrong-fire-a-patch-employee-snapping-a-photo-2013-8

Fei, D. (2014, February 9). My baby and AOL's bottom line. *Slate*. Retrieved from http://www.slate.com/articles/double_x/doublex/2014/02/tim_armstrong_blames_distressed_babies_for_aol_benefit_cuts_he_s_talking.html

Fish, B. (2011, February 14). CEO reputation can't be measured by profits alone. *Online Reputation Management*. Retrieved from https://www.reputationmanagement.com/blog/ceo-reputation-not-just-profits

Gara, T. (2013, August 13). Abel, I'm sorry: Tim Armstrong apologizes for live firing. *Wall Street Journal*. Retrieved from http://blogs.wsj.com/corporate-intelligence/2013/08/13/abel-im-sorry-tim-armstrong-apologizes-for-live-firing/

Kaufman, L. (2014, February 9). Facing criticism after remarks, AOL chief reverses 401(k) changes. *New York Times*. Retrieved from http://www.nytimes.com/2014/02/10/business/media/facing-criticism-aol-chief-reverses-change-to-401-k-plan.html?_r=0

Peters, J. W., & Kopytoff, V. G. (2011, February 11). Betting on news, AOL is buying the *Huffington Post. New York Times*. Retrieved from http://www.nytimes.com/2011/02/07/business/media/07aol.html

Romenesko, J. (2013, August 8). Listen to AOL CEO Tim Armstrong fire Patch's creative director during a conference call [blog]. Retrieved from http://jimromenesko.com/2013/08/10/listen-to-aol-ceo-tim-armstrong-fire-his-creative-director-during-a-conference-call/

Yarow, J. (2013, August 14). This is the photo that led to Tim Armstrong losing his cool and suddenly firing an AOL employee in front of 1,000 people. *Business Insider*. Retrieved from http://www.businessinsider.com/the-photo-that-led-to-tim-armstrong-firing-abel-lenz-2013-8

11 Engaging Communication and Case Studies

The high-tech age requires high-touch balance in the same measure.
—*John Naisbitt, author of Mega Trends and High Tech High Touch*

When people first met Elvis Presley face to face, many said he made them feel like they were the only person on the planet in that moment. Mohammad Ali, perhaps the greatest heavyweight boxer of all time, said of meeting the King of Rock and Roll in the flesh, Elvis "was the sweetest, most humble, and nicest man you'd want to know" (www.elvis.net). John Lennon described the Beatles' one and only meeting with Elvis as tense in the first few moments because The Beatles were very nervous. Elvis quickly cracked a joke, broke out the instruments, and connected with the Beatles by sharing stories about life on the road (Lennon, 2002). Despite being hailed as the King of Rock and Roll, Elvis was extremely tuned-in when interacting with others. The 1950s, however, was a different era. Today, we are inundated with endless distractions. Nevertheless, some organizations excel at engaging communication, as this chapter illustrates. First, research and concepts explore what "engaging" communication looks and sounds like, and second, four case studies show organizations striving to enact it: Southwest Airlines, Wegmans, Google, and Zappos.

Engaging Communication

Engaging communication contrasts with impersonal communication. Rather than being automated and distant, ***engaging communication*** connects with the whole person. It starts with obvious communication behaviors such as warm eye contact, smiling and supportive facial expressions, a friendly tone of voice and other positive vocal expressions, animated gestures and body movement, and walking around and mingling in the office in a relaxed manner (Teven, 2007, 2010). These concrete behaviors strengthen the relationship between supervisors and employees. Engaging communication, however, goes beyond mere nonverbal behavior. Personal, supportive, and empathetic, it creates an encouraging dynamic between supervisors and subordinates that pursues *I-Thou* communication (Buber, 1970). In contrast to Buber's *I-It* communication mentioned in Chapter 10, an ***I-Thou*** perspective sees the other person as a human being who is naturally endowed with an inherent value, dignity, and worthy of our respect. From Buber's perspective, Holba (2008) states that it is in "I-Thou moments where we find deeply genuine and connective communication encounters" (p. 497). Even though we may find ourselves in different or even "unequal" roles, an *I-Thou* mindset encourages dialogic communication. Arnett (2012) explained, "There are examples of mutuality or reciprocity between unequals, displayed in communicative life between teacher and student in which there is more leaning toward the *Other* from the teacher than leaning toward the teacher from the student" (p. 145). Buber's *I-Thou* concept is philosophical and ethical. Practically speaking, all interactions cannot be in an *I-Thou* spirit. Our roles sometimes require moving quickly and moving on. Too many times, however, interactions drift toward shallow, routine exchanges because of the pressures mentioned in Chapter 10. The *I-Thou* ethic, thus, is the ideal to strive for in organizational life.

The reasons for engaging communication go beyond the pursuit of a philosophical ideal. From a practical standpoint, it helps organizations succeed. Campbell, White, and Johnson (2003) show a clear connection between employees' communication satisfaction and productivity and organization effectiveness. As Teven (2010) stated, "Although several factors are related to employee morale, the single most important one in enhancing job satisfaction is superior-subordinate communication" (Teven, 2010, p. 71). I focus mainly on engaging communication between supervisors and subordinates and then between organizational members and customers for a valid reason. As Bisel, Messersmith, and Kelley (2012) explained, "The supervisor-subordinate relationship is a microcosm of the organizational universe" (p. 129). In most cases, leaders directly supervise a specific set of employees. Each employee experiences a one-on-one or dyadic relationship with his or her supervisor.

Each ***dyadic relationship*** has its own characteristics and quality. Much research has been done on the way leaders interact with their subordinates. In essence, "Interpersonal communication within the context of leader-member relationships is crucial in determining the quality of those interactions" (Campbell et al., 2003, p. 191). For instance, Liden and Graen (1980) showed that engaging supervisors reported providing a "greater amount of job-related feedback, support of actions, and personal sensitivity (understanding of the person's problems and needs, and awareness of his/her abilities and potential)" (p. 465) to employees who became top performers. In contrast, lower-performing employees who did not enjoy the same level of engaging, supportive communication from their supervisors were more likely to experience increased stress and decreased job involvement (Kacmar, Witt, Zivnuska, & Gully, 2003). As Teven (2010) put it, employees "will simply work harder for a supervisor whom they like" (Teven, 2010, p. 80). Employees and the organization thrive within a supportive communication environment.

The body of research regarding many facets of this area often derives from ***Leader-Member Exchange*** (LMX) theory. The most impressive are the positive results it helps produce (Kacmar et al., 2003; Liden & Graen, 1980; Liden & Maslyn, 1998). When leaders cultivate engaging relationships, their employees receive ample resources, desirable assignments, emotional support, greater motivation, and excellent performance ratings from their supervisors. The benefits go both ways. These subordinates have higher productivity, greater initiative, lower turnover, increased commitment to the work, long-term loyalty, higher satisfaction, and give higher ratings to their supervisors. Engaging communication benefits everybody.

In addition to the behaviors mentioned above, high-quality relationships develop when the supervisors and subordinates tend to certain aspects of their relationship. Liden and Maslyn (1998) found three key ingredients that both members of the high-quality dyadic relationships felt toward each other: They *like* each other, demonstrate *mutual loyalty*, and show *professional respect* (see p. 50).

> ***Liking/Affect:*** Both members of the dyad like each other. They share mutual affection. This liking is based mainly on interpersonal dynamics rather than professional similarities or values. This mutual affection is the type that may result in a friendship.
>
> ***Loyalty:*** Each member of the dyad expresses public support for the other person's goals and personal character. This loyalty generally involves faithfulness to the individual that is consistent across situations.
>
> ***Professional Respect:*** Each member of the dyad perceives that the other has built a reputation of excelling at his or her work inside and outside of the organization. These perceptions can be based upon the dyad's shared work history, personal experience, feedback

from people inside or outside of the organization, or knowledge about awards or other indications of professional recognition and achievement. Because respect is partially established by others' feedback, it is possible for one or more members of the dyad to feel professional respect toward the other before working together.

Engaging Communication Can Be Subtle

Unfortunately, most supervisors do not have mutually positive relationships with each individual they lead. As research discussed in Chapter 10 shows, leaders tend to form ***in-groups*** and ***out-groups***. You have probably also noticed how subtle behaviors can identify favorites and shape our relationships. A leader may make just a little more eye contact, laugh a bit longer, use slightly more supportive language, or show a patient facial expression with individuals in his or her in-group in contrast to communication with out-group members. Young (2007) and Rowe (1990) explained that, while these actions are small, their effect is not trivial. A leader may affirm one employee's presentation by looking and sounding fully engaged throughout it (e.g., sustained eye contact, leaning forward, occasional nods, enthusiastic tone of voice, etc.) but appear slightly preoccupied during the next employee's presentation (e.g., glancing at his phone, arms folded, distant look in his eyes, flat tone of voice, etc.). Small nonverbal cues can speak volumes and promote various impressions.

Tiny differences in word choice, tone of voice, volume, rate of speech, eye contact, body orientation, gestures, and other body language send a cumulative message. According to Rowe (1990), employees who do not receive these displays of affirmation can feel less confident and be less productive. Livingston (2003) showed that employees who received supportive communication and positive labels increased their performance while employees who did not showed decreased productivity. Leaders may be unaware they are sending both positive and negative messages, especially in ways that undermine employees' work (Rowe, 1990). The behaviors are often so minor—partial smile, unenthusiastic handshake, inconsistent eye contact—that leaders are not aware of their impact.

Classic research on teachers illustrates the way communication nuances can shape the efforts of students (Rosenthal & Jacobson, 1968). In an experiment, teachers were told certain students in their classes were gifted when, in fact, they were assigned randomly. Even though they had similar pre-test scores to the other students, those "gifted" students' performance on the post test dramatically improved compared to their classmates. In part, the teachers' positive attitude, expectations, and subtle communication behaviors influenced the students' commitment to learning. Research on ***leader-follower relationships*** shows similar results (Livingston, 2003). Employees generally accept leaders' unspoken appraisal and perform up to or down from those expectations. The good news is that positive expectations and communication can turn an average performer into an outstanding employee (Eden & Ravid, 1982).

Engaging Communication Takes Courage But Has Benefits

Establishing positive, high-quality relationships with employees involves *I-Thou* communication that engages others more fully and produces clear benefits. Not only do we get to enjoy higher-quality relationships at work, a benefit unto itself, but these relationships also result in better performance, higher productivity, higher employee satisfaction, and higher organizational morale for all. While authentic engaging communication takes courage, the four case studies below show engaging communication between and among organizational insiders and the customers they serve.

Cases Involving Engaging Communication

Developing a Great Place to Work: The Southwest Airlines Legacy

Southwest Airlines, headquartered in Dallas, TX, consistently ranks high on *Fortune* magazine's "most admired companies" yearly list (World's, 2015). It also appears high each year on *Forbes'* list of "best places to work" (America's, 2015). Not surprisingly, Southwest's customers like the airline as much as its employees do. In an industry riddled with low customer satisfaction, Southwest stands out as the airline with the fewest customer complaints coming in at a miniscule 0.33 complaints for every 100,000 passengers (Potter, 2011). According to the Bureau of Transportation statistics, Southwest Airlines has carried more domestic passengers each year than any another airline since 2011 (http://www.rita.dot.gov). Its 46,000 employees fly over 100 million passengers a year, most of whom are loyal repeat customers (Gallo, 2014). This customer loyalty, however, does not stem from perks or fancy services. In fact, the airline has few extras and does not even offer first class seats. Customers board in groups and select their own seats, a choice most of them enjoy. What the airline lacks in luxuries, however, it makes up for in other ways. Southwest is a low-cost airline and the only one that does not charge passengers to check bags. Perhaps more so than its low cost, this carrier is best known for its playful employees and outstanding customer service. While variables like budgets, the best flying routes, and relationships with venders and suppliers are all important, the way Southwest's people treat each other and customers has a huge impact. Thus, the focus of this case is to look at how Southwest's leaders and employees created a longstanding great place to work. That starts with Herb Kelleher and Colleen Barrett.

Southwest's Leaders

Herb Kelleher, the company's co-founder, served as the company's president and CEO of Southwest from 1981 until 2001. He stepped down as the CEO and occupied the role of the company's chairman until 2008. During his time as the company's leader, Kelleher built the company into the powerhouse it is today. He did it with his unique approach. In fact, Kelleher's leadership "style" is legendary and set the tone at the airline. He did almost anything to connect with and even entertain his employees. He regularly dressed up in outlandish costumes at company events. For instance, he dressed up as a biker, complete with an actual Harley Davidson. He impersonated Elvis, wore go-go boots, and even cross-dressed just to make employees laugh. Kelleher is serious about providing a world-class experience for passengers but not serious about himself. He once said, "Anybody who likes to be called a 'professional' probably shouldn't be around Southwest Airlines. … We want people who can do things well with laughter and grace" (Freiberg & Freiberg, 1996, p. 65). Instead of stuffy and serious, leaders and employees are "remarkably uninhibited and empathetic individuals who believe that the … [goal] is to make a profit by serving people and making life more fun" (Freiberg & Freiberg, 1996, p. 65). Kelleher's flair for the fun and the dramatic knows no bounds.

In one instance in the early 1990s, Southwest began using the advertising line "Just Plane Smart." Unfortunately, Stevens Aviation, an established company that services mostly private jets, had just begun using the line "Plane Smart" to market its services. To avoid a costly lawsuit, the CEOs of both companies agreed to "settle it like men" by arm wrestling in an arena often used for professional wrestling. The event was dubbed "Malice in Dallas" by Southwest. The winner would earn the right to use the slogan as they pleased. Southwest produced a video that captured the events leading up to the match that featured a smoking and drinking Herb Kelleher as he "trained" for the event (see Southwest, 2009). The videos compare Kelleher to iconic fighters such as Muhammad Ali and the fictional character Rocky Balboa. The match itself played out in colorful and dramatic fashion in a professional wrestling ring with a wig-wearing announcer who called the match in front of a large crowd. Stevens Aviation CEO, Kurt Herwald, recently revealed that Southwest hired professional wrestling insiders to choreograph the event for maximum dramatic impact ("3 Lasting," 2013). It was a brilliant move. The event was an unrestrained spectacle. In the end, Kelleher lost two of the three rounds of arm wrestling to a much younger Herwald. In gracious fashion, Herwald unexpectedly then gave Southwest the permission to continue using the slogan, which was not part of Kelleher's plan ahead of time ("3 Lasting," 2013). The event raised $15,000 for charity, but Southwest and Stevens Aviation were the big winners. Southwest received free publicity that would have cost an estimated $6 million to purchase ("3 Lasting," 2013). Many years later, the event is still being covered in textbooks and well-known online magazines like *Inc.com*. Stevens Aviation, a little known company at the time, enjoyed four years straight of 25% annual growth and a transformed corporate culture and reputation.

Similar to Kelleher, Colleen Barrett was a long-time leader at the airline and served as president of the company until 2008. Barrett played a fitting counterpart to Kelleher. She echoed the message Kelleher sent to employees with the well-known maxim at Southwest, "[don't] take yourself too seriously" (Arnoult, 2013, para. 13). For her part, Barrett embodied the playful and sometimes outlandish "Southwest spirit." She also had a reputation for deep care and commitment to employees. Kelleher and Barrett's personalities shaped and permeated the company's culture in numerous ways.

Let's Have Some Fun

If you had to sum up working for and flying on Southwest in one word, it would be *fun*. Part of the fun emerges by placing a value on each employee's unique personality. Kelleher once explained, "We try to let people be themselves and not have to surrender their personality when they arrive at Southwest" (Freiberg & Freiberg, 1996, p. 116). One employee said, "Senior people don't get jaded here. … Employees are able to be their own person. This stimulates hard work and loyalty. … People just don't quit here" (Freiberg & Freiberg, 1996, p. 117). This authenticity makes it much easier for everybody to have fun. The following long-time manager shares a story about a prank a ramp agent played on her when she asked if she could guide a plane in with his lighted batons.

> The ramper with whom I had been working was allowing me to have my wish and there I was, standing on a tug so the pilots could see me better, making the gestures with the batons exactly the way the agent was instructing me to do. … [He said] "Okay, give the signal I taught you." So I started waving the batons in a circular motion, exactly the way he had instructed. Suddenly, the taxiing aircraft began making a 360-degree turn on the tarmac. I was mortified. What had I done? Of course, about that time, the ramp agent doubled over in laughter. … The joke was on me. (Grubbs-West, 2005, pp. 53–54)

The ramp agent had secretly contacted the pilot and told him to spin the plane in circles. The pilot even let the passengers in on the joke. The company encourages the fun, even in their advertising. One print ad read, "Work at a place where wearing pants is optional" (Freiberg & Freiberg, 1996, p. 204). The playful ad was promoting the company's casual dress policy and went on to say, "Not to mention high-heeled shoes, ties, and panty hose. Because at Southwest Airlines, we do things a little differently" (p. 204). Employees enjoy enormous freedom compared to most companies. The airline trusts their carefully selected people to use common sense. Employees also have plenty of fun with passengers. Flight attendants frequently customize the pre-flight safety announcements in humorous ways. When flights get delayed, they play games with the passengers, sing songs, host light-hearted competitions, perform skits, and engage customers in numerous other ways to pass the time in an enjoyable way.

Part of Southwest's hiring approach makes this fun atmosphere remain effective. The company has a clear policy to hire people based upon their attitude and ability to handle relationships and communication well. Put simply, Southwest hires for attitude and trains for skills. Kelleher stated, "We look for attitudes; people with a sense of humor who don't take themselves too seriously. We'll train you on whatever it is you have to do, but the one thing Southwest cannot change in people is inherent attitudes" (Freiberg & Freiberg, 1996, p. 67). A ramp manager elaborated on this philosophy:

> One thing we cannot teach is attitudes toward peers or other groups. There's a code, a way you respond to every individual who works for Southwest. The easiest way to get in trouble at Southwest is to offend another employee. We need people to respond favorably. It promotes good working relationships. … You find an individual with an upbeat and positive attitude—and you'll find that everything that needs to be done, will get done. It's very contagious. (Gittell, 2003, p. 86)

At Southwest, attitude isn't everything but it is a prerequisite to getting hired and doing the job well. The result is a company full of playful, fun-loving, and high-caliber leaders and employees who take their tasks seriously but not themselves.

Caring About Employees

Another distinct ingredient that makes Southwest a great place to work is that people genuinely care about each other. This attitude can be traced directly to the top. Herb Kelleher, for all his flair and showmanship, shows people great care when he interacts with them. A pilot said the following about Kelleher:

> Herb is a true charismatic leader. He's not your average CEO. He really cares to let people know he cares. When he talks to you, he is really focused on what you are saying. No one can pry him loose. I've seen this. He sets the example of respect for everyone. (Freiberg & Freiberg, 1996, p. 58)

Kelleher credits his mother with teaching him how to treat people with care and respect. "She said," to Kelleher, "You should treat people with respect. She said positions and titles signify absolutely nothing" (p. 59). Colleen Barrett, the long-time president, enjoys the same reputation among employees. A manager reflected on Barrett, "Colleen remembers everyone and everything—if you have a birthday you'll get a card from her. She's up there with Jesus Christ, in our eyes" (Freiberg & Freiberg, 1996, p. 58). In fact, one of the first lessons new leaders are taught at the airline is "Don't try to learn your job. You first priority is to get to know your people!" (Grubbs-West, 2005, p. 97). Southwest consistently prioritizes treating people well.

If you listen to Southwest leaders long enough, it becomes obvious that they even often side with their employees over customers. Passengers can sometimes act unreasonably. When this happens, the airline does not follow the common motto, *the customer is always right.* About this Kelleher once said, "The customer is sometimes wrong. We don't carry those sorts of customers. We write them and say, 'Fly somebody else. Don't abuse our people'" (Freiberg & Freiberg, 1996, p. 268). Kelleher actually answered some customer complaint letters himself. For instance, one passenger who flew Southwest regularly wrote to the company after every flight to complain about virtually every detail. After numerous return letters from Southwest employees, the customer continued to complain. It wore the employees down. Finally, Kelleher himself responded in a short but sweet letter of his own: "Dear Mrs. Crabapple, We will miss you. Love, Herb" (Freiberg & Freiberg, 1996, p. 270). While most companies don't have the fortitude to handle their worst customers this way, Southwest's employees know in moments like this that their leaders will look out for them. Barrett explained Southwest's philosophy on caring for employees, "If you treat your employees well and they feel good enough about themselves they are going to treat each other better. That will overflow into how they treat the customer" (Arnoult, 2013, para. 19). Employees and leaders frequently mention "family" and "love" when discussing their workplace relationships. Even companies that do business with Southwest notice the difference. Tom Kalahar, for example, runs Camelot Communications, the airline's outside media-buying agency. He stated, "It makes me feel good to see my people happy to be working with Southwest. … Having Southwest as one of our clients is one of the best benefit programs I have for my people" (Freiberg & Freiberg, 1996, p. 220). Company leaders care for their employees, and in turn, employees treat each other and customers in the same fashion.

Communication as a Priority

Southwest also places a high priority on quality communication among departments. On the surface, this communication looks common. An employee explains:

> There's constant communication between customer service and the ramp. When planes have to be switched and bags must be moved, customer service will advise the ramp directly or through operations … operations keeps everyone informed. … It happens smoothly. (Gittell, 2003, p. 37)

An external study of Southwest revealed that the company's commitment to high-quality relationships and communication reinforced and created what the study called "high levels of relational coordination" (Freiberg & Freiberg, 1996, p. 91). The study connected this to important outcome measures such as improved "flight departure performance, particularly faster turnaround times, greater staffing productivity, fewer customers complaints, fewer lost bags, and better on-time performance" (p. 91), all of which contribute to customers' overall experience. Further, one of the most amazing features of Southwest's culture is how often the term "respect" comes up when interacting with others. A pilot explained, "We're predisposed to liking each other—I like the flight attendant and even that guy [operations agent] over there and I don't even know him. I guess it's mutual respect" (Gittell, 2003, p. 35). Communication at Southwest is not simply about exchanging relevant information. When done with respect, communication also cultivates high-quality relationships.

The expectation for respect extends to how the airline handles inevitable conflicts. Friction in the airline industry is common, particularly between people from different working groups. In the past, the airline handled conflicts departmentally through bureaucratic channels and the individuals involved made little progress. Over time, the company developed the interpersonal approach that gets the specific individuals to talk directly to each other in one-on-one fashion. An administrative assistant explains as follows.

> When something really serious happens and you can't work things out, the two managers involved call a "Come to Jesus" meeting, a face-to-face between the people who have the problem. You take the day off and bring everyone together. It doesn't happen much, but it happens. It's a matter of mutual respect. (Gittell, 2003, p. 103)

One flight attendant manager recalled a meeting with a flight attendant and pilot that worked out so well, she "got chills on my neck because of how wonderfully this worked out. … it was such a blessing" (p. 103). Southwest's secrets to handling conflict is that the company views each conflict as an interpersonal, one-on-one communication issue in contrast to the often immovable departmental or workgroup *us vs. them* approach.

Leaders' Legacy

The Southwest story continues and so does its success. Even though Kelleher and Barrett both retired from the airline, their legacy lives on in the company and culture they built. Gary Kelly, who took over as CEO, president, and chairman in 2004, has been at the company since the mid-1980s. He too embodies the Southwest spirit. For instance, the company threw a large costume party to celebrate its 40th anniversary. In past years, Kelly, a man, has dressed up as Dorothy from the *Wizard of Oz* and a female character from the film and Broadway show *Hairspray*. He even shaved his legs for the occasion. For the 40th anniversary party, however, he said, "I was determined to be a man this year" (Mouawad, 2010, para. 2). He dressed up as Woody from the *Toy Story* series of films. Beyond the fun, however, the company's fundamentals are as strong as ever. The company's entire approach helps the airline exceed industry standards in every way. It's still a great place to work. Employee turnover is at an astoundingly low 2–4% (Makovsky, 2013). The company has the highest paid mechanics, flight attendants, and pilots in the airline industry (Mouawad, 2010). The company is also positioned well for continued long-term profits (McGrath, 2015). Perhaps most impressively, Southwest is on a run of 40

Questions:

- Why does it take courage to put employees before customers?
- If it works so well for Southwest, why don't more airlines take this approach?

consecutive years of profitability, an unparalleled accomplishment in any industry (Gallo, 2014). At least in the case of Southwest, having fun is one key way to run a successful company.

Wegmans Food Markets Says "Employees First, Customers Second"

In 1930, the Wegman family opened their first supermarket. Over the next several decades, Wegmans Food Markets emerged as a shopping phenomenon in New York State. Most people don't normally see the world of grocery stores as a particularly interesting industry, workplace, or destinations. Still, it has continued to set the standard for excellence, particularly in its treatment of employees, customer service, and the shopping experience. As strange as it may sound for those who have never shopped at Wegmans, the supermarket competes with companies like Google as one of the nation's best employers. In fact, *Fortune's* "Best places to work" list has ranked Wegmans near the top every year since the list started in 1998 ("100 Best," 2015). The company ranked #1 in 2005 and is frequently in the top 10. Similarly, *Forbes* ranked Wegmans #9 on its America's Best Employers list ("America's Best," 2014). The company, headquartered in Rochester, NY, has won countless awards that both reflect and establish its reputation as an excellent employer. Employee satisfaction and superior customer service have propelled Wegmans' success. While the rest of the country was pulling itself out of a recession, Wegmans has doubled its revenue in the past decade and opened stores in new areas like Maryland, Virginia, Massachusetts, and Brooklyn, NY. This case examines what this family-owned chain does in its 80+ stores to make Wegmans a consistently superior place to work.

The Wegmans Experience

What most new customers notice first is the in-store experience. A consultant and industry expert, Burt Klickinger, has studied the supermarket industry for over 35 years. He stated, "The first thing you need to know about Wegmans is it's as special as people say" (Ferdman, 2015, para. 4). Compared to the size of most competing stores, "Wegmans is the equivalent of eight to 10 other supermarkets" (Ferdman, 2015, para. 8). Its produce section alone is twice the size of an average competitor's entire store. Roughly one-third to half of each store resembles a beautiful open-air European food market (Beldon, 2003). The market offers a "unique blend of gourmet and everyday food products" (Kalita, 2004, para. 6). CEO Danny Wegman confirmed, "We target the customer who is very passionate about food" (Kalita, 2004, para. 8). The variety and choices are astounding. For example, the company offers hundreds of different types of cheeses alone (Beldon, 2003; Bingham & Galagan, 2005). A writer visited Wegmans to put employees to the test and reported his experience:

> If you want to find out why Wegmans rules among supermarkets, try this. Go to a Wegmans' cheese department and ask for something really obscure. We tested this at the Wegmans in Fairfax, Virginia, by asking for a *Tomme de Savoie*, a savory, semi-hard cheese made in the part of France that surrounds the southwestern corner of Switzerland. For the record, Wegmans carries 700 kinds of cheese, but not *Tomme de Savoie*. And here's the cool part. The saleswoman not only knew instantly that the *Tomme* was not among Wegmans' 700 offerings, but she knew why. It's made with raw cow's milk and therefore can't be sold in the United States. This degree of knowledge is one of the secrets of Wegmans' success. (Bingham & Galagan, 2005, p. 32)

Jason Skelly, a manager at Wegmans stated about the variety and service, "Folks who want the full experience, we can get you that. … We can get you the six-ounce sea bass, as well as the education on how to handle that sea bass. There are several layers to what we do" (Kalita, 2004, para. 12). In most supermarket chains, this level of service is uncommon.

Part of Wegmans appeal is its theatrical layout and showmanship. It offers tastings of new products and recipes throughout its stores. As the CEO, Danny Wegman, gave a tour of a new location, he "pointed out the wood-fired brick oven [in the full-service bakery], noting that it burns a cord and a half of hardwood a week. Customers can watch the split wood being fed into the fiery furnace" (Beldon, 2003, para. 15). He continued, "It's really animation for the customers. … We like the way it bakes bread, but we like the showmanship of it" (Beldon, 2003, para. 16). The showmanship extends beyond customers' weekly shopping trips. They can also sit and dine in the store's Market Café, which seats from 100 to 300 people depending on the location. Customers can buy packaged prepared food or choose from several buffet style arrangements like "home style," veggie, Asian food, and organic salad bars. They can purchase made-to-order subs, pizza, and other offerings. Wegmans offers freshly made sushi and a full-service coffee shop offering cappuccino and gourmet flavored coffee. Importantly, these various restaurants are not segmented from each other the way you might see a separate eyeglass shop or hair salon at a Walmart Supercenter. At Wegmans, the various eateries, coffee shops, and kiosks intermingle to maximize customers' browsing. The stores also offer bakeries, one of its most profitable departments, and flower shops. A limited number of locations even have high-end restaurants connected or adjacent to the traditional market café area. Wegmans exceeds what most shoppers expect from a trip to the market.

Another touchstone of the Wegmans experience is how well everybody treats customers and each other. Danny Wegman explained why it's important to select the right type of employees: "Anybody can build the stores we build. It's the people who make the difference of shopping at Wegmans or shopping somewhere else. … We hire people who like serving people. If you do, we feel we can train you in any particular skill. It's hard to train you to like someone" (Kalita, 2004, para. 21). By selecting employees with the desired disposition toward people, they more naturally say, "Good morning. How are you? How are your kids?" (Kalita, 2004, para. 15). One employee explained it in simple terms: "If they have a hurt ankle, you ask how they're feeling" (Kalita, 2004, para. 15). After selecting the right employees, the next step is instilling Wegmans' values. "The first [value] is caring," explained Danny Wegman. "When we hire, we try to find people we believe will be caring: caring about our customers and caring about their Wegmans teammates. And then we have to spend some time together and learn to trust each other. That's all part of what goes on when we open a new store or bring on a new employee" (Bingham & Galagan, 2005, p. 34). He explained interactions with the staff:

> When employees have a problem of some kind, we step forward and help them solve it. Permission to do that doesn't have to come from me. It can come from anyone. We've made that very clear. That's what we believe in and that's how we treat each other. Part of that is training, but part is living it. And talking about it. We do a lot of storytelling to get feelings across. It's part of our training effort to recap stories. (Bingham & Galagan, 2005, p. 34)

Danny Wegman is particularly proud of the reputation for service and caring the company has earned. He remarked, "I hear that when folks are in a bad mood, they go to Wegmans to cheer up. People greet you with a smile and ask you if you want a taste of something. Customers get a happy fix and that makes our people feel spectacular. It's circular" (Bingham & Galagan, 2005, p. 35). Wegmans' people make it a special company and a special place to shop.

Treating People Well: "Employees First"

The true secret to Wegmans' success is the leaders' interesting twist on how they see the business's priorities: "Employees first, customers second" (Hudson, 2005, para. 6). Danny Wegman explained the company's approach: "I've said it many times, but it bears repeating. Our employees make Wegmans a place where customers feel happy and cared about, and my job is to make sure our employees feel that way, too" (Once, 2015, para. 2). One writer summed up Wegman's philosophy: "The rationale is that if employees are treated in a first-class way and made to feel valued, they'll take care of customers well. Happy customers will return" (Hudson, 2005, para. 7). Kevin Stickles, the company's vice-president for human resources, explained the company's thinking:

> The first question you ask is: "Is this the best thing for the employee?" That's a totally different model [than most companies]. … When you think about employees first, the bottom line is better. … We want our employees to extend the brand to our customers. (Rohde, 2012, para. 2)

Doing what's best for employees manifests in a number of ways. A main ingredient in Wegmans consideration of its employees is simply being kind. Danny Wegman stated, "When I visit our stores I see how our employees care about each other and about our customers. Because of our people, we have been able to grow our business without compromising our values" (Wegmans, 2012, para. 4). Company employees echo this treatment. Online at Indeed.com*, current and former employees shared their experience at Wegmans:

- [Wegman's] practices what it preaches in everything we do. The company has treated me like gold since day one and everyone at Wegmans is given the same treatment, training and attention. It is truly a family environment and teaches people that want to learn. (Great, 2015a)
- Working at Wegmans has truly been an awesome experience. The people that I work with are awesome and all of the managers are extremely nice. It is a very high team specific environment which I love. (Productive, 2015)
- It is a very family oriented company to work for. The corporate and store management really know how to take care of their employees. Over the past 10+ years I have been with the company I have enjoyed everyday because my team and department manager make it feel like it is my home away from home. We all consider ourselves family considering practically all of us have been together since we all started together, in my current store. One of the most enjoyable things I love is seeing the customers that I have built relationships with over the years come into my department/store just to say "Hi, how are you?" Those customers make it that much better of a work environment. It ensures me that I have made a difference in their lives. (Great, 2015b)

Being kind is not the only way the company does what's best for its employees.

The company also meets employees' needs in tangible ways such as generous employee benefits. Danny Wegman states plainly, "We want the folks at Wegmans to be able to have a good life. … We figure if you [as an employee] can't do that, then you're always worrying about that" (Glynn, 2006, para. 16). As such, employees also enjoy a long list of additional benefits such as health coverage, dental coverage, 401(k) retirement savings plan, Wegmans' retirement plan, a scholarship competition for college students employed at the company, paid time off, life insurance, adoption assistance, and many others (Walters, 2011). In addition to this foundation, Wegmans approaches employee compensation and benefits thoughtfully. Gerry Pierce, the company's senior vice president of human resources, stated, "When you are looking at benefits, there are a lot of things that have value with people that don't necessarily cost whole dollars. … Sometimes those things are worth more or as much as direct pay items" (Walters, 2011, para. 9). For example, when asked by the company to rank the importance of various benefits, employees cited a flexible work schedule, company reputation, and health benefits as their top three choices (Walters, 2011). Interestingly, base pay and time off were at the bottom of the list.

Like many supermarkets, Wegmans employs a high percentage of high-school and college students, and it also treats them very well. Since 1984, the company has given away over $100 million in scholarships for its student employees. Further, even part-time workers who average 24 hours or more each week are eligible for health insurance coverage. The company also invests in part-time employees' professional development at the company. Wegman's has a youth apprenticeship program that involves approximately 250 young employees each year. Danny Wegman stated, "It's one of the most exciting things I see us do. To me it models every value that's important to us as a company. They're listened to. There are people in the company who care about them" (Bingham & Galagan, 2005, p. 36). In the program, young employees lead a team project in their individual department, study the work for five months, and deliver a presentation on it at the end. Danny Wegman explained the benefits:

> The kids are learning and realizing how they can make a difference, and by listening, we model a behavior we all think we should practice anyway. We should listen to each other and respect folks. It doesn't matter if they're 16 years old. They're the ones doing the work. They see the opportunities. (Bingham & Galagan, 2005, p. 36)

The company's approach to even its youngest, part-time employees helps the workers but ultimately benefits the customers and the company. One of the main ways is through retention. As one writer put it, "No one leaves because there is a great sense of both family and team at the same time" (Glynn, 2006, para. 25). The value of *family* is strong at Wegmans and goes beyond mere metaphor. After all, Wegmans is a private, family-run business. Colleen Wegman, the company's president, said, "We often say that we're an extended family at Wegmans because of our values" (Stone, 2010, para. 14). Moreover, the company likes to hire employees' family members, a practice normally discouraged in government and public companies. Some stores have four generations working at the same time. As one employee put it, "The thinking is that if one family member is a good worker, then the spouse or offspring will be just as good" (Bass, 2005, para. 12). Many of Wegmans' practices put employees first in ways that help the company in the short and long term.

It Works for Wegmans

Wegmans' approach is uncommon, but so are its results. Wegmans beats competitors in almost every measure available. The company's turnover rate (i.e., employee attrition) is remarkably low. Amazingly, only 4–5% of Wegmans employees leave each year (Lucas, 2012). To put that number in perspective, national average for grocery stores is a dismal 39% (Buchanan, n.d.). Wegmans is not just a great place to work; its leaders and employees have created a great place to shop. *Consumer Reports* ("America's Best," 2015) rated Wegmans "America's Best, Freshest Supermarket." The magazine awarded Wegmans the highest rating in its food's freshness and quality, in the stores' cleanliness, and in employees' courtesy. Not surprisingly, Wegmans continues to grow. Sales have doubled over the last ten years. Store sales average over $1 million per store each week compared to the national average for grocery stores of $350,000 (Beldon, 2003; Wegmans, 2015). In 2010, Danny Wegman was voted CEO of the decade in Rochester, NY, in a poll conducted by the *Rochester Business Journal* (Stone, 2010). As one analyst stated, "[I]f you look back over the last 100 years … Danny should be CEO of the century" (Stone 2010, para. 24). Wegmans recently announced plans to open a store in Brooklyn, NY, which will be the chain's first store in New York City and a long-anticipated landmark for the company. A former Wegmans customer who moved to Brooklyn tweeted when hearing the announcement, "@Wegmans The lord heard my prayers. I'm crying as I type this" (Wegmans, 2015, para. 14). It is no surprise that the chain does better every year. In a 2016 survey of over 10,000 customers, the company was voted the best grocery chain in the country and placed 4th on *Fortune's* 2016 list of best places to work (Kell, 2016).

Author's Note: I currently live near a Wegmans and have shopped there regularly. I can personally attest that the stores are always gleaming, and the produce section alone is a ready-made "photo op." Employees make eye contact, greet me like a friend, and often use my name, I suppose by looking at my credit card. Employees' nametags display how long they've worked at the company and it is common to see employees who have worked there over 10 years. Wegmans is, without exaggeration, one of New York State's top tourist destinations (Bass, 2005). As a friend recently said, "If you visit friends in Colorado, the locals take you on a hike in the mountains. If you visit New York State, the locals take you to Wegmans." In fact, when I first visited the Rochester area, a relative immediately took me to visit Wegmans. I have visited the flagship store in Pittsford, NY, as part of the preparation of this case study. It is hard to exaggerate the level of excellence managers and employees have achieved. I even "tested" employees working in the massive cheese department as one writer suggested earlier in the case. They were knowledgeable, friendly, and appeared honored to work at Wegmans.

Questions:

- How much influence does the Wegman family's leadership have over the company's culture?
- Do you think this approach could work in other grocery chains? How about other industries?

*Indeed.com is a job site search engine that allows employees to rate their current and past employees. The feedback is anonymous and honest. While not all Wegmans' feedback was positive, the overwhelming majority was upbeat and supportive.

Google's Data-Driven Approach to Help Employees Love Their Jobs

Most people know about Google the company mainly because they use google.com to search the Internet. The company's business interests span a much wider spectrum than most people realize. The company offers gmail, cloud computing, and numerous other software applications and services like Google Maps, Video Hangouts, Google Docs, and Google Calendar. Google also owns what many users think are entirely different companies like YouTube. The company generates most of its revenue through the paid advertising done via all of these services. The company was founded in the late 1990s and quickly became known as one of the most innovative places to work. Shortly thereafter, the company codified the phrase "Don't Be Evil" as its official slogan. The motto is "built around the recognition that everything we do in connection with our work at Google will be, and should be, measured against the highest possible standards of ethical business conduct" ("Code of Conduct," n.d., para. 2). This code of conduct applies to the relationship between the company and its users but also to each employee, executive, and board member. The company employs nearly 45,000 people all over the world. While it is truly international, Google's largest corporate office is in Mountain View, part of California's Silicon Valley region where hundreds of high-tech and Internet companies reside.

In practice, the company appears to live by its motto. Google is also one of the most desirable places to work in the US. In 2015, the company was ranked the #1 best place to work by employees in *Fortune* magazine. It's been at or near the top of the list for nine years running. Google CEO and co-founder Larry Page was also named the nation's best CEO to work for according to employee surveys ("Glassdoor Employees' Choice," 2015). Page received an impressive 97% employee approval rating. This case looks at the practices and methods Google uses to engage employees and create a great place to work.

Google's "Insane" Perks Are An Investment

In the early 2000s, Google quickly became known for its many employee perks. Entire articles have been dedicated to outlining the breadth and depth of the Google lifestyle (Smith, 2013). A major perk is the free food. Google boasts literally dozens of cafeterias, cafes, and snack counters. One employee stated, "you're never further than 150 ft. (or so) away from food, so micro kitchens with coffee, drinks and snacks are close by" (Smith, 2013, para. 4). Free food obviously saves employees time and money. Food is also labeled as green, yellow, or red to inform employees about the healthiness of each choice. Employees at Google's Mountain View campus can get free rides to work on a Google bus with free Wi-Fi. Pets are also welcome and, as explained by an employee, can contribute to a more positive atmosphere: "The benefits of allowing dogs in the office far outweigh the costs, and the increase in job satisfaction for those with dogs or who like dogs far outweighs the mild annoyance" felt by those who don't like dogs (D'Onfro & Smith, 2014, para. 21). Employees can award each other "massage credits" for good performance and cash them in for a free one-hour massage. Google also provides a variety of free exercise and fitness opportunities such as classes and equipment.

One employee said, “The opportunity to get outside and run around if you had some energy to work off, knowing you could just shower and switch into some other clothes helped alleviate a lot of the fidgety energy I felt” (D’Onfro & Smith, 2014, para. 31). The company provides fresh towels for after-shower workouts and onsite laundry machines so employees don’t have to store their sweaty clothes all day. Many of Google’s offices even provide little scooters so employees can zip around from meeting to meeting in a fun and playful way that also contributes to their physical and mental health.

The employee perks go well beyond the fun, high profile types. Google provides a wide range of benefits aimed at caring for employees’ less visible interests. For example, in addition to working with smart, motivated, creative people—a benefit in itself—Google asks employees to spend 80% of their time on their primary area of responsibility and 20% of their time working on “passion projects [employees] believe will help the company” (D’Onfro & Smith, 2014, para. 33). Employees are even allowed to take up to three months off to explore other interests. Though these sabbaticals or leaves of absence are unpaid, employees continue to receive healthcare benefits and are welcomed back to their old jobs. Amazingly, if an employee dies, Google makes several important financial commitments. In addition to traditional life insurance, the surviving spouse receives 50% of the employees’ salary for 10 years and $1,000 per month for each child. One employee stated, “When I mentioned this benefit to my wife, she cried … She actually cried that the company would do that for her if something happened to me” (D’Onfro & Smith, 2014, para. 30). The company offers generous healthcare coverage and matches 50% employee 401k contributions. Thus, while the company does have numerous tube slides and firehouse-style poles to get to lower floors in a playful way, it offers benefits that reach into employees’ deeper concerns.

To some people, it might seem as if Google is simply flush with cash and giving employees anything they want. However, the employee perks mentioned above were the result of a business centered cost-benefit analysis decision-making process. Ultimately, these decisions are not just “neat things” for employees. In win-win fashion, Google’s leaders help the company by providing employees with what they want. Providing employees free food is great for the employee but also means that employees won’t leave campus, get stuck in traffic, hold up meetings, and slow down the progress on their work. From a financial standpoint, the cost of providing an in-house meal is small compared to the hourly pay of a Silicon Valley employee. Google calls its human resources department People Operations (POPS for short), the department responsible for coordinating and measuring the relative effectiveness of each of these benefits. A manager of POPS explained the thoughtfulness of Google's approach:

> We make thousands of people decisions every day—who we should hire, how much we should pay them, who we should promote, who we should let go of. … What we try to do is bring the same level of rigor to people decisions that we do to engineering decisions. Our mission is to have all people decisions be informed by data. (Manjoo, 2013, para. 9)

One writer explained POPS this way:

> Google's HR department functions more like a rigorous science lab … At the heart of POPS is a sophisticated employee-data tracking program … not just [about] the right level of pay and benefits but also such trivial-sounding details as the optimal size and shape of the cafeteria tables and the length of the lunch lines. (Manjoo, 2013, para. 6)

POPS considers every action and decision in light of data the department collects. One such decision, for example, was *how often should the company remind employees to contribute to their 401k plans*? POPS discovered that it was better to remind employees more frequently to contribute to their retirement fund to get results. Interestingly, however, employees responded when emails from POPS suggested "aggressive" goals rather than comparatively modest goals: "If you implore an employee to contribute $8,000 to his retirement rather than, say, $2,000, he'll tend to save more—even if he can't afford $8,000, he'll put in more than he would have if you'd suggested $2,000" (Manjoo, 2013, para. 16). Through rigorous data collection and analysis, POPS found that the ideal waiting time in the cafeteria was between three to four minutes because it was "short enough that people don't waste time but long enough that they can meet new people" (Manjoo, 2013, para. 16). POPS also discovered that placing eight-inch plates next to the 12-inch plates resulted in employees choosing smaller, healthier-sized portions. POPS measures virtually everything.

Perhaps Google's most noteworthy benefit in recent years occurred when the company extended maternity leave from an already high 12 weeks. The company now offers new moms 18 weeks paid leave for each new child. To put this number in perspective, only 12% of privately employed workers in the US receive paid maternity leave of any kind (Portillo, 2014). Further, of the moms that return to work after having a child, about 25% go back to work just 10 days after giving birth (Portillo, 2014). Without paid time off, these new moms have few options. Like most decisions at Google, however, the company noticed a problem and made the right adjustment. Turnover rate among its female employees was much higher than for male employees. When POPS looked into it further, the department found that most of the females who left the company were new moms. They would leave to give birth but would not be ready to come back after 12 weeks off. Instead, they left the company. Turnover like this is very costly in a variety of ways. When Google extended these benefits, the company cut turnover for new moms by a striking 50%, which brought the number in line with company norms for male employees. Thus, the decision to extend maternity benefits to 18 weeks was, in part, a smart financial decision as much as it was an additional benefit to new moms. Susan Wojcicki, CEO for YouTube, a Google company, spoke about the company's policy after her fifth maternity leave:

> Mothers were able to take the time they needed to bond with their babies and return to their jobs feeling confident and ready. … And it's much better for Google's bottom line—to avoid costly turnover, and to retain the valued expertise, skills and perspective of our employees who are mothers. (cited in Gillett, 2015, para. 5)

New moms also have the option to return to Google on a part-time basis and use Google's free daycare service when they return. In an article from *Business Insider* (Gillett, 2015) entitled "20 great places for new moms to work," even most other mom-friendly companies offered fewer paid weeks off. Bank of America offers 12 paid weeks off, Hewlett-Packard (HP) offers 14 weeks, Facebook also offers 18 weeks off, and Microsoft offers up to 20 weeks off.

Bottom Line: It's About the People

Even though outsiders know Google for its technology and innovation, its business really comes down to people. The peers employees get to work along side are the best aspect of working at Google. POPS does more than decide on various perks and benefits and do all they can to retain their people. They are also the driving force behind the company's rigorous selection process. Google has the opportunity to hire from a generous applicant pool. According to a Google insider (Wilkes, 2012), the company receives 1.5 million applications per year, which equates to 300 applications for each position opening. The company's people-friendly reputation allows managers to hire the best of the best. As one applicant put it:

> We are surrounded by smart, driven people who provide the best environment for learning I've ever experienced. I don't mean through tech talks and formal training programs, I mean through working with awesome colleagues—even the non-famous ones. (D'Onfro & Smith, 2014, para. 8)

Another employee (Vidra, 2013) reflected on what he likes best: "It will sound a bit cheesy, but in my opinion the best employee perk is the people you work with" (para. 1). The employee continued, "I've worked in several other .coms and have never been more challenged and energized professionally from my colleagues than at Google. People are generally happy to work here" (para. 1). Another employee (Moura, 2013) underscored the value of people and relationships: "All of the other mentioned perks are great, but it's really all about the people" (para. 1).

It's not an accident that most people approve of the leadership and the people they work with. Another role that POPS plays is helping managers. On numerous occasions the department collects data on what makes some Google managers more successful leaders than others in terms of employee ratings. For example, managers who received high scores were described as "a good coach," "a good communicator," "doesn't micromanage," etc. (Manjoo, 2013, para. 13). With this data, the company pursued and coached the underperforming managers in the skills displayed by the more effective managers. The overall scores for managers at Google began to rise following this project and have continued to rise since. While no company is perfect, Google provides many examples of how investing in people and treating them well is often a smart business decision.

Author's Note: I was fortunate to facilitate a workshop on executive communication skills at Google's Mountain View campus not long after starting this book. Employees and leaders were easy to work with and appeared extremely happy to be there. During my free brisket lunch, I noticed numerous employees doing laps in the pool and later watched others play beach volleyball around dinnertime. The "vibe" felt very much like a fun college campus in all the best ways, including smart, hard-working people who knew that working at Google indeed represented a special time of their lives. True to form, some employees had their dogs at work and I even noticed a veterinarian's office right there on campus. In addition to the numerous outstanding perks mentioned earlier, the quality of décor was also superior but not easily translated into words. Instead of common bland colors and names like "Conference Room A," the particular building we worked in had a classic rock theme with floor-to-ceiling pop culture murals and rooms with names like "Sweet Caroline," a 1969 son by Neil Diamond. The interior design was detailed, thoughtful, and stimulating. As one writer put it, "Google's offices are really incredible places.

Questions:

- How do you think Google's leaders view their employees? How does it show?
- To what extent does a company have to be "rich" to use Google's approach to treating employees well?

They're filled with all sorts of odd, playful touches. They make going to work look like it would be fun" (Yarow, 2013, para. 1, 2).

Zappos.com: In the Business of Happiness

Zappos is an online retail company that sells clothes, shoes, and many other items. Its slogan, "Powered by Service," is more than words. The company started in 1999, around the time when so many other "dotcom" companies popped up across the US. When the economic bubble of online companies was in full collapse, Zappos continued to grow. By 2008, the company brought in an astounding $1 billion in sales. How did Zappos excel in an era when so many other new companies failed? The company is known for much more than its amazing economic success. Zappos' leaders focus almost entirely on people. Tony Hsieh (pronounced "shay") and Zappos built that success on a reputation as an incredible place to work that provided an amazing customer experience. In 2009, Zappos was ranked 23rd on *Fortune's* annual list of best companies to work for ("100 best," 2009). Like many online organizations, it has no retail storefront and instead sells entirely over the phone and online, a unique challenge when selling items as personal as shoes and clothing. Many of the 1500 employees located in its Las Vegas headquarters are customer service phone representatives with several layers of managers above them. Even though they never interact with customers face to face, employees still consistently "Wow" customers. Its website states, "WOW is such a short, simple word, but it really encompasses a lot of things. … whatever you do must have an emotional impact on the receiver. … We seek to WOW our customers, our co-workers, our vendors, our partners, and in the long run, our investors" ("Zappos," 2013a, para. 1–3). This case looks at exactly how Zappos created a corporate culture that reaps these enthusiastic responses from customers and employees.

Zappos' Culture

A key to Zappos success is leader's value for relationships. The company lives its stated core values ("Zappos," 2013c), one of which is the importance of positive, open communication: "It's important to always act with integrity in your relationships, to be compassionate, friendly, loyal, and … treat your relationships well. … if the trust exists, you can accomplish so much more" (para. 3). Zappos builds these relationships, in part, through informal interaction between leaders and employees. Its managers are expected to spend 10–20% "of their time goofing off with the people they manage" (Chafin, 2009, para. 41) outside of their normal work responsibilities. Hsieh stated, "part of the way you build company culture is hanging out outside of the office" (Chafin, 2009, para. 41). Leaders also expect employees to get to know each other throughout the company and have developed creative ideas to ensure this. For instance, when logging onto their computers, employees must also match a name with a photo of a randomly selected fellow employee before they can begin work. The company even keeps a record of each employee's score (Palmer, 2010, para. 13).

Leaders also encourage employees to be themselves and have fun at work. In contrast, many call centers strive for uniformity and structure. One reporter stated, "Zappos headquarters looks more like a playground than an office. Every cubicle is festooned with knick-knacks" (Medina, 2010, para. 12). Hsieh described what Zappos leaders strive for: "I want to be in an area where everyone feels like they can hang out all the time and where there's not a huge distinction between working and playing" (Medina, 2010, para. 14). Zappos strives to strike a balance between professionalism and fun. Its unofficial symbol to capture this balance is the mullet style haircut. Mullet wigs hang from various places throughout the office space to capture the attitude, "business in the front, party in the back" (Medina, 2010, para. 3). Zappos provides nap rooms for employees to sleep between 30 and 60 minutes per day depending upon how busy it gets, an unheard of practice in the call center industry. Instead of conformity, Zappos' leaders "want people to express their personality in their work. To outsiders, that might come across as inconsistent or weird" ("Zappos," 2013b, para. 3). Leaders genuinely want employees to let their unique personalities shine through.

At the same time, Zappos leaders also know that the company's distinctive culture will not fit every potential employee. Hsieh developed a creative solution to the "bad hire" problem that plagues many organizations. The phrase, "bad hire," describes somebody who performs well throughout the interview and hiring process but does not end up thriving at the organization once the real work starts. In many cases, a bad hire is obvious to both the newly hired employee and the hiring manager. In many cases, both parties end up sticking it out to try to make it work with limited success. Zappos comes at this issue differently than most companies. About a week or two into a new hire's training, a manager meets privately with each new employee and makes "the offer," a now well-known feature of Zappos' culture. The manager tells the employee, "If you quit today, we will pay you for the amount of time you have worked, plus a $2,000 bonus" (McFarland, 2008, para. 4). Zappos has increased the dollar amount of the bonus over the years to make sure the offer is genuinely tempting for less-than-committed new hires. A mere 2–3% of employees take the cash. As a result, there are no I-just-work-here employees at Zappos. Virtually everybody wants to work there.

Customer Service

Customers also experience Zappos' commitment to people. Most call centers use a sophisticated system of "metrics" or measures to make sure each employee is working up to his or her capacity. For instance, many companies measure each employee's success by tracking call duration and number of calls in a given shift or "average handle time." Hsieh stated, "This translates [in other companies] into reps worrying about how quickly they can get a customer off the phone, which in our eyes is not delivering great customer service" (Hsieh, 2010, para. 14). Christa Foley, senior manager of HR at Zappos said, "We have found that we have to 'un-train' folks that do come from a long history of call center work so that they can be successful in our environment" (McNeal, 2013, para. 5). Hsieh stated, "We just care about whether the rep goes above and beyond for every customer" (Hsieh, 2010, para. 15). Zappos employees also do not use any prepared phone scripts to steer the conversation awkwardly toward the close of a sale. Nor do they "upsell" by recommending additional products or services to their customers. Hsieh stated, "We don't have scripts because we trust our employees to use their best judgment when dealing with each and every customer. We want our reps to let their true personalities shine during each phone call so that they can develop a personal emotional connection (internally referred to as PEC) with the customer" (Hsieh, 2010, para. 15). One of the ways Zappos does this is by using customers' area code to automatically route calls to employees who have a personal connection to that geographic area (McNeal, 2013). If a customer calls from Colorado, for example, the automated system might direct that call to a phone representative who attended Colorado State University. This provides an instant piece of common ground to discuss as the employee processes the customer's order. Leaders also empower employees to make independent decisions without asking for permission. Zappos' goal, as senior brand marketing manager Michelle Thomas explained is to, "provide the best possible customer experience, and do so in a fun and high touch manner" (Edwards, 2012, para. 14).

Zappos has accumulated numerous stories that are told and retold about the unexpectedly exceptional service (Edwards, 2012). One employee sent flowers to a female customer who ordered shoes in a new size because her feet were damaged from medical treatments. Another employee sent a free pair of shoes via overnight delivery to a best man who arrived at a wedding without proper shoes. Still another employee left the Zappos building to purchase a specific pair of shoes from a competing store because Zappos' warehouse had run out of that particular shoe. Perhaps the most often told story about Zappos' customer service is about Hsieh's pizza delivery story (Hsieh, 2010):

> After a long night of bar-hopping [in Santa Monica, CA], a small group of us headed up to someone's hotel room to order some food. My friend from Sketchers tried to order a pepperoni pizza from the room-service menu, but was disappointed to learn that the hotel we were staying at did not deliver hot food after 11:00pm. … In our inebriated state, a few of us cajoled her into calling Zappos [located in Las Vegas] to try to order a pizza. She took us up on our dare … The Zappos rep was initially a bit confused by the request, but she quickly recovered and put us on hold. She returned two minutes later, listing the five closest places in the Santa Monica area that were still open and delivering pizzas at that time. … [the story illustrates] the power of not having scripts in your call center and empowering your employees to do what's right for your brand, no matter how unusual or bizarre the situation. (para. 19–22)

Stories like this weave an organizational memory and reinforce the level of service and autonomy Zappos expects from employees. Leaders support employees' efforts with a few key customer-friendly policies. The company offers free delivery with no minimum purchase-requirement. Incredibly, Zappos offers a no-questions-asked free return policy. In fact, the company encourages customers to use its free return policy to purchase multiple sizes of shoes and clothes, keep the size that fits, and send the rest back. Customers have one full year to return a product, and Zappos states, "If you purchase on 2/29 of a Leap Year, then you have until 2/29 the following Leap Year to return those orders. That's four whole years! Woot!" (Shipping, 2013, para. 5). The policies are so flexible they sound as if customers wrote them instead of a corporation. Zappos' approach is clearly working. The company does little traditional marketing or advertisement and achieved most of its success before social media marketing became popular. It has grown almost entirely by word-of-mouth from satisfied customers, and an impressive 75% of sales come from repeat customers (Charlton, 2009).

Delivering Happiness

Zappos' recipe for success is simple: It makes people happy. Hsieh stated,

> At Zappos, our higher purpose is delivering happiness. Whether it's the happiness our customers receive when they get a new pair of shoes or the perfect piece of clothing or

> the happiness they get when dealing with a friendly customer rep over the phone, or the happiness our employees feel about being a part of a culture that celebrates their individuality, these are all ways we bring happiness to people's lives. (Gallo, 2009, para. 4)

Jenn Lim, who has been a consultant to Zappos for over 10 years, stated, "I've had the fortune of seeing Zappos go through these various phases, from being an online shoe seller to focusing on customer services to zeroing in on employee happiness to, ultimately, delivering happiness" (McNeal, 2013, para. 2). Happy employees make happy customers. Christa Foley, senior manager of Human Resources stated, "By correlating employee happiness with traditional metrics of customer happiness (e.g., repeat customers, net promoter score) we can easily see how they're directly related" (McNeal, 2013, para. 6). After studying Zappos and its CEO, one reporter concluded, "Other business innovators work with software code or circuit boards or molecular formulas. Hsieh prefers to work with something altogether more complex and volatile: human beings themselves" (Chafkin, 2009, para. 9). Zappos truly does strive to deliver "Wow," and by most accounts is succeeding.

Zappos' Leaders Still Experimenting with the Culture

In 2015, Zappos was in the news for a slightly different reason. CEO Tony Hsieh was still not satisfied with the culture Zappos had created. He felt it was still too traditional and wanted to tinker with it even more by introducing a radical idea called Holacracy, which is an essentially self-management model (Groth, 2015). Hsieh's goal is to break "down our legacy silo'ed structure/circles of merchandising, finance, tech, marketing, and other functions and create self-organizing and self-managing business-centric circles instead" (Groth, 2015, para. 4). Moving away from a traditional managerial structure toward employee circles has not sat well with everybody. Employees have criticized Hsieh's idea for being too ambiguous and criticized Hsieh for experimenting with Zappos' culture too much. Still, Hsieh is fully committed and essentially asked employees who could not get fully committed to the Holacracy approach to leave the company and accept a generous severance package. Some writers took this an aggressive, domineering move

Questions:

- How can Zappos break all of the "best practices" and still surpass most other companies in the call center industry?
- Do you believe Hsieh has gone overboard by insisting on a Holacracy? Do you think his change will ultimately succeed?

(Greenfield, 2015), but the goal of Holacracy, in part, is to reduce managerial positions and structural boundaries. This severance package, which included the equivalent of at least three-months salary, was similar to "the offer" that ensures that only employees who truly want to be at Zappos remain. Approximately 14% of employees took the offer and left rather than adopt the Holacracy approach (Snyder, 2015). This number is still far below typical annual turnover rates of 33% in the call center industry (Huebsch, n.d.). Nevertheless, are critics right? Has Hsieh gone too far this time? While Zappos takes more risks than most companies when pushing its culture to the limit, the company's approach has thus far assured that only employees who really want to work there remain. As long as that happens, the company should remain positioned to continue delivering happiness to its customers. Only time will tell if Hseih's latest move will take Zappos to the next level or stall the company's climb.

Chapter Discussion Questions

- To what extent do you see an *I-Thou* view of people in these organizations?
- How much do these leaders shape the cultures of these workplaces? Does the engaging approach require courage? Why?
- Why do you believe the approaches used by these organizations are unique in their respective industries? Why don't all organizations adopt these practices?

Key Terms

- Engaging communication
- I-Thou
- Dyadic relationship
- Leader-Member Exchange
- Liking/Affect
- Loyalty
- Professional respect
- In-groups
- Out-groups
- Leader-follower relationships

References

Arnett, R. (2012). Beyond dialogue: Levinas and otherwise than the I–Thou. *Language and Dialogue, 2,* 140–155.

Bisel, R. S., Messersmith, A. S., & Kelley, M. (2012). Supervisor-subordinate communication: Hierarchical mum effect meets organizational learning. *Journal of Business Communication, 49,* 128–147.

Buber, M. (1970). *I and Thou.* New York, NY: Charles Scribner's Sons.

Campbell, K. S., White, C. D., & Johnson, D. E. (2003). Leader-member relations as a function of rapport management. *International Journal of Business Communication, 40,* 170–194.

Eden, D., & Ravid, G. (1982). Pygmalion versus self-expectancy: Effects of instructor- and self-expectancy on trainee performance. *Organizational Behavior and Human Performance, 30,* 351–364.

Gawande, A. (2009, March 30). Hellhole: The United States holds tens of thousands of inmates in long-term solitary confinement. *New Yorker.* Retrieved from http://www.newyorker.com/reporting/2009/03/30/090330fa_fact_gawande

Holba, A. (2008). Revisiting Martin Buber's I-It: A rhetorical strategy. *Human Communication, 11,* 495–510.

Kacmar, K. M., Witt, L. A., Zivnuska, S., & Gully, S. M. (2003). The interactive effect of Leader–Member Exchange and communication frequency on performance ratings. *Journal of Applied Psychology, 88,* 764–772.

Kell, J. (2016, April 14). Wegmans was just named the best grocery chain in America. *Fortune.* Retrieved from http://fortune.com/2016/04/14/best-grocery-store

Lennon, J. (2002). Ze king and I: John describes The Beatles meeting with Elvis … in his own words. *Absolute Elsewhere.* Retrieved from http://features.absoluteelsewhere.net/ZeKingandI/john_talks_meeting.html

Liden, R. C., & Graen, G. (1980). Generalizability of the vertical dyad linkage model of leadership. *Academy of Management Journal, 23,* 451–465.

Liden, R. C., & Maslyn, J. M. (1998). Multidimensionality of Leader-Member Exchange: An empirical assessment through scale development. *Journal of Management, 24,* 43–72.

Livingston, J. S. (2003). Pygmalion in management. *Harvard Business Review.* Retrieved from https://hbr.org/2003/01/pygmalion-in-management

Mirivel, J. C. (2012). Communication excellence: Embodying virtues in interpersonal communication. In: T. J. Socha & M. J. Pitts (Eds.), *The positive side of interpersonal communication* (pp. 57–72). New York, NY: Peter Lang.

Rosenthal, R., & Jacobson, L. (1968). *Pygmalion in the classroom.* New York, NY: Holt, Rinehart & Winston.

Rowe, M. P. (1990). Barriers to equality: The power of subtle discrimination to maintain equal opportunity. *Employee Responsibilities and Rights Journal, 3,* 153–163.

Teven, J. J. (2007). Effects of supervisor social influence, nonverbal immediacy, and biological sex on subordinates' perceptions of job satisfaction, liking, and supervisor credibility. *Communication Quarterly, 55,* 155–177.

Teven, J. J. (2010) The effects of supervisor nonverbal immediacy and power use on employees' ratings of credibility and affect for the supervisor. *Human Communication, 13,* 69–85.

Starr, B. (2015, April 17). Missouri National Guard's term for Ferguson protesters: "Enemy forces". *CNN*. Retrieved from http://www.cnn.com/2015/04/17/politics/missouri-national-guard-ferguson-protesters/
Young, S. (2007). *Micro messaging: Why great leadership is beyond words.* New York, NY: HarperCollins.

Southwest References

3 Lasting Lessons from Malice in Dallas. (2013, July 22). *Inc*. Retrieved from http://www.inc.com/3-lasting-lessons-from-malice-in-dallas.html
America's best employers. (2015). *Forbes*. Retrieved from http://www.forbes.com/best-employers/#tab:rank_page:2
Arnoult, S. (2013, February 28). Colleen Barrett talks Herb, go-go boots and service with a smile. *Runway Girl Network*. Retrieved from http://www.runwaygirlnetwork.com/2015/02/28/colleen-barrett-talks-herb-go-go-boots-and-service-with-a-smile/
Freiberg, K., & Freiberg, J. (1996). *Nuts! Southwest Airlines crazy recipe for business and personal success.* Austin, TX: Bard Press.
Gallo, C. (2014). Southwest Airlines motivates its employees with a purpose bigger than a paycheck. *Forbes*. Retrieved from http://www.forbes.com/sites/carminegallo/2014/01/21/southwest-airlines-motivates-its-employees-with-a-purpose-bigger-than-a-paycheck/
Gittell, J. H. (2003). *The Southwest Airlines way*. New York, NY: McGraw Hill.
Grubbs-West, L. (2005). *Lessons in loyalty: How Southwest Airlines does it—An insider's view.* Dallas, TX: Cornerstone Leadership Institute.
Makovsky, K. (2013, November 21). Behind the Southwest airlines culture. *Forbes*. Retrieved from http://www.forbes.com/sites/kenmakovsky/2013/11/21/behind-the-southwest-airlines-culture/
McGrath, M. (2015, May 18). Southwest and American Airlines top list of companies poised for best 2015 earnings per share growth. *Forbes*. Retrieved from http://www.forbes.com/sites/maggiemcgrath/2015/05/18/southwest-and-american-airlines-top-list-of-companies-poised-for-best-2015-earnings-per-share-growth/
Mouawad, J. (2010, November 20). Pushing 40, Southwest is still playing the rebel. *New York Times*. Retrieved from http://www.nytimes.com/2010/11/21/business/21south.html?_r=0
Potter, E. (2011). Most-complained-about airlines. *Travel and Leisure*. Retrieved from http://www.travelandleisure.com/slideshows/most-complained-about-airlines/2
Southwest Airlines "Malice in Dallas" [video]. (2009). Retrieved from https://www.youtube.com/watch?v=51a5xuxxxZQ

Wegmans References

100 Best Companies to work for. (2015). *Fortune*. Retrieve from http://fortune.com/best-companies/wegmans-food-markets-7
America's best employers: #9 Wegmans Food Markets. (2014). *Forbes*. Retrieved from http://www.forbes.com/companies/wegmans-food-markets

Bass, M. (2005, May 29). A company that gets it right. *The Berkshire Eagle*. Retrieved from www.berkshireeagle.com

Beldon, T. (2003, April 25). Grocery rivals, beware: Wegmans is coming. *The Philadelphia Inquirer*, p. C1.

Bingham, T., & Galagan, P. (2005). A higher level of learning. *Training & Development, September*, pp. 32–36.

Buchanan, R. (n.d.). Employee turnover in a grocery. *Chron*. Retrieved from http://smallbusiness.chron.com/employee-turnover-grocery-15810.html

Ferdman, R. A. (2015, May 14). Unlike Brooklyn, D.C. area's already hip to Wegmans. *The Washington Post*, p. A15.

Glynn, M. (2006, March 12). Running supermarkets is a family affair for Wegmans. *Buffalo News*, p. C1.

Great company. (2015a). Wegman's [company review website]. *Indeed.com*. Retrieved from http://www.indeed.com/cmp/Wegmans/reviews

Great place to work. (2015b). Wegman's [company review website]. *Indeed.com*. Retrieved from http://www.indeed.com/cmp/Wegmans/reviews

Kalita, S. M. (2004, February 26). A new type of food chain. *The Washington Post*, T1.

Lucas, S. (2012, November 21). How much does it cost companies to lose employees? *CBS News*. Retrieved from http://www.cbsnews.com/news/how-much-does-it-cost-companies-to-lose-employees

Productive and fun place to work. (2015). Wegman's [company review website]. *Indeed.com*. Retrieved from http://www.indeed.com/cmp/Wegmans/reviews

Rohde, D. (2012, March 22). The anti–Walmart. *Reuters*. Retrieved from http://blogs.reuters.com/david-rohde/2012/03/22/the-anti%E2%80%93walmart/

Stone, M. (2010). Poll: Wegman selected as area's top chief executive. *Rochester Business Journal.* Retrieved from http://www.rbj.net/article.asp?aID=182621 on 2015, July 9.

Walters, C. (2011, June 10). Taking a closer look at benefits: the Wegmans way. *Rochester Business Journal*. Retrieved from http://www.rbj.net/article.asp?aID=187917

Wegmans. (2015). 15th consecutive year: *Fortune* places Wegmans on "100 best companies to work for" list, ranking #4 [Press Release]. Retrieved from http://www.wegmans.com/webapp/wcs/stores/servlet/ProductDisplay?langId=-1&storeId=10052&catalogId=10002&productId=734552

Wegmans Food Markets, Inc.: An overview [website: Company Overview]. (2015). Retrieved from http://www.wegmans.com/webapp/wcs/stores/servlet/CategoryDisplay?storeId=10052&identifier=CATEGORY_2441

Google References

100 best companies to work for. (2015). *Fortune*. Retrieved from http://fortune.com/best-companies/google-1

Code of conduct. (n.d.). *Google*. Retrieved from http://investor.google.com/corporate/code-of-conduct.html

D'Onfro, J., & Smith, K. (2014, July 1). Google employees reveal their favorite perks about working for the company. *Business Insider*. Retrieved from http://www.businessinsider.com/google-employees-favorite-perks-2014-7

Gillett, R. (2015). 20 great places for new moms to work. *Business Insider*. Retrieved from http://www.businessinsider.com/the-best-places-for-new-moms-to-work-2015-6

Glassdoor employees' choice award winners revealed: Google's Larry Page #1 highest rated CEO in 2015. (2015). *Glassdoor*. Retrieved from http://www.glassdoor.com/blog/glassdoor-employees-choice-award-winners-revealed-googles-larry-page-1-highest-rated-ceo-2015

Manjoo, F. (2013). The happiness machine: How Google became such a great place to work. *Slate*. Retrieved from http://www.slate.com/articles/technology/technology/2013/01/google_people_operations_the_secrets_of_the_world_s_most_scientific_human.single.html

Moura, G. (2013). What is the best Google employee perk, and why? [Discussion Forum]. *Quora*. Retrieved from http://www.quora.com/What-is-the-best-Google-employee-perk-and-why

Portillo, C. M. (2014, December 17). In defense of paid maternity leave: 5 shocking facts from YouTube CEO Susan Wojcicki's *WSJ* op-ed. *The Business Journals*. Retrieved from http://www.bizjournals.com/bizwomen/news/latest-news/2014/12/in-defense-of-paidmaternity-leave-5-shocking-facts.html?page=all

Smith, K. (2013, March 6). Google employees reveal their favorite perks working for the company. *Business Insider*. Retrieved from http://www.businessinsider.com/google-employee-favorite-perks-2013-3

Vidra, E. (2013). What is the best Google employee perk, and why? [Discussion Forum]. *Quora*. Retrieved from http://www.quora.com/What-is-the-best-Google-employee-perk-and-why

Wilkes, S. (2012). How many people, on average, apply to each open entry-level programming/developer position at Google? [Discussion Forum]. *Quora*. Retrieved from http://www.quora.com/How-many-people-on-average-apply-to-each-open-entry-level-programming-developer-position-at-Google

Yarow, J. (2013). Check out Google's crazy offices in Zurich. *Business Insider*. Retrieved from http://www.businessinsider.com/googles-zurich-office-2013-12?op=1

Zappos References

100 best companies to work for. (Fortune, 2009). Money. Retrieved from http://money.cnn.com/magazines/fortune/bestcompanies/2009/snapshots/23.html

Charlton, G. (2009, November 4). Q&A: Zappos' Jane Judd on customer loyalty [blog]. Retrieved from http://econsultancy.com/us/blog/4912-q-a-zappos-jane-judd-on-customer-loyalty

Edwards, J. (2012, January 9). Check out the insane lengths Zappos customer service reps will go to. *Business Insider*. Retrieved from http://www.businessinsider.com/zappos-customer-service-crm-2012-1#ixzz2nwPk3WYX

Gallo, C. (2009, May 12). Delivering happiness the Zappos way. *Business Week*. Retrieved from http://www.businessweek.com/smallbiz/content/may2009/sb20090512_831040.htm

Greenfield, R. (2015, March 30). Zappos CEO Tony Hsieh: Adopt holacracy or leave. Retrieved from http://www.fastcompany.com/3044417/zappos-ceo-tony-hsieh-adopt-holacracy-or-leave

Groth, A. (2015, March 16). Internal Memo: Zappos is offering severance to employees who aren't all in with Holacracy. *Quartz*. Retrieved from http://qz.com/370616/internal-memo-zappos-is-offering-severance-to-employees-who-arent-all-in-with-holacracy

Hsieh, T. (2010, December 21). Branding through customer service. *Huffington Post*. Retrieved from http://www.huffingtonpost.com/tony-hsieh/branding-through-customer_b_799316.html

Huebsch, R. (n.d.). Standard employee turnover in the call center industry. *Chron*. Retrieved from http://smallbusiness.chron.com/standard-employee-turnover-call-center-industry-36185.html

McFarland, K. (2008, September 16). Why Zappos offers new hires $2,000 to quit. *Business Week*. Retrieved from http://www.businessweek.com/stories/2008-09-16/why-zappos-offers-new-hires-2-000-to-quitbusinessweek-business-news-stock-market-and-financial-advice

McNeal, M. (2013). A case for culture: Why aligning employee and company values around "delivering happiness" matters. *Marketing Insights, 3*, 44–45.

Medina, J. (2010, December 26). Las Vegas gets new city hall, and a mullet. *New York Times*. Retrieved from http://www.nytimes.com/2010/12/27/us/27vegas.html?_r=0

Palmer, K. (2010, August 10). The secrets to Zappos' success. *US News*. Retrieved from http://money.usnews.com/money/articles/2010/08/10/the-secrets-to-zappos-success

Shipping and Returns. (2013). *Zappos.com*. Retrieved from http://www.zappos.com/shipping-and-returns

Snyder, B. (2015, May 8). 14% of Zappos' staff left after being offered exit pay. *Fortune*. Retrieved from http://fortune.com/2015/05/08/zappos-quit-employees

Zappos family core value #1. (2013a). *Zappos.com*. Retrieve from http://about.zappos.com/our-unique-culture/zappos-core-values/deliver-wow-through-service

Zappos family core value #3. (2013b). *Zappos.com*. Retrieved from http://about.zappos.com/our-unique-culture/zappos-core-values/create-fun-and-little-weirdness

Zappos family core value #6. (2013c). *Zappos.com*. Retrieved from http://about.zappos.com/our-unique-culture/zappos-core-values/build-open-and-honest-relationships-communication

Zappos family core value #7. (2013d). *Zappos.com*. Retrieved from http://about.zappos.com/our-unique-culture/zappos-core-values/build-positive-team-and-family-spirit

12 Tips, Tools, and Resources to Move from Impersonal to Engaging Communication

Would you describe the relationships at your organization as cold or high quality? Do people generally act supportive toward each other, or is the atmosphere tense? Most organizations could use more positive and engaging communication. The cases in Chapter 11 show highly successful companies can succeed by treating people genuinely and supportively. The tips, tools, and resources in this chapter can help any organization move from impersonal to more engaging communication.

Contagious Engagement Model

As mentioned in Chapter 1, leaders' behaviors are particularly contagious. Leaders at all levels of the organization serve as powerful examples for others to follow. If we want to cultivate engaging communication, we must "practice what we preach." The Zappos, Wegmans, Southwest, and Google cases in Chapter 11 inspire the following simple diagram for engaging communication.

The cultivation of this model requires at least two steps: (a) managing our distractions and other impersonal habits effectively, and (b) improving our supportive communication behaviors.

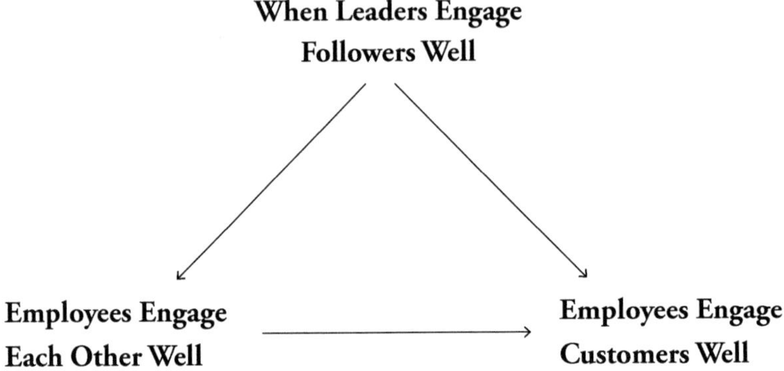

Thin Slicing: Creating the Wrong Impressions in Conversations

The first step toward more engaging communication is to reduce undesirable habits and distracting behaviors. By far, the biggest distraction in conversations these days is technology. Every time we check our phone, send a text message, or take a call, it sends a message to people in the room. We may downplay our use of technologies as minor and justify our need to "stay connected." Each moment seems minor to us but these behaviors can prompt people to form an undesirable impression of us because of the "thin slicing" process we use to interpret others' behaviors. This term refers to the way we observe and make judgments about another person based upon a brief excerpt or moment from the person's overall behavior stream (Houser, Horan, & Furler, 2007). Ambady and Rosenthal (1993) showed, for example, that students made accurate predictions of teachers' personality, style, and approach after viewing video clips as short as 6–15 seconds. Similarly, Babad (2005) showed that students could accurately predict how teachers would treat both low and high performers after watching a mere 10-second video clip.

This research shows that most of the impressions we form come primarily from visual and other nonverbal cues, and, despite what we may wish to believe, those judgments are often accurate when compared to long-term evaluations of our behavior. For example, 50–75% of observers find it inappropriate when somebody checks his or her phone during business meetings and off-site lunches even when the mood is informal (McGregor, 2013). Using technology is the most common offender. Many other small behaviors send messages too, particularly in one-on-one or group settings. People will notice if we only seem interested when

Box 12.1. Impersonal Communication Cues.

When somebody ...	**It can send the message ...**
Sends an email from the next office	It's a hassle to you talk face to face.
Walks by me without saying hello	You're not in my in-group.
Makes little eye contact with me	You're not here.
Only talks to me about work	You're not a whole person.

Box 12.2. Engaging Communication Cues.

When somebody ...	**It sends the message ...**
Drops by the office just to say hello	You're in my in-group.
Listens carefully	Your opinion matters.
Makes warm eye contact	I like you.
Asks about my weekend	We're building a positive relationship.

the topic directly relates to our area of expertise, if we stay out of the conversation for too long, if we shuffle papers, or are otherwise distracted. On the upside, this thin-slicing phenomenon means engaging communication can quickly create a positive impression, which we will explore later in this chapter. See Boxes 12.1 and 12.2 for your impersonal and personal communication cues.

Nonverbal Leakage

The term "leakage" describes the small nonverbal behaviors we do when deceiving others (Cody & O'Hair, 1983). When we attempt to conceal the truth, for example, we are more likely to touch our face, avoid eye contact, change our facial expression, etc. This concept is helpful beyond typical deception scenarios. Most observers, for example, will not likely pinpoint precise behaviors but may feel that a leader is acting "phony" or disingenuous when his or her true feelings for them leak out. If we pretend to like people or fake interest, something will seem a bit off to them. The differences in behavior may seem subtle, but the messages are clear. Our true feelings are difficult to hide, especially over the long run. Even if we do our best to feign interest in somebody to appear more engaging, we cannot sustain it consistently during the flow of conversation at a meeting. Leaders' behaviors are held to even higher standards than employees'. As shown in Chapter 11, people can easily sense leaders' treatment of preferred employees.

Readers may have experienced, for instance, supervisors or co-workers who maintain a neutral or expressionless face when communicating so as to not indicate any negative feelings toward the other person. This is a mistake for at least two reasons. First, most people will interpret a stone-faced expression as negative rather than neutral. The absence of confirmation in an expressionless face can easily be seen as a disconfirming reaction. Second, in 100% of the cases of the professionals I have observed, they give people they like big smiles. They give the neutral expression to people they don't like as much. Faking or reducing negative messages will not create engaging communication. Behaviors must go hand in hand with an *I-Thou* (Buber, 1970, 1947) mindset toward others. When we cultivate a belief system in which all people are valuable, deserve respect, and possess an inherent dignity, our engaging communication will be genuine and make the intended impression.

Mindset Minute: How Do You See People?

Our view of other people directly shapes the way we interact with them. If we do not approach people with a favorable view of their nature, no amount of coaching or tips on engaging communication will make much difference. Do you ever see people as impersonal objects? It's hard to see people as unique beings when we accept institutional or commercial labels. As a first step, develop an *I-Thou* mindset through practice. We should strive to see other people as inherently valuable, deserving of our respect, and possessing an innate dignity.

Do you know anybody who makes it hard to care about them? I know a young man in his mid-twenties, for example, who can seem detached. A casual observer at work might conclude that he just doesn't care or thinks he's a "cool guy." It is tempting to mentally disqualify the young man, to see him as someone who just isn't committed to the job, to see him as an *It.* I almost did. However, I learned that that the young man had lost both of his parents in the previous two years. He now provides for and raises two much younger siblings as if they were his children. His detached disposition is the result of a broken heart and the weight of his responsibilities. I no longer see him as an *It* because I listened to his story. We all have a life story. The philosopher Plato once said, "Be kind. Everyone you meet is fighting a hard battle." When we commit to viewing others as whole people rather than narrowly defining them, we move closer to the *I-Thou* mindset needed to engage them effectively.

Small Talk Is Big

As we manage or reduce our undesirable distractions and impersonal communication habits, we must build our engaging communication skills. Small talk is one indispensible way to connect with others. It happens in the space between greetings and task-related communication but serves crucial functions. As Mirivel and Tracy (2005) explain, "once a spate of interaction is described as *small talk,* it is quite easy to treat it as unimportant" (p. 6). Many scholars and professionals alike see small talk as "peripheral or even a distraction in the workplace; it is often denigrated as not the 'real stuff'" (Pullin, 2010, p. 458). Most people pay little attention to conversation until somebody says, "Okay, let's get started" (Mirivel & Tracy, 2005, p. 2). After all, what could talk about weather, sports, food, and entertainment possibly accomplish? According to Knutson and Ayers (1986), however, small talk actually plays a critical gap-filling role. It is a low-risk way to build new relationships, validate existing relationships, and is gateway conversation to exchanging task-related information. Also, it helps people get to know each other as whole human beings outside of our organizational roles and plays an indispensable role in cultivating positive relationships. Small talk can build rapport and trust, reestablish harmonious relationships, create mutual understanding, and advance the organization's "business goals" (Pullin, 2010, p. 471). Moutoux and Porte (1980), for example, found that supervisors' small talk directly and positively influenced satisfaction, morale, and productivity.

Allen Weiner (2006), a consultant, speaker, and author, provides a few simple ways to make small talk. He suggests we ask, "What do you do on the weekends?" or "What do you do on Saturdays?" instead of the blanket statement, "Tell me about yourself." In his decades' worth of consulting to executives, a question about how we spend our weekends or Saturdays is much more likely to lead to an interesting conversation that gets the other person talking. He reflects about one lively conversation he had during a mid-seminar break after asking his "Saturday" question where he did more listening than speaking, "Because I was mostly listening, was it 'small listening'? Of course not. The time I spent listening resulted in his making a connection with me that proved helpful in the course of the seminar" (p. 112). Among other ways to make small talk, Weiner also recommends the following:

(a) Ask for advice in topics of the other person's expertise (e.g., "Should I buy branded drugs or generics? Does it really make a difference?"). (p. 112)
(b) Talk about our foibles or small weaknesses. He states, "When I talk about mine, people talk about theirs. Sometimes that helps us make a connection." (p. 113)

Some people seem naturally gifted at making small talk. However, one of the easiest ways to jumpstart small talk conversation is to get the other person talking.

Emotional Labor and Leadership

Over the past few decades, research on emotional labor picked up speed and has many possible applications to improve our engaging communication. In many careers, our emotions are an important part of the actual work (Hochschild, 1983; Tracy, 2000). Travel and leisure employees such as flight attendants, cruise ship employees, and hotel staff provide a desirable emotional experience. They must often maintain this positive emotional state, including under stressful situations. In commercial scenarios like this, employees are paid as much for their personalities as for the other tasks they perform. In essence, the central aspect of their job is to provide a "package of emotion" that customers pay to experience. Emotional labor has another side. Employees such as firefighters (Scott, 2005), prison guards (Tracy, 2005), or financial advisers (Koesten, 2008) must satisfy conflicting emotional demands to do the job well. Research directly examining the emotional labor of leaders is still rare (e.g., Fisk & Friesen, 2012). However, the application of existing emotional research can enlighten every leader's fulfillment of his or her job description.

The outcome is visible when we communicate with others. People engage in emotional labor in two primary ways: *surface acting* and *deep acting* (Hochschild, 1983; Tracy, 2000). In the first case, we "put on" a smile and act the part, but the emotions we display are not the ones we feel. The second occurs when we deliberately put ourselves in an emotional state whereby we display genuine emotions. In Hochschild's (1983) book, a flight attendant described how she often associates the faces of unfamiliar passengers with people she knows and is fond of. By doing so, she creates an emotional bridge and feels an affinity for a stranger rather quickly. Once she makes that connection, she easily engages the passenger in a more authentic positive, supportive way.

Employees and leaders at all levels can learn a valuable lesson from this research. We may not automatically feel an affinity with each person we lead. However, we can take steps that will help us care about and connect with all of them through *I-Thou* glasses and authenticity. As a first step, we can consult research on Leader-Member Exchange to focus on three areas of connection. As discussed in Chapter 11, Liden and Maslyn (1998) showed that employee-leader pairs reported high-quality relationships when they mutually "felt" three primary tendencies for each other: Liking/affect, loyalty, and professional respect. Leaders can use these three reference points to build connections with followers, particularly those who may feel they are in the leader's out-group. The following are first steps in the right direction:

(a) *Affect* or "liking." In other words, they liked each other personally as friends do.
Tip: Explore areas of similarity through small talk.
Tip: Invest more informal time going to lunch, having a coffee, etc.
Tip: Learn about their non-work-related interests.

(b) *Loyalty.* Both employees and leaders showed loyalty and support for each other across situations.
Tip: Directly express support and loyalty (e.g., "I've got your back on this.").
Tip: Act as an advocate when opportunities arise.
Tip: Show clear, consistent support for employees' projects. Give them the benefit of the doubt when others might not.

(c) *Professional respect.* Honor each other's professional accomplishments through shared work history, public reputation, or known achievements.
Tip: Start by looking for traits you may already respect and state them directly (e.g., "I respect your work ethic.").
Tip: Ask for details about any awards or accomplishments on display in the office (e.g., "Ah, I see you won an alumni award from your college. What was that like?").
Tip: Brag about his or her accomplishments when the occasion presents itself.

These are simple entry points to developing stronger connections in each area. The goal of deep acting is not to score some temporary points for noticing an award on an employee's desk. The point is to take steps to feel each of these genuinely toward the other person.

Profiles: What Does Engaging Communication Look, Sound, and Feel Like?

It should be clear by now that engaging communication starts with an *I-Thou* mindset and must be as authentic as possible. If it is genuine, we will apply most of the behaviors from Chapter 11 without much effort: warm eye contact, smiling and supportive facial expressions, a friendly tone of voice and other positive vocal expressions, animated gestures and body movement, walking around and mingling in a relaxed manner, etc. In addition to the broader perspectives offered in the Zappos, Southwest, Google, and Wegmans case studies, I offer personal experiences that focus on minor behaviors from two small businesses that excel at engaging communication with customers.

Burrow's & Mr. Frank's. While living in Little Rock, Arkansas, I once went shopping for a pair of glasses. After a few unsatisfying experiences at chain stores, I found a family owned store called Burrow's & Mr. Frank's. There, an employee immediately greeted me warmly, introduced herself, and asked me how she could help. She then walked me over to a man named Lon, who I later learned was the owner. Like the employee, Lon greeted me warmly, shook my hand, and listened carefully as I explained the type of glasses that interested me. Patiently, he showed me some amazing styles that all looked wonderful. When we talked about the price, I was shocked: $700. It's not that the glasses weren't worth it. This little store in Arkansas has a high-end, world-class selection I would pit against the finest stores in New York City or Los Angeles. Still, I told him I was looking for something a little more affordable. He showed me several more styles, and I finally ordered a pair that looked good and fit my budget.

When I returned to pick up my glasses, Lon greeted me like an old friend. He sat me down at a small table with a leather top. He removed my glasses from their case as if he were handling fine jewelry. He shaped the earpieces and adjusted the nose pads several times with the care of a sculptor. After each adjustment, he placed the glasses on my face to observe. When his work of art was complete, he sat back and smiled for a moment. He held up a mirror for me to look at and asked, "What do you think?" as if the answer was obvious. Lon and the rest of his staff were masters at engaging communication. I'm sure I spent less money than most customers, and yet Lon and his staff treated me as if I were their only client. When people asked about my new glasses, I happily told them about my experience. A week later, my good friend showed up with his own new pair of glasses from Burrow's & Mr. Frank's. He confided that he'd spent even more than $700! Despite Lon's high-end products, his business is thriving. Unlike the chain stores, he doesn't open on Saturdays. His loyal customers are more than willing to wait until Monday. A 2014 review on Google said the following about the store: "I am not a paying customer at this shop. … I popped into this shop this afternoon and despite my not having purchased anything from them, they adjusted my spectacles, free of charge and with a smile. … Outstanding service here." Lon and his entire staff treat everybody like this.

Mr. Lemon. While I was an undergraduate student at Rhode Island College, I delivered pizza for a small local chain. On hot days, the manager would often send a driver to a nearby popular frozen lemonade stand, Mr. Lemon. Frozen lemonade is a sub-cultural feature of Rhode Island, my birthplace. We taste and compare it as if it were fine wine. Mr. Lemon, a family-run business, is perhaps the best frozen lemonade in the entire kingdom of Rhode Island. One online reviewer said about the taste, "If sunshine, happiness, and delight were frozen and served in a cup, you would have Mr. Lemon." The store literally has thousands of regular customers. As good as it is, however, the secret to Mr. Lemon's success is not its lemonade. The owner and employees are master communicators. Here's a near-verbatim account of a conversation I had with the owner (i.e., "Mr. Lemon") about 20 years ago when my pizza manager, Mike, sent me on a frozen lemonade run. Keep in mind, I was wearing my pizza delivery "uniform."

Mr. Lemon:	Alex, how are you doing?
Me:	Great. How are you?
Mr. Lemon:	Fantastic. Hot day. What can I get you today?
Me:	I'll have four medium "Tootie Fruities."
Mr. Lemon:	No problem. (He started working on my order). Hey, your brother Josh stopped by a few weeks ago. His wife is having a baby, huh?
Me:	Yeah, it's crazy.
Mr. Lemon:	Do you think it will be a boy? Wouldn't that be great?
Me:	Hey, either way. He's excited.
Mr. Lemon:	(Hands me my order). That'll be $8. Are you working with Mike tonight?
Me:	Yeah, Mike is on tonight. (I hand him the money plus a tip).
Mr. Lemon:	Oh, thank you very much. You tell Mike I said hello.

The amazing part is that my experience that day was not unusual. In fact, it's the norm. Mr. Lemon and his sisters have similar conversations with every customer in line, no matter how busy. I don't know how they do it, but they refer to almost every returning customer by name. They ask you about your life. They ask you about your family's life. They ask you about work and people you know. They remember the details in follow-up conversations. They treat thousands of individuals as if they are part of a small in-group. Online reviews of Mr. Lemon's service are outstanding. One read, "Nicest people in the world." Another stated, "They don't know me from a hole in the wall, but every time I'm there, I'm treated like royalty." Still another put it more dramatically and humorously: "Mr. Lemon is the last good place in an otherwise dark and hopeless world."

I went to Mr. Lemon dozens of times per year while in college but moved away from RI after graduation and haven't lived there in over 20 years. On a recent visit, I took my wife to show her what I had been talking about. I had no expectation that the staff would actually remember me decades later. That would be unreasonable. I decided beforehand not to remind them I used to come there frequently. When I arrived, Mr. Lemon himself was at the counter. He did not appear to recognize me at first. Still, he asked me about our plans for the day and was as warm and engaging as ever. As the brief conversation progressed, he looked more carefully at me as if he were studying my face. When we completed the order, he looked right in my eyes and said genuinely, "It's good to see you again." Even after a 20-year absence, the associated aging, different clothes, and other identity–blurring realities that come with time, I'm convinced he was on the verge of remembering me without any help or hints. Mr. Lemon's employees all demonstrate this amazing connection with people.

We do not always recognize engaging communication in the moment because the interaction goes so smoothly. When we analyze it a bit, however, the staffs at Burrow's & Mr. Frank's and Mr. Lemon's share some characteristics. First, they are genuine. Their care for people is obvious. Second, they perform all of the engaging communication behaviors discussed here. Like Elvis Presley, they make you feel like you are the only person on the planet when they are talking to you. We can learn much by observing the individuals already around us who demonstrate a special skill for connecting with others, a skill that at one point they learned.

Conclusion

The foregoing tips, tools, and resources will help manage the impersonal distractions and habits we may have developed over the years and provide initial steps to pursue more engaging communication practices. Behaviors like immediacy and small talk are certainly helpful but mostly so when they are rooted in authentic appreciation for other people. You can use the survey below to evaluate your own fundamental skills for tuning in to the people around you and gauge the areas you need to develop first to engage people more.

Survey

If you are a supervisor of any sort, this survey helps looks at the relative quality of your relationships with the people you lead. The survey is taken from Liden and Maslyn's (1998) research on Leader-Member Exchange. Each person who completes this survey will likely offer a slightly different picture of the relationship because each relationship between leader and follower is a unique dyad. The surveys should provide a starting point to understand the current level of quality in your relationships. You should give it to at least several people you lead. Arrange to collect them anonymously. To score, add all the items together and divide by 12. An average score of 5.0 or greater indicates a high-quality relationship.

Instructions: Please fill out and return this survey to your supervisor. Please be honest and ensure that your responses are anonymous.

1 = Strongly disagree
2 = Disagree
3 = Somewhat disagree
4 = Neither agree nor disagree
5 = Somewhat agree
6 = Agree
7 = Strongly agree

_____ I like my supervisor very much as a person.
_____ My supervisor is the kind of person one would like to have as a friend.
_____ My supervisor is a lot of fun to work with.
_____ My supervisor defends my work actions to a superior, even without complete knowledge of the issue in question.
_____ My supervisor would come to my defense if I were "attacked" by others.
_____ My supervisor would defend me to others in the organization if I made an honest mistake.
_____ I do work for my supervisor that goes beyond what is specified in my job description.
_____ I am willing to apply extra efforts, beyond those normally required, to meet my supervisor's work goals.
_____ I do not mind working my hardest for my supervisor.
_____ I am impressed with my supervisor's knowledge of his/her job.
_____ I respect my supervisor's knowledge of and competence on the job.
_____ I admire my supervisor's professional skills.

References

Ambady, N., & Rosenthal, R. (1993). Half a minute: Predicting teacher evaluations from thin slices of nonverbal behavior and physical attractiveness. *Journal of Personality and Social Psychology, 3*, 431–441.

Babad, E. (2005). Guessing teachers' differential treatment of high-and-low-achievers from thin slices of their public lecturing behavior. *Journal of Nonverbal Behavior, 29*, 125–134.

Buber, M. (1947). *Between man and man.* (R. G. Smith, Trans.). London: Routledge & Kegan Paul.

Buber, M. (1970). *I and Thou.* New York, NY: Charles Scribner's Sons.

Cody, M. J., & O'Hair, H. D. (1983). Nonverbal communication and deception: Differences in deception cues due to gender and communicator dominance. *Communication Monographs, 50*, 175–192.

Fisk, G. M., & Friesen, J. P. (2012). Perceptions of leader emotion regulation and LMX as predictors of followers' job satisfaction and organizational citizenship behaviors. *The Leadership Quarterly, 23*, 1–12.

Hochschild, A. R. (1983). *The managed heart: Commercialization of human feelings*. Berkeley, CA: University of California Press.

Houser, M. L., Horan, S. M., & Furler, L. A. (2007). Predicting relational outcomes: An investigation of thin slice judgments in speed dating. *Human Communication, 10*, 69–81.

Knutson, P., & Ayers, J. (1986). An exploration of the function of small talk in friendship relationships. *Journal of the Northwest Communication Association, 14*, 4–18.

Liden, R. C., & Maslyn, J. M. (1998). Multidimensionality of Leader-Member Exchange: An empirical assessment through scale development. *Journal of Management, 24*, 43–72.

McGregor, J. (2013, November 11). Study defines cellphone etiquette. *Washington Post*. Retrieved from http://www.journalgazette.net/article/20131111/BIZ/311119992/1031/biz

Mirivel, J. C., & Tracy, K. (2005). Premeeting talk: An organizationally crucial form of talk. *Research on Language and Social Interaction, 38*, 1–34.

Moutoux, D., & Porte, M. (1980). Small talk in industry. *Journal of Business Communication, 17*, 3–11.

Pullin, P. (2010). Small talk, rapport, and interpersonal international communicative competence. *Journal of Business Communication, 47*, 455–476.

Scott, C. (2005). The socialization of emotion: Learning emotion management at the fire station. *Journal of Applied Communication Research, 33*, 67–92.

Tracy, S. J. (2000). Becoming a character for commerce: Emotion labor, self-subordination, and discursive construction of identity in a total institution. *Management Communication Quarterly, 14*, 90–128.

Tracy, S. J. (2005). Locked up emotion: Moving beyond dissonance for understanding emotion labor discomfort. *Communication Monographs, 72*, 261–283.

Weiner, A. (2006). *So smart but ...: How intelligent people lose credibility and how they can get it back*. San Francisco, CA: Jossey-Bass.

Conclusion and Implications

The emphasis of this book has been to show a collection of case studies that exemplify two paths: cautionary tales and positive examples. With 31 cases and four sections, various facets explore courageous communication practices. This chapter summarizes the model of courageous communication covered in the foregoing chapters and some broader level "takeaways" from the entire collection. To reiterate, *communication is courageous when it a) stands against common but minimally effective and even harmful practices and b) pursues more effective and sustainable strategies, even if doing so is unpopular in a given context.* Below, I provide a summary of the courageous communication model. As the case studies show, the four themes often align and complement each other in practice.

Collaborative Communication

Collaboration is primarily about working together in a mutually beneficial relationship. With this approach, we design ways to share authority, responsibility, and accountability (Schwarz, 2006). Collaboration also means letting go of more individualistic and controlling tendencies to create space to do shared work. It requires sufficient information and supports positive relationships that build

> ***Takeaway 1:***
>
> Too much control results in resistance and does little to help organizations achieve their goals.

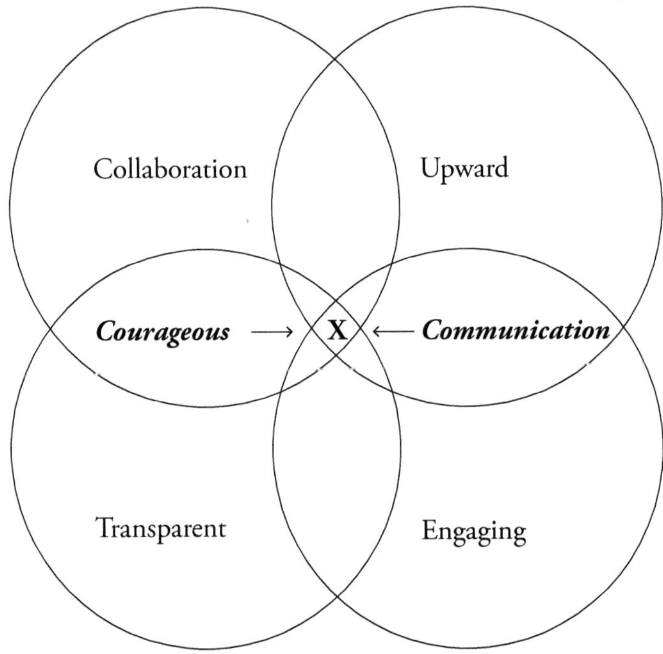

> ***Takeaway 2:***
>
> Collaboration generates ideas and a more satisfying culture.

trust, integrity, consensus, ownership, and alignment. Collaboration is driven by authentic dialogue between and among individuals and can happen in virtually any organizational setting. Stakeholders share values that guide them to pursue goals that become possible with a team approach.

Upward Communication

Bottom-up communication is drawn up the hierarchy by organizational leaders. Dedicated channels are some of the organization's best ways of collecting intel to make educated decisions. However, because of possible distortions, communication should move with minimal filtering from the lower levels to decision-makers.

> ***Takeaway 3:***
>
> Top-down communication is important but is not adequate to make high-quality decisions.

Good upward communication can include both quantitative and qualitative data and should sample a wide variety of participants, especially front-line supervisors, front-line employees, and customers. Because these three groups lack authority and resources, leaders are responsible for initiating surveys, focus groups, and other methods of collecting feedback (Larkin & Larkin, 1996). The goal is to provide decision-makers with a well-rounded, or representative picture of the organization's situation rather than a narrow or skewed version. Upward communication should happen at planned intervals to ensure a consistent flow of information, especially for important organizational changes.

> ***Takeaway 4:***
>
> Responsible leaders gather feedback to make better decisions.

Transparent Communication

Transparent communication is founded on the requirement to speak up, or as Weick (1990) phrases it, "the necessity to talk" (p. 589). Transparency displays an organization's process openly for all relevant parties and encourages members to discuss anything that stands out as unusual. This helps organizations identify potential problems, errors, or misunderstandings sooner. Transparent communication also involves a gentle touch when dealing with individuals. Candid conversations require care and honesty. Organizations that communicate openly within their walls avoid small problems from escalating into crises and are better equipped to communicate transparently with external stakeholders when the need arises.

> ***Takeaway 5:***
>
> Secrecy allows problems to grow.

> ***Takeaway 6:***
>
> Transparency identifies issues when they are smaller.

Engaging Communication

Engaging communication seeks more authentic and human connections among individuals. Despite the daily pressures of work and the temptation to automate most interactions, engaging communication makes an investment in the relationship between fellow employees and between leaders and followers. It involves warm, supportive, attentive, and empathetic nonverbal and verbal communication cues. Ideally, engaging communication expands in-groups to include a much wider array of individuals. In addition to its organizational advantages, it also demonstrates the inherent worth of all human

> ***Takeaway 7:***
>
> Impersonal interactions separate people.

> ***Takeaway 8:***
>
> Engaging communication builds relationships.

beings (Buber, 1947, 1970). Engaging communication, thus, is fundamentally communication among equals.

Practical Implications

The collection of case studies also leads to some practical and conceptual implications. The first one is that collaborative, upward, transparent, and engaging communication practices hold many untapped advantages. Collectively, the research and case studies in this book show the numerous benefits of courageous communication:

- More passionate, committed employees
- Higher productivity
- Higher employee morale and job satisfaction
- Lower turnover
- Greater coordination among departments
- Innovative cultures
- High-quality decisions
- Increased social capital
- Decreased chance of crises
- Quicker recovery from crises
- Increased sales and growth
- Better stakeholder relationships
- Greater investor confidence

By almost every industry measure, the courageous organizations outpace their competition and set new industry standards. If these communication practices are so beneficial, however, then why don't all organizations adopt them?

Second, collaborative, upward, transparent, and engaging communication requires a level of courage for which not all people or organizations are ready. When we collaborate, we risk not getting credit, our ideas not getting used, or reaching the perceived limits of our own creativity. Asking for upward communication risks hearing feedback that may make us feel bad about our own performance or past decisions that have not worked. Communicating transparently involves talking about our failures and shortcomings publicly and responding supportively when others do the same. Engaging communication risks breaking through our relational comfort zone to connect more genuinely with others. Further, these practices require courage because they go against many long-standing organizational norms, industry standards, and accepted professional "best practices" as well as reach forward to take organizations to new levels. It is no wonder Hornstein's

(1986) book on *Managerial Courage* has the subtitle, *Revitalizing Your Company Without Sacrificing Your Job.* In some organizations, merely suggesting a different direction can be seen as "not getting it" and may result in instant out-group placement by others. Organizations are highly politicized contexts, and doing something new comes with inherent risks despite the potential rewards.

The third implication is that, in practice, traditional approaches are not isolated. They reinforce each other in predictable ways. The cautionary cases demonstrate this clearly. For example, Foxconn demonstrated a clear *control-and-resistance* dynamic. Leaders justification of their heavy-handed approach included elements of *impersonal* communication, such as dehumanization. For example, Foxconn's CEO referred to employees as "animals" and saw nothing wrong with "sweatshops." Similarly, Jim Beam employees were treated in both *controlling* and *impersonal* ways. Merck demonstrated clear *top-down* tendencies for handling Vioxx and an organized campaign of *secrecy* about its most damaging data. In every cautionary case study, organizations that demonstrated one aspect of the traditional communication approaches (controlling, top-down, secretive, or impersonal), demonstrated at least one other from the same list. Further, the opposite was not true. Traditional approaches to communication did not pair up with courageous approaches. For instance, highly controlling organizations were not otherwise good at transparent, upward, and engaging communication.

The same was evident in courageous communication approaches. The case studies showing one of the courageous communication practices also showed evidence of other courageous approaches. Nestlé Purina, for example, took *upward* feedback seriously, and its leaders also spent time *engaging* workers face-to-face to develop employees' long-term career at the company to prevent turnover. Similarly, Dominos used *upward* communication and then shared results *transparently* within the company and publicly. Founders and primary contributors of Bigger Pockets, a highly *collaborative* organization, are refreshingly transparent about their successes and failures. Thus, while we may define aspects of communication in journal articles and textbooks narrowly, the communication practices in these case studies align and cluster in predictable ways in actual organizations.

Fourth, the benefits of courageous communication do not extend to controlling, downward, secretive, and impersonal communication. The overuse of these practices set the organizations back. Nevertheless, to reiterate a previously made point, a basic level of controlling, downward, secretive, and impersonal communication is acceptable and even necessary at times and not inherently negative. Clearly, for instance, organizations should provide a safe and orderly atmosphere where leaders communicate important information down the chain of command. Also, some issues such as personal health or other private information should be handled discretely. Further, some interactions with co-workers and customers can be automated with little harm. In contrast to these basic applications, however, this book looks specifically at organizations that overused these approaches even when they hurt organizations' effectiveness. Leaning heavily on these traditional approaches often made matters worse. Judging by the availability of cautionary case studies, the scales in many organizations today still tilt toward an overuse of traditional communication approaches and much less use of courageous communication.

Conceptual Implications

Courageous communication, like courage itself, is not easy to define. The four themes explored here should by no means limit future conceptualizations. These themes enlist elements of courage and courageous communication articulated by others (e.g., Hornstein, 1986; Jablin, 2006; May, 2012). They challenge established organizational practices, involve risk, and endorse proper actions for organizations' long-term health and effectiveness. This book adds to the conversation on courage four principles to enrich the ethical foundations for a communicative theory of courage. First, *dialogue* supports the genuine and mutual exchange between communicators that enables a collaborative spirit. Second, *utilitarianism* for *promoting the greatest good for the greatest number of people* emphasizes the need for gathering reliable upward feedback to make sound decisions. Third, *significant choice* underpins the importance of transparent communication for leaders, employees, and customers to make informed choices about organizations. Fourth, the concept of *I-Thou* reinforces the value of engaging and personal interactions between people, in part, because human beings have an inherent value and dignity that is worth cultivating through communication. These four ethical principles and the practices they support weave a conceptual framework for courageous communication. Beyond its practical benefits, it reaches for an ideal much higher than many organizations currently strive.

In addition to demonstrating courageous communication, the case studies in this book demonstrate the constitutive nature of communication. As Craig (1999) would have predicted, communication was not a mere secondary issue for these organizations. It was the creative mechanism that created the organizations' reality and shaped them for better or worse. The Boy Scouts case, for example, showed that, while no organization is immune to potential sexual abuse scandals, the communicative environment of the organization made future abuse more likely. The data shows that the organization's secrecy amplified the problem. Similarly, the secretive way of handling potential academic fraud at the University of North Carolina, Chapel Hill, allowed their shadow curriculum, questionable athletic eligibility, and education quality of its students continue for years longer than it might have otherwise. In the same way, the impersonal or engaging way organizations treat employees is not a peripheral issue; it is a central feature of organizational culture. The way Zappos and Southwest treat employees has a direct impact on their sales, growth, and long-term success as companies. In contrast, organizations like Abercrombie & Fitch, AOL, and Amazon reportedly do not treat employees well, and the impact of this shows in terms of retention, legal action, public reputation, and revenue. In both positive and cautionary situations, the organizations' communicative practices created contexts where treating people either well or poorly was considered normal and acceptable.

Furthermore, the cases demonstrate the constitutive nature of communication through how the practices of leaders spread throughout the organization. On the down side, at Enron, for example, the controlling disposition of its top leaders was contagious. Other executives assumed this aggressive posture while at the same moment organizational outsiders saw this behavior as completely unprofessional. The bullying behavior of one key player on the Miami Dolphins team, the leader of the offensive line, spread to other members of the offensive line and was tolerated to some extent by the organization despite producing one of the weakest offensive lines in the league. Similarly, NASA leaders cannot rid the agency of an increasingly casual approach to serious safety concerns. The constant and self-inflicted pressure of schedules, budget issues, and reduced standards made another accident seem almost inevitable.

On the upside, some organizations enjoyed the benefits of the contagious aspects of communication. Google's leaders created an employee-centric culture, which, in turn, helps the company attract and retain the best people in the industry and continues to position Google for future success. Dr. Ring's courageous public discussion of his wrong-site surgery mistake at Massachusetts General Hospital broached a taboo topic in healthcare and encouraged other physicians to follow protocols more carefully. The courage of leaders, in particular, produces a clear ripple effect. As such, they have a special responsibility to employ communication practices with the goal of long-term effectiveness. In fact, they have a unique opportunity to distinguish themselves and their organizations by communicating in good faith. In numerous case studies, leaders gained a national profile for their courageous communication.

Conclusion

In conclusion, the tips, tools, and resources at the end of each section are inspired partially by the case studies and drawn partially out of existing literature. They provide closure for each part of the book and serve as future reference. Based upon these case studies, previous research, and my own professional experience in organizations, many use outworn, unsuitable tools for the problems they face. Like 6-year-old Michael in the opening paragraph of the introductory chapter who swung his new hammer above his head without realizing the potential danger he was causing his nearby friends, many organizations and professionals today are using tools that might be perfectly suitable for narrow purposes but not for long-term positive outcomes. Unfortunately, these old tools have caused and continue to cause damage when they are overused. Simply reducing these traditional practices, however, will not distinguish organizations. For that, they must be courageous and apply the tools set forth here.

References

Buber, M. (1947). *Between man and man.* (R. G. Smith, Trans.). London: Routledge & Kegan Paul.

Buber, M. (1970). *I and Thou.* New York, NY: Charles Scribner's Sons.

Craig, R. (1999). Communication theory as a field. *Communication Theory, 9*, 119–161.

Hornstein, H. A. (1986). *Managerial courage: Revitalizing your company without sacrificing your job.* New York, NY: John Wiley & Sons.

Jablin, F. M. (2006). Courage and courageous communication among leaders and followers in groups, organizations, and communities. *Management Communication Quarterly, 20*, 94–110.

Larkin, T. J., & Larkin, S. (1994). *Communicating change: How to win employee support for new business directions.* New York, NY: McGraw-Hill.

Larkin, T. J., & Larkin, S. (1996). Reaching and changing frontline employees. *Harvard Business Review, May–June*, 95–104.

May, S. (2012). *Case studies in organizational communication: Ethical perspectives and practices.* Thousand Oaks, CA: Sage.

Schwarz, S. (2006). *Creating a culture of collaboration: The international association of facilitators handbook.* San Francisco, CA: Jossey-Bass.

Weick, K. E. (1990). The vulnerable system: An analysis of the Tenerife air disaster. *Journal of Management, 16*, 571–593.

Index

D

E

F

G

H

I

J

K

L

M

N

O

P

R

S

T

U

V

W

Y

Z